FIGHTING CHANCE

FIGHTING CHANCE

An NFL Season with the Seattle Seahawks

Fred Moody

Sasquatch Books
Seattle

Library of Congress Cataloging-in-Publication Data

Moody, Fred.
  Fighting chance.

  1. Seattle Seahawks (Football team). 2. National
Football League. I. Title.
GV956.S4M66 1989 796.332'64'09797772 89-10293
ISBN 0-912365-22-6

Design by Jane Rady
Front cover photo by Mark Harrison, *The Seattle Times*
Back cover photo by Corky Trewin, Timeout Sports Photo
Back cover portraits: top left, Brian Drake, SportsChrome East/West;
  top right, Mitchell B. Reibel, SportsChrome East/West;
  bottom left, Dave Black, SportsChrome East/West;
  bottom right, Brian Drake, SportsChrome East/West
Interior photos by Rod Mar

Typeset in Century
by Typeworks, Vancouver, B.C.

Sasquatch Books
1931 Second Avenue
Seattle, Washington 98101

Other titles from Sasquatch Books:
  Seattle Best Places
  Northwest Best Places
  Washingtonians

For Anne

Contents

Acknowledgments

One of the great pleasures afforded me during the course of this project was watching legitimate journalists at work. The beat reporters covering the Seahawks provided me—often inadvertently—with inspiration and insight. Particularly helpful were John Clayton of Tacoma's *Morning News Tribune*, Clare Farnsworth of the *Seattle Post-Intelligencer*, Todd Fredrickson of Everett's *Herald*, Greg Johns of the Bellevue *Journal-American*, and Gil Lyons of the *Seattle Times*. These gentlemen endured my bumbling incursions into their well-mapped territory with inexhaustible patience and grace, and frequent bemusement.

Inspiration of a more entertaining sort was provided by aging enfant terrible Harley Soltes and his understudy, Rod Mar.

My understanding of both the game of football and the life around it was enhanced immeasurably by Cherise Bailey, Sue Krieg, Terry Largent, Connie Millard, and Gia Robinson, for whose honesty and insight I am eternally grateful.

I am also particularly indebted to Seahawk public relations director Gary Wright and his assistant, Dave Neubert, two sardonic gents who know how to keep a writer in line.

Special thanks are due David Brewster and Chad Haight, for their largesse, faith, forgiveness, and inability to keep a writer in line.

In lieu of a muse, I was provided Katherine Koberg, whose ingenious editing has spared me infinite embarrassment and saved the reader from a fate worse than *Vanna Speaks*.

A number of other people also provided invaluable material, tactical, and emotional assistance. Most memorable are Charlotte Kores and Walt Loeffler of the Seahawks, Wayne Wallis and Diane Glover, Jim and Karen Diederick, Jan and Mark Allister, Andora Sharpe, Mary Brennan, Spencer Huntington, Anne Depue, Jon Ransom, Elena Song, Pat Moody, Sam Hudson, and Glen and Jean Moehring.

Most of all, my wife, Anne, and my daughters, Erin, Caitlin, and Jocelyn, made tremendous sacrifices and endured months of neglect from their would-be husband and father for the sake of this book. There were times, I am sure, when they thought they were trapped in a remake of *The Shining*.

Man, the most courageous animal, and the most inured to trouble, does not deny suffering *per se*: he wants it, he seeks it out, provided that it can be given a meaning.
— Friedrich Nietzsche, *The Genealogy of Morals*

The proof is the fact and the fact has no meaning except what is given it by those who establish the facts.
— Henry Miller, *Tropic of Capricorn*

PART I

PRESEASON

Mike McCormack's Face

To the Northwestern pessimist, it is only April. To the optimist, it is already April. At the exact midpoint between the closing of one Seattle Seahawk season and the opening of the next, football hunger is no less palpably in the air than is the warm, sweet scent of emerging springtime. So focused is the Northwestern subconscious on football that even the opening of baseball season cannot distract it. The April 5 *Seattle Post-Intelligencer*, for example, kicked off the 1988 major league season with a football metaphor: "A's Stewart throws Seattle for a loss with 2-hitter."

Sports pages would be filled during the ensuing weeks with stories on the illness and retirement of Seahawk safety Kenny Easley and of the related signing of the team's quarterback-of-the-future, Kelly Stouffer. Occasionally, speculation surfaced that Seattle's Nordstrom family, a department-store dynasty that also served as majority owner of the Seahawks, may at last have found a buyer for its share of the team, on sale for two years. And on April 28, when Seattle's CityClub met for lunch at the Four Seasons Olympic Hotel, it was to ponder no less serious a matter than the coming National Football League season. Held once a week, each CityClub luncheon includes a speech by an invited guest on some topic of civic interest. Previous speakers in the early months of 1988 included Seattle police chief Patrick Fitzsimons, U.S. Senator Dan Evans, and Montlake Elementary School principal LaVaun Dennett. This day, CityClub's honored guest was Seahawk president and general manager Mike McCormack.

Resplendent in civilian pinstripes, McCormack cut a dapper figure at the luncheon. Looking rested and relaxed, he was in fine offseason form, relishing his role as visiting dignitary. He smiled readily, his eyes twinkling like a sprite's, and shook hands with princely politesse. His manners were unselfconsciously out of date: Whenever a woman approached his table, he stood, bowed briefly, then waited until she was seated before he sat down again.

A former offensive tackle, McCormack is a massive man. He is tall and thickset, with white hair, bright pink skin, and pale, luminous eyes. He

1

moves with an agility and grace so surprising in someone his size that it seems almost threatening. Upon first meeting him, you are too over-whelmed by this spectacle of size and color and light to realize, until much later, how odd it feels to shake his huge hand. It is like coming to grips with a prehensile steak.

Even more remarkable is McCormack's face, an expansive, subtly ex-pressive stage upon which the whole rich array of human emotion can play in a matter of seconds. McCormack, for some reason, is incapable of ex-pressing any emotion—simple affection, for example, or mild irritation—without employing his entire face. While this condition makes him seem incapable of concealing his thoughts, it also makes him a terrific interview subject. Verbally he may deliver the football man's typically unenlightening answer to a reporter's question, but his traitorous face all the while is sing-ing like a canary.

He smiled indulgently, fond and proud, while a local hack introduced him as "Nordstrom's most successful store manager," then summarized his long and storied career.

A standout offensive lineman at the University of Kansas in the late 1940s, McCormack was an all-star his senior year. The NFL's New York Yanks made him their number-one draft choice in 1951, then relinquished him to the military for two years before wrapping him in one of sporting his-tory's biggest packages—a 15-player trade—and shipping him off to the Cleveland Browns in 1954. Blessed with tremendous power and speed (he could run 40 yards in 4.8 seconds—a remarkable feat for a man his size), McCormack came to be regarded by Browns founder Paul Brown as the finest player he had ever coached. In nine seasons with Cleveland, McCormack played in six Pro Bowls, three NFL championship games, and eventually was inducted into the NFL Hall of Fame. Retiring after the 1962 season, he spent three forgettable years selling insurance before returning to football as assistant coach for the Washington Redskins in 1966. After six years there, he served as head coach for the Philadelphia Eagles from 1973 through 1975, as assistant coach for the Cincinnati Bengals from 1976 through 1979, and as head coach for the Baltimore Colts for two seasons before becoming Seattle Seahawk director of football operations in 1982. When Seahawk head coach Jack Patera was fired that year, McCormack served as interim coach for the balance of the season. In January 1983, he was named Seahawk president and general manager. He promptly set about redirecting the fortunes of an expansion franchise he was convinced now had the talent to contend for the Super Bowl. Twenty-three days after becoming team president, he sought out and signed a new field general, the

Buffalo Bills' Chuck Knox, regarded as one of the NFL's all-time greatest coaches.

Under McCormack, Seattle brought Seahawk salaries from near the bottom of the NFL heap to somewhere near the top. (Just how near the top is a matter of conjecture. While McCormack ranks Seattle "fifth to eighth" in player salaries, the NFL Players Association ranks Seattle second.) After being shut out of the NFL playoffs through their first six seasons, the Seahawks under McCormack made the playoffs in three out of the next five seasons. Now, going into 1988, the team had high hopes. With McCormack in the front office, Seattle had gone from perennial doormat to perennial contender, from a 35–57 won-lost record after its first six years to a 53–32 record for the last five.

In many ways, McCormack defined the Seahawks. The 1988 edition would be almost entirely his team. Of the 105 players scheduled to report to training camp that July, all but seven would be McCormack-era acquisitions. The team's coaching, personnel, and scouting department heads all were McCormack signees. He also—partly by default, partly by design—sets the tone for the Seahawks' relationship with fans and media. Coached by an all-but-inaccessible eccentric and owned by a deliberately invisible family, the Seahawks have made McCormack their point man. Virtually all off-field controversies and matters of public interest are funneled through him. A master of unpredictability—sometimes secretive, sometimes open and engaging, occasionally playful, nearly always truculent—he keeps sportswriters at an amiable arm's length. One day he might jump in front of a photographer, blocking his attempt to photograph an injured player. The next he might go out of his way to spare a reporter embarrassment by telling him that a player he is writing a feature on is about to be cut from the team. Always his emotions are right on the surface, a circumstance that allows reporters to view him more as a fellow human being than as a faceless corporate executive. It also makes him, in the concluding words of the hack's introduction to the CityClub audience, "that staple of a sportswriter's diet: good copy."

To warm applause, McCormack took to the dais to deliver his speech, which he began with an apology to the women in the audience: "You'll have to forgive me. I'm not used to talking before members of the fairer gender . . . " He went on, with obvious pride, to point out that under his stewardship, the Seahawks had the National Football League's sixth-best record over the previous five seasons. The team performed even better off the field than on it, selling out all but a handful of games through its first 12 seasons. The waiting list for season tickets, he observed, is 10 years long.

What few seats came available for the 1988 season went to fans who signed up in 1979. While modestly attributing much of his franchise's achievement both to the nationwide success of the NFL and to the Northwest's love of football, he was also quick to attribute a good part of it to the way the Seahawk organization is run. He lavishly praised the Nordstrom family's hands-off ownership policy, and described the team's goal-setting procedures, preparation for games and player drafts, and so on, trying occasionally to draw connections between the world of football and the world of business.

Before long, McCormack invited the audience to ask questions, and hands went up all over the room. His listeners clearly were more interested in the Seahawks' on-field prospects than in their business practices, and they questioned McCormack on everything from the reasons behind Seattle's acquisition of rookie quarterback Kelly Stouffer to the state of the Seahawk kicking game. He furnished answers so readily, and with such good cheer, that he gave the impression he'd be happy to spend the rest of the afternoon there.

Even things that turn him purple with rage during the season struck him this afternoon as hilarious. He got his biggest laugh of the day with a grin-graced remark on Seattle punter Ruben Rodriguez: "We like Ruben," he said, "even though he does occasionally kick one straight up in the air."

As often happens at luncheons of this sort, there were reporters in attendance, and when the torrent of pleasant questions from the audience proper finally slowed to a trickle, Steve Raible, sports broadcaster from KIRO, the local CBS-television affiliate, interjected with an unpleasant one. "Mike," he asked, "is there anything new to report on the Kenny Easley situation?"

McCormack's eyes turned distant and dead and his face stony. His torture-by-journalism face, it was at once submissive and hostile. As reporters tend to do, Raible had brought up the offseason's most controversial football story, and in so doing—to judge from the look on McCormack's face—he had ruined the whole afternoon.

Seattle safety Kenny Easley, along with backup quarterback Gale Gilbert, had kept the Seahawk name prominently displayed in the papers all offseason, focusing Seattle's attention for months on the dark side of professional football. Gilbert was fighting sexual assault charges brought against him by two different women. The charges, countercharges, allegations, dubious defenses, and zany details of Gilbert's attempted seductions, while keeping sports fans alternately entertained and appalled, were bringing considerable embarrassment to the image-conscious Seattle franchise. Eventually Gilbert would be acquitted in the first trial, would plead guilty in the second, would be released by the Seahawks, and would try to catch on with the Canadian Football League's Calgary Stampeders. That career move would be thwarted by the Canadian government, which would deny him entry into Canada, and Gilbert would mercifully disappear from public view.

Easley was another matter. Seven stellar seasons as Seattle's greatest defensive player had come to a controversial end after the 1987 season. An exceptionally reckless player, Easley had seen his skills decline year by year as professional football, in the form of shoulder, knee, and ankle injuries, exacted its inevitable toll. In addition, Easley, who is black, served as the Seahawks' union representative during the 1987 player strike and for his trouble received considerable hate mail—much of it racist.

The player strike—the NFL's second in five years—lasted only four weeks. The league canceled its games on the strike's first Sunday, then played three more weekends with teams staffed by strikebreakers. The strike was effectively broken when the nation's television networks elected to broadcast the strike games, thereby siding with ownership against the league's workforce. Week by week, both television ratings and attendance at strike games across the league improved, the tide of public sympathy turned gradually against the players, and union solidarity eroded, the players returning in ever-greater numbers to their teams.

While listing a variety of grievances, the strike really was over a single issue: free agency for players. Under the current system, a player was the property of the team that drafted him until that team traded his rights away, and football players wanted at least the limited freedom to bargain that was enjoyed by professional basketball and baseball players.

Embittered at both Seattle management and Seattle fans, Easley asked to be traded at the end of the '87 season. His resentment and physical decline, combined with the chance to sign a highly regarded quarterback prospect named Kelly Stouffer, led the Seahawks to trade Easley to the Phoenix Cardinals. The Cardinals had drafted Stouffer in 1987, been unable to sign him, and now had until draft day 1988 to trade him or lose their rights to him altogether.

Before the Seahawks could risk trading for Stouffer, they needed to have him signed to a contract. The trade had been consummated only after a flurry of white-knuckle negotiations between McCormack and Stouffer's agent, Mike Blatt. Then, six days before the CityClub luncheon, McCormack and Blatt came to terms, Stouffer signed with Seattle, and Easley flew off to Phoenix to take his physical.

McCormack punctuated his negotiations with Blatt with a characteristic, if unfortunate, moment of candor with the press. First, he called Blatt a liar. Then, told that Blatt had said Stouffer's signing was held up because

Easley had not yet shown up in Phoenix for his physical, McCormack got in one last dig. "Agents," he said, "do not know the ways of the NFL."

Before the 1988 season ended, that last remark would come back to haunt McCormack by way of a turn of events so bizarre it should do away forever with the naive notion that life's coincidences are accidental.

First, though, there came a tragic turn of events for Easley. After being thoroughly gone over by Phoenix's orthopedists, he passed with flying colors, and Cardinal pro personnel director Larry Wilson called McCormack with the good news. Shortly thereafter, Wilson called again. Phoenix doctors, he said, in looking over the results of some routine lab work, discovered that Easley was on the verge of complete kidney failure, and his playing days were over.

As he told his CityClub audience about Wilson's second phone call, McCormack's expression shifted again. His face was clouded with all the disbelief and anger and agony that combine to make up unfeigned human grief.

This sort of emotional revelation is extremely rare in football, where masculine stoicism reigns supreme. Even for someone as mercurial as McCormack, it was a remarkable display, and a reverent hush descended over the gathering of fans before him.

However unprecedented, though, it was not what made the luncheon unforgettable. In the ensuing months, memories of McCormack's lamentation would fade, while two of his answers to fans' questions at the luncheon would take on, in memory, the aura of prophecy. Asked about last season's players strike, McCormack answered, "It seems like the teams that had the most turmoil went the farthest last season, and the teams that hung together fared the poorest. You wonder if the modern athlete responds to the kind of family atmosphere we've been trying to build around here."

Moments later, asked to assess Kelly Stouffer's abilities, McCormack brightened considerably, then concluded his remarks with a statement that makes no sense unless it is regarded not as mundane prediction but as inspired vision. "He'll be playing," McCormack intoned, "sooner than his coaches plan for him to be."

With those two pronouncements did Michael Joseph McCormack, however unofficially, kick off the heroic hobble that officially would begin high up in the Rocky Mountains, on the fourth day of September, and would end 119 days and 17 pitched battles later on the banks of the Ohio River, in the gathering dusk on the last day of the Year of Our Commissioner 1988.

Author! Author!

By 11:55am on Wednesday, July 13, the media room at Seahawk head-quarters was packed with pundits. His Eminence, Seattle head coach Chuck Knox, was scheduled to appear at high noon for a formal declaration of the opening of the team's 13th preseason training camp. Conversations in the room were animated, and the writers eager. Since Knox, however, is at least as well known for his bromide-laden speeches as he is for his winning football, the reporters' excitement was considerably diluted by the prospect of sitting through another full season of Knox's press-conference platitudes.

Before it had even begun, then, the season was opening to mixed reviews.

At 11:59, Seahawk public relations director Gary Wright walked into the room, shouted a peremptory "Let's go!", and led the shuffling herd across the hall to a perfectly appointed, blond-wood-paneled conference room, the walls decorated with huge portraits of each year's number-one draft choice. At 12:02pm, Knox, preceded by Mike McCormack, strode into the room and sat down at a long table covered with microphones and tape recorders.

McCormack, wearing his aggressively bland meet-the-press face, sat down beside Knox and said, in a lifeless monotone, "A couple of announcements." The team's customary preseason scrimmage with the Houston Oilers, he said, would be held at the Tacoma Dome, with proceeds benefiting the Mary Bridge Children's Hospital. He announced the signing of veteran center Blair Bush, then concluded the opening portion of the program with a mumbled, "We're working on the remaining veterans, free agents, and draft choices."

The Bush signing was to be the first in a flurry of contracts to be inked just as camp was opening. After the collapse last season of the players strike, the NFL Players Association had gone to court, claiming that contract talks were at an impasse and that a collective bargaining agreement was unattainable. Under the expired agreement—which was still in force, since a new agreement had not been reached—all players, whether signed

7

or unsigned, were the property of the team that had last drafted or employed them and were prohibited from selling their services on the open market unless the team that "owned" them gave them their release. Under labor law, the union pointed out, a judge could declare an impasse in negotiations and make all players instant free agents, able to bargain and sign with whatever team they chose.

As the case was argued before federal judge David Doty in Washington, D.C., over the summer, contract negotiations across the country came to a halt. If Doty ruled for the players, all contracts would be voided and every player in the league would suddenly become a free agent only two months before the scheduled beginning of the season. The result would be total anarchy, with teams locked in a bidding frenzy to sign players, build rosters, and teach their systems to their new charges almost overnight. The pro football season would be reduced to playground football, with teams choosing up sides and having at it. The specter of impending disorder had coaches and general managers heading into training camp in a state of tight-lipped consternation. By July 11, the day Doty was to render his verdict, Seahawk headquarters was crackling. "You can't talk to anybody today," I was told that day by a laughing team functionary. "People are a little . . . *tense!*"

Doty, apparently enough of a football fan to share NFL coaches' fear, decreed that although the players were on sound legal ground and although their pending antitrust suit was likely to be resolved in their favor (a resolution that would render the NFL's college draft and player reserve system illegal), to grant an injunction now would cause such chaos throughout the league that he couldn't bring himself to do it. With the status quo thus reinstated for at least one more season, negotiations resumed, and by training camp's first day, all but 10 of 105 Seattle players would be signed.

As McCormack withdrew into dour silence, Knox greeted the gathering and launched into a description of the training camp regimen. That coming Saturday, he explained, the Seahawks' 36 rookies and 34 of the team's 69 veterans would report to advance camp and would begin practicing the following day. The rest of the team would report for physicals next Wednesday and begin practicing Thursday. Practices would be held at 9:15am and at 2:45pm each day. The 105-player roster would be cut, as dictated by NFL rules, to 60 players on August 23—three days before the final preseason game—and to 47 players on August 29, six days before the season opener against the Denver Broncos.

Knox was barely recognizable to those who had last seen him during the previous season. For one thing, he was wearing a green cardigan sweater of a hue so bright that it practically glowed. For another, he was wearing socks to match. Most surprising was his countenance. Where normally he looks exhausted and eaten alive by anger—his skin sallow and slack, his eyes watery and red-rimmed, and his jaw ferociously set—today he exuded childish cheer. The color had been pumped back into his cheeks, his eyes were dry and clear, and he was speaking so vigorously that his listeners, long accustomed to getting four or five words out of him for every 20-word question they asked, began to suspect that the real Knox had been replaced by a poorly prepared stand-in.

"Coming into this season," he chirped, "we need to improve our coaching: profit by mistakes that were made and work to get better. We need our veteran players to improve, and we need an infusion of young talent to come in and make significant contributions. Our special teams play has to improve. Our overall play last season was bad. We need to improve our schemes [Seattle's formations and methods of attack both on offense and defense], create a better motivational framework, and have better practice organization."

Five minutes of effervescent monologue—unprompted by question, untainted by cliché—went by before Knox at last made a passing allusion to one of his favorite Knoxisms. "We're very excited about the season," he said. "It's a big challenge for us."

As is the case with many of Knox's one-line pronouncements, this one was the tip of a cryptic iceberg. The word "challenge" is always intended to remind his listeners of his tired mantra, "There are no problems in life—only challenges." Asked about any matter that most of us would regard as a problem (the size and age of his porous defensive line, for example), Knox invariably replies, "It's a challenge," by which he means, "Yes, it is a big problem, but I am so determined to find a way to overcome it that nothing in the world can keep me from doing so by means of my will and my ingenuity." By employing that statement to kick off the 1988 campaign, however, Knox wasn't simply beating his chest. He was letting the press see, just for a moment, how disappointed he had been by the previous season. By calling the upcoming football season "a big challenge," he was alluding to the weaknesses that had undone him in 1987 and admitting that they had not been overcome by the '88 player draft.

The '87 season had indeed been disappointing, and afterwards Knox entered into an offseason of troubling reassessment. He had seen his rebuilding effort, begun in 1983, finally come to fruition in 1986, albeit one game too late. His team, 5–6 that year with five games to go, suddenly turned invincible, winning the rest of its games and finishing the regular season with the NFL's hottest offense. Hot as the Seahawks were, however, their 10–6 won-lost record was good enough only for a tie with three other teams in their conference, and three more teams did better than that. This left the Seahawks one of four teams vying for two wild-card playoff spots, and in the end they were left out of postseason play because of the league's complex tie-breaking formula.

That a team on such a roll should go home empty-handed, while far less inspiring teams went on to the playoffs, struck *New York Times* columnist Dave Anderson as so ludicrous that he proposed having that year's punch-less New York Jets "trade their playoff spot to the Seattle Seahawks for an offense to be named later." Seattle's five-game roll at the end of that season also established them in the national media as preseason favorites to make the 1987 season's Super Bowl. Instead, they failed to win more than two straight non-strike games all season long, finished a troubled 9–6, and played poorly in their wild-card round playoff loss to the Houston Oilers. When Knox came back to Seattle, he faced a chorus of criticism from fans, many of whom suggested that he be fired.

He also had to face up to some sobering numbers. The Seahawks had managed a winning streak longer than two games only once since 1984. In 1987, they had been inconsistent on offense, with a well-played game most often followed by a disastrous one, and on defense had been far worse than their 9–6 record indicated. They ranked 22nd in the 28-team NFL in total defense, 26th in rushing yards allowed, and, surrendering 4.7 yards per running play, finished dead last in that category. At that rate, as McCormack pointed out, teams could beat Seattle without ever bothering to throw a pass.

Almost immediately, Knox and the rest of the Seattle braintrust had set to work analyzing their team's needs. Most glaring, in Knox's view, was the need to improve the play of his linemen and linebackers, whose in-adequacies were to blame not only for Seattle's inferior run-defense numbers but for their poor pass-defense numbers as well. The latter, according to Knox and McCormack, were due not to weak pass coverage but to a weak pass rush. "We've got three cornerbacks," Knox said at the press conference, "who can run, who can play, but defensive line is a position we've been trying to upgrade for a couple of years. We need a speed pass rusher." McCormack and Knox felt that Seattle's biggest need on offense was for a good all-around tight end, a position requiring both the blocking skills of an interior lineman and receiving skills good enough to make the end a significant part of the team's passing attack. Next, they wanted a backup to the team's prime mover, running back Curt Warner, who would be entering camp recuperating from his third operation in four years. "Curt Warner's going to carry the load," Knox explained. "What we need if he gets hurt or nicked or something is a guy who can go in there and sustain something." And at wide receiver, the Seahawks were on the verge of trouble: The ages of perennial superstar Steve Largent and veteran Ray Butler had made shoring up the receiver position the top priority in the last player draft.

McCormack was most concerned with improving the overall depth of his roster. Ideally, at each position a team would have a backup player who was three or four years younger than the starter. "What you like is a blend," he explained a few days before the press conference, "so that as one gets older you have someone else ready to replace him." After the 1986 season, Seattle was dangerously thin and old at linebacker, lacking even adequate backup players, and had made Pittsburgh linebacker Tony Woods their first pick, Stanford linebacker Dave Wyman their second. Then, in the supplemental draft, they acquired Oklahoma linebacker Brian Bosworth. In one offseason, they signed three new, talented linebackers—who, as things turned out, would all be starting in 1988.

Going into the '88 draft, held on April 24, the team had no first-round choice—that had been part of the price for Bosworth—and thus had to wait until the 48 most-wanted players were gone before Seattle's turn came. As luck would have it, the draft was uncommonly rich in wide receivers, and Brian Blades, a promising wideout from Miami, was available when Seattle's number came up. Next time around, they picked Syracuse wide receiver Tommy Kane. "Those were not difficult decisions," McCormack says. For the second straight year, the draft had been richest at one of the positions the Seahawks most needed to improve.

The draft, however, had done nothing to help Seattle's most pressing problem: its defensive front. There were no 6'4", 285-pound speedsters to help pressure the quarterback, and Knox was left with three defensive linemen who were too old and too small to take on their modern offensive counterparts.

Forced to work with a defensive roster made up of obsolete linemen and inexperienced linebackers, Knox announced, he had decided to deploy a defense that would compensate for his team's built-in liabilities. The '88 attack would feature a more aggressive "one-gap" attack in place of the former relatively passive "two-gap" defense. "We want to free our linebackers up," he explained, "so they can beat offensive linemen with speed and quickness. And we will have more of an attacking scheme than in the past."

Knox's audience pricked up its ears at the unsolicited utterance of *actual football terminology*. Having walked into the room with eyes glazed over from lack of expectation, they now were doubly surprised. Not only was Knox in a talkative mood, he was saying something of genuine interest! "One-gap! . . . Two-gap!" His listeners, taken aback, looked as if Knox had just flung open a window, letting a sudden gust of enthusiasm into the stuffy room.

Scintillating as the language sounded, however, the change Knox had in mind was actually fairly subtle. When two teams face off at the line of scrimmage, there are five offensive linemen opposite three defensive linemen. The offensive line is broken down into alternating blockers and gaps, with each defensive lineman confronted by two gaps—one on either side of the man facing him. In the two-gap scheme, a defensive lineman charges, hits his blocker, then decides which gap to fill. The linebacker, meanwhile, looks first to see how the play is blocked, then charges forward to fill the gap his teammate on the line has left vacant. The whole defense, in the two-gap scheme, is programmed to react to the offense's initiative rather than to attack on its own. In the one-gap scheme, lineman and linebacker alike are preassigned single gaps to attack, and when the ball is snapped, they charge the gap in question, hoping to beat the blocker there, then look for and react to the ball carrier.

Knox also planned to enhance defensive aggression by having his linebackers and safeties dog and blitz—rush the quarterback—more often rather than wait to see whether the offense was passing or running with the ball before deciding whether to rush or drop back into pass coverage.

The switch of schemes was an attempt at developing a defense that seized the initiative from the opposing offense. Knox wanted to restore to the Seattle defense a level of aggression not seen since 1984. The change also was a simple illustration of one of Knox's strongest-held beliefs: that a coach's job "is to put his players in the most advantageous position possible to make a play." Since he had small, quick defensive players rather than big, immobile ones, Knox was forced to use a scheme that would better utilize their quickness while reducing their significant size disadvantage.

He was making a similar move at linebacker. Since his linebackers, being young, were quicker afoot than they were amind, the two-gap scheme was risky. It called upon linebackers to make too many decisions under fire— the kind of decisions that demand experience and savvy. By asking them to rely more on their bodies than on their brains, Knox was simply finding a way to employ his linebackers' strengths as attackers rather than having to compensate constantly for their weaknesses as thinkers.

Upbeat as Knox sounded about his strategic changes, they were made more by default than by design. Since he was more or less stuck with the same players as the year before, he had no choice but to change the system that deployed them. "The defensive performance just wasn't there last year," Mike McCormack explained to me later. "Could that be the schemes? Or was it a combination of scheme and players?" If they opted to focus on the scheme, it was because they had no alternative. "We decided it was the scheme, because you can't replace 22 players on the defensive side of the ball. So try a new scheme, to make them more aggressive."

On the offensive side, Knox's options were even more limited. For years, his offense had been vulnerable to storming defenses which would overload up front in order to force Seattle to abandon its strength—the running game—and rely on the unreliable arm and mind of quarterback Dave Krieg. "We're going to make changes in our audible systems," Knox said, referring to the quarterback's coded system for changing plays at the line of scrimmage. "We need to try to anticipate problems rather than try to react to them after they occur."

Anticipation being the emerging theme of the press conference, Knox pressed on. "To anticipate a question, 'What are we going to do if Fredd Young doesn't report?' . . . We'll move Tony Woods to the right side and start Bruce Scholtz at left outside linebacker."

At Knox's mention of Young, McCormack executed a nearly imperceptible wince, and someone asked if there was any possibility that he would accede to Young's demand to renegotiate the remaining three years of the four-year contract he had signed last season. "No," McCormack replied tersely.

McCormack's manner reawakened the prodding instincts that cause reporters to ask questions to which they know they won't get printable answers. Someone asked whether or not Kenny Easley, who had been unavailable for comment ever since his career-ending kidney ailment had been discovered, would be arriving to take a team-administered physical examination, as was required by a technicality in his insurance coverage. "Yes," McCormack said, his face ossifying. "But there are physicals and there are physicals . . . In other words, I would not plan on holding a press conference with Kenny Easley when he shows up for his physical."

It was time now for the next item on the journalistic agenda: Brian Bosworth's recent statement in New York's *Village Voice* that Knox "is a good offensive coach, but he doesn't know shit about defense." Asked to comment, Knox allowed as how he believed Bosworth was misquoted, then said with a smile, "Usually people say I don't know anything about offense!" This elicited a laugh from his audience, then brought on the inevitable question about Bosworth's forthcoming masturbate-and-tell book, *The Boz: Confessions of a Modern Anti-Hero.*

Knox was waiting for this one. "That book, whatever it is, won't have anything to do with what we do or how we do this season. The book isn't gonna block anybody or tackle anybody. You people will run out and buy it . . . that'd be something wouldn't it? Reporters *paying* for a book? . . . and as always, there will be some instant rush and people will be quoting the book, paraphrasing the book, and asking questions about what was meant to be and intended to be. Then it will just be put up on the back shelf . . . "

From the back of the room came an interruptive question: "Any other books you want to comment on, Chuck?"

For once, Knox looked embarrassed. He stared out at his laughing audience for a moment, confused and silent. The reference was to his own book, *Hard Knox*, due out in October.

Knox is so secretive that nothing could be more out of character than for him to produce an autobiography. To those familiar with his public persona, it made no sense. It was clear that even as his book was about to appear, he was at least as ill at ease with what he had done as his readers-to-be were surprised.

Yet authorship, you would think, must come naturally to Knox. A coach is nothing so much as an author, with the football season his work-in-progress. After conceiving and planning his work during the offseason, the coach enters the season with an ideal plot, complete with happy, heroic ending, already outlined in his mind. All that remained before the writing of the final draft of Knox's *1988 Season* (the 16th volume in *The Knoxiad*) was to develop his characters, a task he was set to begin in four days. After that would come the exhausting challenge of imposing his work of fiction upon 12 other authors, each seeking to subvert the others' work for the sake of his own. Out of this 16-week collaboration among coaches would evolve a more interesting story than that envisioned by Knox. For each of his attempts at creation is destined always to develop in the same way: Knox, the author, is also the central character in a far grander work, authored by an unseen hand. That story chronicles Knox's struggle to survive the clash of his dream work with the grimmer workings of reality. And in this coming season, it would soon be clear, reality would have in store for him surprises and twists of plot worthy of the most imaginative of fiction writers.

CattleCall

*All happy families are alike, but an unhappy family is unhappy
after its own fashion.*

—Lev Tolstoy, *Anna Karenina*

Like an incandescent baseball, the mid-July sun shone fiercely down on
the grunting and squealing athletes toiling below, as if to serve notice that
they were playing the wrong game. The players, in full football regalia,
gasping for air and dreaming of shade, would occasionally gaze at the
sidelines, where coaches, scouts, reporters, and other privileged spectators strolled languidly along, dressed in shorts, baseball caps, and light
summer shirts. While the players broiled, the onlookers basked, and more
than a few of the athletes must have wondered whether the same sun
shone down on both groups.

The 102 hopefuls on the field represented the best football talent that
money, expertise, time, and fortune could ferret out. They had been
filmed, timed, poked, prodded, measured, weighed, bled, quizzed, graded,
and matched against a list of strengths and weaknesses in the existing
Seahawk roster before being invited, or commanded, to attend Seattle's
training camp. Some, it could be seen at a glance, stood no chance of making the team. Others stood no chance of not making it. But for most, the
jury was more or less still out.

Acquiring pro football talent is an art disguised as a science. For all of the
mathematical measurements taken of a player's strengths, skills, range of
motion, reflexes, and work habits, the final analysis comes down to intangibles and instincts. Football's talent search is essentially a high-tech roll
of the dice. However promising—or unpromising—a player's size and speed
and strength, his ability to thrive in the professional ranks can almost never
be accurately predicted. In the end, coaches must simply put him out on the
gridiron and see what happens.

Seattle's 1988 preseason roster included a telling blow to the pride of
football's scientists: wide receiver Steve Largent. The only current

Seahawk to have played for Seattle from the dawn of the franchise, Largent
began his career by being cut from the Houston Oilers roster during the
1976 preseason. The Seahawks picked up Largent that year only after persistent prodding from offensive coordinator Jerry Rhome, who coached
Largent in college and thought he could play pro ball. Now, going into 1988,
Largent was one of the greatest players in football history. He held four all-
time NFL receiving records and was within less than a season's reach of
four more.

While Largent was the most spectacular example of the shortcomings of
football science, he was by no means the only one on the Seattle roster. Of
the previous season's 22 starters, eight had come to Seattle as "free
agents," players who either had gone undrafted or had signed with Seattle
after having been cut by other teams. Of the 61 players in camp who had a
year or more of NFL experience, fully 27 had come to Seattle via the free-
agent route. (Before signing with Seattle, those 27 players were considered by the entire NFL to be worth less than hundreds of others who were
drafted and signed ahead of them, then ultimately released without ever
playing in a game.) By contrast, only 20 returnees originally were drafted
higher than the sixth round.

Held every spring, the NFL player draft is a rigidly controlled parceling-
out among the league's teams of the rights to sign players coming out of
college. Teams are ranked in each year's draft in reverse order of their finish the season before: The worst team drafts first, the best team last. This
ranking obtains throughout the two-day affair, with teams drafting in the
same position in every round until all of the supposedly draft-worthy talent
is used up.

For the Seahawks, every draft is preceded by a full year's preparation.
The franchise divides the U.S. into five areas, each with its own scouts.
The scouts look at as many college players as possible, assigning each a
grade from 1 to 10. Their work is then supplemented by two more scouts
who look at the top-graded talent, then by Seahawk player personnel director Mike Allman, who looks at the top 150 staff-rated players. "That way,"
says Mike McCormack, "we get at least three looks at our top 150 kids."
Reports and rankings are turned in at the end of the season to the Seahawk
coaching staff. The coaches then attend the NFL physical, a meat market at
which the whole nation's potential pro talent is examined. After that, having
ranked the top 10 to 15 players at each position, the Seahawks send their
position coaches around the country, visiting and working out each player.
Then, in the first three weeks of April, the scouts and coaches confer, compare numbers, debate, and assign a final grade to each player, ending up
with a list of the top 500 prospects, ranked in grade order.

Knox, McCormack, and Allman are reputed to be among the NFL's best when it comes to spotting legitimate professional potential in an aspiring youngster. Their ability, though, is largely a matter of gut instinct. Seattle's grading system, while "scientific" in form, is little more than an attempt to quantify coaches' and scouts' impressions about a prospect. "I've never seen a 10," says McCormack. "He would be a superhuman specimen. I've seen some 9.1s, some 9.2s . . . Usually your quarterbacks, your running backs, an outstanding one would be in the 9 range. There is a lot of 8.2s. Most of your first-round picks will be in the 7 range. Then you work down to 3s, who are maybe free agents or not a real good draft pick. Threes usually are players who have one thing but not a lot of things. He might have great size, let's say, but not much foot speed—hasn't played up to his body. Or a real outstanding runner, but maybe too small."

The Seahawks go into the draft in much the same way they enter a game. They prepare as thoroughly as possible in order to draft according to a plan rather than according to impulse. While they hope to fill holes at particular positions through the draft, they also want to compile the most talent-rich roster possible. Mostly, they want to avoid passing up a highly ranked athlete for one who, while filling an immediate need, might also still be available in a lower round. "If you reach and pass up a lot of good athletes, a lot of athletes that you have ranked high," says McCormack, "to draft someone that might be available in another round, then it hurts you, because you lower the quality of your talent."

The Seahawks did exactly that in the 1985 draft. Desperate for a fullback who could block for star running back Curt Warner, they made mediocre fullback Owen Gill their number-one draft choice. Abandoning their customary disciplined approach, the team passed up more than 30 athletes rated higher than Gill, hoping to strengthen themselves at fullback. They ended up not only without the back they sought—Gill proved to be an incompetent blocker, and never played a down for Seattle—but with one less athlete to help build their 1985 roster. That year, not entirely by coincidence, they finished 8–8.

The next year, the Seahawks were compensated by fate when John L. Williams, a superb blocking back, was available to Seattle in the first round. To a chorus of leaguewide criticism—conventional wisdom insisted Seattle needed to draft an offensive lineman—they selected him. During the ensuing preseason, it was immediately apparent that the Seahawks had found in Williams the player they had sought in Gill. The NFL's youngest starter that year, Williams was the only rookie running back to start all 16 games, and was the American Football Conference's leading rookie rusher, with 538 yards. He also proved to be a flawless blocker for Warner, who with

Williams's help enjoyed the best season of his career. Entering 1988, Williams was firmly installed as the linchpin of the offense, serving as Warner's lead blocker and having emerged as an all-purpose back. He had been Seattle's 1987 leader both in yards-per-carry average and in pass receptions out of the backfield.

Williams's was to prove one of the very few positions, on or off the field, that Knox would not have to worry about as camp opened. On July 15, the day before advance camp, the Nordstroms announced their purchase of their minority partners' 49 percent of the Seattle franchise. With the team now entirely in their hands, it was widely believed, sale to outside interests was in the offing. Curt Warner, tabbed by Knox to be his primary offensive weapon, was recovering from ankle surgery and would see very little playing time during preseason. Unpredictable wide receiver Daryl Turner, who had missed May's three-day minicamp, had not yet reported, and no one seemed to know where he was. Starting defensive end Jeff Bryant, who had yet to sign a contract, and Fredd Young, unhappy with the contract he had signed, were staying out of camp. Young's backup, Greg Gaines, arrived at camp with a damaged disk in his back, was set to undergo surgery, and would be out for three months. Celebrity linebacker Bosworth, who had elected to forgo arthroscopic surgery on a sore shoulder during the offseason, was in pain. Knox, who just weeks before had planned on redesigning his defense around his veteran linebackers, now found that three out of eight of them were either missing or injured.

At the end of the camp's first week, Young's holdout took a turn for the pathetic. By then, even Young's agent, Bruce Singman, had given up on him, insisting that the pact Young had signed the year before was a reasonable one. A new agent, Jeff Dankworth, was reviewing the history of Young's contract negotiations and preparing to represent him. Young, subject to fines of $1,000 per day for being under contract and not showing up at practices, was also courting more extreme financial disaster. Should he continue to stay out of camp, the Seahawks, under the terms of the 1982 collective bargaining agreement, could serve him with a letter insisting that he rejoin the team. If he refused to do so, he would be put on a player reserve list for the entire season, during which he would not be paid and would not be allowed to play anywhere. Even if he gave in, he would be penalized. Once the letter was served, his salary would be frozen, thus denying him the $75,000 raise due him in '88.

Young's ire was directed not so much at his own contract as it was at the difference between his and Bosworth's. By unhappy coincidence, Young had signed a three-year contract, with an option year, the day before Bosworth signed a 10-year, $11 million blockbuster deal. Young, an unheralded player out of New Mexico State, had been drafted by Seattle in the third round of the 1984 draft. He turned out to be a far better player than even he had ever imagined, and was rewarded going into 1987 with a contract that could net him $380,000 that season ($260,000 in base salary, a $50,000 signing bonus, $50,000 for being a Pro Bowl starter, and $20,000 for being named All-Pro). Bosworth, during that same season—his first— would be paid $350,000. Young's base salary was to rise to $350,000 in 1988, $425,000 in 1989, and $467,000 in his option year, 1990, with the opportunity each year to earn significantly more by making performance incentives. Over the same period, Bosworth was to earn yearly salaries of $400,000, $500,000, and $600,000, with no performance-incentive opportunities. With the incentives, then, Young's salary was slated to be higher each year than Bosworth's. What gnawed at Young was that he had to perform to be paid, while Bosworth didn't. He also had been required to prove his worth in the pro ranks before being offered a good contract, while Bosworth was paid simply for showing up. Bosworth was granted a $2.5 million signing bonus, with deferred payments to begin in 1997, before playing so much as a single down, and arrived in Seattle a full-blown marquee idol, being courted by poster, movie, book, and commercial-endorsement people, while Young remained a virtual nonentity.

When Bosworth graduated from the University of Oklahoma in 1987, he was reputed to be the nation's best football player and football's most colorful character. He was known nationwide as "the Boz," an outrageous, outspoken wild man, as irreverent off the field as he was powerful on it. A standout linebacker and good student, he graduated one year before his college football eligibility expired, and entered a special supplemental draft, in which all 28 NFL teams participated in a lottery for the rights to him. When the Seahawks won the lottery, Bosworth vowed not to play for them and held out—publicly demanding a trade and privately negotiating a contract—until midway through the 1987 preseason. By the time he finally arrived in Seattle, he was already a superhero. He was the first bona fide, show-biz-savvy celebrity to sign on with a Northwest sports franchise. Before playing a single down in Seattle, he had already become a larger-than-life Northwest institution, a legend before his playing time.

Upon showing up at the '87 training camp, Bosworth immediately declared himself "pissed off," saying, after practice one day, "I come in here and I'm only in camp four days, and hell, people expect me to make sacks and interceptions. People think that I'm the Second Coming. It ain't like that. In college, you deal with a few real players and a lot of average players. In the professional ranks, every player is a great player. It takes a little time to get used to it."

Accordingly, Bosworth played that season more like a mortal rookie than an instant immortal, and soon found himself simultaneously keeping both a high and a low profile. Nationwide, he labored mightily to keep the Boz in the public eye, while in Seattle he tried to keep Brian Bosworth out of sight. During the 1987 players strike, while his teammates walked picket lines in Seattle, he jetted around the country, appearing as a video jockey on MTV and showing up on as many television talk shows as would have him. Less than one-third of the way through the season, offended by un-flattering comparisons between his prodigious skill at self-promotion and his as-yet-unremarkable skill at pro football, he stopped talking to Seattle reporters altogether. By season's end, he was granting interviews only to reporters from national media.

Bosworth's ennui, and dissension among all the players, dogged Seattle all season long. The month-long strike divided the Seahawks bitterly. When the 1987 campaign ended with an overtime loss in the first round of the playoffs to the Houston Oilers, there was widespread conviction among players and fans alike that the Seahawks, a team divided, had played below their potential.

For nearly everyone, last season's travails were now forgotten. Even Bosworth arrived at the '88 camp sporting a self-professed "new attitude." But Young either couldn't understand or couldn't stomach the fact that pro football has become as much entertainment as sport. When a top college player is negotiating his first pro contract, his position in the draft and his celebrity status give him leverage that lesser-known players, or players from lesser-known colleges, do not have. The player with the right college credentials and the ability to hype himself can demand far more for his ser-vices than they are worth when measured purely in football terms. While Bosworth's athletic potential was grossly magnified by his notoriety as he was coming out of college in 1987, Young's potential had been grossly mini-mized by virtue of his being unknown as he was coming out of college in 1984.

Throw in the shy, inarticulate Young's instant dislike for the glib and glamorous Bosworth, and you have a classic rags-to-riches-to-rage story, reaching a culmination of sorts when Young finally showed up for training camp after sitting out for a week. He arrived on the practice field on Sun-day, July 24, with "50 Blues" written on his ankle tape. Bosworth, the sea-son before, had been denied his desired uniform number, 44, and had taken to writing either that number or "44 Blues"—an allusion both to his state of mind and to the name of the company he had formed to market Bos-worthian products—on his ankle tape before games. Young was alluding to Bosworth's commercial endeavors, to his own uniform number (50), and to the $50,000 difference between his and Bosworth's 1988 base salaries.

The wit apparently was lost on Young's teammates, who, out of embar-rassment for him, tried to ignore the message. Young attended both prac-tices Sunday, then walked onto the field Monday, abruptly turned around before practice began, went back to the locker room, changed clothes, and left. "I guess I'm leavin'," he muttered to the parking lot guard on his way through the gate. For reasons he chose not to discuss with anyone, he was back that afternoon, "50 Blues" and all. Tuesday he showed up for the morning practice session, then disappeared in the afternoon. Asked at the end of that day whether Young's unpredictable behavior was becoming a problem, Knox tried to inject some predictability into his troubled camp by answering, "There are no problems in life, only challenges."

During the camp's first week, I came upon evidence of one particularly compelling challenge. *Seattle Times* columnist Blaine Newnham, sitting out-side the team's cafeteria waiting to interview a player, suddenly found Mike McCormack looming over him. Two days before, Newnham had written that the expected sale of the Seahawks by the Nordstrom family, should it take place, would severely damage the franchise. "Enjoyed your editorial," McCormack said to Newnham. "*Very much.* And I hope it'll be a help. A help to the cause." Then, lowering his voice to a whisper, he continued: "To keep them from selling." McCormack, who had once worked for legendary franchise-wrecker Robert Irsay, owner of the Indianapolis Colts, knew full well the critical role ownership plays in the building of both winners and losers. In the Nordstroms, McCormack had found winning ar-chitects, and the challenges posed by their loss struck him as insurmount-able. "It would be a shame if they sold," he said later. "I think the Nordstroms are the best owners in football. And I've been around some who have not been considered the best."

I thought of McCormack often during this training camp, but never so sympathetically as on the day of Seattle's first preseason game, on August 4, against the Phoenix Cardinals. I entered the Kingdome that day ahead of a tall, thin, distinguished ghost of a gentleman, graying at the temples and wearing a dark business suit. Just inside the Kingdome gate stood another man, distributing free Seahawk team posters. As I passed the hawker, I heard him yell to the Suit, "Free poster, sir?" I turned around to watch. The gentleman stopped in his tracks, let a barely perceptible, confused look flit across his face, and stared at the poster for a few seconds. "Looks good!" he said at last, taking one. Then John Nordstrom, the Seahawks' managing general partner, headed for the elevator, leaving me to wonder what other pro franchise owner could walk unrecognized into his team's home stadium. (For that matter, what other owner would take the poster?)

Whatever other virtues Nordstrom might bring to his franchise, his greatest—and the one that set him apart from his NFL brethren—was his refusal to seek ego gratification through franchise ownership. The Seahawks were the only team in the league without mention of its owner in its media guide, and the Seattle ownership was fabled for its refusal to meddle in football decisions.

Training camp was marked most noticeably by a brutish angst, differing from McCormack's only in that it was more palpable. For some players, camp was a struggle to survive; for others, it was a struggle to endure the boredom of preseason and get on with the real football, with its real hitting and real stakes, that was scheduled to commence on September 4, when the Seahawks traveled to Denver to take on their perennial archrivals, the Broncos. Denver had gone to the Super Bowl the previous two seasons, while Seattle had never been there, and for established Seahawk players the entire training camp was to be devoted to answering a single challenge, first posed by Curt Warner as camp opened. "Let's face it," Warner said. "Denver isn't the most overpowering team. We've beaten Denver on several occasions, we've split with them year in and year out, yet for some reason, they end up in the Super Bowl and we don't. Now, I don't know what it is—but I don't think they're a better football team than us."

Warner entered camp looking relaxed and cheerful, more like someone on vacation than someone gearing up for 16 weeks of body-battering work. He walked through this training camp—his sixth—with the air of visiting royalty. "The thing that I've learned," he said in the early going, "is that you can't come in here geared up. Because it's a long, drawn-out process. So I just try to come in here with a relaxed attitude."

He recognized that his was a uniquely privileged position. The amount of work he would be getting in the coming season was guaranteed; no one was watching him to determine whether he was worthy of bearing Seattle's offensive burden. "In my position," he said, "you're using less energy worrying about the situation you're in. Some guys are just going to try to work their way into shape. But there are a lot of guys who are going to take it seriously because they're trying to make the football team."

One of those guys was reserve center Stan Eisenhooth, fighting desperately for one of the last spots on the roster. Eisenhooth was listed as the third center on a team that would keep only two. For him, training camp was an exercise in perpetual anxiety and all-out effort. Every move, however slight, was critical to his survival. "The basic objective for me," he explained, "is to fight my butt off and get back to where I was." Signed as a free agent after the 1986 draft, Eisenhooth spent two straight seasons on Seattle's injured reserve list, first with a shoulder injury, then with a broken hand. In the interim, Seattle signed another center, Grant Feasel, who worked his way ahead of Eisenhooth on the depth chart. To survive, Eisenhooth would have to have a perfect camp. "The coaches are looking at everything," he said. "How we're managing through the heat, how we're trying to stay consistent with what we're doing. If they tell us we're doing something wrong, they want us to correct it, and not do it again. That's what you try to concentrate on—not making too many mistakes. The way to catch the coach's eye is to just be consistent and do the right thing."

Knox strives mightily to keep his players' anxiety finely honed. He tries to give every player a challenge—or at least the illusion of one—in the form of someone competing for his position. In this he invariably succeeds, except in the case of a few players who either are in a class by themselves (as are Warner and Largent) or whose positions are particularly difficult to fill.

Knox had, for example, been unable to find a punter credible enough to provoke even a modicum of anxiety in incumbent kicker Ruben Rodriguez. Rodriguez strolled through this camp like someone with a lifetime contract. I asked him one day about his regimen—or his lack of one—and he smiled the most easygoing smile I have ever seen. "I don't have to worry about keeping my job," he answered.

Camp for him was devoted mostly to waiting for the season to start. While his teammates were sweating and pounding their way through practice twice each day, Rodriguez and place-kicker Norm Johnson could be seen standing around, languidly kicking, tossing, or walking after balls, or occasionally snapping them to quarterbacks in some of the drills. "It's basically kick back, you know," Rodriguez said. "Just work and make sure that inside your own mind you're doing something to better yourself. And after you're done with that, you spend a lot of time just sitting on the side bored and bored and bored. We've got drills right before practice time that we do, like 45 minutes or so. And 15 minutes after practice, that's all. Other than that, it's just a lot of sitting around."

Rodriguez's routine consisted mostly of kicking 20 punts per day, while coaches videotaped him both from the front and from the side, and charted and graded each kick. Each evening, he would take the tape home and study it, looking for the reason behind each kick's success or failure. The previous season, he had come to training camp with a pulled hamstring and had performed poorly. "This year," he said, "I've had 116 punts and I'm averaging 44 yards, so it's a lot better. Hang time [the time the punted ball remains in the air] is a lot better too—probably about two-tenths of a second better [longer] than last year."

Rodriguez's rookie season had been plagued by inconsistency, and he finished with subpar numbers. His net average (kick distance minus yards returned by opposition) was only 34 yards per kick, a good 6 yards less than his goal. For every superb punt, he sent two or three straight up in the air or off the side of his foot. "I need to get a good start now," he said, "and just keep that consistency going throughout the season."

Less than two weeks into camp, Seattle demonstrated the value it places on consistency, when McCormack abruptly traded wide receiver Daryl Turner—whose five pro seasons had been one long descent from stardom to inconsistency—to the Cleveland Browns for a fifth-round draft choice. Three days after the trade, at the press conference announcing his arrival, the Browns suddenly called Turner aside and told him he had failed his physical, explaining that they had discovered a spinal defect that could result in paralysis. The trade was voided. McCormack, when notified, protested and pointedly observed that a team can always find a way for a veteran player to fail a physical. Then he waived Turner, who simply disappeared.

(Two months later, the reason behind the Browns' backbone play surfaced. Cleveland, on the verge of completing the trade, was notified that Turner had failed an NFL drug test for the second time, which meant that had he made the Browns roster, he would have begun the season by serving a 30-day suspension.)

Attrition reduced the Seahawk roster to 92 after two weeks, and the players headed into the four-game preseason schedule either fighting for their professional lives or quietly working themselves into regular-season shape. "Let's face it," said Warner on the eve of the preseason opener against the Phoenix Cardinals, "we're not going to win the Super Bowl if we win all four preseason games." As a sign of how little the game mattered, he was to be held out of it, in order to hasten rehabilitation of his ankle. Eisenhooth, on the other hand, was anxious to move up the depth chart. "Every time we get in there," he said of himself and his fellow lower-echelon players, "we just have to show them that—hey!—we know what's going on, too."

When the dust from the game cleared, the scoreboard read Seattle 21, Phoenix 7, and Eisenhooth was glum. He had been in for only three plays and had not done well. "Personally, I didn't have a very good one out there," he said. "I *have* to have a good week now. It seems like I had limited time out there. And if you only get three, you gotta get three great ones." Camp for him had turned into a day-to-day roller-coaster ride. "For the whole week up to this game, I felt real confident in myself, really good. But they're only gonna keep two centers here. Every play is important, and I had a couple bad plays. I made stupid mental mistakes tonight. I can't make them again—that's how it is."

A week later, after playing the Detroit Lions in the Pontiac Silverdome, he was ecstatic. His team had "won" in overtime, 16–13, and he had been the team's center both for the entire second half and for the overtime period, when his team drove into position for a game-winning Norm Johnson field goal. "Blair [Bush, Seattle's starting center] and Grant both got hurt right there on the same series," he blurted out, sitting in his team's cramped Silverdome locker room, "and I went out there and just tried to calm down, because BOOM when something like that happens, I get all uptight, but I . . . OK. It took me a couple of plays to figure it out. I just did what I had to do. I hope. I don't remember. I have a hard time remembering a lot of plays until I see them again. I had fun out there, so you know, that's what . . . I feel good."

Warner, having tasted his first postoperative game action, was just as satisfied, if considerably less exhilarated. "Today," he said, "I just wanted to get hit a few times and fall on the turf and see if it still hurts and if it's still there. It's never as bad as you think it's going to be. Once you get hit a couple of times, you realize that, 'Ah, it's not so bad . . . ' Matter of fact, I kind of liked it out there!"

Two days after the next forgettable dress rehearsal, against the Buffalo Bills in the Kingdome on August 19—the Seahawks scoring 30 points to the Bills' 13—Eisenhooth saw what looked like the beginning of the end of his career when Seahawk coaches moved him from center to tackle. Leaving the field after his first day at his new position, he tried taking a philosophical tack. "Maybe I can become a multi-tackle," he said.

On the morning of August 23, players arriving for work found assistant coach Rusty Tillman lurking around the entrance to Seahawk headquarters. Tillman is Seattle's "Turk," the assistant coach assigned to tell players they are about to be cut from the team. The Seahawk players crept past him, many of them frightened. Tillman quietly approached 15 players that morning—12 free agents and three low-round draft picks—and said the same thing to each: "Coach Knox wants to see you—and bring your playbook." This is the ritual cutdown-day greeting delivered to the unfortunate on every NFL team. When a player hears the summons from the Turk, he knows his professional football career is over.

Tillman ignored Eisenhooth—which meant, at the very least, that the aspiring "multi-tackle" had a job for at least six more days.

It was odd how players, once released during camp, seemed almost to cease to exist. When Seahawks were cut, they instantly vanished. All traces of them evaporated, save for occasional fleeting glimpses, on harshly sunlit days, of their shimmering shades lurking outside the practice-field fence, waiting to be recalled to life.

Aside from the August 23 cutdown, camp afforded the spectator almost nothing of interest. Daily practice sessions, being repetitive exercises in refining techniques and learning the rudiments of the Seattle system, were often almost unbearable to watch. They were the sort of procedure only a coach could love. The preseason games were practice sessions thinly disguised as games. Devoid of real strategy or real game planning, they utterly lacked drama or suspense. In Seattle, the only resemblance preseason games bear to real games is in the ticket pricing: At $10, $15, $21, $25, and $30 per seat, prices are the same for these scrimmages staged purely for the purposes of player evaluation as they are for real games played with real rage for real stakes. Since every Seahawk game is a sellout, season-ticket packages are an all-or-nothing proposition: Buy tickets to all games—including preseason—or buy tickets to none of them. If fans want to see Seattle play Denver for the division title in December, they have to pay for the Seahawk-Cardinal game in August.

The Seahawks' policy is simply a function of the team's popularity. In Detroit, the Lions would have risked selling no season tickets at all if they tried Seattle-style blackmail. Even with tickets priced at a rock-bottom $15.50 and $6, the Lions could only manage to fill a third of the Silverdome for their practice against the Seahawks.

For most of the camp's six weeks, I was preoccupied and unnerved by the close view I was afforded of blood and pain. Watching football on television, or even from the stands, we never quite take in the full extent of the game's violence. Most of the time, we watch the ball, and see running backs and wide receivers move more like dancers than like fighters. Even when we see ball carriers and tacklers collide, the force of their impact is lost in the thrill of the game. Armored and helmeted, they look like androids, or robots, and we don't see the very real, and very human, pain and injury that they suffer. During scrimmages, every play I watched brought a cascade of violence, with its attendant chorus of pops and squeals and groans. And interior linemen often left the field at the end of practice in uniforms flecked and smeared with blood.

The more I watched the Seahawks' camp, the more I wondered what had made pro football so immensely popular. Founded in 1920, the National

Football League had to fight against public apathy and franchise bankruptcy into the 1950s. A 22-team league in 1926, the NFL was down to 10 teams in 1931, and as late as 1960 was still regarded by Madison Avenue as a distant second to college football in the glamour department. By 1970, though, professional football had taken hold on all three major television networks, its championship game (first dubbed the "Super Bowl" in 1966) had become a national extravaganza, and the NFL was well on its way to becoming sporting history's greatest monolith.

I wondered how such a game could have captured the national imagination at such a time. The decade from 1960 to 1970 was an era of social and political upheaval, a decade marked by nationwide civil disobedience, widespread rejection of established values and systems and beliefs, and the refusal by record-breaking numbers of the country's draft-age males to serve in the military. It was a time when violence in any form fell dramatically out of fashion. Yet it was also a time when football, a game laced with military terminology, governed by militaristic minds, played by obedient foot soldiers to whom it would never occur to question authority, and shot through with bone-crushing violence, became the nation's favorite sport.

I think that even the most dedicated and obsessed of football's followers have their moments of doubt about the worth of this blood sport. One morning midway through camp, I arrived early and found myself down on the field watching practice with only one other spectator: a beat reporter far better known for his ardor than for his insight. The team was already hard at work, filling the air with sounds of effort and intense contact. I had just pulled out a notebook when two players, running at full speed, collided right in front of us with an explosive "pop!", punctuated by pained grunts. Both hit the ground, momentarily dazed, then jumped up and moved nonchalantly on. It was a sickening, glorious, barbaric sight, and I was just working my way through the notion that this level of violence might be football's most engrossing feature, when I was bumped from my train of thought by the voice of my companion. "You know, it's really a pretty weird fuckin' game when you think about it," he said.

One immediate consequence of football's violence was that Knox, having started the preseason with 12 linebackers, found himself one month later, after the preseason's first three games, with only six healthy enough to practice. He was further vexed by the continued holdout of defensive end Jeff Bryant. Going into the final preseason game in San Francisco against the 49ers, though, Knox was upbeat. And with the Seahawks' arrival at their San Francisco hotel, all the drudgery of preseason vanished, and coaches, players, reporters, and fans alike could feel the approach of the season opener against Denver, now only nine days away.

The San Francisco game proved to be far more entertaining than anything else in preseason, with the possible exception of Knox's inaugural press conference. The fun began with the Seahawks' exit from their San Francisco hotel on the way to Candlestick Park. When Bosworth walked through the lobby, an eloquent hush descended and every pair of eyes in the place tracked him out the door. Behind me, I heard a woman start giggling uncontrollably. I turned to take a tasteless look. "Was that him?" she squealed. "Was that really him? Oh, I'm *so* embarrassed!"

It continued at Candlestick, where I came across McCormack sitting alone in the press box some two hours before game time. He had spent the day dealing with reporters' inquiries on the latest Fredd Young rumor. "He says he'll be back tomorrow," McCormack muttered before I could ask. "But I'm not holding my breath."

As for the game, the teams devoted all but one drive in the first half to a grim exchange of punts, the 49ers kicking seven times, the Seahawks five. Three of Rodriguez's punts were from inside San Francisco territory, and he tried to kick high and short, having the ball bounce inside the 49er 10-yard line, where it would either be downed by a teammate or, hitting football's fabled "coffin corner," bounce out of bounds in the shadow of the San Francisco end zone. Instead, he failed all three times, kicking into the end zone twice (with the result that the ball was brought out to the 20 for the 49ers), and kicking too short the third time, the ball fielded at the 20 by 49er returner John Taylor.

The game was so unspeakably dull that Rodriguez's losing battle with his own foot was the first half's only dramatic feature.

To be fair to Rodriguez, the wind was wreaking such thorough havoc that players were struggling even to track the football, much less throw, catch, or kick it. Watching receivers run their carefully charted and timed pass patterns, only to lunge clumsily after the loony ball, I could see, in stark relief, the fragility of football's game plans. For coaches, the game is as much a search for order as it is a search for domination and victory. A professional coach is like a devoted scientist, employing every means at his command to control circumstance, chance, and human failings and emotions by means of the ingenuity of his diagrams. He tries to orchestrate an assault on the intangible, directing a game in which his schemes are staged exactly as drawn, in which all obstacles can be anticipated and surmounted, and which he will win by virtue of having planned for and found a way to control every possible twist of fate. Knox's favorite statement of his ambitions in this regard is the frequent invocation of Dodger franchise architect Branch Rickey's well-known aphorism, "Luck is the residue of design."

Unfortunately, the fates at Candlestick had a few wind-delivered twists in store that not even Knox could anticipate. After lulling him with a seamless six-play touchdown drive at the start of the second half—thereby staking Seattle to a 14–0 lead—followed four plays later by yet another San Francisco punt, the fates began to blow the residue of his designs all over the field. Midway through the third quarter there came a span of 3 minutes, 44 seconds in which the Seahawks gave the 49ers the ball three times on the threshold of the Seattle end zone, and San Francisco mounted three touchdown drives—one taking only 47 seconds, the other two 3 seconds each—on their way to winning the game, 27–21.

The third 49er touchdown was set up by a Rodriguez punt of such mysterious significance that it struck the game's spectators as a cryptic message sent from Beyond.

As Seattle lined up in punt formation, with Rodriguez settling in uneasily near the back of the end zone, the entire stadium fell silent. Not a soul in the place failed to sense that a powerful spectacle was about to unfold. Rodriguez stepped forward, center Grant Feasel's snap sent the ball sailing back along a wind-mediated curve into his hands, and all 22 advancing, retreating, and colliding players conformed in their movements exactly to the diagrams in their playbooks. Rodriguez—head inclined, eyes focused, arms extended at the proper angle from his body, still stepping forward with the correct manner and timing he had practiced thousands of times in his career—released the ball and whipped his kicking foot forward. In that split second before his foot made contact with the ball, everything on the field seemed to freeze, and I was treated to a vision of perfect football order: every player in exactly the right location and posture.

Then, with a savage *swooosh*!, Rodriguez's foot swept by the ball, making only incidental contact. The football slowly described a high, lateral arc, bobbing gently in the wind, and set sail straight for the sideline as Knox watched the unfolding of a coach's worst nightmare: anarchy on the gridiron. The players arrayed about the field broke in hopeless confusion from their scripted paths, running hither and yon, looking every which way for the ball. Rodriguez was the first to see where it was headed, and he took off after it. He arrived in time to see it land, just out of reach, at the half-yard line, and take a perfect sideways bounce out of bounds. He had managed, at last, not only to hit football's coffin corner, but also to lend new meaning to the term.

On the postgame stat sheet, Rodriguez's effort would be recorded prosaically as a "minus 6 yard punt." But even as San Francisco was taking the lead with a one-play, 1-yard, 3-second touchdown drive, I understood that the intangible had counterattacked, introducing the tiniest of deviations from the designed position of the football as the punter's foot rose up to meet it.

Oddly enough, Knox was in high spirits afterward. "We're making progress," he said. "We're not the football team that we're going to have to be a week from Sunday, but we've made a lot of progress the last two weeks, and we had a great training camp. We just have to build on it."

He seemed unfazed even by Rodriguez's portentous punt, saying, when asked about it, "You never like to see a punt like that. You didn't see me over there doing backflips, did you?"

Reporters confused by Knox's good cheer were just as confused by Seattle's preseason statistics. Over the four-game span, the Seahawks had put up conflicting numbers. In compiling a 3–1 record, Seattle finished at the top of the AFC West preseason standings, tied with the Denver Broncos. But that record was puzzling, at best. Seattle's starting unit had played only the first half of each game, with the remainder each time played by a mixed bag of second-unit players and deep reserves. Seattle's three wins had come against teams with a combined 1–8 preseason record, while their lone loss came against the now 3–2 San Franciscans. Yet the Seahawk starting unit had lost its three meetings with losing teams and won its half against the 49ers, its only quality opponent, while Seattle reserves had done exactly the opposite.

After talking with Knox, I waded through a sea of equipment, discarded tape, bandages, and postgame quotes in search of wisdom, which I found issuing forth from offensive line coach Kent Stephenson. I asked him how coaches cope with the sort of disaster Seattle had faced when San Francisco was given its three touchdowns. "Fate has a lot to do with this game," he said. "You know, you can throw the ball on the ground and it'll go a different way every time. You can't let yourself be distracted by things you can't do anything about. If you do, you take away your focus from what's important in a ball game. What you try to do, is those things that you can control, and those things that you do have a handle on, you study them deeply and hope that you've covered all those kinds of situations out on the practice field. Control the things that you can control, and the rest of the things—an official's call, the bounce of the ball, a deflection that goes to them instead of us—those kinds of things you have to deal with, and feel that over the year it's going to be a 50 percent thing, just like flipping a coin."

This was a bracing bit of metaphysics—a declaration of faith in the ultimate fairness of the universe.

Almost immediately, it seemed misguided. Back up in the press box, news was sweeping through the Seattle media section that the sale of the Seahawk franchise was nearing consummation. The Nordstrom family, the winds were whispering, had all but completed the sale to someone named Kenneth Behring, a California multimillionaire. To me, it was sad news— and far sadder, I think, to Knox and his players. The Nordstroms were enormously popular owners. Their loss, just as the season was beginning, could prove—as ownership changes in pro sports almost always do—to be far more of a problem than a challenge to the franchise's employees. Athletes and coaches, like thoroughbred horses, are too high-strung to take in stride even the smallest changes in order and routine. The odds in Denver, already stacked against Seattle, were about to rise clean out of sight.

PART II

SEASON

Introitus Interruptus

4

One beginning and one ending for a book was a thing I did not agree with. A good book may have three openings entirely dissimilar and inter-related only in the prescience of the author, or for that matter one hundred times as many endings.
—Flann O'Brien, _At Swim-Two-Birds_

Stan Eisenhooth played only one down against San Francisco, and that only because tackle Ron Mattes's shoe fell off in the middle of a play and Eisenhooth had to come in for him while he retied it. Eisenhooth spent the weekend preparing himself to be released on Monday, the day of the NFL's final player cuts. On Sunday night, he called his family back East to say that his career likely was over and that he would be coming home soon. The next morning, he remembered later in the week, "I came in, and I wasn't greeted by Rusty. So that took a lot of heat off. I sat down in my locker, went to the meeting, and nothing was said, so I said, 'Fine with me!' So I'm happy that they're giving me the opportunity to be here and stay here and work at tackle and work at center and work at guard."

When his coaches had moved him from center to tackle the week before, he had been convinced that his days were numbered. "All I could think about then was that they usually move someone that late, it's like, outskis, you know. They move you just to get you out of the way, and then you're gone. That was in my mind, but then I said, 'Well, if that's going to happen, at least I'm going to go out having a good practice and everything,' so I just took every day and tried to have a good one. And said, 'At least I'm going to make 'em think.' "

For his coaches, keeping Eisenhooth had been one of two extremely difficult decisions to make in the offensive line. "As it wound down," said Kent Stephenson, "we had to make a decision at guard with Alvin Powell and Jon Borchardt. And what you have is youth—a young, outstanding athlete [Powell] that's learning the game—and a veteran [Borchardt] that knows the game inside and out and is very technical, but who had been in it

10 years and his legs were starting to wear out just a little bit. We had a close call at tackle with Curt Singer and Stan Eisenhooth. There, versatility had something to do with it. Eisenhooth's ability to play other positions. You weigh all kinds of factors when you make those kinds of decisions. Curt Singer had had a good camp, but he'd been hurt a lot. That was tough, it wasn't his fault and it wasn't our fault. It was just the breaks of the game."

When it comes to cutting players, coaches must be absolutely pitiless, if only because making the wrong decision ultimately could cost them their own jobs. Their aim is simply to build the roster that can get them the most wins. "You never take the long view," said Stephenson. "I've been a football coach long enough to know that *this* is the season that counts. This game, then the next game. And as cruel as it sounds, you always hope you have guys who can come in and replace existing players. Because that makes you a better football team. I don't mean to sound coldhearted or anything, but we're a better football team if somebody can come in and be better than who we have. That's the first thing we're looking for: Can this guy come in and be a starter for us?"

One guy who had been a perennial leading candidate for cutting was running back Randall Morris, a persistent underachiever whose survival each season had less to do with his strengths than with the weaknesses of each year's draft. This season, because of the acquisition of Kevin Harmon, Morris looked like a goner. Yet cutdown day came and went and there he was. Seattle coaches, to the surprise of everyone—particularly Morris—had decided to keep both him and Harmon. After Monday's practice, Morris sat, smiling broadly, on a bench outside the Seahawk locker room, holding court with the Seattle media. Normally not much of a talker, today he was a veritable quote machine, the words pouring out in a flood of relief and joy. "I walked in slowly," he said, "so nobody would see me, 'cause Rusty, he's got the job of axing people, telling 'em that Chuck wants to see 'em. And I was avoiding Rusty. And then I saw him, and he didn't say anything, and I said, 'Well!' Did like this"—he demonstrated an exaggerated double take—"for a minute, you know 'cause as soon as he sees you, if Chuck wants to see you, he usually tells you right then and there. I saw him and he didn't say anything, so I went to my locker and put on my sweats and went to the meeting."

Asked if he had felt relieved, he answered with a laugh. "Yeah, yeah! I said, 'Thank you Big Fella!' " Then he started fondly remembering other close calls, dwelling longest on his favorite: "Usually when you walk in those front doors over there, Rusty's right around there. My first year, when we were in training camp, we were in the dorms instead of here. And Rusty knocked on our door, and he called my name, right? And if he comes in your room early in the morning, that means you're gone, you're cut. So he said, 'Randall! Is that you?' I said to myself, 'Oh, man, I'm cut already?' It's, like, the first game! And I said to Rusty, 'Yeah.' You know, real sad. He says, 'Is that Al Ricky over there?' I said, 'Yeah.' So he went over to my roommate, he said, 'Al, uh, coach wants to see you. Bring your playbook.' So then at lunchtime, he said, 'I scared you, didn't I?!' He messed with me! Oh, I was so scared! I remember—that's the only time he ever talked to me, right there!"

I was beginning to think they were keeping Morris around just for his storytelling ability.

His tale finished, Morris stood up and grandly shook hands all around. It was a strange moment. Reporters aren't used to being treated so courteously by players. Each one, in turn, muttered something congratulatory: "Uh, way to go, Randall . . . " "Nice job, Randall . . . " Then Morris went into the locker room, and the reporters went back to pondering Knox's cuts.

Seattle's roster was Knox's classic blend of youth and experience. Only two starters on offense had played fewer than five years, two had played 10, and one—Steve Largent—had played 12. Krieg, Knox's starting quarterback, was entering his ninth year. And while his second offensive unit was considerably younger, it included only one rookie—receiver Brian Blades, who had come from the University of Miami, one of the most polished college football programs in the country. Backup quarterback Jeff Kemp was entering his eighth year, and Knox had added considerably more experience and savvy to his second unit by signing nine-year veteran tight end John Spagnola, newly released by the Philadelphia Eagles, the day before final player cuts.

To Seattle's young defense (six of its starters had three or fewer years of experience, the combined first and second units included seven second-year players and two rookies, and 10-year linebacker Keith Butler had just been cut), Knox had added experience in the form of two veteran free-agent safeties, nine-year player Nesby Glasgow and six-year vet Vernon Dean, both of whom could play "starting" roles in his nickel defense. To back up Joe Nash at nose tackle, he had acquired 10-year player Ken Clarke.

According to Knox, the infusion of veteran players was intended to counter the effect of rebuilding with youth, as he had been doing since arriving in Seattle in 1983. "We're keeping young football players here," he said. "In the six years we've been here, we've had a tremendous turnover, and we've continued to win. And usually, when you have that much turnover, you don't win; you're in a rebuilding phase." Where other teams might be willing, as many often are, to suffer through a few losing seasons while their overyoung rosters mature, Knox wanted to win as much as possible now. "It's a question," he explained, "of trying to keep the football players that you think can make the best contribution to your football team over the course of this season."

That approach had cost two promising young players their jobs. Because he had elected to keep Glasgow and Dean, Knox had to release defensive backs Mark Moore and David Hollis, players who, one or two years down the road, would be better than Glasgow and Dean would be. But, as Kent Stephenson had said, "You never take the long view. *This* is the season that counts."

Knox's troops, broken down by position, numbered eight linebackers; six running backs; five wide receivers; four safeties and four cornerbacks; three players each at offensive tackle, offensive guard, quarterback, defensive end, and nose tackle; two each at center and tight end; and one punter and one place-kicker. Most players had more than one role. Rookie linebacker Darrin Miller, for example, backed up at inside linebacker, was a special-teams player and could snap for punts; starting guard Bryan Millard was also a backup tackle; Eisenhooth could back up at guard, tackle, and center, and play on special teams; backup quarterback Jeff Kemp also held for place kicks, as could Largent and Krieg; Doug Hollie backed up at both defensive ends; and so on, down to tight end Mike Tice, who doubled as the team's emergency quarterback.

Seattle was able to keep three quarterbacks and an extra running back because of a rule change from the previous season. Last year, rosters had been limited to 45 players. This season, teams were allowed to keep 47, with two to be declared inactive before each game. The two extra players afforded a team insurance against sudden injury. Nearly all teams would carry a third quarterback as one of their inactive-roster players. Going into the season, Seattle slated one inactive slot for quarterback Kelly Stouffer, the other for Kevin Harmon.

The Seahawks' 47-man roster actually numbered 48. Fredd Young, finally served his ultimatum, had returned, and Seattle was given two weeks to work him into shape before having to count him as an active player. And at least one other change was expected soon. Eventually, Jeff Bryant would have to agree to a new contract, and backup defensive end Doug Hollie would undoubtedly be cut to make room for him.

Bryant would come to terms for the same reason Young returned. His only other choice would be to be entered onto one of the jumble of NFL "reserve" lists and not play football at all. Under football's reserve system, every player, whether or not his contract has expired, is the property of whatever team has last signed or drafted him. Should a player want to play for a team other than the one that owns his rights, his only recourse is to persuade or force his team to trade him. Bryant tried to do that and failed, other teams noting that the salary he had turned down (a two-year contract at $525,000 for the first year, $575,000 for the second) was for more than they were willing to offer. Young, although back in camp, stood a better chance of forcing a trade. Not only was he already signed to a contract, but he had more potential.

The reserve system was designed to reduce a player's negotiating power, make teams more competitive, and keep salaries low. The only way an athlete can free himself from a team's bondage is to become so poor a player that his team, reasoning that no one will want him, finally gives him his outright release. Over the years, as players have struggled to find ways to wriggle between the reserve-system lines, the system has grown to a level of complexity only a lawyer could love. There is a reserve list to cover every conceivable reason, real or contrived, that a player may have for not suiting up to play. Kelly Stouffer, for example, when drafted by the St. Louis Cardinals, refused to sign a contract and was put on the "Reserve Drafted Unsigned" list until traded to Seattle. Players who announce their retirement can be placed on the "Reserve Retired" list if teams fear they may try to come out of retirement to play for another team. Young, had he not returned to camp, would have wound up on the "Reserve Left Squad" list. Had he never shown up at camp at all, he would have gone on the "Reserve Did Not Report" list. Other lists include "Reserve Suspended," "Reserve Physically Unable to Perform," "Reserve Injured," "Reserve Nonfootball-related Illness," and my personal favorite, "Reserve Drafted— Goes to Another League." The only contingency left uncovered by the League is death, although rumors persist that the NFL is considering the addition of "Reserve Deceased" to the list of lists.

Injury and illness lists allow for a certain amount of intriguing political and tactical play. A player injured while playing or training for football is placed on Injured Reserve, while a player injured in some other manner—lifting weights at home, say, or in a car accident—is placed on the Physically Unable to Perform list. Players who have fallen ill, or fallen prey to drug or alcohol problems, often wind up on the Nonfootball-related Illness list. When Seattle's final roster was announced, linebacker Greg Gaines, who hurt himself lifting weights in the offseason, was listed as Physically Unable to Perform, while linebacker Sam Merriman, offensive tackle Dave Des-Rochers, nose tackle Roland Barbay, and wide receiver Louis Clark went on the Injured Reserve list.

Injured Reserve differs from the other two injury-and-illness lists in one important respect. The list often is employed to stash healthy players (in

1988's case, DesRochers and Clark) a team cannot yet use but doesn't want to release. Theoretically, an IR player is required to be legitimately injured; the NFL randomly selects IR players to be sent to a neutral physician for proof that their injuries are real. But in practice, a team can always find a way to use the list as a repository for players for whom it sees a future use. Ron Mattes, for example, spent a year on Injured Reserve learning to switch from the defensive line, where he'd played in college, to the offensive line. Stan Eisenhooth spent two years on Injured Reserve, one year with a shoulder injury, the next with a broken hand. While both players could demonstrate real injury, both also were less severely hurt than many of their active-roster teammates. They were simply being stored for future use.

Stashing is regarded as a tolerable, good-ol'-boy form of deception to be winked at rather than censured. During training camp, Injured Reserve handicapping is one of the main forms of entertainment for reporters. This season, the Seattle press may have set an all-time record for prognostication, tabbing DesRochers as a definite IR prospect less than two weeks into camp.

A compelling image of the NFL's airtight reserve system was furnished that week in the form of the newly returned Fredd Young. After an unrepentant day of practice, he stood on a chair in front of his locker, furiously flinging stuff into a garbage can some 10 feet away. Glowering, clad in his underwear, still sweaty and scarred from his efforts on the field, glancing occasionally at a relaxed and cheerful Brian Bosworth holding court four lockers away, Young looked like Cain plotting revenge as he regarded the favored Abel.

It cannot have improved his mood any to see Bosworth's just-released book excerpted, quoted extensively, and discussed at great length in Northwest newspapers, or to read that it already was number seven and still climbing on the *New York Times* best-seller list.

Young and Bosworth had hogged the sports headlines all camp long. Bosworth, besieged daily, had long since refused to discuss his book, his teammates were sick of being asked about it, and Knox had had it up to here with questions about both players. "Fredd Young looks good," he said emphatically after Young's first day back. "Fredd Young is a football player. He's got the quickness. He's got great natural ability. He moves around on the football field." Asked about the tension between the two linebackers, Knox insisted, "I don't think it has any effect whatsoever. You see, football is an individual game played within a team framework. One guy has to block one defensive guy. One guy has to beat this offensive blocker and get to the guy with the football. . . And so the book is not going to block, it's not going to tackle. You can have players on the team—which has been forever—this guy likes this guy better than that guy. That's got nothing to do with coming in and doing the job that you signed on for. So it's a profession. You've got a job to do, you come in and you go to work every day. You come in and you make the team and you play as hard as you can play every Sunday. It's just that simple."

Tell it to Fredd, Coach.

By the silence that greeted his lecture, Knox could tell that his audience didn't think it was just that simple. Growing more heated, he continued. "I think a lot of that has been blown out of proportion, too. But that gives you people something to write about. That's why you guys come around looking for those kinds of things. Those guys kind of write their stories for you people. You guys don't have to do it, then. You don't have to be creative. You just have to quote what you thought you heard somebody say or what somebody else said that they said, and if you weren't there you got it from somebody else. And then somebody puts a tag line on it and away you go, whether it's right or not. And that's the nature of the business. But that has nothing to do with how we're going to play."

It had everything to do, however, with how Knox relates to the press. This little diatribe was the first performance of a leitmotiv that would grace his press conferences throughout the season. The harangue was also a classic illustration of Knox's rhetorical method. The suggestions that reporters care more for scandal than for football, that they never quote anyone accurately, that they deliberately exaggerate, and that they are too lazy to ferret out and write about the truth all make up the core of a football man's perception of the press. Reporters hear these insinuations from players and coaches all the time. Where Knox's stand out is in the way they are received by their targets. With other footballers, reporters simply turn a deaf ear until they can get their interview subject back to the business at hand. Yet for some reason, reporters all but revel in Knox's assaults. There is something so charming about his delivery and his careful choice of words that he seems entertaining where other sports figures come across as merely hostile. And so at the end of this lecture, as with so many of his moral asides, Knox's audience laughed heartily.

His journalism seminar apparently concluded, Knox was asked if he was optimistic about the season. "Well, I'm always optimistic," he answered. "I've been optimistic now for some six weeks. OK?" Alluding then to his longing for the return of Jeff Bryant, he said, "I just have a little beacon light out there and I look out and see if somebody might be following it over to our headquarters here, so to speak. So I hope that we can get him in, certainly. But I have no grounds to be optimistic—other than that I'm an optimistic guy."

With the team roster now more or less in final form, the Seahawks were ready to slip into their customary, comfortable season's rhythm, a week of practice, a game, a week of practice, a game . . . For fans, the regular season begins with the opening kickoff of the first game. For players, it begins with the final player cuts, after which they commence preparing exclusively for their first opponent. Traditionally, that week is a time of relief and concentration. All the distractions and insecurities are at last dispensed with, and teams can get down to the serious business of professional play.

That, at least, is what is supposed to happen. This year, fate had a few gut-wrenching distractions in store and waited only one day after Monday's final player cuts to begin revealing them.

First came the announcement at a hastily called press conference on Tuesday that the Seahawk franchise had been sold to a pair of California multimillionaire Kens, land developer Kenneth Behring and contractor Kenneth Hofmann. The noon briefing was so heavily attended that it had to be moved downstairs from the press conference room to the Seahawks' biggest room, a place normally reserved for team meetings. At the head of the room, hanging from a blue backdrop, was a huge replica of a Seahawk helmet, flanked by two Seahawk jerseys: numbers 19 and 88. Before that arrangement stood a long table, draped in blue, on which sat a jumbled assortment of microphones and an NFL football flanked by two Seattle helmets. Some 50 chattering reporters, photographers, radio voices, and television technicians sat studying the display as they awaited the arrival of Behring.

The din suddenly stopped when a door at the front of the room opened and Behring, McCormack, and Knox came through. The silence seemed inspired more by surprise than by curiosity, for Behring looked hilariously miscast. Wearing a pink knit sport shirt and tan slacks, and sporting the bejowled, soft-eyed face of a basset hound, he looked like a retired boilermaker heading out for a round of golf. Behring is an extremely short man, and when he sat down, his face disappeared behind the wall of microphones and his puzzled eyes peered out over them, amazed at the size of the crowd that had gathered to meet him.

The agenda of the press conference that followed can be divided into five categories: proffering as little information as possible about the sale; charming the pants off the Seattle media; denying that the Seahawks would ever be moved to Oakland; learning to be more circumspect; and uttering paradoxical prophecies.

Item Number One was summarily dispensed with. Behring identified his co-purchaser (Hofmann, who, according to Behring, would buy 49 percent of the team), said the purchase was a "straight cash transaction," and told reporters that, yes, the price was close to the $80 million figure that had already been reported in the newspapers. Later, it developed that the sale price was actually nearly $100 million, $19 million of it in the form of liabilities assumed by Behring.

The second item went no less smoothly, as the assembled press corps took an instant liking to the new owner. Blessed with an unprepossessing face and an unpretentious manner, Behring has charisma to burn. "I try to get along with everyone," he said at one point. "One thing my mother told me: 'You'll never make it on your looks, so you better develop a personality.'" He proved engagingly rough-hewn, humble, and given to self-deprecating turns of phrase. "Unfortunately," he said when summarizing his life, "I never went to college." When introduced, he bowed deferentially as he extended his hand. And rather than play the cool, detached high roller, he made no attempt to hide his boyish glee at the prospect of buying an NFL franchise. Throughout the session, he kept breaking into an unabashed smile. Like a kid who comes downstairs on Christmas morning expecting a lump of coal and finds instead a new pony, he kept gazing dreamily out at his audience, as if astounded at his unbelievable luck.

He scored his biggest points by taking a gratuitous shot at Mariners owner George Argyros, a notoriously penurious, hated figure in Seattle. "I'm not sure he even wants to win," he said. "I don't know where he's trying to go, or what he's trying to do."

With that, he brought down the house.

Behring lives near Oakland, a city that had lost its NFL franchise to Los Angeles five seasons before and had been trying to regain one ever since, so suspicion was high that he intended eventually to move the Seahawks down there. But he skillfully parried Oakland questions with paeans of praise for the Northwest. "You've got the best football fans in the country," he kept insisting hyperbolically. "This is the greatest football town in the country! You'd certainly never take a team out of a town where it's loved so much—the fans'd kill you!" Asked about Oakland for maybe the 20th time, he blurted out, "I don't even like that town, to tell you the truth." Too late, a Seahawk staffer leapt in, shouting, "That's off the record!" Behring, laughing, repeated the plea so uncertainly that he sounded like a foreigner trying to master a newly encountered English phrase.

This of course only served to make him seem more ingratiating. The press loves nobody so much as someone who doesn't know how to be slick. The more Behring talked, the more you could see the Legend of Kenneth

Behring beginning to take form. He got more laughs from his audience of professional skeptics than a skilled comic does from an audience of drunks. When the press conference ended, there was even a smattering of applause—an unheard-of breach of protocol.

Still, the press conference had not been without its warning signs. Every time Behring addressed a question about the degree of his involvement in football matters, Knox and McCormack would smile in such a pained, forced way that you could see, through their eyes, nothing but trouble on the horizon. Flanked by those smiles, Behring's lines took on unintended implications. "I'm not here to change anything," he said at one point, "I'm here to help." Later, he said, "I want to be involved, but I want to have people around me who are better at this than I am." Trying again, he said, "Why do you think I'm here? If it wasn't for these gentlemen"—he patted Knox and McCormack on their backs—"I wouldn't even be interested!"

It seemed that he was protesting a bit too much, particularly when he said that his son, a Florida high-school all-stater whose college football career had been ended by a knee injury, wanted to be "involved" in the franchise. He said that McCormack and Knox "will know that I'm here." And he said, in countless different ways, that his emotional attachments to football and to his new franchise were so strong that he couldn't help but tinker. "I'm in the whole way," he blurted out at one point. "And it's more than money—I'm emotionally involved. I'll want to be informed, I'll want to be in on the important decisions." He constantly allowed as how he couldn't stand to lose: "I think winning is Number One"; "I'll guarantee you, we'll be competitive enough to be a winning team"; "I'm afraid that I'll want to win so much that if I see something like a bad kick, I'll want to get a uniform on and try to kick one myself."

Knox's icy smile froze over completely when Behring declared that his new acquisition was a Super Bowl–caliber team. "I felt a certain momentum that was happening, and I wanted to be a part of it," Behring said. "I've loved football all my life. I want to be with a winner. It's just a certain feeling, a winning feeling."

He insisted, however, that he was not out to win financially, and in so doing, he unwittingly stripped away a little of his unassuming facade. "If I were looking for a business venture, this is not what I would get into. To be financially profitable, we feel you should make 25–30 percent on your money."

Whoa!

Hard as it was to reconcile Behring's homespun appeal with that rapacious a profit motive, it was no less hard to reconcile it with his profession. He was said to be involved in 500 land development projects, including 10 golf-course communities in Florida. It was hard to buy the notion that he had managed all that by virtue of being a sweet, aw-shucks kind of guy. His best-known deal was Blackhawk, a 5,000-acre project on the slopes of California's fabled Mount Diablo. Behring had taken on—and beaten—the Sierra Club on that one, turning the wilds there into a huge development of million-dollar-and-up homes.

His enthusiasm for the Northwest seemed a little dubious as well. "This area has a real future," he enthused. "I'd like to build a nice golf-course community up here. There's a real need. I built 10 golf courses in Florida..."

Whoa, whoa!

Behring regarded the timing of the sale, coming as it did only four days before Seattle's season opener, as optimum. "We didn't want it to be a distraction to the players," he said. "So we decided we should do it either before the season started or after the season was over." Knox, anxiously counting down toward the Denver game, doubtless couldn't imagine a worse distraction coming at a worse time.

The Nordstrom family has always had a magic touch that places them above public reproach and imbues their enterprises, whether retailing or pro sports, with an aura protecting them from the kinds of problems that routinely dog their competitors' undertakings. So as the press conference broke up, it was hard not to fear that the Seattle franchise, now bereft of the Nordstrom mystique, was headed for a downturn in fortune.

The next day, Knox, in spite of the return that morning of Jeff Bryant, seemed more worried about the future than he had seemed on Monday. Asked about Behring's high hopes, he answered, "Well, when you start a season fresh, anything is attainable. It may not be realistic when we're sitting here with a pretty young defensive football team. We're starting three linebackers, each one is listed in his second year. One of them, really, is in his first year, because he didn't play last year—that's Dave Wyman. We have uncertainty in our defensive line—Jeff Bryant came back today, and he hasn't practiced. We have a Pro Bowl linebacker [Fredd Young] that's practiced once with shoulder pads and headgear on Monday, he'll be out in full gear today. So to talk about a Super Bowl with that type of situation . . . We can dream and I'm optimistic, but there are some question marks."

Knox went on to reiterate that he hoped for improved play from everyone, then took time out to dress down Ruben Rodriguez. "We have to punt better than we punted in San Francisco, obviously. But Ruben Rodriguez punted well for us last year. And he has to be able to punt consistently well to keep his job. There's no question about that. That's the job, that's the game, that's the job description. You must be able to punt the football well.

That's why you're here. That's just something that he has to do. And punters are like field-goal kickers. You kick well here for one team, you seem to have everything right in a groove, in a rhythm, and all of a sudden something goes wacko. I don't know what it is with them. But we're not going to have a kicking caravan in here right now. Ruben Rodriguez is the guy that's going to be doing the punting in Denver on Sunday. But there are a lot of punters that are out there. There are a lot of punters on the waiver wire. There are Pro Bowl punters . . . "

This was Knox's way of telling Rodriguez that Seattle had invited several kickers in that week for tryouts.

Later on Wednesday, Knox heard news that shoved Seattle's punting problems far to the back of his mind. Starting cornerback Terry Taylor was to be suspended for 30 days for violating the NFL's drug policies. McCormack, walking out to reporters on the practice field late in the afternoon, was so overcome with emotion that he barely managed to read the team's brief statement on the suspension. Knox, for his part, couldn't even talk about it, choosing instead to issue what must surely be the briefest prepared statement in the history of the written word: "It's unfortunate for Terry Taylor, but we will adjust and get the next best man that we can."

The league refused to divulge any details on Taylor's transgression, but his suspension meant he had failed two drug tests. Under new NFL rules, a first failure is a confidential matter between the failed player and the league, and a second carries an automatic suspension. News soon surfaced that Taylor had tested positive for cocaine during both the 1987 and 1988 camps. He was to be banned from football until at least September 30.

The next day, Seattle re-signed defensive back David Hollis in time for him to practice with the team in the afternoon. Afterward, defensive backfield coach Ralph Hawkins could only shake his head when asked how he would adjust to the absence of Taylor. Replacing Taylor in Seattle's standard defense was not that serious a problem, Hawkins explained, as Melvin Jenkins was a more-than-adequate replacement. Hawkins's biggest problem was redesigning Seattle's complicated nickel defense. "We're trying all sorts of different combinations," Hawkins said, "and some people who were in there before might have to come out. And it's late in the week. We haven't decided what we're going to do. We have no idea. We haven't settled on anything. We're trying to find out in practice what looks the best." He gave every impression of being a man completely out of options. After a long pause, he looked up at his interrogators with a mischievous gleam in his eye and continued, "There's an old saying that you've heard around here: 'Play the hand you're dealt.' "

Then he laughed, ghoulishly.

Chez **5** Dodge

We fell to wrestling again. We rolled all over the floor, in each other's arms, like two huge helpless children. He was naked and goatish under his robe, and I felt suffocated as he rolled over me. I rolled over him. We rolled over me. They rolled over him. We rolled over us.

—Vladimir Nabokov, *Lolita*

The day before the Seahawks flew to Denver, Seattle strong safety Paul Moyer made an odd observation. "This team has lived off adversity," he said. "We play our best with adversity."

Perhaps Moyer was simply groping for a reason to feel optimistic, as athletes are prone to do. But I had long since learned to pay close attention to what he says. A five-year veteran who had played his entire career with Seattle, Moyer until this season had been a role player on defense and a special teams standout. With blond hair, blue eyes, a square jaw, and an aquiline nose, he is an all-American classic, the second coming of Chip Hilton. When I first started reporting on Seahawk games, I thought reporters gravitated to him simply because he is one of the few talkative players on the Seattle squad. But I had come to understand that he is as analytical and as forthright as he is glib, and that he always gets right to the heart of whatever matter is at hand.

So when he said that the Seahawks "lived off adversity," I took a long mental look at their history and realized that from the day of Knox's arrival five seasons before, the Seahawks had been consistent in only one respect: They always played either far below or far above expectations. Expected to go nowhere in 1983, they inched into the playoffs, then advanced against all odds to the AFC Championship game. The next season, rated a Super Bowl contender, they took themselves out of contention in the season opener when Curt Warner, alone in the open field, tore a knee apart and was sidelined for the rest of the year. Given up for dead, Seattle instead went 12–3 through the season's first 15 weeks and headed to the Kingdome for a season finale against the 11–4 Denver Broncos, whom they had beaten in Denver three weeks before. Favored to win, they instead lost. The loss left them tied with Denver atop the AFC West and cost them the division championship when the tie-breaking formula awarded it to the Broncos. The year after, with a completely restored Curt Warner back in the lineup, they entered the season with a restored contender's reputation and promptly ruined it, finishing a dismal 8–8. Eleven weeks into the 1986 season, they were 5–6 and written off by the rest of the league when they suddenly revived and won their last five games, falling one win short of making the playoffs. Tabbed by prognosticators as a sure Super Bowl team the season after that, they struggled to finish 9–6, then were eliminated in the first round of the playoffs. In each season, it had taken the expectation that they would go nowhere for them to get anywhere, while the expectation that they were going places had killed their chances of ever getting off the ground.

It was a peculiar pattern, and one which made handicapping the coming season almost impossible.

As if to further shore up Moyer's confidence, Fredd Young opted not to show up for the flight to Denver, heightening the sense that the team flying out of Seattle early Saturday afternoon was on a suicide mission.

By the time the Seahawks landed in Denver, Bozmania—or Bozphobia—was raging. Local media coverage of Denver football is frenetic even under the dullest of circumstances. There are four nightly sports-talk radio shows, three weekly Bronco television shows, exhaustive newspaper coverage, and an apparently insatiable hunger among the public for Bronco news. Bosworth, whose moneymaking instincts are to salesmanship what his 4.5 speed is to football, had included in his book some carefully manufactured "hatred" for Denver quarterback John Elway, saying, among other things, that he wanted to "shoot" him and that Elway looks like "Mr. Ed." This sort of transparent hype is the stuff of which pro wrestling bouts are made. Yet in Denver, fans took it so seriously that Broncophiles were venting their heartfelt rage at what they took to be Bosworth's heartfelt rage by constantly publicizing his book and buying it in record numbers.

While Bosworth's teammates avoided public comment on his round-the-clock self-promotion, there were occasional indications that they were tired of constantly hearing and seeing his name. Even Bosworth's closest friend on the team, linebacker Dave Wyman, was sick of the selling of the Boz. Upon being shown a seminude picture of Bosworth in *Rolling Stone*, he looked at it blankly, muttered—for Bosworth's benefit—"What an asshole," and walked angrily away from his pal.

More telling was team reaction to the cover photo of Bosworth on the

August issue of United Airlines' in-flight magazine *Vis-a-Vis*, alerting the traveler to the presence inside the magazine of a purported Bosworth story entitled "My Seattle." This prose milestone, a thinly disguised combined commercial for Bosworth's book and for one of the cities served by United, is as criminally inaccurate as it is unreadable. "But it's scuba diving that I really love," writes "Brian Bosworth," "and the water off Seattle, though sometimes too cold for an Oklahoma boy like me, is the most beautiful I've ever had the pleasure of plunging into. The reefs around the San Juan Islands are spectacular." The reader, remembering that Bosworth is a Texan and having a hard time remembering the San Juans' spectacular reefs, struggles on, coming at last to the pièce de résistance: "The Silver Dome, where I play football, is an example of the kind of construction that continues to go on here."

Since United Airlines and Seattle's Denver hotel (the Westin Tabor Center) are parts of the same conglomerate, a copy of *Vis-a-Vis* had been thoughtfully put in every room. A Seahawk advance man, arriving in Denver a week ahead of the rest of the team, was so alarmed at the effect sightings of the magazine might have on Seahawk players that he swept through the team's rooms, cleaning out every last copy.

That potential distraction thus dispensed with, the Seahawks could get down to the business of anxiously awaiting the next day's kickoff. They passed the time sitting in their rooms, attending an evening team meeting, and occasionally venturing through the hotel lobby.

However mightily they tried, they just could not make themselves inconspicuous. Off the field, football players are comically out of scale. They are no less noticeable in an American hotel lobby than they would be in Lilliput. Autograph hounds, circling the Westin lobby like sharks, surrounded them whenever they emerged from an elevator. Nonfans would edge away when they saw players approaching. Early Saturday evening, hotel guests in the lobby jumped aside in fear when Seattle's offensive linemen came sweeping through, side by side, on their way to supper. And Sunday morning, one elderly woman, about to enter an elevator, stopped in her tracks. Looking out at her were three behemoths—Seahawk tight end coach Russ Purnell, tight end John Spagnola, and defensive end Alonzo Mitz—with their game faces already firmly set in place. "Eeeeee!" she squealed. Then she withdrew.

With kickoff slated for 2pm, the team left the hotel via bus at 11:30. Shouldering their way through crowds of fans, experienced players could sign one or two autographs between elevator and bus without breaking stride. One by one, they filed through, with strangely blank and concentrated gazes. Defensive end Jacob Green, wearing an elegant dark, pinstriped suit, looked like a church elder on his way to Sunday services. His face, though, eyes bulging, mouth hanging slightly ajar, gave him away.

Shortly behind him came a skittish Dave Krieg, wearing a rumpled nylon windbreaker that looked as if it had traveled to Denver in the pocket of Krieg's pants. Try as Krieg might, he just can never manage to look the part of a supercool NFL quarterback, the way the telegenic Elway does. Getting on the bus with his teammates now, he could be mistaken for a kid who'd won some fans' contest, first prize being a ride to the stadium on an NFL team's bus.

Had the author of the Book of Genesis, before ever putting pen to paper, seen Mile High Stadium this Sunday afternoon, he would have ended the story of the creation of the world with, "And on the seventh day, God created Football." The skies were a pristine, clear blue, the temperature 77 degrees, and the light autumn-crisp and bright. It was a dreamy day, designed for football. The stadium, a horseshoe-shaped affair with a white, rearing stallion atop the scoreboard at its open end, is the home both of the football Broncos and the Triple-A baseball Denver Zephyrs, and can be configured perfectly for either sport. The stands on the west side can be hydraulically lifted and moved either backward, to uncover left field, or forward, up to the football field's sideline, both procedures taking 24 hours to complete. Built on spindly steel girders, like a gigantic kid's erector-set project, the stadium shoots at a gravity-defying angle to an astonishing height. It is beautiful as only old stadiums can be, and it evokes poetic football visions of heroic effort and inspired strategy, of unforgettable games, of sparkling, sunlit autumn air filled with flying blood, dust, sod, and the grunts and yowls of wounded men.

Arriving at the stadium two hours before game time, I toured the grounds around the stadium and walked through the stands. Fans either came streaming directly into the stadium or lounged on the grass outside, barbecuing and eating picnic lunches. Nearly everyone wore orange— Denver's colors being orange and blue—many wore cowboy hats, and many more were drinking. Yet the throngs were silent. There was no shouting, and conversations were held in such muted tones that I had to strain to hear the sound of voices. Everywhere was the reverential air of people entering church. Inside the stadium, the causeways were quiet, save for the sounds of shuffling feet and the occasional chants of vendors hawking beverages.

Safely back in the press box, engorging myself on properly thematic barbecued beef sandwiches (press box caterers are big on regional cuisine), I watched Ruben Rodriguez boom kick after spectacular kick during pregame warmups. It had been a hard week for him. Not only had Knox made it clear that he had to punt better to keep his job, but Seattle newspapers had been speculating on his forced departure. He reacted with glum determination, saying on Thursday, "I read that stuff, but they don't know the shit that goes on out there. I know they had other kickers in here, but I just don't care." Perhaps not, but something, clearly, was pumping high-octane fuel into his foot.

Given the solemn air in the stands, the air in the press box turned out to be surprisingly sacrilegious. However devoutly the Denver press corps hypes the Broncos in print and on the air, it apparently is chafing fiercely at the promotional bit. One Denver reporter, eyeing a press release announcing that "Number 12" Bronco jerseys (newly issued in honor of Denver fans) could be bought at several local retail outlets, threw the thing disgustedly on the floor, muttering, "What a crock!" Even the National Anthem seemed to infuriate some of these guys. "What horseshit!" I heard one man exclaim during the pregame rendition. To which his companion sarcastically replied, "Come on—this is what it's all about!"

The anthem over, I sat down and made a quick catalog of the anti-Bosworth signs posted in the stands: "Boz is short for Bozo," "Hey, Boz, write any good books lately?", "Burn the Boz."

Denver, apparently, suffered from a critical wit shortage.

Down on the field, the coin toss having been dispensed with, the teams lined up for Denver's kickoff to Seattle. Next to me, a late-arriving radio reporter squeezed himself into his chair, surveyed the stadium, and sighed, "*Chez* Dodge." The crowd began to roar. And suddenly the game began.

Denver's Rich Karlis sent a picture-perfect kick to David Hollis, who had usurped Randall Morris's place as kickoff returner. The insubstantial Hollis, overanxious to make an impression on his coaches, caught the ball 3 yards deep in the end zone and foolishly decided against downing it there. Running it out, growing less visible with each step, he was unceremoniously slammed down at the Seattle 15. On came the Seahawk offense to run the first official 1988 Seattle play from scrimmage. A Curt Warner run off right tackle, it gained only 2 yards, Warner's blockers unable to budge Denver off the line of scrimmage.

On the next play, John L. Williams, delaying, curled out of the backfield, was left uncovered by the Broncos, caught Krieg's pass on the run and took off up the left sideline, gaining 26 instant yards and immediately silencing the Denver crowd. Krieg then handed the ball off to Warner, who darted through a huge hole on the left side of the line, burst between two linebackers, and was suddenly in the open field with only one man—cornerback Mark Haynes—between him and the Denver end zone.

This was nearly identical to the play the Washington Redskins had employed almost constantly in running Denver out of the stadium in the previous Super Bowl. As with any running play, once the layer of defensive linemen and linebackers is breached, the ball carrier is on his own, freelancing through a chaotic disarrangement of flying, fallen, and recovering bodies. All diagrams and schemes and coaching philosophies forgotten, the game becomes simply a contest between two sets of athletes, relying on instinct, reflex, and physical skill. For the first two or three seconds, a play is slam chess; after that, if it hasn't ended, it's a free-for-all.

Warner gave Haynes a head-and-shoulder fake so convincing that it turned the cornerback completely around. Unfortunately for Seattle, though, Warner so lost himself in admiration of his handiwork that he paused to watch Haynes flounder, allowing Bronco safety Dennis Smith to come flying in from behind and knock the ball loose. The Broncos recovered the fumble on their own 38, the crowd came roaring back to life, and the coaches, sending in new units with new plays and schemes, recovered their control of the game.

Denver began its offensive with a Super Bowl reprise of its own. As expected, the Broncos went right at cornerback Melvin Jenkins, sending wide receiver Vance Johnson streaking down the right sideline. It was a replay of the first play of their last Super Bowl, in all but one respect: The last time, Denver had scored a touchdown; this time, with Jenkins matching Johnson stride for stride, the ball fell incomplete. On the next play, Elway's pass was batted down by Jacob Green. Next, Johnson ran an out-pattern to the left sideline, Seattle's nickel defense opening like an umbrella before him, and Johnson, catching the ball 8 yards downfield, was immediately smothered by cornerback Patrick Hunter. It was classic Seattle third-down-and-long defense, designed to absorb the offensive attack rather than attack the offense, keeping receivers in front of the defensive backs, surrendering yardage only up to just short of the first-down marker. "We played real smart," Paul Moyer said afterward. "We kept everything in front of us. When they caught the ball, we came up and we hit 'em as hard as we could."

Punter Mike Horan came on then and kicked to the Seattle 10, where Bobby Joe Edmonds fair-caught the ball.

The first exchange of blows, then, had basically been a standoff, the Seahawks starting their second possession only 5 yards farther back from where they had begun their first. Denver, however, enjoyed a significant field-position advantage, and the Broncos packed the line of scrimmage, hoping to stop the Seahawks cold and force them to turn for deliverance to the inconsistent Ruben Rodriguez. John L. Williams, carrying on first down, managed to gain 3 yards on sheer physical strength, there being no opening in the line for him. Denver packed the line of scrimmage again, and

Krieg faded back to pass. Ray Butler, enjoying a 5-inch height advantage over cornerback Jeremiah Castille, ran a perfect out-pattern around Castille to the left sideline, turning for the ball just past the first-down marker. Krieg threw the kind of pass then that he throws only when he is red-hot. Centimeters out of the leaping Castille's reach, it settled easily into Butler's outstretched hands. Hitting his receiver in that spot, with the defender in front of him, was like hitting, from 35 yards away, the point in a room where walls and ceiling meet. As Butler came down, however, with both feet inbounds, the ball slipped through his hands. On the next play, under pressure from a no-holds-barred Denver rush, Krieg's pass was deflected by dogging linebacker Simon Fletcher.

On came Rodriguez to kick a low, 37-yard punt under heavy pressure. Denver's Kevin Clark returned it 9 yards to the Seattle 41.

The stage now was set for the Seahawks to fold. Under Knox, they had gone 1–4 in Mile High Stadium, and their losses there had been characterized by fumbles, dropped passes, and serious mental lapses. Only 3 minutes into this game, they already had tallied items in two out of three of these categories. With the Denver crowd roaring at full throttle and the Denver players luxuriously licking their chops, Seattle dug in to defend itself against the onslaught.

The Broncos had resolved during the offseason to shore up their almost nonexistent running game, and had traded for fading Dallas star running back Tony Dorsett. Having lived exclusively on the arm of John Elway for the last five seasons, Denver coach Dan Reeves was determined to change dramatically. He wanted to run the ball at least 25 times per game, particularly against the notoriously weak Seattle rushing defense.

Denver immediately unveiled its new running attack, sending Dorsett straight up the middle first for 6, then for 5 yards. With first down now on the Seattle 30, Denver lined up with Dorsett alone in the backfield, then shifted tight end Clarence Kay into the fullback slot. At the snap, Kay preceded Dorsett through a hole at right guard and flattened Bosworth as Dorsett burst through for 5 more yards. Trying the same play again, Kay was met this time by Dave Wyman. Lowering his head, he blasted Wyman with an earthshaking hit. Wyman reeled, but stood his ground, and Kay—out cold—fell forward, unable even to bring his arms up to break his fall. He hit the turf like a felled tree. Nash, meanwhile, popped the ball loose from Dorsett, and the semiconscious Wyman fell on it.

The play over, Kay still lay there, face down, hands tucked under his waist, elbows outflung. Working carefully, so as not to move his neck, a team of medics took a full 5 minutes to slip him onto a stretcher and roll him off the field. He was scarcely past the sideline when play resumed. "Just wheel him off," the man beside me said with a sarcastic laugh, "and get another one in there!" It was one of those chilling moments when the players seem to be the least valued, most easily replaced components of the NFL product.

Seattle wasted little time in returning—or trying to return—the ball to Denver, gaining 7 yards in two plays, then allowing the Broncos to bat down another Krieg pass. Rodriguez kicked another poor punt, this a 42-yarder netting 34 yards after the return. Denver, however, had been penalized for its zeal. Overloading the middle, the Broncos had sent linebacker Bruce Klosterman bursting through a seam beside center, with speedster Sam Graddy following close behind. When fullback Tommy Agee stepped up to block Klosterman, the linebacker simply grabbed him by the shoulders and pulled him to the side, clearing the way for Graddy to block the kick, which he missed doing by a mere matter of inches. It was a beautifully designed play, but it was illegal. Denver was flagged for holding and Seattle got the ball back 10 yards upfield, with a new first down.

What seems most maddening about football is its insistence on eluding the grasp of the game's technicians. The modern coach is first and foremost a scientist, employing stopwatches that time players to the hundredth of a second, sophisticated video and photographic equipment, complex computer programs and analyses, and every imaginable mathematical, medical, management, and technological tool, all in his effort to control the flow of a game. Yet games most often are won or lost because of tiny, uncontrollable shifts of emotion, which make a mockery of the technocrat's efforts.

The combined effects of Kay's injury and the Denver penalty had effected just such an emotional shift. The Broncos were reeling, and Seattle was quick to take advantage. Back to pass on first down, Krieg hit Butler, crossing over the middle, with a perfect 13-yard pass. Seattle's sliver of advantage, though, immediately slipped away: Butler dropped the ball. Recharged, Denver smothered Seattle's receivers on the next play, and Krieg deliberately overthrew Butler deep. On third down, Krieg was sacked.

To the renewed roar of the Denver crowd, Rodriguez came on, took the snap from center, and strode with textbook grace into the ball. The second his kicking foot made contact, the stadium grew quiet. The ball shot off Rodriguez's foot, sailed over the head of the rapidly retreating Kevin Clark, hit the ground an astonishing 58 yards downfield, took one 10-yard bounce, and sidled out of bounds at the Bronco 6-yard line. With a single 68-yard swing of his leg, Rodriguez had pinned the Broncos against their own goal line, reversing a field-position battle that had been going inexorably against Seattle from the opening kickoff.

The Broncos made a pretext of taking back the initiative, but after gaining 22 yards on three plays—the last a 16-yard pass—they stalled. Elway threw behind Vance Johnson, then was sacked by Alonzo Mitz, after an interminable scramble. On third-and-22, Denver's Gerald Willhite gained 7 yards on a draw play, and the Broncos' Mike Horan punted 48 yards.

Three plays later—the last a clutch 6-yard completion to Steve Largent on third-and-five—Seattle had a first down on its own 44, and was off and running. Butler ran a 19-yard out-pattern, then turned upfield, catching Castille unaware. Realizing that Seattle was about to score a touchdown, Castille grabbed Butler, was flagged for pass interference, and the Seahawks found themselves on the Bronco 35. From there, it took seven plays to score: four outright runs, one short pass, and two runs disguised as passes.

The highlight of the drive came on a third-and-three play from the Denver 12. The Seahawks lined up in their shotgun formation, with three wide receivers on the left, with one on the right, and with fullback John L. Williams to the right of Krieg. As Krieg began his snap count, Steve Largent, the middle of the three left-side receivers, started in motion to the right, as he nearly always does when Seattle lines up unbalanced. Instead of waiting until he had moved all the way across, though, Krieg called for the ball just as Largent passed in front of Butler. The 5'11", 191-pound Largent turned upfield and threw a block on 6'3", 230-pound inside linebacker Karl Mecklenberg, who was lined up as a defensive end.

At first I thought that Seattle coaches had sent their most prized player on a suicide mission. Mecklenberg, however, was so intently studying Krieg that he never saw Largent coming. The wide receiver hit him full speed, blasting him in the chin with his shoulder, and Mecklenberg—4-inch, 40-pound advantage and all—was knocked off his feet.

Largent's was not the only surprise move to come at the snap of the ball. Guards Edwin Bailey and Bryan Millard, instead of retreating in their pass-blocking stance, pulled left. Krieg handed the ball to Williams, crossing in the same direction, and Williams followed the two guards through the area cleared by Largent. To his credit, Mecklenberg leapt up, pursued, and tackled Williams downfield, but not before Williams gained 7 yards, earned a first down, and set the stage for a Curt Warner 5-yard touchdown run around right end, coming on the next play. At the 13:29 mark of the second quarter, Seattle led, 7–0.

The Williams run had been a subtle and well-disguised seizing of opportunity. Proof that the Seahawks had a more varied attack and a greater array of disguises than did Denver, it also demonstrated Knox's and offensive coordinator Steve Moore's eagerness to counter their own tendencies.

And while an indication of the unpredictability of the Seahawk offense, it was by no means an isolated one. On their previous five first downs, Seattle had tried undisguised running plays only twice, throwing two passes and running a quarterback draw the other three times. Now, on third-and-three—a sure passing situation—they had sent in four wide receivers, lined up in passing formation, and sucker-punched the Bronco defense. The spectators, silent as Puritans during a fire-and-brimstone sermon, could begin already to see the outline, dimly forming, of their team's damnation.

Except for a seven-play, 62-yard Bronco drive culminating in a tying touchdown at the 3:27 mark, the teams devoted the rest of the second quarter to exchanging the ball, Denver punting once and throwing one interception, Seattle punting twice. The teams finished the half dead-even in points and nearly even in statistics—a tally that gave the Seahawks enough of a psychological advantage to send them back out for the third quarter breathing fire. Opening the second half on offense, the Broncos lost 1 yard on a Tony Dorsett carry, then threw a pass behind Ricky Nattiel and into the hands of Melvin Jenkins. Jenkins returned the interception 20 yards to the Denver 6, and Krieg, improvising, hit Ray Butler in the back of the end zone three plays later, putting the Seahawks up 14–7.

Five punts later—three by Denver, two by Seattle—the Seahawks came out on offense on first-and-10 at their own 28 and lined up without realizing that they were staring right into the face of disaster.

The series began innocently enough, with Krieg hitting Largent for a 15-yard gain on first down. Then, sending his favorite receiver on a short crossing pattern, Krieg saw him work his way open, and threw high as Largent ran full speed across the middle. Leaping, Largent stretched, grabbed the ball . . . and blacked out. He never heard the collective gasp from the stands, nor did he see, or hear, or feel what caused it. Running hell-bent in the opposite direction, safety Mike Harden had come upon a defensive back's dream: a wide receiver, his body extended, waiting helpless and unaware for a defender's concussive hit. Aiming right for Largent's face, Harden propelled himself shoulder-first into the receiver's facemask, shattering it, jarring the ball loose, and sending Largent crumpling to the ground, where he lay writhing and unconscious. It took Seahawk medics nearly 7 minutes to revive him, after which they guided him gently to the sidelines, where he was diagnosed as having suffered a concussion. Only dimly aware of what was going on, Largent watched the rest of the game from there.

In aiming for Largent's face, Harden entered a murky moral zone between the hard defensive play and the deliberate attempt to maim. Largent, who afterward professed indifference to the violence of the hit, nevertheless took the facemask home as a keepsake and uttered not a word of objection when the league office subsequently fined Harden $5,000.

As if brought alive by the assault, the Seahawks rode Krieg's arm downfield, taking a 21–7 lead with 3:32 left in the third quarter.

The scoring drive was remarkable both for the hit on Largent and for the complete disappearance of the Seattle running game, which sputtered through the first half, then came to a complete stop in the third quarter. All but 23 of the drive's 72 yards were gained in the air, with 22 of the rushing yards being gained on a Krieg quarterback draw-cum-Denver-penalty out of shotgun formation. Unable to run, and deprived by Mike Harden of their best receiver, the Seahawks had chosen the game's lowest moment to resort to some ingenious bread-and-butter gimmickry. First came Krieg's draw play, then a 30-yard screen pass to John L. Williams, moving the ball to the Denver 15 and giving Seattle fans a rich foretaste of the season to come.

The John L. Williams screen is a nifty bit of orchestrated anarchy first introduced by Seahawk coaches the season before, during a win in Chicago against the tough and talent-rich Bears. In that game, it had turned into a 75-yard touchdown romp. It has proven almost impossible to defend against, for two reasons. Williams in the open field is impossible to tackle (in this game, he had habitually run right through the likes of Mecklenberg on his sweeps, and the Broncos had repeatedly had to gang-force him out of bounds after failing to bring him down); and Seattle can run the play out of every one of its formations and has employed it in all manner of situations, under practically every down-and-distance circumstance there is. It has been disguised as a deep pass play, as a handoff to Curt Warner, as a Warner pitchout-sweep, as a Krieg rollout, and even as a Williams run straight ahead. It has been thrown to Williams on the right, left, or in the middle. In every case, Seattle appears at the snap of the ball to be running some other play and, while the defense reacts to the fake, three linemen and Williams discreetly creep off like illicit lovers to some prearranged spot, wait for the ball, and then take off.

In this version, Krieg faked a pitchout to Warner, who was breaking right, then followed him as if to roll out and pass downfield. Then he turned and threw across to the left, where Williams and his minions were waiting.

At 21–7, the game turned into a spectacle of futility, with both offenses stopping themselves cold, save for one Denver touchdown drive near the end of the game. I tried turning my attention to divining the meaning of Seattle's win-in-the-making, but was distracted by my awe for both teams' punters.

For the 13 minutes following Seattle's last touchdown, the game was a breathtaking duel between these two. Six straight possessions—three by each team—all ended in punts. Most amazing were Horan's efforts, all three of which, incredibly, were downed inside the Seattle 3-yard line. Each time, the Seahawks responded with short-lived, cautious offensive efforts, ending in Rodriguez punts of 40, 44, and 60 yards. At game's end, Rodriguez and Horan would have punted nine times each—Horan for 403 yards, Rodriguez for 428. They were the day's best and most consistent performers.

Seattle ran out the clock with a 54-yard, 4-minute drive, its second-longest offensive effort of the game. Coming hard on the heels of Denver's last touchdown, it was a minirevival, of sorts, of the moribund Seahawk running game. Eight of the nine plays were runs, and two of the drive's three first downs were earned on the ground. The ground game had eaten up far more time than yardage, however. The biggest play of the drive was a 21-yard pass from Krieg to Williams, and five of the eight running plays had gained 2 yards or less.

As the fourth quarter's final seconds ticked off the clock, I considered the nature of the game. Pitting two archrivals, expected to finish one-two atop their division, it had been, in effect, a playoff game, played with high-stakes, postseason intensity. But it also had been a season opener and had been plagued by inconsistency and mistakes, the staples of inaugural games. Most of all, it had been characterized—defined, in fact—by weakness. While Seattle's pass defense made more clutch plays in this game than it did all the previous season, Elway clearly had an off day, often missing open receivers. And Seattle, coming into the game planning to win with ball control, eating up time by running against a weak Denver rushing defense, relied instead on offensive gimmickry, timely passing, and Denver turnovers. Seattle trying to run the ball against Denver was a peculiar spectacle: two teams pitting their weaknesses against one another. In the end, the Seahawk rushing total—178 yards on 42 carries—was deceiving. Twenty-seven of the yards were Krieg's, and Warner had averaged only 3.3 yards per carry.

When you beat your archnemesis 21–14 in his own stadium, though, such considerations mean nothing, and the Seattle players, leaving the field, were jubilant. Bosworth roared and pumped his fists in the air. Others were whooping, others were quietly smiling. Joe Nash, mindful of where he was and who was glaring angrily down at him from the stands, decided to wait until he was safely in the Seattle locker room before starting to celebrate. "Keep your helmets on!" he cautioned the teammates preceding him into the tunnel.

Knox, pinned in a corner of the locker room by a swarm of reporters, tried to downplay the significance of the win. "It's a win in the division," he said. "That's always a big win. We beat a team that's won the division the last two years, and we beat them here. So that's a big win. But it doesn't mean anything if we don't go on and win next week. That's the nature of the business."

Asked if he was surprised, he bridled a bit. "I've said all along that we're gonna come up here and play a good football game. We prepared well, we had a good training camp. I'm just proud of our football team and I think they put to rest any of this talk about distractions, because they came in here and took the bit in their mouth and got the job done... I mean, everybody made plays out there today. That's what you've got to do."

Knox had elicited his best play out of his defensive backfield, the unit expected to have the most trouble. Facing one of the game's greatest quarterbacks, the Seahawks had held Elway—or, at least, helped Elway hold himself—to 21-of-45 passing, for 259 yards, had intercepted him twice, and had covered receivers thoroughly enough to cause him to be sacked three times by one of football's worst pass-rushing units. "We were just out there playing good, solid defense," said free safety Eugene Robinson. "And we were talking. Getting guys in the right position where they could make the play. There was a lot of communication—all over the field. You need the communication! Last year, we had breakdowns in communication. But when we communicate, nobody can stop us. We were calling out their patterns, seeing their different formations and watching for their tendencies, being alert."

Two lockers over, Paul Moyer tried putting things in perspective. "I really didn't play very well, but I don't even care," he said with a smile. "It's probably one of the most emotional wins I ever had. Just because we've been waiting all year for this, you know, and we'd gone through so much during camp, during the week, the tragedy with Terry Taylor, but we came together. And I told a lot of people down the road that we play real well with adversity. And we did today, too... Actually, I don't know how well we played, but we played well enough to win."

Next to him, Melvin Jenkins was quietly cultivating the cornerback's trademark—a gunslinger's icy, triumphant demeanor. "My wife said to me, 'You know they're gonna come after you?' And I said, 'I know—and I'm glad.' They came right at me the first play. I knew it was gonna happen like this, but I prepared myself all week, you know, I knew they were gonna attack me because of the situation that happened with Terry Taylor. So I was ready. I just wanted to prove myself—show that I could play with the best."

I made my way into the coaches' locker room, where I came upon Steve

Moore sitting alone in the middle of the room, his eyes distant. When I asked him if he knew why his team had had trouble running the ball consistently, I could see immediately that he knew the answer. I could also see that he didn't want anyone else to know it. "Well, uh... no!" he answered. "I mean, I've got some impressions, but you'd have to look at the film. It was a very complicated game out there, and I've got an impression, but I'd rather not comment on that."

Turning back to the players, I ran headlong into a toothy Ruben Rodriguez grin. "I told everybody I owed 'em from last week—you know, the screwup I had last week—and I did," he said. "I felt good today. I went out there during warmups and was hitting 'em great, and I said, 'This is my game. This has gotta be my game.' I just want to get everything back now, and keep going."

I ran a gauntlet of whoops and shouts, to the far corner, where Warner, the quietest player in the room, was as puzzled as he was happy. "I'm telling you, I don't know what was going on out there," he said. "They were doing a lot of stuff. Naturally I would have liked to have more yards—I'm sort of disappointed. But I'll tell you what—either they had the holes filled or I can't see anymore. They just shut our running down."

The players were clearing out fast, heading for the team bus. The crowd waiting outside was friendly. When a smiling Bosworth emerged, it was, surprisingly, to cheers rather than boos. Shortly after, Krieg came out, sporting a subtle rebuke to his detractors—who always compare him unfavorably to Elway—in the form of a "John Elway Show" hat.

The ride to the airport was surprisingly quiet. Players pored over the play-by-play sheets, held cordial arguments over statistical arcana, and went over some of the game's plays. You would never have guessed that less than an hour before, they had been embroiled in the game of their lives. There was no trace of relief or surprise at having won, and not a hint of the turmoil they had been through during the week leading up to the game. All of the fear and trembling, apparently, had been confined to the sports pages and the hearts of Seattle fans.

When the bus reached the airport, it cruised slowly past Ken Behring's private jet on the way to the team's chartered airliner. Bosworth stared hard at it, impressed and excited. From the back of the bus came the friendly taunts of Seahawk offensive linemen: "That your jet, Brian?" "Where's yours, Brian?" Dreamily, he murmured, to no one in particular, "Wouldn't that be something? Just have your own jet, just take off... whooooosh!" He looked for all the world like a gigantic 10-year old boy, out on a field trip with his fellow students from some special school for the oversized.

The Skin **6** of Dreams

For rookie quarterback Kelly Stouffer, preseason had presented the first opportunity to play live football in nearly two years. Because he had refused to sign with the team that drafted him in 1986, he was sent into pro football exile for a year, hanging around his home town, Rushville, Nebraska, trying to keep his skills sharp by throwing a football against a curtain hung in his old high school gym. It was as tense as it was tedious a time, for few football players succeed in beating the player draft system. For most aspiring pro athletes, to lose a year of play and training is to lose a career.

Stouffer, though, was a rare find. At 6'3", 210 pounds, he was a model modern quarterback. And he had an arm that brought tears to pro scouts' eyes. "He has a lot of the natural things that you can't coach," Mike McCormack said during training camp. "The height and the ability to see downfield over those big linemen. And throwing from up here"—he cocked his arm, putting his hand against his ear—"with a quick arm and quick release, instead of throwing out of the well."

Because he held out for a year, though, and because he attended a college—Colorado State University—with an undistinguished football program, Stouffer had little more to recommend him than the skills he was born with. "If he had gone to a Miami," said McCormack, "where there's almost a professional program, if he'd gone down there to an intricate passing offense and all that, he'd have been a little better prepared. He shows his rustiness here, he shows that he hasn't played in about 20 months, and that he did not come out of a sophisticated program."

Accordingly, Stouffer's return to full-fledged football had been brief. Once the season started, he returned to another form of exile—one of the two inactive-player spots on the roster. From there, he studied the game by watching and listening on the sidelines both at games and on the practice field, posing as the coming game's opposing quarterback during defensive practice, watching game films, and attending quarterback meetings.

As the season began, it seemed at times that Stouffer's coaches felt they had stumbled upon a treasure of potentially limitless value and of such delicacy that the slightest mishandling of it would reduce it to ruin. Every move they made with him seemed more calculated to avoid damage than to confer greater strength and ability. Given the durability, age, and experience of Dave Krieg and Jeff Kemp, they figured, they had the luxury of taking their time with Stouffer.

From all indications, Stouffer seemed content to wait and study and learn. But there were times when his position coach, Ken Meyer, seemed impatient with his superiors' painstaking quarterback development program. On Wednesday after the Denver game, Meyer seemed particularly glum. "He's not getting much work now," he said grimly, when asked about Stouffer's progress. He paused for a second, then brightened. "But he's learning well. He had a good grasp of the Denver game. He made a lot of helpful suggestions. He really understood what was going on out there."

One who understood far less what was going on out there was Fredd Young, who had pulled a Stouffer act of sorts by refusing to take to the field for the Seahawks. McCormack, who at the beginning of training camp said of the Young fiasco, "I thought I had that one put to bed for three years," grew increasingly irritated as Young's attempt to wriggle out of his contract extended through the entire training camp and into the season. Publicly professing the conviction that Young eventually would give in, McCormack privately worked for weeks on trading him. Finally, on the Thursday after Seattle's win over Denver, he swung a deal with the Indianapolis Colts, sending Young there for the Colts' 1989 and 1990 first-round draft picks. Under a new contract with the Colts, Young would make $900,000 in '88, the first year of a five-year, $5 million pact with Indianapolis.

The deal came through in the nick of time for both Young and the Seahawks. The NFL's two-week roster exemption for Young, granted on August 28, was due to expire in two days. Had he not been traded, Seattle would have been forced to put him on its Reserve Left Camp list and would have had to keep him there, without pay, until after the season.

In the final analysis, the Young-Seahawk duel could best be described as a battle in which Young and McCormack went eyeball-to-eyeball until Indianapolis blinked. Young was determined not to play for Seattle, and McCormack was determined to let him go for nothing less than two number-one draft picks. The two men were fighting not so much a battle over money as a battle over principle: Young for the right of a player to sell his services to the highest bidder, and McCormack for the right to control a player he had acquired on the NFL slave market. In staging a one-man strike, Young, however unwittingly, was trying to strike a blow for player freedom, just as Stouffer had done. And in refusing to sell Young for less, McCormack was striking a blow for owners' control over their most talented players. "There's always a lot of concern that this could set a bad precedent," McCormack said. "That's why we were adamant that we had to get two number ones. Now, if a player feels that he can hold out and get traded, we've established a pretty high price."

McCormack characterized his battle with Young as one in which both sides lost. By trading his adversary to Indianapolis, however, he won a decisive victory. He sent his disgruntled former employee to a franchise run by a madman and extracted such a high price that it would take the Colts years to recover. Under owner Robert Irsay, the Indianapolis (formerly Baltimore) Colts had languished, racking up an 84–135 won-lost record from 1972 (the year Irsay acquired the team) through 1987. The Colts had only four winning seasons in all that time, the last one being 1987, when they went 9–6, and the last before that being 1977. Since 1972, Irsay had been through nine head coaches—one of them McCormack—two cities, and a *Sports Illustrated* exposé of his bizarre behavior, peculiar business practices, and maddening management style. McCormack will never say so publicly, but in his own secret view he must have known that in sending Young to Irsay he was joining together two people who richly deserved one another.

The Colts were the only team in the league willing to pay McCormack's asking price. They did so both because they felt that Young was a good enough player to take them all the way to the 1989 championship, and because they thought their last such bold move had been well worth the price. The year before, having drafted a linebacker, Cornelius Bennett, who refused to come to terms, they had worked a complex trade sending Bennett to the Buffalo Bills and unhappy Los Angeles Rams running back Eric Dickerson to Indianapolis. As part of that deal, they gave up their first- and second-round picks in the 1988 draft and their second-round pick in the 1989 draft. It seemed a fortune to pay, but Dickerson is one of the greatest athletes who ever lived, and with him in their backfield, the Colts rebounded from 1986's 3–13 record to 1987's 9–6. Now Young apparently was regarded as a defensive counterpart to Dickerson, for the Colts had given up almost as much for him.

When the soap cleared from their two big deals, the Colts were slated to go three years without a first-round pick and two years without a second-round pick. Six weeks after acquiring Young, they would be 1–6, on their way to a 9–7 season, with no hope in sight of improving their team through the player draft. Such are the risks of the all-or-nothing approach to roster-building.

Heading into the season's second game, Knox had more immediate acquisition and disposal problems to contend with. Hoping to inject more speed into his defensive backfield, he released David Hollis to make room for newly acquired cornerback Lou Brock, Jr., released in training camp by the San Diego Chargers. A second-round pick in the 1987 draft, Brock spent the '87 season on injured reserve, suffering from a blood infection, then failed to make the '88 Charger squad. "We need another corner with some speed," Knox said on Wednesday, "a cover guy who can help out in our nickel package. Our scouting reports on him, coming out of college, were high . . . and that's about it for Lou Brock."

It was a curious move. In Hollis, Seattle lost a competent kick returner and reliable defensive back; in Brock, they gained an unproven cornerback who had been unable to make one of the NFL's weakest teams.

Knox's comments notwithstanding, Seattle must have had some doubts about Brock. After giving him a tryout on Monday, they sent him packing, then suddenly called him back from aboard a plane waiting to take off at Sea-Tac airport. Now Brock was excited and neologistical. "Not to be braggadocious," he said, "but I wasn't too concerned. I just felt that there was going to be an opportunity for me. I just need to throw everything that happened behind me and look forward to playing for Seattle and making Seattle a contender."

To reporters gathered around him on Wednesday after practice, Brock did not have the look or sound of an NFL player. Soft-spoken, short, and insubstantial, he seemed to fade a little more from view with each word he uttered. His interviewers seemed embarrassed for him and devoted most of the session to asking why he had chosen football over baseball, the sport in which his father had gained fame as a base-stealer.

Knox, true to form, was anything but braggadocious as he assessed his team's chances the coming Sunday against the lightly regarded Kansas City Chiefs. Having won on the road in Denver, he was worried about a letdown at home against the Chiefs, who were coming off a 4–11 season, had lost the week before to the Cleveland Browns, and had not won in the Kingdome since 1981. His week's efforts were dedicated to keeping his team anxious rather than overconfident.

He felt that the Seahawks had received more than their share of breaks in Denver, and he was worried about uncontrollable breaks turning things the Chiefs' way a few days hence. "Sometimes things happen in a football game that may not be indicative of what one thinks happened," he said cryptically, when asked if he was worried about inconsistent play from his team. "You come off a big win or something and go out there and have everybody going and everybody really prepared very, very hard for this week and then you leave the ball laying out there or you have a kick hit the upright or you get a touchdown called back, and the next week the head of officials tells you that it was a bad call. And then people say, 'Well, you were up last week, you were down this week'—and that might not in fact be the case at all."

Sometimes things are said at a press conference that are not indicative of what one thinks was said. The first sentence of that statement was so hypnotically nonsensical that it lulled Knox's audience into missing his point. A coach, he was saying, is no more able to control the outcome of a game than he is able to dribble a football. However thoroughly he can prepare to do battle with an opponent, he can do little to prepare to do battle with randomness. He was trying to make reporters see that while there may be a few hundred possibilities a coach can manage in a given game, there are millions more raging out of control.

That Knox's confession was more prophetic than even he realized was not to become immediately apparent, the weather on the Sunday of the Kansas City game being too glorious to allow for gloom. Seattle's skies were clear, and temperatures were in the low 70s. Fans, in humming hordes, came cascading through downtown, through Pioneer Square, and along the waterfront, finally creeping into the Kingdome like insects crawling under a rock to escape the sun.

During the hours leading up to a Seahawk kickoff, downtown Seattle is transformed by the crowds streaming to the stadium. Bookstores and bars are packed with browsers and customers, sidewalks overflow, and streets are clogged. Dressed predominantly in Seahawk blue-and-gray, carrying football paraphernalia, and hooting and hollering, the fans look like invaders come to wipe out downtown civilization.

Nowhere do they look more invasive than on the ferry from Bainbridge Island. On any other day, the boats from Bainbridge are filled either with quiet nuclear families or three-piece-suited commuters. But on Seahawk Sundays, the morning boats—the 10:15 and 11:15—are taken over by a standing-room-only crowd of people decked out in all varieties of football jerseys or absurd homemade costumes declaring the wearer's allegiance to the Seattle Seahawks. The colorful, noisy spectacle is at once enchanting and creepy. Over the course of the year, only one other boat ride to Seattle is worse—the annual malodorous return of cyclists from spring's Chilly Hilly bicycle tour of the island.

Maneuvering through the thick throngs on the streets, I detected not a glimmer of preoccupation with the team's soap-operatic start. Already this season, sports fans had been taking in a steady diet of stories on Fredd Young's mental state, Daryl Turner's travails, Gale Gilbert's legal problems, Kenny Easley's health, and Brian Bosworth's ego. Yet for all the prominent display these stories enjoyed in the papers, they seemed to have no influence one way or the other over fans. The stadium would be packed, as it is every Seattle football Sunday, and fans would be focused only on the game.

That the game should be the focus for everyone was a sore point with Knox and McCormack, who had frequently begged reporters during the final days of training camp to stop writing about Young and start writing about the excellent training camp Seattle was having. Sportswriters, for that matter, were no less fed up. "We're all sitting here," one beat reporter wailed the day Indianapolis offered its two draft picks for Young, "saying, 'Take it and get the guy out of here!' Because we all want to start writing about football again."

That was sort of what they got to write about after the season's second game. The battle against Kansas City was not so much a football game as it was a game of hot potato slathered with slapstick and sandwiched between thick slices of boredom.

The Chiefs made an early pretense of helping to stage an interesting game. Taking the opening kickoff 4 yards deep in the Kansas City end zone, returner Keyvan Jenkins tried to run it out and was stopped by two teammates, who grabbed him and forced him down on one knee—clear evidence that the reputation of Seattle's kickoff team, which had taken a beating in 1987, had been rehabilitated after its solid work in the Denver game. Beginning from its own 20, then, the Kansas City offense started out crisply, until Chief quarterback Bill Kenney hit receiver Stephone Paige for a 9-yard completion and a first down at the Chief 46, and Brian Bosworth came exploding into Paige's ribs, forcing a fumble recovered by Joe Nash at the 48. The Seattle crowd, its ecstatic reaction bouncing off the Kingdome roof, sent the Seahawk offense riding onto the field on a sonar tidal wave.

Seattle started off with five textbook running plays that proved the wisdom of Knox's esteem for the ground game. On the first, Curt Warner shot through a hole at right tackle and darted his way downfield for 9 yards.

Next came John L. Williams, gaining 7 over left tackle. Then Warner swept around left end for 8, and Williams bulled his way into the left side, gaining 1 yard and setting up third-and-one at the Chief 23. Seattle then sent him over right tackle, where the play stalled. Williams bounced to the outside and took off around end before any of the Chiefs could recover. Three yards past the line of scrimmage, only one Kansas City player, safety Deron Cherry, had a shot at him. As Cherry closed, Williams gave him a fierce stiff-arm to the face and took off, the speedy Cherry in pursuit. Incredibly, the heavier Williams stayed in front all the way to the goal line, where Cherry tried a last-gasp flying tackle from behind, bringing John L. down a fraction of a yard too late. Williams, stretching, got into the end zone.

To the tune of a deafening roar from the stands, the game officials conferred—always a sign of trouble—then waited while the video-replay official reviewed tapes of the touchdown. The roar gradually died down, then lapsed into incredulous silence as the score was disallowed, the ball placed just inside the 1-yard line. Briefly, vociferously, the fans booed, their opinion roiling down from the roof with eardrum-crushing strength. Then stunned quiet held sway again as the fans watched their homeboys rush three times into the line of scrimmage, each time coming up with nothing. The entry of Norm Johnson, coming on to kick a field goal, was greeted by a resumption of the booing—this time for Knox, rather than for the officials.

Perhaps they were booing because sometimes things happen in a football game that are not indicative of what an official thinks happened. Perhaps they were booing because they saw, in Kansas City's goal-line stand, signs of familiar Seattle failings. Or perhaps, in booing Knox, they were adhering to humanity's long-standing custom of blaming the messenger for bad news. For this touchdown four times denied was exactly the sort of twist of fate Knox had alluded to in his midweek prophecy.

At any rate, Kansas City opted against accepting the offered momentum, gaining only 3 yards in three tries before punting from the Chief 23. Seattle, starting out again from its own 36, devoted its series to inept moves that reminded fans of the franchise's early expansion days. After a 3-yard Warner run, Krieg dropped back to pass, saw the pocket around him collapse almost immediately, was hit, and fumbled. Guard Edwin Bailey recovered, and Seattle was faced with third-and-14. Krieg then threw a near-completion to Steve Largent, and Ruben Rodriguez, still basking in the glow of his Denver performance, came on to kick into the teeth of an all-out Kansas City rush. Fullback Tommy Agee, calling signals and blocking assignments, alerted Rodriguez that the Chiefs were coming after him rather than setting up a punt return. Rodriguez went into hurry-up mode, walking, before the snap, toward where the ball would come, so as to get the kick off faster. The snap was low, though, and he fumbled it.

Immediately, the punting play's customary stateliness dissolved into a riotous search for the wriggling ball. Rodriguez managed to retrieve it, but was abruptly hit. Before going down, he shoveled the ball to Agee, who further contributed to the confusion by launching the ball airward when he was hit. Depending upon what you call Agee's release, Kansas City either recovered the ball or intercepted it.

The Chiefs now had a first down at the Seahawk 23, but couldn't cash it in. Six plays later, facing fourth-and-six at the Seattle 9, Kansas City sent place-kicker Nick Lowery in to tie the game at the 1:11 mark of the first quarter.

Fans had no sooner resigned themselves to an afternoon of watching two punchless offenses do battle, than Bobby Joe Edmonds returned Kansas City's kickoff 34 yards to the Seattle 41, from where the Seahawks launched a 13-play touchdown drive. Kansas City responded with a five-play dance, 15 yards forward and 10 backward, before punting the ball away. Seattle came back with another extended drive, this one covering 53 yards in 10 plays. The first play of that drive was a fan's delight—a flea-flicker. Krieg handed off to Warner, running right, and Warner handed off to Largent, running the other direction. Largent then lateraled to Krieg, who looked deep downfield—where Ray Butler was covered—then passed to tight end Mike Tice for a 10-yard gain. Three plays later, on third-and-six, Steve Largent took one half-step toward the sideline, then broke straight downfield for 15 yards, dipped his shoulders slightly inward—freezing strong safety Lloyd Burruss—then curled sharply toward the sideline, meeting a perfectly-lobbed ball 8 more yards downfield, catching it, and stutter-stepping out of bounds. It was a magic moment—one of those plays that work so perfectly that the spectator feels it possible to diagram entire lives, entire epochs.

That play, though, marked the last designed moment of the day. From then on, all was futility and comic failure. It took Seattle seven more plays to travel the final 16 yards to the end zone, and it took Kansas City only three more plays (2-yard run, sack, interception) to give the ball back to their hosts.

The interception, which gave the Seahawks a first down at the Chief 18, came with 1:48 remaining in the half. At the 51-second mark, Dave Krieg hit Brian Blades in the left corner of the end zone with a perfectly timed pass, Blades making a sensational catch with cornerback Kevin Ross hanging onto his arm.

The score now 24–3, the air reeking of the spilled blood of the visitors, the crowd in a cannibalistic furor, Norm Johnson lofted a high, slow kick to the Kansas City 4, where Paul Palmer fumbled it, picked it up, and stumbled 4 yards forward before being felled by Alonzo Mitz. At the 45-second mark, Kenney dropped back into his own end zone to pass, was blasted by Jacob Green, and fumbled, Green recovering for the fourth touchdown of his career, and the first since 1985.

Five pointless plays later, executioner and victim retired to their respective quarters, to rest from their labors and ponder the mysterious realm of football emotion. These two teams, whatever their fortunes elsewhere, were helpless in one another's stadium. Since Knox's arrival in Seattle, neither had managed to beat the other on the road.

Lost in the metaphysical morass was Krieg's first-half performance. He had completed 10 of 13 passes, one of his incompletions had been an outright drop, another had been caused by pass interference, and none of his completions had required extraordinary effort on the part of his receiver. Passing on third down, he was four-for-four (discounting the pass interference play), for three first downs and one touchdown. A solid performance by a seasoned, well-prepared quarterback, Krieg's first half would prove to be the best and most consistent facet of the Seahawk attack, on both sides of the ball, in either half. Yet the next day, newspapers and the minds of fans would be filled almost exclusively with memories of Seattle's defensive performance, and the game would go down in history as one won by the Seahawk defense. The game and its aftermath would raise, again, the persistent question of Krieg's place in the Seattle pantheon: What is it about this guy that keeps fans from worshipping him?

Probably the same thing that led his teammates to nickname him "Mudbone."

The second half, won by Kansas City 7–0, was excruciating. Down 31–3 and with no chance of getting back in the game, the Chiefs came out to endure a pointless half of football for the sake of rulemakers, advertisers, and statisticians. It was the kind of half that makes you wish football would adopt the practice, employed in chess, of allowing a combatant to surrender when the game is hopelessly lost. Kansas City threw 42 second-half passes and ran only five times, while the Seattle defense dropped into deep zone coverage on every play, allowing short, meaningless completion after short, meaningless completion. The strategy was sound—the Seahawks were using the Kansas City offense to kill the clock—but the entertainment value was nil. I couldn't imagine what was keeping fans in their seats. You would think that even bloodlust, which often seems the principal attraction of this sport, would be hard to sustain in the face of a complete lack of suspense.

Seattle took a number of players out of the game at halftime. Cornerback

Patrick Hunter, with an injured ankle, was replaced by rookie backup Dwayne Harper; Joe Nash was out with a knee injury; Tommy Kane was in for Brian Blades; and Edwin Bailey had been replaced by Alvin Powell.

After outperforming the Kansas City offense in the first half to the tune of 15 first downs to four, Seattle did exactly the opposite in the second, earning four first downs—only one in the third quarter—to Kansas City's 15. As the half ground on, the game began to take on the pattern of entire Seahawk seasons. Just as Seattle fortunes had improved in years past whenever adversity mounted, and declined in times of relative good fortune, so in this game did the team's performance and effort decline when its scoring advantage rose. After feasting on a steady diet of Seattle breaks and Kansas City breakdowns during the first half, the Seahawks came out in the second half so diminished by a lack of hunger and anxiety that they couldn't bring themselves to play with passion. It was an understandable lapse, but the mediocre play it produced seemed to come too naturally to Seattle. As the clock wound slowly down, the second half of this game showcased as a weakness a condition long considered one of Seattle's greatest strengths: Regarded as a team that can overcome athletically superior foes by playing furiously and with reckless abandon, the Seahawks today looked like a team that cannot win a game without playing over its head.

Going down to the locker room afterward, I managed to dismiss that theory as the inevitable product of ennui. But Knox, after winning 31–10, looked and sounded more like a losing coach than a winning one. "I was unhappy with the second half," he said. "When you're up 31–3, it's hard... but I think every time you go out there you have to play hard." He was equally disenchanted with his special-teams play. "Those kind of mistakes," he said of the first-quarter punting snafu, "will beat you more than anything." His players had come out of the game in poor health, and Knox was worried about having to play the next few games without nose tackle Joe Nash. "We got banged up," he said. "Nash may have to be 'scoped.'" The next day, after examining Nash's knee, team doctors put off arthroscopic surgery, but said he might be out four to six weeks.

However unhappy Knox might have been, he was not unhappy enough to break ranks with his fellow footballers and ally himself in any way with the media. He was as spirited in his pride as he had been in his criticism. He assured reporters that his players' mistakes were flukes, saying of his team's failure to score a touchdown after having a first down at the Kansas City 1, "Our first offensive drive was a well-executed drive, except we couldn't get it in. We have to do better there—and we will. We have a great attitude and we're playing hard." When reporters recovered sufficiently from hearing an actual boast from Knox, they asked if perhaps his team's 2–0 record, given everything that had gone wrong in preseason, might be a trifle misleading, and Knox bristled. "We had the finest training camp in the six years I've been here," he said heatedly.

In the locker room, players were apologetic. "It was kind of a letdown," said offensive tackle Ron Mattes. "You get so far ahead of an opponent, and you don't want to let down, but it's human nature. You don't have no fire. We didn't put 'em away when we had a chance to put 'em away. If we had drove the ball right down the field and got a few more scores, they would have quit right there. The way it was, it seemed like our defense played the whole second half."

Paul Moyer was similarly disappointed. "At one time," he said, "it was— what?—third and 20, they ended up getting a first down. We just can't do that. I don't think we read patterns very well. And I don't think we squeezed some stuff . . . I know I didn't."

One player who had acquitted himself well from beginning to end was Bosworth, whose development as a pass defender had progressed remarkably over last season. In both games thus far, he had shown great anticipation—the sign of a savvy, well-prepared player—and had no trouble covering tight ends and running backs running pass patterns through his area. He let an interception slip through his hands once each game, but even that was proof he could keep receivers from getting open. His greater grasp of the passing game, coupled with his wiser, more aggressive play against the run, was already beginning to justify the Seahawks' immense investment in him.

Patrick Hunter, though, professed to be unconvinced. Sitting two lockers away from Bosworth, he was ragging him unmercifully. "Man, I only played one half, and I still made more tackles than you!" he shrieked. (He had made three, to Bosworth's two.) "Get out there and play the game!" Bosworth, undressing, simply smiled. His body, eloquently testifying to the hard effort he had put forth on the field, was covered with welts and cuts and scrapes and bruises. And the contentment shining like soft light through the array of blotches and scars on his face testified no less eloquently to the game's outcome. When you win big, the game's blemishes and bruises—assuaged by the lopsided final score—are nearly imperceptible.

By now, the stadium was dark and nearly empty. Outside the locker rooms, wives and other interested women milled around, waiting for players to emerge. Reporters under deadline forced their way through and ascended in the elevator to the press box, where they wrote and transmitted their stories. More than an hour after the game, Seahawk video director

Thom Fermstad came through, pushing a cart piled high with blue footlock-ers. He was making his way back out to Kirkland, where he would work far into the night at team headquarters, editing and copying film of the game.

As with any on- or off-field facet of NFL football, the editing and distribu-tion of game videotapes is strictly regulated. (Although the NFL switched from film to videotape in 1986, the medium is still referred to as "film.") On the Monday after each game, each team is required to send to its second upcoming opponent a set of 18 videotapes, covering its last three games. Each set of game tapes includes two recordings each of the game's offen-sive, defensive, and special-teams plays. One tape gives a wide-angle view, from above the sideline, of all 22 players, and the other, made from the up-per stands at one end of the gridiron, takes in the action on a narrower "field," some 40 yards long and extending from one outside linebacker to the other. The tapes also must include a shot of the scoreboard, showing score, quarter, time remaining, down, and distance, before every play. Both recordings are made from points high in the stands, and the players, on tape, look like tiny, scrambling ciphers.

The videotape-exchange rules are part of the NFL's wide-ranging parity formula. By mandating that every team have access to the same amount of tape, of the same quality and format, as every other team, the league seeks to reduce the advantage richer teams have over poorer ones. Like sharing of television revenues and gate receipts, and like the player-draft and reserve systems, the film system is designed to prevent a team from maneuvering for advantage anywhere but on the playing field itself.

Nowhere is the coach's obsessive search for control of a game more ob-vious than in his use of videotape. And nowhere, I suspect, is videotape studied more obsessively than at Seahawk headquarters. Seattle's three-man video crew (Fermstad, video projects director Mike Wacker, and as-sistant Craig Givens) shoots from 2,500 to 3,000 cassettes of practice and game tape per season, and each crew member works from 60 to 80 hours a week on game preparation and tape editing.

On Monday morning, each position coach is given tape of the previous day's game to use in critiquing his particular players. Mondays begin with meetings of offensive and defensive units, at which each play is studied and each player issued a composite grade based on his play-by-play perfor-mance. On Tuesday evening the video crew finishes breaking down and distributing tape sets for the upcoming game and begins work on tapes of the next opponent after that. "We're always working from one to one-and-a-half weeks ahead of the team," says Wacker.

While practice tapes are straightforward—they are used by players and coaches to assess players' learning of their assignments—game tapes, which are used to study opponents' tendencies and to build game plans, are broken down into ever-more-detailed categories. Seattle coaches, after subjecting games to computer analyses that divide and subdivide plays by formation, down-and-distance, situation, and so on, ask Wacker and his crew to break tapes down into 30 different categories, including such specific circumstances as "first down passes inside the 20," "short-yardage runs," "short-yardage passes," "dogs and blitzes," "goal-line passes," and on and on and on and on, with variations week to week depending upon the idiosyncrasies of the team in question. Each tape will have at least three games' worth (and often more, since Seattle keeps a library of all its past games and has separate film exchange programs with other teams) of a particular type of play or look. "A lot of it," says Fermstad, "is driven by paranoia. The whole idea is to leave no stone unturned. But some guys go film-crazy. There's a point where you break down things so far that you can't take it all in."

Players' and coaches' understanding of the game was considerably improved—or exacerbated—by the switch from film to video. "In the old days," Wacker says, "they would just pass reels around, and players would stay here late to look at film. But video has really enhanced the power of film. Players are given their own copies." Now players receive game plans, consisting of written notes and videotapes, on Wednesday mornings, and every player spends a bare minimum of an hour each night, at home, studying recordings of his opponents.

The amount and type of tape studied varies at each position. Linemen typically study the moves, techniques, and tendencies of the individuals they will be fighting. Cornerbacks and wide receivers study one another, with receivers also looking at whole defensive backfields to study zone coverages and player groups' reactions to given alignments and patterns. Quarterbacks and free safeties look at the most tape, since they must call signals, change assignments, and alert teammates to the meaning of a given formation, or shift, or motion. Players will study everything from the number of times a team runs left out of a given formation to the movement of a running back's eyes during a snap count. Always, a player is trying to pick up clues an opponent might unconsciously be sending.

Standing amid the clutter in the Seahawks' hectic video room, taking in the coach's-eye-view of the mobile pawns and pieces on the television screen, I could see at once both what was most fascinating and most maddening about football. Every strength and weakness was laid bare for the viewer to see. The reason behind each play's success or failure was as obvious on tape as it was obscure when seen live. Everything looked so understandable, so . . . *manageable*. The tape-mediated game made players' athletic ability seem insignificant, even irrelevant, in comparison to a coach's football intelligence and strategic skills. How could a coach, I wondered, his head filled with all these visions from above, reconcile the feelings of power arising from that view with the powerlessness he feels when the games are actually played? Real games, coached from the sideline, are beset by problems; taped from above, they present mere challenges. No coach, I decided, has ever lost a game on tape. Studying it from above, designing it from above, he is a god—all-powerful, all-knowing, invincible. It is only when he descends to the level of the mortals who must play the games that he gets in over his head.

The Stepford Wives

Who walks his own high-handed way, disdaining
True righteousness and holy ornament;
Who falsely wins, all sacred things profaning;
Shall he escape his doomed pride's punishment?
                                    —Sophocles, *Oedipus the King*

For the season's first two games, Seattle defensive coaches improvised their way around their team's greatest weakness: a small defensive line whose players were slowed by age. Instead of starting three men and backing them up with two or three more, Seattle rotated its six defensive linemen in and out throughout both games. It was a way of keeping their rushers rested enough to maintain pressure on ball carriers and quarterbacks late in the game.

The ploy was an attempt to stave off the erosion caused by a shortage of defensive linemen coming out of college and by too many winning seasons in Seattle. "Defensive line is one of the toughest places to find people in the draft," Knox explained Wednesday, after the win over Kansas City. "And it's the easiest place to make a mistake, because colleges run and pro teams pass." Because they are called upon to defend exclusively against running attacks, linemen often show more pro potential in college than they actually have. At the professional level, they must learn to read offensive formations and movement, watch for fakes, diagnose a play instantly, then react against either run or pass.

Since 1983, Knox and his staff had been looking for new defensive linemen. Typically, though, surefire ones are among the first five picks in a player draft, and the Seahawks, having had no losing seasons in the Knox era, always drafted too low to get good linemen. "We got three guys out there that are 30 pounds smaller than those people they're playing against," says defensive coordinator Tom Catlin, "and they're our best guys, so we're playing them." All three starting Seattle defensive linemen—Nash, Green, and Bryant—had come into the league five or more years before, and in the intervening time offensive linemen outgrew them. "It was our intention to try to shore up the defensive line with some big stud people, but we never draft high enough," says Catlin. "They're always gone by the time we get to pick."

Hence the six-man rotation, which had worked so far. After two games, Seattle defenders had nine sacks, had deflected 20 passes (more than they had batted down after 15 games in 1987), and had pressured opposing quarterbacks into throwing prematurely 22 times.

They would be forced out of that strategy for at least one game, however, by nose tackle Joe Nash's knee injury, which kept team doctors guessing throughout the week. On the Monday after the Kansas City game, his knee was so improved that Sunday's prognosis (arthroscopic surgery, six weeks of recovery) was upgraded to a mere two weeks of rest. On Wednesday, the confounding knee worsened, and Nash expected to miss four games. Then, when examined on Thursday morning, his knee looked so much better that Knox described the recuperation as "amazing," saying that Nash might even be able to play a little against the San Diego Chargers the coming Sunday.

Even if he did play, though, he would be used sparingly and Seattle's system would have to be revamped. "Now," said Knox on Wednesday, "we're a little bit out of sync with Joe Nash out."

Things were even worse in the defensive backfield. Cornerback Patrick Hunter had a severely sprained ankle and would have to miss the Charger game. With Terry Taylor still suspended, Knox would have to start second-year backup Melvin Jenkins at one corner, rookie Dwayne Harper at the other, and back up both with newcomer Louis Brock, who hadn't played in a game since playing for the University of Southern California in 1986. "We're scrambling around on defense," Knox said. So much so that he tried to sign the twice-cut David Hollis again, only to find that Hollis, hoping to find steadier employment, had signed during the week with the Kansas City Chiefs.

Had Knox managed to sign Hollis, he would have cut him for a third time by Saturday. For while the team seemed resigned to the loss of Taylor, Taylor himself had found that two weeks of going without his weekly $29,500 in salary was more than he could stand. On Thursday he met with NFL Commissioner Pete Rozelle to appeal for reinstatement. When Rozelle stonewalled, Taylor took the NFL to federal court on Friday and won a temporary restraining order that would allow him to play against San Diego. Since courts were closed on Saturday, the League had no time to file an appeal and probably would have been disinclined to do so anyway, since getting involved in a court battle over mandatory drug testing could open a constitutional can of worms that might take years to digest.

On Saturday, then, the Seahawks quietly reinstated Taylor, kept the recovering Hunter on the roster, and released Brock.

Taylor's name surfaced briefly at Knox's Wednesday press conference, in a slightly different connection. An out-of-town television reporter asked Knox a pointed question about Taylor's suspension vis-à-vis Knox's sponsorship of a Seahawk "Blow the Whistle on Drugs" campaign in the public schools. With athletes serving as role models, the reporter wondered, how can a team with a player suspended for apparent drug use take part in an antidrug campaign? "I don't necessarily agree that athletes are who the role models are," Knox answered. "A role model could be your father, your uncle, or the guy down the block."

He was on sound sociological ground here, but he immediately shifted to shakier turf. He explained that Blow the Whistle on Drugs was "a teaching packet, consisting of spaced repetitions throughout the day of warnings about drug use." The idea, apparently, was that the warnings, repeated several times a day for years, would give the antidrug ethic all the allure of a fad. "It starts in first grade," Knox said, "so that by sixth grade, when peer pressure dictates the length of your hair and what kind of jeans you wear, if you get on drugs, you're out of the group. Tapioca! Goodbye . . . "

Tapioca?

Here was the consummate football mind at work. Football, as passed down from coach to player, is a simple exercise in programmed learning. The game's prime teaching tool is repetition. Players are run through the same drills and plays for weeks at a time, until in a game they can move and react instinctively, unhindered by thought. Knox's idea was to extend the same method from the athletic arena to life's battleground, conditioning children to react instinctively against drug use. He believed that these little repetitive lessons, over time, would so mold children's minds and hearts that they would grow into adolescents incapable of being attracted to drugs. Just as an offensive guard can be conditioned to move off the line of scrimmage in a certain way, a child, whatever material and psychological horrors it has endured, can be conditioned to ignore the powerful, manifold consolations of drugs. In Knox's view, it was clear, the psyche was a simple organ, something like a dog's salivary gland.

He struck me then as a man to whom the whole complex panorama of human experience looked like game film. Seen through his eyes, the world must be a tiny spectacle in which everything is easily perceived, easily managed, and readily submissive to his ingenious designs. Was there nothing, I wondered, that he felt incapable of defeating through proper preparation, proper planning, proper programming?

His extension of football's coaching principles into the world at large struck me as definitive proof of the wrongheadedness of people who insist on modeling life after sports. And judging from the roomful of smirks and rolling eyes that greeted his immodest proposal, his cabal of critics had decided either that football had driven him mad or that he had tapioca for brains.

Although too proud a man to admit to concern about what is written or said about him in the media, Knox was not proud enough to let the reporters' obvious scorn go unpunished. Asked about the offensive attack he would face that coming Sunday, he segued into an attack on the press's football ignorance. "They're moving the quarterback around," he said of the Chargers. "They're rolling him out. Now they're over here, pocket right, pocket left, you know—words, terms like . . . something you guys like to hear: different launch points? That's something for you guys to grab on to. They got a *launch point* behind the center, a *launch point* over here, a *launch point* over here. Some people call it pocket right, pocket left, some people call it roll right and roll left, but *launch points* is one that's been mentioned. 'Vary the *launch points.*' Kind of like some of those missiles? You have 'em over here, so you can't focus with your rush pattern. You could write an article on that: *launch points.*"

Whether out of disrespect for Knox or for San Diego, no one did.

The two San Diego games on the schedule figured to be Seattle's only sure walkovers. The Chargers were in lousy shape. The team's only period of respectability—built primarily around quarterback Dan Fouts, wide receivers Charlie Joiner and Wes Chandler, and tight end Kellen Winslow—was from 1978 to 1981. Now Fouts was retired, Joiner was on the San Diego coaching staff, Chandler was playing for the San Francisco 49ers, and Winslow, suspended for discontent, was likely to retire any day. As Charger coach Al Saunders put it on the Wednesday before the game, "In the early eighties, late seventies, this was a very, very talented football team. But they kind of all got old together, all the great players, along with a whole group of offensive linemen. Now we're going through a tremendous rebuilding period."

The tremendous rebuilding period had yet to produce tremendous results. Going into the Seattle game, San Diego was riding an eight-game losing streak stretching back into last midseason and had been soundly beaten, 34–3, in Denver the week before. The Charger offense had scored only one touchdown in its last 51 possessions and was led by two of the league's most pathetic quarterbacks: Mark Malone, a walking definition of mediocrity who had toiled five years as a backup for the Pittsburgh Steelers, then started without distinction for them for two seasons before being traded for an eighth-round draft pick to the Chargers; and Babe Laufenberg, who had been cut by six teams over five seasons before finally finding a home of sorts in San Diego.

Even Saunders was hard-pressed to say anything good about his signal callers. Asked about them, he answered, "There's two guys that... that ... uh ... These two guys are a pleasure to be around, in terms of the quality of person they are. They don't have big egos."

Tremendous!

To judge from the San Diego papers, Malone and Laufenberg made too easy a target to merit sarcastic media attention. That was reserved mostly for Saunders, whose job was rumored to be on the line. "There are times when Al Saunders sounds like a man delivering a eulogy for someone he has never met," the *San Diego Union*'s T.J. Simers would write the morning of the Seahawk-Charger game. "This guy, who is supposed to inspire the Chargers before each game, could put a hungry newborn baby to sleep."

Saunders seemed to take his predicament with good humor. "I feel like somebody put a grenade in my shorts," he laughingly told Seattle reporters Wednesday.

If ever there were a game to inspire overconfidence, it was this one. Yet Seahawk practices this week seemed no less purposeful or crisp than had those before the games with Denver and Kansas City. Dave Krieg continued to practice as if his team's Super Bowl chances were riding on every midweek pass he threw. Seattle's offensive line, as was its custom, stayed late on the field, either sitting and talking together or working overtime on pass-blocking drills. And every day, the last player off the field was backup quarterback Jeff Kemp, son of former presidential candidate (and current Secretary of Housing and Urban Development) Jack Kemp.

Kemp had come to Seattle from the San Francisco 49ers in 1987, in exchange for a fifth-round draft choice. He had played six years in the NFL before that, first for the Los Angeles Rams from 1981 through 1985, then for the 49ers for one season. A perennial backup, he had started only 21 games in seven years—20 as a replacement for an injured starter, and one (a 1987 Seattle win over the Detroit Lions) because the starting quarterback was on strike. Diminutive, barely skilled enough to survive in the professional ranks, he kept his career alive by dint of intelligence, grit, hard work, and an insatiable hunger for a starting job. Yet there was a chin-up, stiff-upper-lip quality about Kemp that kept him battling against the odds in a very sportsmanlike way. Never did he confess to feelings of unhappiness or bitterness or frustration, and only once all season would he outwardly— and unwittingly—let slip, for a second, the stoic mask concealing his longing for starterdom. He was the quintessential backup quarterback—able to keep his pride in check and to get the most out of his meager athletic ability.

Watching him during the week as he ran sprints after practice, his face set in a polite, determined scowl, I wanted to run out onto the field and beg him to stop. There was something poignant about his determination to work and dream so hard. Now in his eighth year of overwork, he was still keeping himself in shape only to stand on the sidelines on Sundays. What on earth, I wondered, kept him from slacking off? Why didn't he give it up, take his economics degree from Dartmouth and get on with his life?

Behind me, I could hear a jaded Dave Krieg submitting to an interview. "I guess to get real technical and intricate," he was saying, "I just look for the guy that's open and either throw it or scramble around or throw it away."

Later that night, I knew, some columnist would be agonizing over a column that just refused to write itself.

And so the week ground along, all focus and routine, until the morning of the game—when, for the benefit of the superstitious, there were staged three ominous portents.

The first sign of trouble came, three hours before game time, in the form of Jacob Green, who emerged from the gift shop of the team's San Diego hotel with the relaxed look on his face of someone on the first day of a long vacation.

The next came an hour later, when I entered Jack Murphy Stadium and noticed a huge, disembodied smile suspended in the pale bright sky to the north, just over the stadium's rim.

A round concrete bowl that is home both to the baseball Padres and the football Chargers, the stadium's configuration serves neither sport particularly well. But something about the place makes you happy to be there. A relaxed party atmosphere prevailed, and fans seemed devoid of prejudice for or against either team. Seattle's players, during pregame introductions, were greeted as enthusiastically as were San Diego's, and the two players receiving the loudest cheers of all were Warner and Largent. Then came the Seahawks' third cosmic warning: they won the pregame coin toss and opted to take the ball.

Somewhere in the neighborhood of 99.99 percent of the time, the team winning the coin toss chooses to start out on offense. Yet nearly 70 percent of the time, the team starting out on defense is the first to score. In a game where coaches play percentages obsessively, why don't they ever take the odds and give the other team the ball? I put this question to Steve Moore once and received, for the first and last time ever, an irrational answer from a football coach. Shrugging his shoulders, he said, "You just always feel that you can get something going."

Immediately, Seattle did. After gaining nothing on the first play from scrimmage, a Curt Warner run off right tackle, the Seahawks began their orderly march downfield with a bit of choreographed improvisation from Dave Krieg. Back to pass, with the pocket collapsing around him, he calmly checked his receivers, in order of preference, then sneaked a sidearm pass between onrushing defenders to Warner, who darted downfield for a 9-yard gain. On third-and-one, Seattle staged a pro forma power play, sending Warner up the middle for 3 yards. Next, faking a handoff to Warner, Krieg threw a 23-yard, first-down pass to Largent, left wide open by helpless cornerback Elvis Patterson. Three running plays and 16 yards later, the Seahawks had a first down at the Charger 29.

To that point, the game had gone so much according to Seattle plan that San Diego's presence seemed a mere formality. The Chargers—young, inexperienced, used to losing—were already in disarray. The Seahawks were marching goalward in lockstep. Devouring the game clock by staying mostly on the ground, calmly carving their way through the ritual resistance put up by the reeling Chargers, they staged one orderly play after another, running and passing with such discipline and prescience that they seemed even to be directing the San Diego defense. In seven plays, they had traveled 51 effortless yards—32 by pass, 19 by run—and now were on the verge of scoring. Five minutes into the game, it already looked as if the day would be devoted to legitimizing the life, work, ethics, and world view of Chuck Knox.

Now, on Seattle's fourth first down, San Diego rushed six defenders. Dropping back to pass, Krieg looked deep, then wound up to throw to Butler, who was breaking toward the left sideline. The Seahawk linemen picked up the Charger rush perfectly, pushing San Diego's outside rushers toward the sidelines and past the pocket, blocking the middle rushers outward, and leaving Krieg a perfect corridor through which to throw his pass. Charger defensive end Tyrone Keys, though, waited, then curled around behind San Diego's nose tackle and came charging up the middle at Krieg. Immediately, Seattle tackle Ron Mattes, closing from Krieg's left, and guard Bryan Millard, charging from the right, hit Keys. Mattes, hit as hard by Millard as by Keys, fell down, Krieg's arm shot forward, and Keys staggered, regained his balance, and came up, by chance, right in Krieg's face. Awkwardly, he threw his hands up just as the ball left Krieg's hand. The ball ricocheted off Keys's hands, arched end-over-end back over Krieg's head, and landed right in the hands of Charger linebacker Keith Browner, who was exactly where Knox's diagram called for him to be: behind and wide of the quarterback, pushed there by tight end Mike Tice. Browner caught the ball on the run and took off, sailing unimpeded into the distant Seattle end zone. At the 5:33 mark of the first quarter, with Seattle having controlled the ball for all but 6 seconds of the game, San Diego took a 7–0 lead.

As Browner crossed the goal line, Krieg looked in disbelief toward his bench. Then his shoulders sagged dramatically, as if they suddenly felt the weight of hidden, hostile forces, and he trotted toward the sideline. Taking off his helmet, he watched, rapt, as Browner's touchdown was replayed on the stadium's DiamondVision screen. He saw everyone on his team do exactly what they had been programmed to do. He saw Knox's diagram come to life and run its precise course, only to direct the ball into the waiting arms of the opposition. His faith shaken, he must have allowed himself a moment of private irreverence, in the form of a heretically reworded Knoxism: "Bad luck is the residue of design." Then cosmic order was restored: The Chargers kicked off, Bobby Joe Edmonds returned the ball to the Seattle 26-yard line, and Krieg, having rested from his labors for all of 10 seconds of playing time, trotted with his troops back onto the field.

Determined to ignore the humbling implications of the Krieg-to-Keys-to-Browner imbroglio, Knox again sent his faithful downfield in the same orderly lockstep. San Diego put up more of a fight this time, attacking the line of scrimmage with more players, more blitzing, and more fury, but Krieg kept managing to leaf through his designed options fast enough to keep his team moving forward. Seven plays later, he had moved the Seahawks 56 yards, to where he faced second-and-11 at the Charger 18-yard line.

Seattle came to the line of scrimmage with Largent and Butler both on the right and no wide receiver on the left. As Krieg called his signals, John L. Williams went in motion wide to the left, becoming a third wide receiver. At the snap, Largent faked Charger cornerback Gill Byrd to the outside so thoroughly that he was able to flit virtually untouched past the stumbling cornerback, heading straight downfield. At the goal line, Largent faked to the inside, then broke to the sideline. Byrd, who had trailed Largent's outside shoulder downfield, didn't buy the fake. With his eyes fixed squarely on Largent's helmet, Byrd broke outside with him. Running now a step ahead of Largent, Byrd turned to look for the ball. It was right where he expected it to be. He caught it in the end zone, on a dead run toward the sideline, with Largent frantically reaching over his shoulder in a futile attempt to bat it down.

Then, after 7 minutes, 48 seconds of play, the San Diego offense came on for a cameo appearance. The Seahawks had amassed 108 yards to the

Chargers' none, had moved the ball at will. . .and trailed 7–0. For them, everything but the residue had gone according to design.

The Seattle defense wasted little time in dispensing with the San Diego attack. After three plays, the Chargers found themselves 5 yards closer to their own goal line. They punted, and the Seattle offense came back on the field at the 4:45 mark to give ball control yet another try.

Starting from the Charger 46, the Seahawks ran five times, coming up with third-and-six at the Charger 20. Krieg, back to pass, didn't notice that San Diego had a safety blitz on, and consequently was sacked by safety Vencie Glenn for a 6-yard loss. Place-kicker Norm Johnson, sent on the field to salvage the quarter, chose instead to punctuate it: His field-goal attempt hit teammate Edwin Bailey in the back.

Whee!

The Charger offense, forced back onto the field by that turn of events, lunged drunkenly downfield in fits and starts. After closing out the quarter with two Gary Anderson running plays up the middle, totaling 19 yards, they began the second quarter with a false-start penalty, a 6-yard Anderson run—again up the middle—an incompletion, a delay-of-game penalty. . . and, of all things, an actual complete pass, good for 28 yards, to wide receiver Darren Flutie. Now at the Seattle 31, Babe Laufenberg threw three straight passes so ineptly that the scorers had to guess the identity of the intended receivers. On came place-kicker Vince Abbott, then, to kick a comically slow, looping, 48-yard field goal that came down inches behind the upright, giving San Diego a 10–0 lead. Up until that kick, in his entire career Abbott had made only two of nine attempts from farther than 40 yards.

After the ensuing kickoff, the Seahawks lined up at their 31-yard line for the play that should have wiped out whatever illusions of winning might still have remained in their minds. Ray Butler, running a deep post pattern, caught the Charger defense completely by surprise and streaked downfield a full step ahead of Gill Byrd. Krieg threw the pass of his life, hitting Butler in full stride at the San Diego 21. Byrd, airborne, reached desperately for Butler, as if trying to hitch a ride to the goal line. Somehow, he managed to grab the receiver's biceps, pulling Butler's arms apart and forcing him to drop the ball. For the third time in 17 minutes of play, the Seahawks had been turned away at the threshold of the Charger end zone.

After San Diego took six hilarious minutes to move 14 yards, Seattle took control of the game, reverting to flawless form. Running and passing at will, the Seahawks covered 55 yards—30 by ground, 25 by air—in eight plays, arriving, newly confident, at first-and-10 on the San Diego 25. The Chargers, desperate to slow the drive, resorted to an ingenious stratagem:

They stopped play to pay homage to Steve Largent. Two plays before, to the apparent notice of no one, Largent had caught a 19-yard pass that gave him a career yardage total of 12,147, breaking by 1 yard the NFL record held by San Diego receivers coach Charlie Joiner. Now Seattle was stopped in midstride so that Largent could be presented a commemorative game ball. "He didn't want to stop," Edwin Bailey would say afterward. "He said, 'Let's go and score.' Too bad that it would break all the momentum that we had going."

Sure enough, the drive stopped cold, and Seattle had to settle for a field goal, making the score 10–3 with 1:53 left in the half. After the Chargers closed out the stanza with a characteristic "drive" (eight plays covering 20 yards), the teams left the field to the tune of this succinct observation, tendered by Mike McCormack: "We gotta get our heads out of our rear ends."

The Seahawks returned from their locker room convinced that they were only one play away from taking control of the game. Eight plays into the third quarter, it looked as if they were right. The Chargers, having lurched 22 yards in seven plays, tried a first-down pass from Laufenberg to wide receiver Anthony Miller, the ball passing languidly through Miller's hands into Paul Moyer's breadbasket.

The Seahawks were mistaken, though, in thinking that it was only San Diego they were fighting. It took them all of two plays, 2 yards, and 50 seconds to realize they were confronting an adversary far more powerful than the earthly Chargers. After Warner carried up the middle for 2 yards, Krieg, under pressure, threw low to Butler, and the ball was picked off halfway along its path by Keith Browner.

Lest San Diego entertain any illusions of grandeur, the game's governing forces granted the Chargers 8 minutes and 17 seconds of goofy wandering from the San Diego 48 to the Seattle 3 and back out to the Seattle 13, from where Vince Abbott kicked wide of the goalposts. The San Diego crowd, by now completely in tune with the cosmos, gleefully hooted.

When the quarter ended, Seattle—which had enjoyed an 18:53-to-11:07 first-half time-of-possession advantage—had managed only five offensive plays and one punt in the entire third quarter, for a time-of-possession disadvantage of 2:29 to 12:31. This was a team hell-bent on finding a way to lose.

Four plays later, they found it. Still down by a mere touchdown, the Seahawks allowed the Chargers only two fourth-quarter plays before forcing them to punt. Then, two plays into what eventually would be a 14-play, 72-yard drive to a field goal, Krieg, under pressure, dumped a short pass off to Butler, who parlayed it into a 21-yard gain. As Butler was catching the ball, though, 271-pound Charger defensive end Lee Williams was coming down on Krieg's back. Williams, hanging on for dear life, rode Krieg right into the ground, and Krieg, as he went down, turned his throwing shoulder to cushion his fall. He hit the dirt shoulder-first, and the whole stadium shuddered from the impact.

Fans who had followed the play downfield turned back to see Krieg lying facedown in the dirt, in obvious pain. Finally he fought his way to his feet and half-stumbled, half-ran to the sidelines. Doubled over and leaning awkwardly to the right, he looked lopsided, and his right arm hung limp and flopping from his shoulder.

Kemp came skittering onto the field, was engulfed by the huddle, and the game resumed.

After Seattle's field-goal drive, San Diego lent an added touch of mystery to the proceedings with a nine-play, 76-yard drive to its first offensive touchdown in 58 possessions. To get the touchdown, the Chargers dug deep into their bag of tricks, running what looked at first like their favorite gimmick play, a wide receiver reverse. After taking Laufenberg's pitch, though, and running to the right with it, running back Gary Anderson faked a handoff to receiver Quinn Early, running left. Seattle's defense went with the fake, flowing Earlyward, and Anderson galloped 25 yards, untouched, to score. The Chargers had taken advantage of Seattle's careful pregame preparation. "We had seen the reverse on film," said a glum Thom Fermstad afterward, "but not the fake off of it."

Seattle players, streaming into the locker room after the game, looked utterly devastated. Losing 17–6 to San Diego had taken a Herculean effort. Their uniforms were in tatters and they were far more bruised and cut and hobbled than they had been after the first two games. While from the stands it appeared that the Seahawks were beating themselves, from up close it was clear that they had been thoroughly and physically walloped by their opponents.

First to come through the tunnel from the field was linebacker Dave Wyman, a look of uncomprehending fury on his face. Seconds after he disappeared into the locker room, there was a deafening crash—the unmistakable sound of vented spleen. Next came Largent, with one eyelid hanging grotesquely down, at half-mast. He had injured it late in the game, when he threw a block on San Diego cornerback Elvis Patterson and Patterson inadvertently jammed his finger into Largent's eye. Cornerback Melvin Jenkins followed, with the vacant stare of a trauma victim.

Knox, cornered in the hall, was wide-eyed. His mouth hung open as if he were gasping for air. His customary postgame reserve had deserted him, and he seemed completely at a loss. He had come up against forces that all the preparation in the world cannot combat, and he gave the impression that he would never be able to make sense of the game.

"Dave Krieg, the doctor just told me, has a shoulder separation and will probably be out about six weeks," he began. There was a tiny, uncharacteristic quaver in his voice. Involuntarily, he was acknowledging what he had always refused to acknowledge in the past—that Krieg is an outstanding quarterback and that without him his team was seriously diminished.

"We couldn't make the plays offensively that you have to make to win," Knox continued. "Four turnovers is enough to get you beat anytime. There were too many balls batted around . . . We just couldn't make any plays, you know? We hit a pass, and we don't catch it. We do something else, we get it batted down. We were just out of sync all day. You gotta make plays!" Asked if San Diego's defense deserved any credit, he tried manfully to give it some, but couldn't quite manage it. "They played hard," he answered. "But you saw the plays. We drop a pass, mess it up over here, we mess it up over there . . . "

He cut the interview short then and made his way into the locker room, perhaps to ponder the mysterious workings of chance. In correctly characterizing the loss as one in which proper plays had been called but not carried out, Knox was underscoring, in his indirect way, that his designs and decisions had been sound and that the game had been lost by forces and failings beyond his control. His ineloquent "We were just out of sync all day" was a reluctant, tacit acknowledgment of the limitations of his tactical and motivational powers.

Gone now was the bluster and pride that had marked Knox's midweek press conference.

Losing to the Chargers cost Knox more than just a temporary loss of confidence. The Seattle media began to raise tentative questions (questions that would become ever more persistent as the season wore on) about the character of Knox's team. Why, the query most often would go, do the Seahawks have so much trouble against inferior teams? Implicit in the question were doubts about Knox's ability to motivate his troops, and to best employ his own imagination and combativeness. The Charger loss, Steve Kelley wrote in the *Seattle Times* on Monday, "should come as no surprise. The Seahawks have never been a team that could stand prosperity for more than a couple of weeks." Over at the *P-I*, meanwhile, Art Thiel would write, "While it's not accurate to say the Seahawks never win the little ones, it is reasonable to suggest that a big part of the Seahawks' extreme modesty in achievement relative to talent . . . is a frequent inability by coaches and players to locate a game face when they are favored."

These two columns would prove to be the opening salvo in a season-long barrage of printed and televised suggestions that would amount to the sportswriting equivalent of a Greek chorus.

Grasping now for story angles, the press followed Knox into his team's locker room, where they waded through physical and psychological gore in search of quoteworthy insights. Paul Moyer was among the first to oblige. The loss of the game and the loss of Krieg, he insisted, could help more than hurt the Seahawks. "Obviously, you know, this game hurts," he said, "but, hey, it's adversity time. You know what happens on this team when they get adversity."

This, apparently, was the positive thinker's rabid way of characterizing weakness as strength. The only way we could have beaten the Chargers, Moyer was implying, was to play the game under adverse conditions.

Krieg, injury and all, manfully tried to shoulder all the blame for the loss. "About my performance," he said, "I'm not too excited about that, obviously. If you throw an interception for a touchdown, and a couple more that stop good drives, when everyone else is doing a good job . . . basically, it's just very frustrating to have me stopping the drives. We had a whole bunch of opportunities, but we just didn't put it in the end zone."

Krieg was a mess. He stood shirtless in front of his locker, hemmed in by reporters. The determined look that had marked him from training camp's opening day was gone. And his torso was bizarrely asymmetrical, as if someone had removed the end of his right collarbone. The shoulder on that side looked inches smaller than its opposite number, and Krieg's right arm hung from it like a long thin bag full of bones. "I could feel that it was hurt," he was saying of the play in which he had been injured, "but I just . . . if I could've lifted my arm or shoulder up, then I'd have been all right, but I couldn't do that, I just was too weak to do it, and then I knew something was kinda wrong. It felt like a little ball was underneath my shoulder pads."

In a confessional mood, he started recounting his sins, taking his listeners through the game interception by interception and eagerly taking the blame for each one, particularly the one to Largent. "I was trying to throw it over Steve's head if I could, because he was covered underneath pretty good," he explained. "But I just couldn't get enough on the ball to get it over the top of him." Then he shrugged his good shoulder, as if resigned to the notion that some failings were simply beyond his capacity to correct.

Misreading the gesture and misunderstanding the intent of his confession, I gave up entirely on Krieg, right then and there. I saw that some- where in his subconscious he was resigned to failure. I thought of how, over the course of his career, he had consistently been garrulous after losses and uncommunicative after wins. Everything I could see and remem- ber about him at that moment added up to one obvious truth: He feels more comfortable in a losing role than in a winning one. As great as he could be, he will always figure out a way "not to get enough on the ball," because deep down inside, he sees himself as a loser.

"What really hurts," he was saying now, "is when you throw three inter- ceptions and then get hurt, you feel like, 'Well, what else can go wrong,' you know?"

No one had the heart to tell him that a mechanical problem on the team's airplane would keep him waiting an extra three hours at the San Diego air- port that evening.

Turning away, I saw Kelly Stouffer walking through the room on his way to the bus. He looked terrified. Having expected to spend a season learning the pro game, he now was thrust by Krieg's injury onto the active roster, where he was only a hoofbeat away from playing real football. "Coach, if it be thy will," he seemed to be thinking, "let this cup pass from me."

It did not take long for nearly all the players to clear out of the locker room. It is an article of faith with Knox that you get out of town quickly af- ter a loss. All that remained for reporters, before going back upstairs to write their columns, was the ritual postgame Bosworth interview. Since Bosworth refused to talk until he was showered, dressed, and bejeweled, and since editors refused to allow their reporters to turn in copy without Boz quotes in it, every Seattle game now ended with a Bosworth watch. Back from the shower room, his hair dried and sculpted, his clothes, ear- rings, and trademark Gargoyle sunglasses on, Bosworth exercised ex- cruciating care in donning his socks and shoes while six reporters crowded in behind him. Finished at last, he turned around. He sported a massive bruise on one cheekbone.

"A loss could eventually come back and haunt you," he said. "But again, if we steer the course right, and go back and take care of business the way we're supposed to take care of business . . . we're still in front and we're still on top and our basic job right now is to not look back."

His inquisitors were thrown for a loss. Their only reason for talking with Bosworth, aside from his celebrity status, was his penchant for the colorful quote. Now here he was spouting clichés faster than the cliché-master him- self, Chuck Knox.

First to try a question was the *Times'* Tom Farrey, who weighed in with, "What happened?"

"Where were you?" a suddenly infuriated Boz responded. "You just walk in? Ah . . . they scored more points than we did!"

Regaining control of his alter ego, Bosworth went on in a monotone. "It was just one of those things where they got a few breaks and they got aroused, and one of the things Chuck was saying all week, 'Don't let an aroused team on top.' Then when they got a couple breaks like they did, it was tough—and you know, they played a good game. There's no taking that away from them. We just need to stay the course and come back next week and prepare for San Francisco. What you gotta do is you just gotta stay the course and keep doing the job and hope that Lady Luck will come around or something will happen or somebody will make a good play, and . . . this was just one of those games that in this business will happen to you."

The season before, Bosworth had arrived from college a snazzy, inexhaustibly quotable kid. He had obligingly uttered all manner of hilarious, offensive—and sometimes even insightful and informative—statements. He was a coach's worst nightmare, someone whose lack of circumspection filled newspapers with inflammatory quotes used as motivational tools by opposing coaches. Knox, whose playbooks include a section on dealing with the press, devoted much of the season to muzzling his new superstar.

Now Bosworth had turned into a reporter's worst nightmare. And although I knew that he was simply resorting to the athlete's time-honored tactic of being deliberately boring in order to get reporters to leave him alone, I couldn't manage to fend off the notion that Knox, in his obsessive search for absolute control over his team, his game, and his fate, had murdered Brian Bosworth and replaced him with a bionic clone. I saw Knox then as a mad scientist, eliminating his players one by one and replacing them with mechanical doubles. How else to explain the legions of talkative youngsters who came to Seattle fresh from college only to be turned, almost overnight, into mindless, laconic veterans? How else to explain Bosworth's complete transformation?

I had stumbled upon the Stepford Franchise! Who would be Knox's next victims? Moyer? Krieg after a loss? Ken Behring? The press? This man had to be stopped!

Adding Injury to Insult

Time usually erases the mistakes of contemporaries, but parts of their mirages are preserved in the histories... It has always been and always will be this way, because it is impossible to find any objective criteria.

—Nadezhda Mandelstam, *Mozart and Salieri*

The season's third week brought what should have been a dream matchup for football fans: The Seahawks' Chuck Knox vs. the San Francisco 49ers' Bill Walsh. The two are among history's greatest pro coaches. Knox, in his 16th season, ranked ninth all-time and fourth among active coaches, with a 141–83–1 regular-season won-lost record. On the list of coaches who had worked 10 or more seasons in the NFL, his career winning percentage (62.9) was the seventh-best all-time and second-best among active coaches. He was a four-time Coach of the Year winner, had gone to the playoffs 10 times, was the only coach in league history to have taken three different franchises to postseason play, and twice came within a single play of advancing to the Super Bowl.

Walsh's record, while shorter, was every bit as impressive. Now in his 10th NFL season (his entire head coaching career had been at San Francisco), he sported an 84–54–1 won-lost record, a 60.8 winning percentage, and had taken the 49ers to the playoffs five times. He won two Super Bowl Championships—after the 1981 and 1984 seasons—the last capping an astonishing 18–1 year. His 1987 team, leading the NFL in nearly every offensive category and sporting the league's number-one defense, had run up a 13–2 record, then been upset in the first round of the playoffs by the Minnesota Vikings. Going into the '88 season, his team was expected to make it to the Super Bowl for the third time in eight years.

The Walsh-Knox faceoff in Seattle presented a confrontation not only between two great football minds, but between two perfectly opposite stereotypes. Walsh was white-collar cool, a walking definition of "Californian." He was tanned, tall, trim, and graced with a flowing mane of thick white

91

hair. A classically handsome man with a statesman's jaw, he was glamour personified. He spoke in measured, mellifluous tones, eschewed clichés, and unselfconsciously employed an almost scholarly vocabulary. A Professor Emeritus of Football, he was widely regarded as the game's reigning philosopher-king.

Knox, on the other hand, was pure blue-collar fire, a middle-American millworker. He looked shorter and dumpier than Walsh. Sallow and balding, he had the combative, hard-set jaw of a habitual barroom brawler. Plainspoken, given to homespun clichés, and often blunt, he was widely regarded as a dull, overreaching proletarian who had ascended higher than his destined level by dint of hard work and determination.

Walsh, in short, was the liberal, imaginative innovative darling of the media, while Knox was the conservative, unimaginative underdog of the old school. One stereotype coached from the head, the other from the gut. The game purportedly would pit intellectual genius against street smarts, royalty against peasant, inspiration against craftsmanship, the coach of the eighties against the coach of the fifties, the trendy against the outdated.

The two men's respective images were further highlighted by Walsh's Super Bowl credentials and Knox's lack of them.

Unfortunately for fans, the opposing coaches' reputations were all that this game had going for it. Both teams were struggling with lackluster performances. Both had come off baffling losses to league doormats: Seattle to the San Diego Chargers, and San Francisco to the Atlanta Falcons, of all teams, in Candlestick Park, of all places. Each team's starting quarterback had thrown three interceptions in its loss, and in each game one of the interceptions had been returned for a touchdown. And both teams had serious injury problems, although Seattle, having lost Dave Krieg, was in far worse shape than San Francisco was. Of the 11 players listed on the 49ers' midweek injury report, in fact, all would play against Seattle.

For some reason, the aftereffects of the Charger loss, combined with the beforeffects of the daunting 49er game, made Knox uncharacteristically talkative at his midweek press conference. Perhaps, knowing what was to come that Sunday, he thought he could avoid the game by prolonging the press conference into the following week. Were it not for reporters' mounting worry that their catered free lunch (a regular post-press-conference feature) was growing cold, Knox might still be there, filibustering away.

Kelly Stouffer, being the third quarterback and one of the two inactive players on each game day's 47-man roster, had had virtually no practice running the Seattle offense since the season began. His time during each week was devoted almost exclusively to simulating opposing quarterbacks during defensive practice. So Knox was asked if he would be giving Stouffer a greater share of the first-unit offense's rehearsal time now that Krieg's injury had caused Stouffer to be promoted to second-string quarterback. Knox's answer indicated how complex and systematic a game football has become, with a team trying to study and remember an almost endless array of new formations and modes of attack each week. "You can only get one quarterback ready," Knox said. "Because you take one pattern, and you run it against this coverage today, a different coverage tomorrow and a different coverage Friday. That one quarterback's gotten three defensive looks. Now, you'll get one of those three coverages in a game. He has to see it, so that he knows where to go based on what the coverage does. If the number-two guy takes the snaps on Thursday, that means the number-one guy has only seen two of the coverages. If he gets the coverage in a game that he didn't get in practice, he might be not as likely to make the proper read and the proper adjustment. This is true of every team in the National Football League. Backup quarterbacks get less than 10 percent of the work in practice during the week, for that very reason." Years ago, he went on to say, you could expect to see no more than three simple defensive alignments in a game. "Now," he continued, "you get all kinds of combinations: you get five, six, seven defensive backs in there. You get the dogs and blitz looks, you get all kinds of different fronts [arrangements of linemen and linebackers]. You get different looks in different weeks. And you have to be ready."

In 10th-year quarterback Joe Montana, the 49ers had one of the all-time greats. Backing him up was fifth-year quarterback Steve Young, who was better than most of the league's starting quarterbacks. Last season and through the first three games of this one, Walsh had wavered between the two, pulling the waning Montana at times for the waxing Young, and now they were like teammates in a relay race, fighting over the baton instead of exchanging it. The debate over whether or when Montana should give way to the 49er quarterback of the future was raging throughout the Bay Area. "Montana's the starter and Young's the backup," Walsh would tell Seattle media later that day. "As you know, that's getting a lot of attention down here, for some reason. People are just *consumed* by it."

Coaches generally loathe quarterback controversies almost as much as they loathe reporters, and do everything they can to avoid getting embroiled in one. Knox, however, was envious of Walsh. "You would love that as a coach," he said with great relish. "To have two number-one quarterbacks. You'd like to have that at every position on your football team. I wouldn't care whether somebody gets mad or doesn't get mad. When we put you in there, just go do the job. You say you're number one? Well, if number one isn't playing too well, I'll put the other number one in."

Knox next introduced a theme he was to hammer away at for the rest of the season. The galling loss to San Diego, in which his perfectly wrought designs had consistently gone awry, the portrayal of Walsh as a genius, and the ever-more-intrusive, questioning presence of a new team owner who was convinced the Seahawks should be one of the league's elite teams, moved Knox to denigrate the role and power of the head coach. "See, football players win football games," he said. "Guys who can make plays win football games. If X's and O's would win, you could go out there and buy three or four books that have X's and O's, and put that offense and that defense in. But somebody has to throw it, and somebody's got to catch it. And somebody's gotta defend and somebody's gotta rush. And somebody's gotta punt it, and somebody's gotta catch it. And the more of those people you have that can do that real well, the more games you win, usually." In case some in the room still didn't understand that he was downplaying both his own role in Seattle defeats and Walsh's role in San Francisco victories, he grew more explicit. "See, you don't lead the National Football League in total defense without excellent personnel," he said of the 49ers. "Granted, they've got great coaching. But you don't do it week in and week out with mirrors. We're a younger team. They don't have too many changes from last year. We have 12 new players on our 47-man roster. They've got big-play people. That's why they've been to the Super Bowl."

From there, he turned his attention to chance, pointing out that there are only five out of a game's 130 or so plays that actually count. The whole hours-long spectacle is staged simply to subject the mettle of its performers to a few instantaneous tests. "And they don't have to be great plays," Knox said. "Ball is tipped, you get it instead of that guy gets it. The ball hits your linebacker right in the chest here, and goes bang-bang, and he goes like this"—he brought his hands up to his chest—"he doesn't catch it. OK? If he catches it, their offense is out. The next play, they throw a touchdown. The ball is on the ground here, instead of falling on it, we bat it out of bounds, never having had control, and they get it. OK? We gotta make four out of five just *affordable* plays. That's the game."

Pro coaching jobs are notorious for burning out the men who take them. Every year, at least one bright young (or bright middle-aged) coach walks off the job at the apparent peak of his career. Commentators attribute coaching burnout to the stress of dealing with modern athletes, the stress of having to win constantly, the stress of working for maniacal owners, the stress of working endless hours, the stress that comes with big money... But I think nothing could drive coaches from the game faster than having to confront, week after week, this paper-thin difference between winning and losing.

I didn't realize that at the time, however. Instead, along with the other members of the chorus, I rolled my eyes like a high schooler and let my mind wander while my tape recorder did my listening for me. When Knox finished, I walked across the hall, took my place in the free-lunch line, ate, swapped Knoxisms, and went over the week's soap opera installments.

On Tuesday morning, General Mills had held a press conference with Steve Largent to unveil the new Steve Largent Commemorative Edition Wheaties box to be sold in Pacific Northwest grocery stores. It was a fine and fitting tribute to a remarkable athlete, and Largent is about as stereotypical a Wheaties symbol as you could ever imagine.

Once the Wheaties moment was gone, the Northwest's attention was directed to the other end of the stereotype spectrum, where Terry Taylor lurked, hoping the NFL drug enforcers would just melt away. "It can't get no worse," he had said on Monday. "The best thing would be just to end the whole thing right now. I didn't make the mistake. They did." It looked at first, however, that the NFL planned to appeal the federal court ruling granting Taylor an injunction against being suspended. NFL Director of Communications Joe Browne said on Monday that the judge's decision was being reviewed. On Friday, Taylor and his agent met with NFL Commissioner Pete Rozelle and NFL "drug adviser" Dr. Forest Tennant, after which Rozelle decided to let Taylor play against San Francisco.

Sunday morning, Taylor was hit from another front. The *Seattle Times*, under the headline "Problems plague Taylor," carried a long, investigative story by reporter Tom Farrey on the cornerback's troubled off-field life. Over a two-year period ending in November 1987, Farrey wrote, Taylor had "missed 11 court dates for traffic-related tickets, had 11 warrants issued for his arrest, and incurred $2,816 in court fines, according to King County records." The story also told of a November 1987 assault in which Taylor, in the company of then-Seahawk wide receiver Daryl Turner, punched a woman in the mouth outside of a Bellevue video store. It also revealed that Taylor, who a month before had told the *Times* that he had used cocaine only once in his life, told a federal judge three weeks later that he had a drug problem. At the time of Farrey's story, Taylor had been undergoing weekly drug counseling at team expense for 10 months and had been involved in no criminal or civil matters since the counseling had started. He had also taken and passed 25 drug tests between the two he had failed.

To anyone familiar with big-time sports—whether pro, college, or high-school—the Taylor story was drearily familiar. It was the story of a troubled human being protected from accountability for his actions by virtue of exceptional athletic ability. There are very few professional athletes who have not been pampered in this fashion. Beginning early in high school, sports stars are routinely spared the rigors of personal responsibility. Their sins and crimes and excesses are covered up or quietly taken care of, their academic failings are ignored, and they are kept in a permanent state of blissful irresponsibility. In return for bearing the burden of our dreams, the modern athlete is set apart from the rest of society in a way that both protects and endangers him.

The athlete can pay an extremely high premium for his moral insurance. The greater his penchant for trouble, and the more he is bailed out by his protectors, the greater grows his conviction that he leads a charmed life. Eventually, the succession of coaches, boosters, agents, and general managers who protect the athlete outside the arena in order to exploit his talents inside it either fail or lose interest in him, and his illusions of invulnerability are shattered.

Newspapers are filled with stories of athletes who abruptly and unexpectedly are called to account. Maryland basketball star Len Bias, shortly after being named the nation's number-one draft pick by the Boston Celtics, dies of a cocaine overdose. Cleveland Browns defensive back Don Rogers suffers the same fate. His brother, former UW Husky football star Reggie Rogers, now with the NFL's Detroit Lions, kills three teenagers when his high-speed drunken drive through Detroit suburbs ends in a spectacular crash. Seattle SuperSonic guard Dale Ellis is arrested for domestic violence. Guard Eddie Johnson, rescued by Seattle from cocaine-induced exile to the Continental Basketball Association, is released by the Sonics after one season and ends up in jail on drug possession charges. Gale Gilbert is arrested on sexual assault charges. Terry Taylor and Daryl Turner are suspended for failing drug tests. . .

In every case, the publicized offense was only the last in a series of troubles, all previously hushed up, going back years in the lives of these players. And in each case—at least in each case where the offending athlete remained alive after his transgression—the offender seemed either curiously indifferent to the consequences of his behavior or outraged at the treatment it brought down on him. "Everybody was shocked at what happened to Gale," said one Seahawk employee of Gilbert's travails. "He was just doing what everybody did. The only difference was he got caught."

During my sojourn with the Seahawks, and during briefer visits to other pro, college, and even high-school franchises over the years, I have been consistently appalled by two bizarre and troubling aspects of big-time sports. One is the fans' blind worship of their heroes, who inspire more awe than I have seen accorded anyone anywhere else. The other is the utter childishness of athletes. With few exceptions, they are impulsive, grandiose, immature creatures who, like infants, expect their every need and whim to be instantly satisfied. They whine, wheedle, throw tantrums, and demand unqualified, uncritical love—which they get from every quarter, at least until the inevitable disappearance of their athletic prowess.

Their temperamental deficiencies are aggravated by conditions unique to the sporting world. In American sports, the slightest decline in a player's concentration or ability can be devastating. Athletes live in constant fear of losing their jobs, not to mention the astounding privileges and pleasures that come with them. They also suffer such dehumanizing physical and psychological torments that the anesthetic blandishments of drugs and alcohol—or fervently held religious conviction—seem a virtual necessity.

By the time a football player reaches the professional level, he has little reason to expect his off-field behavior to be held in check. He has always been set apart, held up to moral standards off the field that are as different from those applied to ordinary citizens as his performance standards on the field are from those applied to people in ordinary jobs. Drug use traditionally has been just one more item on a long list of excesses that society tacitly allows the athlete.

Two years ago, faced with a mounting public outcry to reform itself, the NFL instituted as strict a drug-testing program as it could manage after negotiations with the League's players union. First instituted during the 1987 preseason, the present drug control effort calls for urinalysis during preseason. A player who tests positive for drug abuse is prescribed inpatient treatment, outpatient treatment, or simple monitoring of his behavior, and can be subjected to random urine testing. Should he test positive a second time, he is subject to a 30-day suspension. A third positive test would call for his banishment from the league for at least a year.

The program is a shambles, partly because it tries to treat drug use both as a disease and as an offense, partly because it ignores the larger disease—a separate, ill-defined societal standard of behavior for athletes—and partly because it involves drug testing, a procedure of questionable legality. Taylor's was the '88 season's ninth 30-day suspension and the second to be rescinded upon challenge. And since the dubious legal status of drug testing makes the NFL anxious to avoid court battles, the chances of players challenging future drug-test failures is certain. Somewhere down the line, inevitably, the league's policy will be struck down by the courts.

If anything, Taylor's story buttresses the case against drug testing. His pattern of erratic off-field behavior and inconsistent on-field performance should have been enough to tip off his coaches and teammates that something was wrong. He could have been forced into counseling simply by the team's threatening him with the loss of his starting position or his place on the roster altogether. By going the drug-testing route, the NFL gives players with a genuine drug problem one more denial mechanism to help prolong their addiction.

It should also be noted that by all indications save one, Taylor's counseling program was working. He no sooner entered counseling than his off-field legal entanglements ceased. And considering the 25 random tests he passed, one would have to admit, at the very least, the possibility that the test he failed was flawed.

Yet such is the nation's antidrug hysteria, and such is its faith in the infallibility of science, that there were calls in the media for more extreme forms of suspension and treatment for Taylor, and when he came onto the field during the player introductions preceding the game with San Francisco, he was greeted with a smattering of boos.

The game was only seconds old before Taylor's predicament seemed the least of his team's problems. Bobby Joe Edmonds fumbled the opening kickoff, giving the 49ers the ball at the Seahawk 27. And what happened over the course of the next eight snaps of the ball unambiguously signaled the outcome of the game, the essential helplessness of football coaches, and the nature of the NFL universe.

The 49ers ran right up the gut of the Seahawk defense, sending backs straight ahead five times for a total of 23 yards, coming up with third-and-two on the Seahawk 4-yard line. There, unaccountably, Walsh directed his quarterback to pass, a case of overcoaching if ever there was one. Joe Montana's pass, thrown under pressure, fell incomplete, and place-kicker Mike Cofer came on to kick an easy field goal, watch it be disallowed for holding, then miss his attempted reprieve. His kick sailed wackily wide of the goalpost, to the delight of the assembled masses.

The high point of Seattle's next drive, a three-play, 5-yard affair, was a Jeff Kemp pass that hit a wide-open Steve Largent right in the stomach. The low point was when the ball popped out unprovoked and fell incomplete.

As I sat in the press box trying manfully to factor the collective genius of the two head coaches into these awful proceedings, San Francisco, beginning on its own 37, sauntered downfield to score 7 points in seven plays.

By the 2:30 mark of the first quarter, with the score 7–0, San Francisco had blown two of three scoring opportunities, having sandwiched a touchdown between two missed field goal attempts. And Seattle closed out the quarter by three times coming within inches of pulling off game-breaking plays.

The first came after Cofer's second missed field goal. On first down, Seattle center Blair Bush and right guard Bryan Millard opened an immense hole for Curt Warner, who darted through, sidestepped a linebacker, and took off upfield. There was no one between him and the 49er goal line, now 55 yards away. Suddenly, cornerback Tim McKyer came slanting in from the right, dove, and made a touchdown-saving ankle tackle at the 49er 49. Roaring, howling, brandishing a fist, and beating his chest, an outraged Warner leapt to his feet and made as if to attack McKyer. Then, more or less collecting himself, he strutted back to the huddle, still wildly gesticulating, and delivered a quick series of one-on-one exhortations to his blockers.

Three plays later, Kemp, rolling right, was pulled off his feet by a 49er rusher and had to throw a second sooner than he intended. As his pass, looping toward John L. Williams, fell inches short, spectators were treated to a tantalizing vision of what might have been. There, right in front of the bouncing ball, stood Williams, and beyond him stood three blockers, positioned perfectly to wipe out the only three defenders facing them. Beyond them stretched 47 yards of vacant gridiron, at the end of which, shimmering like a mirage, sat the inaccessible San Francisco end zone.

On came the punter Rodriguez, to close out the quarter with a high, languid punt that landed, as diagrammed, on the San Francisco 4, taking a long sideways bounce to the 3, then rolling along a slow curve toward the goal line, with Eugene Robinson and speedy linebacker Darrin Miller in hot pursuit. Robinson, reacting a split second slowly to the first bounce, caught up to the ball 6 inches from the goal line, with Miller, attacking from a different angle, only inches farther away. As both players dove, a little gray, shapeless, furry creature suddenly materialized and nudged the ball over the goal line just as Robinson brushed it with his fingers. The two players skidded past and the ball came to rest just inside the 49er end zone. The little sprite, convulsing, disappeared. By the grace of God-knows-what, the 49ers had the ball out on their 20-yard line instead of inside the 1.

There, as if by prearrangement, had occurred three of Knox's five "affordable"—or pivotal—plays per game. The 49ers made their play—McKyer's superb tackle of Warner—while the Seahawks failed at their two.

Thus ended the first quarter, to be followed, as dictated by the rules, by the second. At the end of the half, San Francisco led 17–0, Jeff Kemp's NFL quarterback career was all but over, and Seahawk demons had conspired with 49er fates to pile up some astonishing numbers. To wit: San Francisco earned 14 first downs to Seattle's two, gained 299 total yards to Seattle's 22, and passed for 155 yards to their hosts' minus-2. There, forever emblazoned in the record books, are Kemp's totals: 12 pass attempts, one completion, three interceptions, and a yardage total too disgraceful to bear repeating. As the numberstruck teams retired to their locker rooms, Kemp, trotting beside Kelly Stouffer as he entered the tunnel off the field, looked as faded and insignificant as a candle flame engulfed by sunlight.

For some reason, the Seahawks emerged as scheduled to endure the second half. Oddly energized by the humiliation of the first half, they started off with a ferocious series of defensive plays. On the third play of the third quarter, Montana completed a flat pass to running back Roger Craig, and cornerback Melvin Jenkins leveled Craig with a hit so fierce that it sent a wave of palpable, electrifying shivers through the crowd, which came out of its torpor to emit a roar of approval. The roar built, in stages, through the next two plays—both vicious, high-speed sacks of Montana—then reached its crescendo when Barry Helton punted 42 yards downfield to an angry Bobby Joe Edmonds.

Fielding the ball cleanly, Edmonds dodged San Francisco's lead tackler and darted to his right. Teammate Vernon Dean took out the next 49er, and Edmonds slipped through a seam between two sets of blockers and defenders. By now, the picket line of blockers had formed perfectly according to plan. Stepping around another blocker and victim, Edmonds slipped an open-field tackle and took off unhindered, escorted by three more teammates. Riding this troika downfield for 15 yards, he stepped around its point, M.L. Johnson, as Johnson wiped out another hostile San Franciscan. Then, as Edmonds's remaining blockers split apart to foil attackers, Helton slipped through to tackle him at the 49er 29.

Three plays later, Seattle faced its shortest third-down distance of the day, third-and-four at the San Francisco 23. Stouffer, inserted at halftime in place of the faltering Kemp, stepped back to pass, and in four heartstopping seconds seduced the entire Pacific Northwest sporting press and public.

Fans long accustomed to watching a succession of Seattle quarterbacks (Jim Zorn, Dave Krieg, and Kemp) dart like small, frightened rabbits behind titanic linemen, peeking between them in a panicked search for receivers, watched rapt as Stouffer just . . . *stood there*. Stock-still, his throwing arm idling, indifferent to peril, he looked studiously over the heads of the monsters colliding around him, coolly surveying the unfolding pattern of receivers and defenders downfield. Into the heads of the 62,382 fans in attendance came blasting the same thought: "That's what pro quarterbacks do!" Then Stouffer threw the ball with such force that Kemp's and Krieg's passes looked in memory like they'd been thrown through water.

Ray Butler, who had shaken cornerback Eric Wright with a nifty comeback move, extended his hands so that they formed guides for the ball into his gut. Then San Francisco's Ronnie Lott, diving from out of nowhere, managed just to get one hand on the ball, deflecting it away. It was a brilliant bit of defensive reaction to a dangerous, perfectly thrown pass.

The play was as critical as it was "affordable," for it spelled the end of

Seattle's lone, short-lived grasp of the game's momentum. On the next play, Norm Johnson missed his field-goal attempt, and the game reverted to first-half form. Three plays after that, Terry Taylor, dragging the ball-and-chain of scandal, fell behind 49er receiver Jerry Rice as the speedster ambled through his pattern, turned on a burst of speed to fly by Paul Moyer and Eugene Robinson, caught a Montana bomb, and carried it proudly downfield to complete a 60-yard touchdown play. Not long after, Rice would catch another of Montana's bombs to complete a 69-yard touchdown play, making the score 31–0.

Bored and disappointed as they had to have been by now, fans nonetheless stayed in their seats, presumably lost in thought over the mystery of football's appeal. Then, near the end of the third quarter, Stouffer rewarded them for their perseverance with the play that convinced his coaches to promote him to starting quarterback for at least the balance of Krieg's convalescence. Taking the snap from center, Stouffer turned and ran into the backfield, intending to fake a handoff to Curt Warner and throw a pass. Having had little opportunity to practice the play, however, he deviated just enough from his path to trip over the heel of one of his teammates. He was sent sprawling. Warner, meanwhile, as called for in the script, had stepped forward and was positioning his arms as if to receive a handoff. Stouffer's nose collided with one of Warner's elbows, and the quarterback fell, dazed. Then, as he explained afterward, "I really don't know what went through my mind. I just knew that I wasn't down because of one of the defensive players, so I knew that I had to get up and try to make something happen." He scrambled to his feet and threw deep, hitting Ray Butler in full stride just as Butler crossed the goal line, 46 yards away. Then Stouffer slumped to the ground, no longer able to put off the pain from his newly broken nose.

After that, the fourth quarter moved along like the slow flow of blood from a wound. When they finally got the game stanched, San Francisco had won, 38–7. Seven weeks later, both teams would have identical 6–5 won-lost records.

Knox's postgame press conference was a bleak affair at which the issue of who would start next week at quarterback was immediately raised. "I'm not even thinking about the quarterback situation right now. I'm thinking about the butt-kicking everybody got," he said.

Stouffer, surrounded by a throng of reporters, exuded the studied indifference of a seasoned professional. "I was just wanting to do what you practice to do," he said. "I wanted to go out there and go through my reads—primary receiver, secondary receiver—have good footwork, and just concentrate on my work. You want to come in there and just explode, and get some positive things going, but in that type of situation, the best thing is to just come in and get a couple completions, get a couple first downs. No one person can make it happen."

Largent, across from Stouffer, still was unable to open his injured eye completely, and his vision was blurred. "It's not as good as I would like it to be," he said of his eye, "but it's not something I would use as an excuse, either."

I made my way over to Robinson's and Moyer's lockers. Robinson, screaming, "I belong to my wife now!" exited early, but Moyer was in a thoughtful mood. "This team is funny," he said. "When we play with emotion, we play very well. Against Denver, we played with emotion. Against Kansas City, I thought we played with emotion. And we just didn't play with it this game. We just didn't have it today. That first half was just total chaos. It was ridiculous."

He was most upset at not having been able to control San Francisco's pass offense. "Their passing game is so conservative, really. They just get it to their running backs. One of their philosophies is just to get it out to them and let them become runners. And that's what they were doing. They were just kind of dinking us, getting 5-6 yards at a time. Then, when we had to make things happen, try to play things a little tighter, they just went over the top of us."

There, in a nutshell, was a perfect description of the Seattle offense. Later, watching a tape of the game, I saw Seahawk plays again and again being run in San Francisco uniforms. Under the influence of Moyer's explanation, I felt the scales fall from my eyes. By midseason, Knox would be under fire, as he is every year, for running a conservative, predictable offense. By season's end, Walsh would be lionized, as he is every year, as one of the game's great innovative thinkers. Yet their strategies were virtually identical, the only difference being their casts of characters.

Still, Walsh was headed for his third Super Bowl in nine years, while Knox, after 15 years, had yet to coach in one. Popular opinion had it that the fault for Knox's futility lay with his coaching. His own opinion, to judge from what he had said earlier in the week, would have it that he has never had the players—the "big-play people"—that get teams to Super Bowls.

The San Francisco loss had been so devastating, though, that Knox may have left the stadium headed for the kind of dark night of the soul that would change his view of himself and his fate. "When you get a butt-kicking like that," he said as he left his postgame press conference, "you evaluate everything."

Moyer was still talking, trying to move his neck into a position that didn't hurt. He had been injured during the waning moments of the game, long after its outcome had been determined. "I'll be all right," he was saying. "I just hit a guy with my head up. It kind of just shot me cold. They just added injury to insult today . . . or insult to injury . . . whatever . . . "

Behind me, cornered by a couple of reporters, I could hear Terry Taylor discussing injuries and insults of a different sort. "She smacked me in the face so I smacked her back," he said of his assault victim. Then, referring to the *Times'* Tom Farrey, he continued. "I wish I could go head-to-head with him. Let's see how good he can write after I whup up on him."

(Screenplay idea: evening soap called "Franchise." Life on National Football League team. Cast of thousands, each episode shifting back and forth among interlocking, preposterous plots. Owner, GM, coach, old players, young players, wives, babes, agents. Drugs, sex, violence, infidelity, big money, intrigue, backstabbing . . . A sort of athletic "Dynasty." Or, to be more true-to-life, a sort of athletic "Fresno.")

Farrey, perhaps by coincidence, left next day for vacation. When he returned, he was assigned full-time to the Sonics.

On Earth, As It Is

Two rigid, rampart-like lines of human flesh have been created, one of defense, the other of offense, and behind the latter is established a catapult to fire through a porthole opened in the offensive rampart a missile composed of four or five human bodies globulated about a carried football with a maximum of initial velocity against the presumably weakest point in the opposing rampart.
—Benjamin Ide Wheeler, 1906

As fond as reporters are of quarterback controversies, the Kemp-or-Stouffer question lacked the magic of the 49ers' Montana-or-Young contretemps. San Francisco writers were chronicling a classic: the story of a fading great's struggle to hold off the rise of an up-and-coming star, with the status of each shifting game by game. In Seattle, reporters were dealing with a nonstory. The Seahawks' starting quarterback, out with a seven-game injury, had given way to two players—one untested and potentially talented, the other a journeyman—who had failed to stage a properly dramatic fight for succession. When one quarterback goes one-for-12 for minus-2 yards, with three interceptions, and the other goes 11-for-15 for 133 yards, with only one interception, and throws a 46-yard touchdown pass seconds after breaking his nose, the debate is over before it can even get started. Kemp vs. Stouffer couldn't even push Taylor vs. Farrey off the front page of the sports section.

One breathless scribe (whose name, out of embarrassment for him, I omit here) was so desperate for a quarterback controversy that he decided, after seeing Stouffer play a single half, to rephrase Seattle's quarterback question. "For Seahawk coaches," he wrote after the San Francisco game, "the question now should be not whether Stouffer should replace Kemp next week, but whether Krieg, when he returns in November, should get his starting job back."

On Monday, the Seattle press gathered to grill Knox on the San Francisco loss and ask him which quarterback would start the following Sunday against the Atlanta Falcons. "Think he'll tell us?" one reporter asked, moments before Knox entered the room. "Nah," answered another. "He'll say, 'We do not make personnel decisions on the day after a game. There's too much emotionalism involved.' "

A few seconds later, Knox walked in, sat down, and was asked if he had decided on next week's starting quarterback. "No," he answered. "We do not make personnel decisions on the day after a game. There's too much emotionalism involved."

Already, it was shaping up to be a dull week.

Knox was depressed. "You get a beating like that," he said of Sunday's loss, "I don't think you have very much that you should feel good about." He was even unhappier with his team's physical condition. So many players were injured that the Seahawks would practice that week without pads, avoiding all contact. "We've got a list of hurt players here," Knox said, "almost as long as my arm."

Aside from Stouffer's nose, the most critical injuries listed were a cracked rib suffered by John L. Williams and a strained arch suffered by linebacker Bruce Scholtz. Scholtz would spend the week—and, for that matter, almost all of the remaining season—barely able to walk. He would wear a walking cast on nongame days, then anesthetize and heavily tape his foot on Sundays. Williams, who had missed the second half against San Francisco, would wait until Sunday morning to decide whether he could play against Atlanta.

Knox also would not know until later in the week if cornerback Patrick Hunter, who had missed two games already with a severe ankle sprain, would be healthy enough to play.

Win or lose on Sunday, Monday is always a day of reckoning for the Seahawks. The coaches arrive early in the morning, and each looks over the previous day's film by himself. Then the offensive and defensive staffs meet separately, with Knox sitting in for a while at each meeting, to critique film of their respective units. After that, the whole team gathers for a postmortem talk by Knox, then players break up by position and go over film with their position coaches.

During film study, every player is graded on every play. "We just determine whether a guy was successful or not," says offensive line coach Kent Stephenson. "Play by play. You either got your man or you didn't. Period."

Against San Francisco, they hadn't. Period. The game was so lopsided that the 49ers had been on offense for 43 minutes to the Seahawks' 17—which made for an extremely short offensive-unit film session on Monday. What little film there was of the Seattle offense was unbearable to watch. Players saw themselves losing individual battles all over the field. In an effort to drive the point home—and also, I suspect, to give the Seattle offense something to do while it waited for the Seattle defense to emerge from its endless examination of conscience—Seahawk coaches required their offensive unit to watch film of San Francisco's offense. They saw blockers and backs and receivers winning individual battles all over the field. "Just seeing the difference," Stouffer said afterward, "was amazing."

On Wednesday, Knox was more close-mouthed than he'd been all season long. His unwillingness to engage in conversation seemed to stem not from coyness or obfuscation—as it usually does—but from exhaustion. "We're gonna start Kelly Stouffer at quarterback this week," he began, to no one's surprise. "We're hoping that he can be the catalyst that can get our offense untracked. I was impressed with his pocket presence, his ability to stand tall in the pocket when the rush is all around him and throw the football."

There was only so much that Stouffer could do, Knox ruefully acknowledged, and he worried that the rest of his team would be unable to get itself ready for Atlanta. "We've got a very banged-up football team, a lot of bumps and bruises and things that are going to limit the amount of work we get done this week," he said. "We're just hoping they'll be healed up enough by Sunday to let the people that are going to be playing go all out."

After a few more flat exchanges, he stood up and left. The press retired to its quarters for the kind of fun-filled commentary reporters allow themselves only when the coach on their beat is losing. "Pocket presence" jokes, which would become one of the season's staples, started flying around the media room. From one end of the room came the question, "If you've got good pocket presence, does that mean you're well hung?" And from another corner came a bad Mae West imitation: "Is that good pocket presence, or are you just glad to see me?"

Already, it was shaping up to be a long season.

Practice that afternoon, while physically slower than normal, was unusually tense and crisp, with most of the anxiety hovering around Stouffer. Offensive coordinator Steve Moore and quarterback coach Ken Meyer stood behind him, Meyer timing his every throw with a stopwatch. Near the end of the session, receiver Brian Blades ran deep, then turned in the opposite direction from where the ball was thrown. Moore, normally soft-spoken and mild-mannered, was furious. He leapt at Stouffer, shouting, "What was that? What was that call? Huh?" Stouffer stood still, palm pressed against his helmet, pondering. It was clear that Seattle would have to go into battle against Atlanta without a good part of its offensive arsenal.

Atlanta, for its part, would be entering the fray without much of anything. The Falcons were so disabled that they should have been allowed to surrender to the rest of the league rather than suffer through the balance of the '88 campaign. With 17 players—eight of them starters—on injured reserve and with four active players seriously hobbled, they led the NFL in mutilated body parts. The week before, in losing to the woebegone Dallas Cowboys, they lost their starting quarterback, Chris Miller, and star fullback Gerald Riggs. Their head coach, Marion "Swamp Fox" Campbell, had a 27–63–1 career coaching record. In 21 seasons, the Falcons had posted winning records only five times, their last winning year being 1982. Suffering from anemic morale and weighted down with the burden of tradition, they were a team besieged by the combined forces of the NFL.

It occurred to me, upon landing in Atlanta, that the lamentable Falcons were a football version of their region's lamentable history. In 1864, General William T. Sherman's Union army came through months of fierce fighting to arrive at, and lay siege to, Atlanta. When the city fell in August, Sherman's victory, in the words of historian Margaret Leech, "revived and inspirited the country." It also revived and inspirited Sherman's army, which marched, indomitable, across Georgia, presenting President Lincoln with the defeat of Savannah in late December.

Now, 124 years later, came another northern army to do battle against the sorry troops representing the city. Knox was taking his army south, trying to recover the morale and health of his troops before taking on far stronger forces, a week hence, in Cleveland.

Atlanta is a historical hothouse, teeming with Civil War–era ghosts. The red earth, the dank air, the lush foliage, and the antebellum architecture all conspired to awaken poetic stirrings in my prosaic northern soul. The most banal gestures and sights took on heightened significance there, and everything seemed symbolic of something else.

How much of that impression was real, and how much the product of an imagination overcome by Southern melancholy, I couldn't tell. Just as I couldn't tell if the next day's game seemed such a moving spectacle because it actually was or because football in Atlanta takes on an aura it lacks in Seattle's mundane mists.

Entering Fulton County Stadium on Sunday morning, feeling particularly susceptible to Civil War memories, I thought back to a Sunday morning in July 1861. In Washington, D.C., that morning, sports fans were packing picnic baskets, loading them onto carriages, and heading out across the Potomac to spend the afternoon watching the Battle of Bull Run. The city's chefs and hoteliers, establishing a tradition that obtains to the present day, trebled the prices of their food and drink, taking advantage of the surge in demand brought about by the impending battle.

The tailgate party and jacked-up concession prices were not the only customs to carry over from the 19th-century battlefield to the 20th-century football stadium. Washington fans needed tickets distributed by the American military—designated the home team at Bull Run—in order to pass into Virginia for the choice seats on the hills overlooking the battlefield. And just as they do for football games today, the media attended as guests of the home team, their passes also obtained from the Union forces.

Once arrived on the hills overlooking the battlefield, the spectators looked down on indecipherable chaos. "It was not possible to make out what was happening on the thickly wooded plain, clouded with dust and smoke," writes Margaret Leech, "but a battle was certainly taking place . . . "

The modern game, while less bloody, is equally confusing. Presumably, when the press asked Union general Irvin McDowell why his heavily favored forces had been beaten, they were told, "I don't know—I'll have to wait until I see the films."

James Weeks, writing in *American Heritage* magazine, documents the Civil War origins of modern football. He writes, among other things, that in 1869, the game that is now regarded as the first intercollegiate football game was played between Princeton and Rutgers, accompanied by spectatorial chants adapted from Union Army cheers.

There are indications that a good part of football's early popularity was due to regard for the game as an alternative to war. Football was prized by many in the late 19th century for its provision of war's moral lessons without war's bloodshed. Writers of the time felt that the game inspired feelings similar to patriotism, and that communities were inspired by these physical contests between groups of soldier-aged youths in much the same way they had been by real battles. No less an authority on war than Stephen Crane credited his football experiences for the power of his *Red Badge of Courage*. "They all insist that I am a veteran of the civil war," Weeks quotes Crane as saying. "Of course, I have never been in a battle, but I believe that I got my sense of the rage of conflict on the football field."

Mournful, tense, and primitive, the Seattle-Atlanta game was like a fight between two battle-weary opponents. Both teams, relying on a host of inexperienced warriors in place of wounded veterans, mounted scaled-down attacks that were hampered considerably by mistakes and bungled assignments. The Seahawk regiment featured a quarterback with a broken nose and only one half-game's worth of experience, a running back with a broken rib, one linebacker with a damaged shoulder and another with a crippled foot, one cornerback (Patrick Hunter, newly returned to the lineup) with a sore ankle and another (Terry Taylor) with a lot on his mind. The Falcons were led at quarterback by Steve Dils, a 10-year veteran who came to Atlanta via the waiver wire to join legions of players so new to the league that one Seattle writer, perusing the Atlanta lineup card, muttered, "Who *are* these guys?"

The battlefield was a mess. From early the previous evening until two hours before game time, Atlanta had been subjected to torrential rains, and Fulton County Stadium's gridiron was a swamp. Seattle defensive coordinator Tom Catlin, after a pregame assessment of the damage and danger posed by the soaking, came off the field shaking his head. "The grass is even worse than the dirt part," he said.

The air was so dense and wet that everything looked smeared. Colors were lush. As temperatures rose into the 70s, mists swirled over the field, often taking the shape of darting, dancing ghosts. Everything from the stadium foundations to the fortunes of the league itself appeared to be rotting, a sensation heightened by the sparseness of the crowd; only 28,619 fans occupied the stadium's 60,000 seats.

The game's tone was set on the first series, a three-play Seattle drive that netted 2 yards, took 1 minute, 30 seconds, and cost Seattle one starter, wide receiver Ray Butler. On the third play of the series, Stouffer bollixed the snap count, sending Largent and Paul Skansi, the receivers lined up on the left, so far offsides that they were 5 yards downfield when the ball was snapped. Butler, on the right side, went deep, getting a step behind cornerback Bobby Butler. But Stouffer underthrew him, and when Butler tried to stop and turn back to the ball, his defender fell, rolling up the back of the Seattle Butler's leg and breaking a bone in the top of his foot.

To the fan looking for good football, the game was disgusting. But to the fan looking for valor, the game was a classic. The teams were not so much fighting one another as they were fighting a common enemy: Luck, or Fate, or History, or Murphy the Lawyer, or attrition . . . or possibly all of the above.

The Falcons' first hint of the sort of day they were in for came on their first offensive series, when Steve Dils, on third down, hit rookie running back James Primus, running a crossing pattern, with a perfect pass, only to see it pass through Primus's hands. After Seattle ran three plays and punted, Atlanta moved 60 yards in seven plays to set up a 32-yard field goal. Then Seattle, as if trying to patent the concept, ran another three-play series before punting. Three plays later, Dils sent wide receiver Stacey Bailey blowing past Hunter into the end zone and hit him with a perfect pass that settled into Bailey's outstretched hands, then oozed . . . slowly. . . slowly . . . through them, slipping free just before Bailey's hands hit the ground. It was as close to being a completion as an incompletion can possibly be, and the price of Bailey's drop proved high. After Dils missed connections with receiver Floyd Dixon, Atlanta's field-goal attempt was blocked.

Now Knox threw percentages out the window and tried to coax a great play out of his team. After 12 minutes of football, during which his offense had earned no first downs and his quarterback was one-for-three in passing, for 9 yards, he sent rookie Brian Blades on a deep post pattern. Blades got a two-step lead on Bobby Butler, turned in to look for the ball, and saw that Stouffer had underthrown him drastically. Butler intercepted the pass and pulled it into his chest as Blades, in a last-ditch attempt to prevent the interception, leapt back at Butler and insinuated his hands into Butler's cradle. Butler went down on his back, with the clawing Blades on top of him. When he hit the ground, Butler was knocked unconscious, and Blades pulled the ball free as he rolled over Butler. Incredibly, the referee came running up to signal a Seattle completion at the Atlanta 12. It was the biggest break Knox was to get all season, and on the next play, it paid off handsomely. Warner ran around right end for a touchdown, and Seattle, stopped cold for all but two plays of the first quarter, closed out the period with a 7–3 lead. What little noise there had been in the stadium stopped altogether.

Atlanta's next series struck an unnoticed but disturbing note for Seattle. Running back John Settle, carrying the ball on six of the Falcons' eight plays, ran off 31 yards on five carries before being stopped for no gain on his sixth, by Brian Bosworth. On his first carry, Settle had met Bosworth at the line of scrimmage, given him a head fake, then easily forced his way through Bosworth's awkward attempted arm-tackle. On the last play, the linebacker drilled him to the ground, but wrapped him up with only one arm—his right. Bosworth appeared unable to use his left arm.

The Seahawks scored 10 more points in the second quarter, while allowing the Falcons to hold themselves scoreless. On the Seahawks' first possession, they mounted a classic Seattle drive, moving 76 yards in nine plays—seven rushes and two passes—over five minutes. It was the first time all season they had sustained a scoring drive with a dependable ground attack.

It was also the last time that half. Seattle's next three drives were for minus-5, 13, and minus-10 yards, respectively, while Atlanta's next three were for 9, 1, and 20 yards. Seahawk fans were not to see such uninspired football again until October 30, when the Seahawks would host the San Diego Chargers. A Seattle field goal, which came with 25 seconds remaining in the half, was set up by an Atlanta fumbled punt return recovered by Melvin Jenkins at the Falcon 16. The Seahawks seized that gift and marched 15 penalty yards backward with it, threw two incompletions, then sneaked forward 5 yards, before Norm Johnson redeemed the miserable series with a 44-yard place kick.

The highlight of the quarter for the Falcons came on third-and-nine during their second possession, when receiver Floyd Dixon beat Hunter deep, Dils hit him perfectly, and Dixon dropped the ball. Take away the psychological and material advantage given Seattle by Atlanta's three dropped passes—two on third down, the other in the Seattle end zone—and take away the astounding official blessing conferred on Blades's 53-yard steal of Bobby Butler's interception, and the Seahawk 17–3 lead easily translates into a crushing Falcon win.

Atlanta, sensing as much, opened the second half with a 10-play, 66-yard drive to a field goal, their march aided by a 15-yard unnecessary roughness penalty on Patrick Hunter. And after the Seahawks managed only 13 yards on four plays, the Falcons struck immediately, with a 45-yard touchdown pass from Dils to Stacey Bailey, left wide open when Melvin Jenkins misinterpreted the play called in the huddle. With 7 minutes left to play in the third quarter, the Falcons had pulled to within 4 points. After the ensuing kickoff, the Seahawks traveled 6 yards backward in three plays, and when they lined up to punt on fourth-and-16 from their own 21, they knew as well as the fired-up Falcons did that they were about to give away the game for good.

Perhaps Atlanta was distracted then by the low-flying airplane everyone could hear approaching the stadium. Or perhaps the Falcons regarded winning the game as a form of betrayal of Atlanta history. Whatever the reason, they committed a holding penalty on Ruben Rodriguez's punt, and the Seahawks were awarded 5 yards, the ball, and a new first down. John L. Williams carried off right tackle then, gaining 5 yards, and the airplane hove into view. It was towing a gigantic banner consisting of a picture of Bosworth's book cover and the words THE BOZ! AT BOOKSTORES NOW. The little plane, putt-putting like a toy, circled the stadium a few times, to the howling of the Seattle press corps. McCormack, sitting too far back to see the plane, asked what was causing all the excitement. When told, he turned bright red—whether from disgust or delight, I couldn't tell—then shook his head, smiling fondly.

The banner, apparently, was all the Seahawks needed. It kicked off an 11-play drive that took nearly 6 minutes off the game clock, culminating in a touchdown with only 40 seconds remaining in the quarter. The centerpiece of the drive was a five-play series of Curt Warner carries, in which Warner simply took control of the game, sliding and darting and bulling his way downfield, moving his team singlehandedly from the Seahawk 44 to the Falcon 6. Midway through the fourth quarter, he and John L. Williams would team up for another touchdown drive, also gained almost entirely on the ground, to put the Falcons away for good. That drive, coming hard on the heels of an Atlanta touchdown, would seal the outcome not only because it would give the Seahawks a fourth-quarter, 11-point lead, but also because it would consume nearly 6 minutes, leaving the Falcons only 2:21 to score two touchdowns. As Williams bulled over from the 1-yard line with the final tally, Atlanta radio announcer Larry Munson, a shamelessly partisan glum ol' boy, summed the game up, mumbling, "It was a tough, tough game, but they got the line of scrimmage on us."

Safely back in the locker room, Knox gathered his troops around him, and led them in a slow rendition of the Lord's Prayer: "Our Father who art in heaven, hallowed be Thy name; Thy kingdom come; Thy will be done on earth as it is in heaven. Give us this day our daily bread; and forgive us our trespasses as we forgive those who trespass against us; and lead us not into temptation, but deliver us from evil. For Thine is the kingdom and the power and the glory. Amen." Then, without a great deal of feeling, they chanted three times, "Hip! Hip! Hooray!"

The prayer, I would find out later, is recited after every Knox game, win or lose. But listening to it after this one, it struck me at first as an odd way to rejoice. It is not a prayer of thanksgiving or of triumph, but a low-key lamentation, a declaration of faith in the midst of struggle.

That, of course, is the point. One game is no more than a single blow struck in the season-long fight for survival. The prayer was Knox's way of reminding his players that their struggle was every bit as difficult after this game as it had been before. Even though they won, they still were in such sorry shape that they would need all the help they could get—from whatever quarter.

Casting my mind back over the game, re-examining it in the somber light of Knox's prayer, I could see nothing but cause for sorrow among the Seahawks. Stouffer's inexperience had been far more noticeable than his prodigious athletic ability. An experienced quarterback, watching the defense react to the offense, anticipates where the openings will be and throws the ball before his target is open. Stouffer, by contrast, held on to the ball too long on most pass plays, refusing to release it until a receiver was already open. On his game-breaking bomb to Blades, for example, Stouffer waited so long to throw that Blades ran out of the range of his arm. Had he anticipated his receiver's breaking open, Stouffer would have thrown the ball sooner and sent it downfield in time for Blades to make a routine catch. As it turned out, it was only by the combined grace of Blades's determination and the referee's blindness that the belated pass was deemed complete.

Stouffer's lack of self-confidence showed in other areas as well, particularly in the third quarter, after Atlanta had abruptly fought its way back into the game. He rifled a pass to the sure-handed John L. Williams, and the ball caromed off Williams's hands. Back in the huddle, Stouffer asked if he had thrown the ball too hard, and Williams said he had. "After that," Stouffer said later, "I definitely short-armed some balls." He still had not developed a natural feel for the short pass and either threw too hard or, overcompensating for the strength in his arm, underthrew his receivers. Since the Seahawk offense is built in large part around the short pass, Stouffer's unmanageable strength was more a liability than an asset. All told, Seattle had won more in spite of him than because of him.

My impressions were reinforced a few minutes later by quarterback coach Ken Meyer, who seemed more relieved than enthused by Stouffer's performance. "He didn't make any mistakes that hurt us," Meyer said. "I'm sure technically there's a lot of odd plays and different things that happened in there, but I think that under the circumstances where we had to have a win, he played well." Steve Moore was worried that Stouffer's inexperience was causing his teammates and coaches to approach games with the wrong attitude. "We wanted him to go in and be a complete quarterback," he said. Noting then that everyone had focused all week on Stouffer's not making fatal mistakes, he went on to say, "But the focus needs to be on making plays. We need to focus on what he wants to do right as opposed to what he doesn't want to do."

Even more troubling had been the play of Bosworth, particularly in the second half. He fared poorly in several of his encounters with John Settle, an unremarkable second-year backup player who had come out of Appalachian State University to sign with Atlanta as an undrafted free agent. Settle, whose 1987 yards-per-carry average had been 3.8, averaged 5.5 yards per carry against Seattle, for 115 total yards, many gained through Bosworth's territory.

Most ominous had been a play early in the third quarter. Settle caught a flat pass from Dils, turned to face Bosworth, and faked right. Bosworth bit only slightly, recovered, and dove at Settle as he ran by on his left. Settle escaped easily and went on to gain 21 yards. The diving Bosworth had not even been able to move his left arm, either to grab at the runner or to break his own fall. He crashed to the ground on his head and shoulder, a crippled humanoid rocket.

Bosworth was so obviously ailing that even now I could see Cleveland's game plan taking form. Their entire offense would be devoted to getting running backs one-on-one with him. And there was little Knox could do about it—unfit as Bosworth was, there was no one to replace him.

The Seattle locker room was somber. Knox seemed particularly downcast. "All in all, it was a good win for us," he said. "But we've still got a long ways to go." His lone moment of expression came when he recalled his team's long third-quarter touchdown drive, which came right after Atlanta opened the quarter with 10 points, pulling within 4 points of Seattle. "We could have let the ball game just get away from us," he said. "But we came back offensively, and when we had to move the ball, we did. When they closed within 4 points, we had enough stuff to come back and go down the field on them."

At best, his players seemed relieved. For offensive guard Bryan Millard, this had been the first game all season that hadn't left him feeling frustrated. "That drive when we got the ball back on the penalty on the punt," he said of the same touchdown drive Knox had cited, "I think we had a long drive . . . shit, I don't know how far it was . . . that was the best drive we had so far this year. That was a tremendous drive. We put a lot of heart and a lot of soul into it, and we worked hard—we got it done real well. It was real nice, to play like that. We needed it—we had to have it."

Stouffer agreed, adding that the emotional condition of the offensive line is the critical difference between winning and losing. "When the offensive line plays well, this offense is always going to play well," he said. "They were just animals on a couple of drives today! They just stuffed 'em, and it was. . . you know, you could just feel it. We were gonna score—that's all there was to it."

To offensive tackle Ron Mattes, that drive, its intensity, and the time it had come in the game all added up to a trouble sign. "It seems like we have to be put in that situation for us to move the ball," he said. "I don't know if we get complacent or what. It just seems like we have to get in a dire situation for us to go out and just play to our potential."

Across from him, Curt Warner was just as subdued. Having gained 110 yards on 22 carries, he had just turned in his first acceptable performance of the year. Instead of celebrating, though, he seemed unhappy at having taken so long to get his game in gear. "I don't know," he said. "It's just been like I've been off for the last three-four weeks, so I was just glad to get back on track somewhat."

I made my way through the locker room then, past a gingerly dressing Steve Largent. Among the records he had been expected to surpass easily this season had been Don Hutson's record for career touchdown catches. With 95, Largent had entered the season needing only five more. With five games gone, though, he had yet to get his first. Now, his injured eye still nearly at half-mast, his movements slow and pained, he looked like a diminished version of himself. Out of sympathy, reporters gave him a wide berth, sparing him the stultifying postgame rigors of quote production.

Or perhaps they spared him out of anxiety at missing the main event of the day, the ritual postgame Boz watch, to take place in a little room between the lockers and the tunnel leading up to the team bus.

Ordinarily, reporters watch and wait for Bosworth at his locker. But his clothes had been taken into the shower room—off-limits to the press—so everyone gathered at the point he would have to pass through in order to get out of the stadium. By now, Bosworth's book had climbed to the number-three position on the *New York Times* best-seller list, so demand for Boz quotes was insatiable. This was particularly true in Atlanta, whose nose tackle, Tony Casillas, had been a teammate of Bosworth's at Oklahoma. The two had despised one another there, and Bosworth in his book had said that Casillas had "boxes of rocks for brains." This bit of wit, of course, stirred controversy in Atlanta, and the flower of Georgia's press corps turned out to cover the expected Battle of Words.

Most of the press—particularly the Seattle press—seemed embarrassed to be there. They were dyed-in-the-wool sportswriters forcibly turned into gossip columnists. They passed the time shuffling their feet, looking at the ground, or whispering occasional wisecracks. "When does His Highness arrive?" someone behind me asked.

Finally, the Highness in question emerged—stoic, blown dry, and Gargoyled—and was immediately engulfed by the forward surge of interviewers. An Atlanta radio reporter shoved his way to the front of the pack and started in. "We talked with Casillas," he panted, "and his comments toward you was you don't exist, and he had some derogatory things to say about peroxide. Do you have any response to Casillas?"

Bosworth's shoulders sagged. "You know," he said resignedly, "Tony and I, we just never hit it off. And I never took anything away from his ability to play the game of football, he's a great football player, but you know, again, I just really don't want to comment on Tony Casillas, he's not really worth my breath . . . "

Although it was clear by now that the tiff between these two *mal mot* machines wasn't going to make anybody forget Frank Zappa vs. Tipper Gore, the radio man pressed on. "He said he wouldn't mind getting you in a boxing match in the parking lot," he shrieked. To which Bosworth answered, "I'm really, I'm not gonna . . . I mean if that's all y'all's questions, I'm not gonna sit here and badmouth another player, I'm just . . . "

Sensing danger, a football writer weighed in with a question on the game:

"Your thoughts on the Atlanta offense today?" "I thought they were a very potent offense," Bosworth answered in a comfortable rush of words. "They've given everybody trouble that they've played, and they've been in the game every game they've played this year, and they've got some good talent up front, they've got a great offensive line, they've got some good backs and great receivers . . . but again, it's just one of those things where you've just got to come out and play every week." Hearing such accolades for a 1–4 team brought a chorus of subdued snickers from the reporters crowding in behind me, but Bosworth didn't seem to notice. "What does John Settle do?" the same reporter asked. "Does he surprise you at all? What makes him so effective?" "He's a lot like Gerald Riggs is," Bosworth answered in a monotone. "He's a load runner, very strong, very strong legs, and a low center of gravity, so he's a really good runner. I have a tremendous amount of respect for John Settle, so . . . uh . . . you know, he did a good job today." Having taken two predictable questions and punched up two predictable answers, he turned, his work finished, and looked for an escape. Leading with his good shoulder, he forced his way toward the door out of the stadium.

The climb out from under Fulton County Stadium proceeds up a long, dark tunnel that switches back and forth like a trail on the side of a mountain. With a bevy of television cameramen in tow, Bosworth proceeded up the tunnel, emerging, to his surprise, into a blaze of wet, soft, late afternoon light. He was confronted by a set of turnstiles over which a mob of people was spilling. Some were brandishing copies of his book, many were waving game programs in the air, and all were screaming. "Brian! Brian!" "Boz!" "Over here!" A high, boiling sea of faces, it looked impassable. Six heavily-muscled security people emerged from somewhere offstage to shield him from the threatening crowd. The guards pressed against him so closely that when they all started moving forward, they had to shuffle rather than walk. Flashbulbs popped madly from all directions. Someone directly in front of Bosworth held a copy of his book up over the fray, and for a second the two figures—Bosworth and the Boz—regarded one another in silence. Then the book was engulfed when the wave of fans shifted. Moving very slowly now, the Bosworth creature made its way through its worshipers, up a ramp along the outside wall of the stadium. In the distance could be seen the Seahawks' bus. Adulatory screams and shouts were coming at him from all directions. "Brian! Boz! The next President of the United States!" He made it nearly a third of the way to the bus when the crowd began to realize he wasn't going to sign any autographs. The shouts, suddenly louder, turned hostile. "Boz! Hey! Fuck you, Boz!" "Boz, you fucker!" His guardians looked scared. "Mr. Personality!" Bosworth and his protectors had been forced over nearer the stadium wall now, and I looked up to see that it was lined with an ominous throng of young, enraged drunks, many of them waving bottles menacinggly and all of them screaming taunts and curses. Now, the security guards looked genuinely panicked, and the crowd had pressed in so tightly that Bosworth had come almost to a complete stop.

I fought my way ahead of him to the bus. Looking back over the crowd, I saw the faces of his guardians regarding the people in front of them with looks of sheer terror. Bosworth's face, though, registered nothing. Disembodied, it perched in the middle of the chaotic crowd like the newly severed head of an overthrown king.

Finally he reached the bus and climbed aboard. The door hissed shut behind him, shutting off the howling outside. Bosworth made his way down the aisle, sat down, and looked briefly out the window. Then, letting his guard down, he registered his only reaction to the whole fiasco: He leaned over, little-boylike, and gently rested his head on the shoulder of the man next to him.

It would fall to nationally syndicated sports columnist Steve Harvey to register the last—and sanest—comment on Bosworth's trip to Atlanta. Harvey's October 12 "The Bottom Ten" column, a weekly feature, ended with this report: *"Scandal?*: The NFL is investigating the charges made by Atlanta tackle Tony Casillas, who said, 'If it wasn't for peroxide and hair spray, there'd be no Brian Bosworth . . . the guy doesn't exist.' If, in fact, Bosworth does not exist, the Seattle linebacker faces a suspension of up to 30 days."

Meat the Press

But that getting there and tackling a guy, getting him down, is another story. Schemes don't do that. If schemes won, we could go out there before the game and take a wheelbarrow full of schemes. Wheel 'em out, put two guys at the 50-yard line, and dump 'em on the ground and say, 'Here, we got all these schemes here, just forget about it today, boys, we got the game won.'

—Chuck Knox, hectoring the Seattle media

Knox was positively misty-eyed after Monday's film review of the game in Atlanta. He was particularly moved by two Brian Blades plays: the wrestling away of the ball from defensive back Bobby Butler on Stouffer's 53-yard pass, and a fourth-quarter wide receiver reverse that set up Seattle's last touchdown. The reverse, which should have been a disaster, set an all-time record for mood swings by a head coach over a 6-second span. Stouffer pitched to Warner, running right, then Warner handed off to Blades, running left. But Atlanta, instead of flowing with Warner as called for in Knox's script, simply waited on the opposite side for Blades, and when he came running across the backfield, he found three defenders waiting for him behind the line of scrimmage. Snarling, they closed in, and Knox started mentally shuffling through his repertoire of third-and-12 plays. Then, with an unexpected burst of speed, Blades slithered between the first two defenders and ran over the third. Thus freed, he angled for the corner of the end zone, getting tangled up with a defender at the 1-yard line. Knox, revived, started riffling through his goal-line offensive plays. But Blades refused to give up. Instead, he fought to stay on his feet, and, as overzealous as a rookie unexpectedly granted a chance to break into the starting lineup, he held the ball out, one-handed, at arm's length, trying to get it over the goal line before being pushed out of bounds. Another defender came flying across and blasted him off the field. The ball, left behind, hung for a moment in the air, then fell to earth just inside the juncture of sideline and goal line. For some reason, it didn't bounce—it just lay there until a Falcon swooped down and gathered it in.

Apparently turned away at the Falcon goal line, Knox started composing a suicide note. The side judge, though, came running up, energetically signaling that Blades's foot had landed out of bounds before he lost the ball. The play was reviewed by the video replay official, who concurred, and Knox made a mental note to resume his stirring defense of the controversial officials' video review system.

Now, safely back in Seattle, he was ecstatic. Blades, tested under game conditions, had proved to be the kind of athlete Knox loves to coach: someone capable of making plays. "Blades will become the starter," Knox said on Monday. "Brian Blades played excellent football for us. He had two big plays. We ran the reverse and there wasn't anything there. He just got that on his own. If you took and put that reverse into the computer, the stat would show it's about an 11-yard gain, but really, what you should put in there is 'Brian Blades, 11 yards.' Because he ran through three or four people and made something out of nothing. Actually, they had the play for a loss. And then he made the great catch, outfought the defender for the football. Those were two big, key plays in the ball game."

They were indeed—not only because both demonstrated Blades's determination and athletic ability, but also because each came within a referee's brain wave of being a critical Seattle turnover instead of a gamebreaker. Had the officials ruled in both cases that Blades's efforts had come up short and that the ball should go over to Atlanta, Seattle more than likely would have lost the game, and Blades would either be forgotten entirely or remembered not for winning the game, but for losing it.

But since fate had smiled on Brian Blades, Knox was smiling too. If nothing else, the plays had proved that Blades had a hot hand, and Knox loves no one so much as a player with a hot hand. Ray Butler, whose broken foot had given Blades his opportunity to strut his stuff, lost his starting position for good.

No one, of course, was acknowledging that Blades had been given Butler's spot permanently. Butler was expected to be back in four weeks. But in the back of every athlete's mind lurks the specter of Wally Pipp, the New York Yankee first baseman who reported to work one day with a headache and let a young ballplayer named Lou Gehrig take his place for what would prove to be the first of an all-time major-league record 2,130 straight starts. As Butler, sidelined by a freak accident, watched Blades showcase his skill against the Falcons, he knew he was being Wally Pipped. An eight-year veteran, he had seen hundreds of players give way, exactly as he was doing, to hungry, opportunistic, younger teammates. On Monday, talking with reporters about his predicament, he was properly reserved. "It's pretty frustrating, because we got guys out there working hard and I want to be a part of it," he said. But his manner was unreservedly depressed.

Inside linebacker Dave Wyman, sitting in front of his locker after practice, was in a self-abnegating mood. "I think I missed more than I made the other day," he said of the Atlanta game. "I think tackling is 90 percent desire. It's something you have to concentrate on." He was asked the sort of ritual question ("Does Settle deserve any credit for running well against you guys?") that always gets a ritual answer ("John Settle played a great game . . . "), but he was too angry to dissemble. "No," he said abruptly, "I don't think that had anything to do with it. I just don't think our head was in the right place."

While many of his teammates were happy enough with Seattle's 3–2 record—good enough for first place in the AFC West—the tally did little to mitigate Wyman's disgust with Seattle's defensive statistics. Having come into the season with improved defense as one of the team's prime goals, the Seahawks, after five games, were giving up an average of 358 yards a game. Worse, they were yielding 133 yards per game on the ground—for an average of 4.6 yards per rush, only one-tenth of a yard better than their NFL-worst 1987 average. In total defense, they now ranked 23rd in the league.

Wyman looks like someone sent to Seattle from Central Casting to play the part of Dave Wyman, linebacker, in a movie featuring a cast of caricatures. He is ugly in a charming way, like an Edsel. He has a lumpy, loutish face only a coach could love. His head is hilariously small for his body, particularly when the body's size is exaggerated by monstrous shoulder pads, and he looks like he cuts his own hair without bothering to use a mirror. He is at his most low-rent when the Seahawks are on the road. Swaggering through some swank hotel (Atlanta's Marriott Marquis, for example), dressed in dirty blue jeans and a threadbare T-shirt with sleeves stretched to the verge of ripping by his outsized biceps, he looks like a rube Army lifer plunked down there as part of some cruel psychology experiment.

His torso is a mess. An agglomeration of engorged, knotted muscles, it is covered with scars of every conceivable size and hue—the legacy of years spent alternately on the field and in the operating room.

But what most defines him as a linebacker is his state of mind. Temperamental and tightly wound, he has no patience with interviewers. He so hates talking about himself that he seems to regard reflection as a sign of weakness or as something inherently dangerous. Yet he is no simpleton. Brutishness aside, he plays one of the most intellectually demanding positions in football (inside linebacker) and he attended a legitimate university

(Stanford). And when caught at the right moment, he can be thoughtful and forthcoming.

At Stanford, Wyman was a legend. Near the end of the 1984 season—he was Stanford's Most Valuable Player that year—he suffered what should have been a career-ending knee injury. He spent four months in a cast, then embarked on a determined rehabilitation project that no one save himself regarded as feasible. Coming back against all medical odds to play for Stanford in 1986—a feat that proved both his strength of will and his limitless love for football—he did well enough to become Seattle's second pick in the 1987 draft.

Immediately, his career foundered. Bothered by chronic shoulder pain, he sank to the bottom of a linebacker-rich depth chart and was traded at midseason to the San Francisco 49ers for a midround draft choice. Then he flunked the 49ers' physical and was shipped back to Seattle. The Seahawks nearly released him, but decided instead to put him on the inactive list, from where he uneasily watched the last six games of the season. Devastated and adrift, he left Seattle at the end of '87 with little hope that he would ever play football again. Then, as fate and determination would have it, he came back this season with an improved shoulder, saw fellow inside linebacker Sam Merriman suffer a season-ending injury in preseason, and found himself in the starting lineup.

Now he felt back on the cusp again. The Atlanta game had been just bad enough to send Wyman on a week-long soul-searching mission, and on Monday, after reviewing film of that game, he seemed desperate to talk to someone—even if the someone in question was a writer.

"This defense is a lot harder than what I had in college," he said. "In college when I was playing, it was run, you got this guy or that guy; pass, you got this area. But there's so many different things you do according to what they do offensively up here. There's a lot to think about. I've been having trouble with it lately. I don't know why—I thought I got good at it in camp, but now it gets kind of confusing sometimes."

His confusion put him at a disadvantage on the field, where he needed to play reflexively. "I think the cerebral side of football takes away from your aggressiveness. I was talking to Brian [Bosworth] about that, and we were both talking about how when we were in college, we were so confident in playing that we were much more aggressive and meaner on the field. I used to get in fights and stuff in college, always punching people and everything. We were saying, you know, it's hard to really be aggressive and have the killer instinct when you're not sure what you're doing."

Longingly, he described the feeling a player has when he is in command of his game. "You get a certain kind of feel on the field," he explained.

"You're in the flow. You just know exactly what's going on. You get up to the line, and things are clicking for you. It's just happening for you and you're right on top of it and you can feel it. And it makes you more excited and aggressive."

Ideally, an inside linebacker does all his thinking before and during the snap of the ball, then reacts instinctively to the unfolding offense. Part of the mental technique is understanding football strategy, and part is recognizing instantly the meaning behind blocking patterns and offensive flows. "You're thinking all the time. You make all the calls, make the adjustments. You're always looking at the down and distance, and tendencies [the plays particular teams are most prone to run out of particular formations], but I tend not to look at tendencies, because—it's good to expect and kind of anticipate things, but if you get too much into that, you start guessing. You just gotta play with what you see, and I have as much success when I just read."

At the snap, Wyman always looks first at the offensive guard, then at the running backs. "You go from the guard to the back," he explained, "and then that usually tells you whether it's run or pass, right there." If it's a running play, he simply goes after the ball, the key being to recognize the play as a run in time to react to it before the lineman has a chance to overwhelm him. If it's a pass, he moves to the area or toward the receiver designated in the huddle as his responsibility. "Once you figure out it's a pass, you drop back, then you get your eyes on the quarterback. Sometimes you have man-to-man coverage, but if you have a zone, it's not just one area, it's a few yards. And if there's a receiver coming through your zone, you have to read what kind of pattern he's running, and you want to get a feel for whether he's gonna hook in or hook out, so you can get a jump on the ball. Then as soon as you get a feel for the receiver, turn around and look at the quarterback, and read his eyes, and read his release."

As if all that weren't enough to slow down a linebacker's animal reactions, there is also the element of deception to contend with. "You can't just fall back into pass defense," Wyman explained. "You have to check for the draw play"—a play in which blockers retreat, as for pass-blocking, and the quarterback drops back to pass, then hands off to the running back, who slips up the middle underneath the pass rush and into a field left vacant by linebackers retreating to defend against the pass. "As soon as the backs clear the quarterback, you take off. Another thing is that a lot of teams use trapping action, where they actually do run blocking, but they throw a pass. That's why you gotta get a feel for the guard, as soon as you see the guard moving, you look in the backfield and see what kind of back read and quarterback read you get."

This goes a long way toward explaining why linebackers are the second-highest-paid players in pro football, after quarterbacks.

Wyman's week would be devoted to stopping the inside running game. "You look at the last game on Monday, and sometimes during the week we'll work on things that hurt us, hurt our defense the previous week," he explained. "See, if you miss something—say we screw up a certain defense against a certain play against Atlanta—there's a pretty good chance that Cleveland's going to see it [on film] and turn around and try to exploit it."

He was particularly galled by the game against Atlanta. Although the Falcons did exactly what the Seahawks had prepared to defend against, the Seahawks were not able to stop them. "Atlanta used a lot of the same plays and schemes against us that San Francisco did," Wyman said. "A lot of the inside running game is similar throughout the NFL. You see the same plays. They might even have used the same blocking schemes sometimes. Atlanta does a lot of things the same as San Francisco anyway, because they're in the same conference and they see each other twice a year. Coaches said that to us last week, that Atlanta would do a lot of things San Francisco does—especially since Atlanta saw SF have some success against us."

With the prompting of his coaches, Wyman had therefore decided that his inability to stop the Falcons stemmed not from inadequate game preparation, but from inadequate emotional drive. "Tackling is a mental thing. It's thinking about it and it's wanting to tackle, and wanting to rip through someone. The best way of showing that is knocking a guy back. You always like to hit a guy and knock him backwards. That's not always ideal—if you're in the open field, one on one with a guy, just getting him is enough. But up the middle, you want to hit a guy and drive him back. Real good hitters—it looks like they're aiming for a spot about 3 yards behind the guy. They don't slow up, they go through. I don't think I've quite got to that point."

He acknowledged that the blame for Seattle's defensive deficiencies was not his alone—his fellow inside linebacker, Bosworth, had fared no better—but he felt that there was nothing Bosworth could do about his weaknesses. "Brian has more of an excuse than I do," he concluded. "Brian has a bad shoulder, and you can see it a lot of times. He can't wrap up with his left arm, so they're getting by him a lot."

Bosworth's shoulder worsened steadily during the Atlanta game, and he played the second half virtually with one arm. He would be held out of Wednesday's practice and would work at a reduced pace the rest of the week, in order for his shoulder to recover enough for the Cleveland game. During the intervening week, the shoulder was Seattle's hottest news item. No human joint had enjoyed so much male attention since the 1971 release of Eric Rohmer's *Claire's Knee*. Papers were full of speculation over the history of the shoulder. How long had it been hurt? Why hadn't it been treated? According to Bosworth, it had been hurting since his sophomore year in college and had worsened steadily during his first pro season to the point where he considered surgery during the offseason.

Then, in a pattern typical for Seattle, Bosworth's and team management's stories diverged. "Deep down inside," he said of his offseason thinking, "I knew I was going to have a problem with it. But I'm kind of chicken when it comes to surgery. I never had one before. So I just kind of postponed it." The next day, Mike McCormack said that it was the team, rather than Bosworth alone, who had decided against an operation.

Given its context—professional football—it was not as odd a decision as it appeared. Pain is as much a part of football as speed, strength, violence, or excessive hype. Three or four games into a season, everybody is hurting, and many players are seriously hobbled between games. The previous season, for example, Curt Warner had been unable to walk after games and was held out of practice several weeks running, but never missed a game— nor, for that matter, even played poorly in one. It is not uncommon to walk into a postgame locker room and see players who minutes before had been running at full speed now inching along like arthritic old men. Exotic taping jobs by trainers, liberal use of painkilling injections, and equipment as technologically advanced as the skin on missiles all are used so effectively that they can turn cripples into supermen.

Players are enjoined by a football code of honor from complaining about pain, but their wives, apparently, are not. Connie Millard, offensive guard Bryan Millard's wife, describes her husband as a rapidly declining man growing old before her eyes. "It's hard for him to get up in the morning, seriously," she says. "He acts like an old man already. I mean, he has to roll over real slow, and push himself up, you know, and I'm just bouncing right up. I'm spry, he's just like barely getting out of bed, and he's only 28 years old! Each year, it's another step harder."

Until the second half against Atlanta, when his shoulder had given out completely, Bosworth had appeared no worse off than many of his teammates. John L. Williams was playing with a broken rib, Terry Taylor with a strained knee, Patrick Hunter with a sprained ankle, and Bruce Scholtz with a chronically strained arch. Steve Largent had played every game hurt in one way or another. Pain in football is not like pain in real life. Where the nonplayer regards it as a warning sign, the player regards it as an inconvenience, an impediment to performance.

Partly, a player feels this way because he doesn't want to lose his job.

Even a star fears being Wally Pipped. And every player's ability to play with pain is evaluated just as closely as is his ability to block or tackle or run with the ball. Knox is rigid in this regard, saying that dealing with injury is not a question of assessing the danger posed to a player by playing hurt, but is, rather, "a question of being able to stand the pain." Eugene Robinson's wife Gia feels that players are forced to play beyond the limits of their endurance. "A defensive back will come in with all this pain," she says, "and they [the coaches] will say, 'We'll shoot it up. You have to be out there.' They push you. They want to win no matter what. They won't hesitate to send you out there hurt."

It is, however, shameful for a player to give in to pain. A player will not sit out a game unless he is so severely hurt that all the technological advances in the world cannot bring his performance up to the level of an uninjured player. Often, as in Bosworth's case, he will not sit out a game even then. "It's not always the coaches," says Terry Largent, who has been watching professional players from close up for 13 seasons. "A lot of times, it's the players. I don't know exactly what the reason is. They want to be a part of the game, they think they can contribute to the game, so they play when they shouldn't." Connie Millard agrees. "They'll do whatever they have to do to try to play," she says. "It's just their own nature."

Football is so dangerous, and the pain players endure so extreme, that there does seem to be something more powerful than simple fear of unemployment keeping injured players on the field. They are as taken with the highs of football as addicts are with drugs. The drive to play is so compelling that athletes will endure anything to satisfy it. They even come to enjoy the pain—or at least to wear it like a medal of honor. "You know, you have that *football feeling*," says Ron Mattes. "I like the weeks where you're still sore when it's time to play. At this point in the season it seems like you're constantly sore and you don't have to worry about being healthy. You just have to continue on playing, and doing the best job. You don't have to say, 'Well, I hope this heals up, that heals up . . . ' It's a numb feeling that you have. That's when I feel I'm in my best groove, and I think that's when everybody else is in their best groove. I like getting in that groove, because you feel more like a football player all the time. The pain is less of a distraction because it doesn't go away and come back. It's always there, and you always have to contend with it, so it doesn't bother you that much. You adjust. It's a good sore! You know you're doing something you like to do. And when the game's over, and I retire, I'll probably miss it."

Knox, for his part, didn't want to hear about pain. He expected his players, whatever their condition, to do what he had put them in position to do. "We've got to tackle better," he said Wednesday. "Because Cleveland can run the football. When you've got a guy one-on-one right there, you've got to make the tackle. And when he runs through your arms and through your shoulders, there isn't anything any coach can do about it."

Reporters always want to talk about strategy, coaches always want to talk about player performance. Time and again on Wednesday, Knox was asked what sort of attack he expected from the Browns and what sort of attack he expected to mount against them. And time and again he brought the topic back to the importance not of schemes and diagrams but of players. "They'll have a wrinkle or two, we'll have a wrinkle or two," he said. "But it's who blocks better, who tackles better, who throws the ball better, who catches it better, who makes the affordable plays when they're presented with an opportunity to do it—that's what's going to determine who wins."

He said this with some heat, more or less in the tone of a teacher growing impatient with a slow-witted pupil. And in the course of his reiteration, he started talking so fast and furiously that he backed himself into a rhetorical corner. "They've got the ability to make a lot of things happen," he said of the Browns. "They've got excellent running backs, they're big, tough defensively, got excellent corners. They're a team that a lot of you people picked to go to the Super Bowl."

Suddenly he stopped, aghast. His audience regarded him first with surprise, then with amusement. Knox had just committed heresy. He had invoked the media in support of one of his football arguments. In doing so, he had implicitly credited reporters with football understanding. It was like hearing Donald Trump embrace communism. "So . . . whether or not that means anything," Knox hastily continued, "it just means they've got good football players and they played well last year." Somehow, that didn't quite redeem him—his listeners now were laughing—so he decided to atone for his softheadedness with a quick attack on the press. "I don't think too many of you people picked Cincinnati to be 5-and-0 at this point, coming off a 4-11 season, when all the talk was fire Sam Wyche [Cincinnati's head coach], some things that happened to him last year, mistakes that were made, that type of thing, it just shows you that sometimes you get a little push going, start making plays, football players start catching the ball, and guys start throwing it and somebody starts tackling somebody, a lot of things happen."

Here in one tormented sentence was contained nearly the entire Knoxian philosophical system. He was highlighting the helplessness of a head coach, sometimes victim and sometimes benefactor of things beyond his control. A good coach, Knox was insisting, is as good when he loses as when he wins. The 4–11 Wyche had run the same plays and drawn up the same game plans in 1987 that the 5–0 Wyche was using this year. In talking about Wyche, Knox was also talking about himself and his predicament in Seattle. He was defending himself against evidence furnished by his own won-lost record over the last four years. As sound as his designs were, they were not enough to win games if players did not carry them out properly. But in the press, coaches are portrayed as powerful figures capable of determining the outcome of games. That perception inevitably affects the way owners see their head coaches. And so in the end, coaches are judged and hired and fired over bounces of the ball and leaps and lapses in human performance that they have no means of controlling.

It was a hard statement to digest—and not only because of its syntax. It ran too fiercely in the face of what Knox constantly tries to do with his designs. His efforts on the practice field and on the sideline during games are unfailingly directed at controlling all those things he was now saying he couldn't control.

Knox was not yet through dressing down the football-ignorant press, whose power over his employment prospects galls him more than anything else about the modern game. Having worked himself into a lather, Knox took the opportunity afforded by the next question to resume, somewhat more deviously, his attack on the media. Is Stouffer, he was asked, progressing ahead of schedule? "Well," Knox said, "everybody has asked me, they've said, 'Now, what is the timetable for Kelly Stouffer, when will he be ready to be a winning NFL quarterback?' There is no timetable. It's not like baking a cake. You don't say you put it in the oven for 45 minutes at 350 degrees or something like that, and it's ready. It's not like the turkey where you put that thermometer in there and that sucker pops up and it means it's done. This is not that kinda game. You have to let him play and see what happens."

For the next month, reporters—either out of forgetfulness or because they hoped to hear a different answer, or because they were from out of town and hadn't interviewed Knox earlier in the year—would ask at least once a week about Stouffer's progress. And every single time, Knox would answer, at increasing length and with increasing heat, that Stouffer was not a cake or a turkey or a student getting a master's degree. It was one more trait in Knox that set him apart from other football people. Most coaches are content to rebuke a reporter by saying angrily that they have already answered the question in question. But Knox prefers a subtler, more painful punishment: the delivery of a longer and longer version of the same inane answer each time a question is repeated. "Well, as I've said many times . . . "

Aaaaaauuuuuugh!

Going to Cleveland to watch a football game is an exercise in athletic archaeology. You travel through layers of time, arriving at the ruins of America's Industrial Age. Huge concrete smokestacks stand idle, and buildings coated with grime look exhausted, like overfarmed cropland. Downtown Cleveland is deserted—trafficless streets, vacant storefronts—as if hastily abandoned eons ago, then left standing, untouched, ever since.

I checked into my hotel the night before the game, found a fellow traveler, and the two of us hailed a cab. The cabdriver was black. "Any good Italian places around here?" my companion asked.

"Yeah—but I can't go into that part of town."

"How about barbecue places?"

"Yeah—but you can't go into that part of town."

He took us to "The Flats," a riverfront reclaimed from its fallen industrial state and turned into a row of restaurants and bars. The strip was packed with pallid, lumpy inebriates—ghosts of Cleveland's turn-of-the-century Slavic emigrations. It was bitterly cold, and the huddled posture of the people shuffling from bar to bar, combined with the barren environment, made it seem human life was barely enduring there. A touch of zest was lent the scene by the abundance of Browns pictures painted on window-fronts, and by the team-logo pennants and sweatshirts and hats and scarves and towels adorning buildings and cars and people everywhere. Frequent football screams rent the night. We were in football country, where the modern game has its roots. Two hours drive away, in Canton, Ohio, sat the Pro Football Hall of Fame. College football tradition in this state goes back over 100 years. Football is so much a part of the culture here, and worship of the game so fervent, that Seattle's football tradition and fan allegiance seem, by comparison, like a lesser devotion. Comparing the two versions of football in their cultural and physical settings is like comparing traditional Roman Catholicism with Unitarianism.

Later at the hotel, standing in the back of an elevator, I watched Bosworth get on and immediately turn his back, pressing as close as he could to the door in front of him. This was his way of avoiding conversation with fans and reporters. He rode down three floors, and scurried off. "Was that the *Boz*?" a man behind me asked. "I think it was," someone else answered. Then the first man said, "Too bad I didn't tell him what an asshole he was!"

Cleveland Municipal Stadium is an immense, crumbling brick edifice, originally built in 1931 in hopes of attracting the 1932 Olympics to Cleveland. (They were awarded to Los Angeles instead.) Its subterranean halls, with their undulating floors and walls, are crisscrossed with twisted girders apparently held in place by thick, crudely applied coats of paint.

Home of both the Browns and the American League's Cleveland Indians, the stadium is configured purely for baseball. The shape of the playing field conforms to that of a baseball field, the stands coming to a point at one end—behind home plate—traveling along the foul lines, then describing a gentle semicircle at the other end, around the outfield. Football is the interloper here and baseball the denizen.

Among other things, this arrangement means that the fans at one end zone seem miles away from the football field, while at the other they are butted right up against the end line. The close-up stands are the stadium's fabled "Doghouse," whose occupants bark, woof, howl, and throw dog biscuits onto the field whenever the mood strikes them.

The stadium, like the city it adorns, is a full-blown cultural experience. The morning of the game, we were crammed into a tiny, low-ceilinged room for a pregame meal cunningly designed to give local reporters a homefield advantage over their visiting rivals from the Northwest. Apparently a breakfast, it consisted of scrambled eggs, white toast, corned beef hash, sausage, bacon, and "chicken fingers," all piled high on one plate. It was figuratively and literally heart-stopping. "Chickens don't have fingers, do they?" I heard a Seattle photographer ask. And Tacoma's *Morning News Tribune* columnist Bart Wright, a portly pundit who looks oddly like a Cleveland native, accosted a press-box waitress as she stomped past. "Don't you have any *fruit?*" he asked plaintively. She looked at him searchingly, trying to get the joke.

Crammed into the glass-fronted, terraced press box, I felt like I had wandered onto a movie set. The press box, the stands with their rusting girders, worn-out wooden seats, and throngs of bundled midwestern bodies—it was all too much of a football cliché to be real.

It also looked warm and wonderful and sustaining. The man sitting down next to me heaved a deep, contented sigh. "It's old," he said, "it's decrepit . . . but it's *home.*" Before I could reply, the stands erupted in a mad chorus of barking and cheering. The Browns had emerged for pregame warmups, many of them in uniforms already muddy and grass-stained—another old-world football touch.

There was more old-time football to come. The Browns, having seen Seattle on film, having lost their top two quarterbacks to injury, and being blessed in their backfield with three powerful, straight-ahead running backs (Earnest Byner, 5'10", 215 pounds; Kevin Mack, 6'0", 235; Tim Manoa, 6'1", 227), figured to run inside all game long. And the Seahawks, fielding an inexperienced quarterback and two experienced running backs against the NFL's number-one pass defense and 20th-ranked run defense, could hardly be expected to take to the air.

The Browns, though, surprised everyone when they started out the game by putting on airs: They threw a pass. It fell incomplete. Then they ran Kevin Mack over left guard, a play their film study had shown would succeed every time they tried it. Mack gained 5 yards. Then, after the Seahawks brought in their nickel defense (purely a pass-defense alignment, the nickel includes four linemen, six defensive backs, and only one linebacker), the Browns went against percentages again: They passed. Again the pass was incomplete.

The Cleveland fans, some 78,605 strong, were outraged. They couldn't understand why a head coach, down to his third-string quarterback and playing against a defense that gives up nearly 5 yards per running play, would choose to throw passes. Why go out of your way to pit your weakness against an opponent's strength?

The Brown coaching staff must somehow have managed to wonder the same thing. After Cleveland punted, Seattle ran three plays and punted, and the Browns, starting over again 3 yards downfield from where their first drive had died, stayed on the ground. Running over right guard on first down, Kevin Mack found a gaping hole where Joe Nash (now flat on his back) and Dave Wyman (now bent in half backward) had been only seconds before. Diminutive cornerback Melvin Jenkins finally dragged Mack down 23 yards later. Mack came back again, running right behind Cleveland center Gregg Rakoczy, and was immediately wrapped around one ankle by Bosworth, dragging him 6 yards before falling. Then Earnest Byner tried right tackle, cutting into the center of the field as the Seattle defense dissolved around him. He gained 16 yards before the unfortunate Jenkins was called upon to bring him down. This three-play, 45-yard slam to the Seattle gut brought the ball to the Seahawk 24, from where the Browns inched their way down to the 1-yard line. Finally, cutting outside right tackle, Mack ran through the embraces of three Seahawks—Bosworth, Vernon Dean, and the now-exhausted Jenkins—on his way into the end zone.

The Cleveland touchdown had been abetted by a critical hallucination on the part of replay official Dave Kamanski on the play before. Reviewing a pass-interference call against Seattle, in which Paul Moyer had tipped the ball just as Eugene Robinson was slamming wide receiver Reggie Langhorne in the back, Kamanski was asked to decide whether or not Moyer had touched the ball. If Moyer had, the pass-interference call would be disallowed, and Cleveland would have a fourth down at the Seattle 11, rather than a first down at the 1. Time and again Kamanski replayed the play, and time and again Moyer came flying in to bat the ball down. Moyer batted the ball in slow motion, in fast motion, backward, and from the points of view of both the sideline camera and the end zone camera . . . and Kamanski at last rendered his verdict: "The ball was not tipped."

The Seahawks struck back in kind. On Seattle's first play from scrimmage after the Cleveland touchdown, left tackle Ron Mattes pulled, ran right, and preceded Curt Warner through the hole at right tackle. Mattes, taking on defensive end Sam Clancy, worked up such a head of steam that he pushed Clancy into linebacker Eddie Johnson, then drove the two of them out of Warner's way. Warner took off down the right sideline, gaining 29 yards before linebacker Mike Johnson caught him from behind, dragging him out of bounds. As Johnson grabbed him, though, he knocked the ball loose, and Warner sailed out of bounds without it. Landing 12 inches in bounds, the ball didn't bounce—it just sat forlornly on the ground, waiting to be embraced. One Cleveland player, too focused on Warner to notice that he no longer had the ball, flew over it, delivering a helmet to the fallen Warner's ribcage. The referee stood next to the ball, waving his arms as if trying to get someone to claim it. Finally, the Browns' Johnson came sliding across the turf, gathered the ball in, and slid out of bounds. The ensuing Cleveland celebration was cut short by the referee's signal that the ball still belonged to Seattle. Replay official Kamanski, called in for consultation, concurred—for reasons that were never explained to the press.

It seemed, at first, like an inconsequential call, for Seattle was forced to punt three plays later. But when Ruben Rodriguez kicked a pitiful, 16-yard punt, forcing returner Gerald McNeil to come racing upfield after it, McNeil fumbled, Seattle recovered at the Cleveland 24, and Warner scored, five plays later, to tie the game. At the 2:10 mark of the first quarter, the score was tied 7–7, both teams owing their touchdowns to official misconduct. And while fans could find more reason to blame the score on the field officials than on either the players or the replay official, they also could legitimately ask themselves the question, "Why is Kamanski here?"

That question, too, was almost immediately forgotten. As if outraged at Kamanski's behavior, the players took control of the contest, turning it into a spectacle so brutal that even the officials were too fascinated to interfere.

Both teams tried to compensate for their glaring deficiencies by bringing heightened emotion and effort to bear on every play. The hitting was ferocious, every player straining to break the game open every time he made contact with an opponent. And since so much of the game was played on the ground—both teams being too weak at quarterback to try sustaining an aerial attack—plays developed slowly, lasted longer, and featured constant, unrestrained, hand-to-hand struggle. Nearly every play, it seemed, ended in the same way. From out of a foaming sea of bodies a ballcarrier, struggling Laocoön-like against the monsters entwining his limbs, would emerge, only to be pulled back under.

But this was merely heroic effort. What made the physical struggle a soul-sustaining spectacle was the poignancy lent it by a more mysterious paradox. The game turned on two crucial second-quarter Seattle mistakes, without either one of which the Seahawks would have been doomed. Already made remarkable by the intensity of its players' efforts, the game was made unforgettable by an upended moral order dictating that the victory should go to the team suffering the most dramatic lapses.

Seattle's first lapse came on the third play of the second quarter, when Melvin Jenkins passed up an almost certain interception for the sake of indulging in a bit of gratuitous sadism. When Cleveland quarterback Mike Pagel, at the Seahawk 32, threw a wobbly pass downfield to wide receiver Webster Slaughter, Jenkins, closing fast, opted to blast Slaughter in the kidneys rather than go for the ball. The pass was thrown so poorly, and Jenkins had such a good break on it, that his chances of intercepting the pass were excellent. Instead, he was flagged for pass interference, giving the Browns a first down at the Seattle 11.

There the drive stalled, Cleveland moving only 4 more yards in three plays, and the Browns brought in their field-goal unit. Jeff Bryant, slithering straight up the middle, reached up and blocked the kick. The ball shot sideways off his hand, bounced once, and landed, as if by design, in the arms of Paul Moyer, who had been pushed wide of the play. With no one in front of him, Moyer took off with the ball, escorted by three teammates. Sixty yards later, Vernon Dean made a mistake that first proved fatal to Moyer's chances of scoring, then proved fatal to Cleveland's chances of winning the game. Instead of blocking Mike Pagel, the only Cleveland player closing on the now-faltering Moyer, Dean turned and looked back over his shoulder to see if someone speedier might be catching up. Left unblocked, Pagel made a diving tackle at the Brown 20.

Pagel had singlehandedly prevented a Seahawk touchdown. He had also separated his throwing shoulder.

Had Jenkins intercepted the pass instead of opting for pass interference, there would have been no field-goal attempt, no block, and no 73-yard Moyer run setting up Seattle's eventual go-ahead field goal. And had Dean blocked Pagel, as he should have, the Browns would not have lost their third quarterback of the season to injury. The Seahawks were on a dubious roll.

Cleveland coach Marty Schottenheimer, perceiving the game's inverted moral order, tried countering with two lapses of his own. First he sent Pagel, in obvious pain, back into the game on Cleveland's next offensive series. Then, after two running plays gained his team 16 yards, he ordered his quarterback, separated shoulder and all, to pass. Wobbling incomplete, the throw was a pathetic sight.

Two more running plays netted 11 yards, and Schottenheimer, in one of the 20th century's strangest moves, ordered up another pass. Pagel dropped back, saw immediately that receiver Webster Slaughter had angled nicely into a short zone in front of linebacker Tony Woods, and tried to throw. Unsteady as the ball was, Slaughter had such good position on Woods that the pass would have been complete were it not for another Seattle mistake. Rookie linebacker Darrin Miller, who had replaced the helpless Dave Wyman on the previous play, became lost in the pass-defense confusion and backed into the wrong zone. Standing in front of Slaughter, Miller reached up and made an easy interception.

Miller's opportunity had come when Seattle coaches, weary of watching Cleveland running backs use Wyman as a doormat, yanked him. Miller played the rest of the game, while Wyman paced the sidelines, now putting his helmet on, now pulling it off, now looking at linebacker coach Rusty Tillman, now looking skyward to regard without amusement the airplane towing a "The Boz! At Bookstores Now" banner . . . all the while asking himself if he had lost it all: his job, his hunger, his ability to play football.

The numbers he saw at halftime were not reassuring. Cleveland had run 21 times for 118 yards—most of the yardage through Wyman's part of the field—averaging a walloping 5.6 yards per carry. Take away Schottenheimer's weird need to call for the occasional pass and Seattle's weirder reliance on its own mistakes, and you have the makings of a Cleveland slaughter.

Instead, Seattle went into the locker room at halftime with a 13–7 lead, having ended the half in typically halting fashion. After recovering a fumbled snap by Brown bottom-of-the-barrel quarterback Don Strock, the Seahawks strung together a drive of sorts when Stouffer managed to complete two passes to Blades, one for 16 yards, the other for 17. They were two of only three Stouffer first-half completions, and the only two catches Blades would make all day. And the other three plays of the "drive" would total 3 yards—all 3 coming on a Curt Warner run in which he turned the wrong way at the line of scrimmage, passing up 20 yards of open field for the sake of taking on two Cleveland linebackers, neither one of whom would have had a shot at him had he gone in the direction called for by the play's design. Norm Johnson's lumbering field goal, clearing the upright by inches at the end of the half, seemed to be more editorial comment than kick.

The second half—a tense 3–3 standoff—was a suspenseful affair, marked by the determined, stolid running of Seattle and the no-less-determined passing of the 37-year-old Strock, brought out of retirement by Cleveland two weeks before. Strock's best and worst moments came during the Browns' last drive of the third quarter. After taking his team from the

Cleveland 3-yard line to the Seattle 25, gaining 56 of the drive's yards through the air, he was intercepted in the Seahawk end zone. He was trying to make the case, I think, for the game being a Cleveland loss rather than a Seattle win.

Suddenly it ended, with Seattle on top, 16–10. Across the floor of Cleveland Municipal Stadium, now the quietest place on earth, Knox and McCormack came running. McCormack, beaming, was pumping his fist in the air. He had spent nine glorious seasons in this stadium as a player, and the pilgrimage back was cause enough in itself for sentimental outburst. The spectacle of his team's struggle to find a way to win a losing battle, played out in this stadium full of personal memories, sent him over the emotional edge. Crawling under the stands, he had to fight back tears.

For Knox, the trip to Cleveland was a trip back to his own mill-town roots. Now the climate and topography and people and football all crowded in around him, reminding him of both the distance and the nearness of his past. As he stepped through the door leading from the field, he looked tearily up into the stands. "Woof! Woof! Woof!" he bellowed. And the fans, crowded against the railing above, responded in kind: "Woof! Woof! Woof!"

Moments later, still overcome, Knox faced the media in a tiny, makeshift room grafted on to his team's locker room. Although he managed to keep his impassive expression intact, his brimming eyes and clogged, hoarse voice gave him away. His speech was halting and heartfelt: "It's just that, you know . . . sometimes the good football teams just . . . you know, it . . . it . . . it's satisfying to be able to come west to east, two weeks in a row, and win. And win outdoors and win on grass, see? And *play*. This is the way football's supposed to be played sometimes. It wasn't, ah. . . any artistic beauty or anything, but there was a lot of hitting going on out there. I'm just glad we won it."

His players, perhaps not as mindful of the role mischievous fate had played in their win, were just as glad but nowhere near as appreciative. Shouts and howls and boyish whoops filled Seattle's cramped locker room. Even when talking with reporters, players were grinning. "I enjoyed that game," said Curt Warner. "I had a good time."

For the second straight week, he had turned in a genuinely professional performance. Against Atlanta, he had averaged 5 yards per carry on his way to a 110-yard day. Against a tougher Cleveland team, he had averaged 4 yards per carry, totaling 96 yards. After four weeks of frustration, those two games left him feeling as if he had finally recovered his form, and he displayed a relaxed, confident postgame demeanor for the first time all season. "My abilities physically, I don't think they change that much from week to week, to be honest with you," he said, as he tried to divine the reasons behind his sudden improvement. "It's just that sometimes mentally I may see things a little better. Sometimes you just say, 'Hey, I'm just gonna fly through here today and not worry about it.' And then there are days where you're kind of like, well, 'Maybe it's here, maybe it isn't here.' You can almost be second-guessing yourself. And that's one thing you want to get out of." He was trying, as Dave Wyman had been doing, to be more reflexive and less reflective.

The difference between a 50-yard day and a 100-yard day is as thin, he explained, as the difference between winning and losing. "You get to the point where I am right now, it's taken me three or four bad games to say, 'Hey, what's up?' But I still try to do the same things, and I still try to make the same reads, and sometimes you see it a little bit better, sometimes your timing's a little bit better. When it's such a delicate balance back there, trying to run that football, sometimes we get the misunderstanding that, 'Hey, maybe he's lost it here or there.' So I don't think I've lost it, because the day that I feel that I've lost it is the day that I say, 'Go ahead and get out of football.' "

Warner's insistence that he had not lost any of his ability was tantamount to a confession that earlier in the year, for the first time in his career, he had been questioning himself. Now, with two straight command performances under his belt, he was swaggering once more. "We can run the football with anyone," he said. "John L. and myself, I think, are as good as anyone in the NFL."

For Stouffer, it had been a day of sidestepping disaster. Knox had asked him to throw only 16 passes, and only three of them, all incompletions, had been long. Stouffer's inexperience with the pace of professional football in general and with the Seahawk offense in particular dictated that Knox call for the pass only when he had no other choice or when the other team could be caught completely by surprise with an attack through the air. "I feel comfortable with just mixing a little pass in here and there," Stouffer said, "and just doing what I'm capable of doing. As I start getting more and more comfortable, and more and more experienced, we'll start doing more things. But right now, we just have to stay with what we're capable of doing."

He seemed to be improving, play by play. After completing only three first-half passes for 30 yards, he had gone six-for-nine in the second half, for 71 yards. "I think in the first half I was just hesitating a litle bit and holding on to the football a little too long," he explained. "It's just something that comes with playing. I can't even explain it. I know in practice things don't really happen like they happen in a game. You have just a hair less time in a game, and you have to react just a little bit quicker. It just comes with playing at this level. You have to rise up to the level you're playing at and just react a little bit quicker."

Standing as tall in the locker room as he had in the pocket, Stouffer grew more authoritative and thoughtful, taking on more and more of the pro quarterback's postgame aspect and aura. Although having started only two games as a professional, he had already ascended from the murky depths of the inactive list to the heights of Seattle football celebrity. Reporters pressed in upon him reverently, writing down every word he said. Now an undefeated NFL quarterback, he was finding that his opinions carried considerable, if newfound, weight with the press corps. Only a month before, he had been unceremoniously pushed away from his locker by the crowd of reporters around Krieg, two lockers away. Now Jeff Kemp had to dress elsewhere, the crowd around Stouffer taking up the entire quarterbacks' corner of the locker room.

Stouffer was far less fazed by his predicament than were his coaches, who found the task of simultaneously molding and employing a starting quarterback more frightening than exciting. Nothing more graphically proved their trepidation than the sudden appearance of Seahawk quarterback coach Ken Meyer at Stouffer's side. Meyer is a reserved man whose emotional displays are limited almost exclusively to mildly pained facial expressions. So it was a shock to hear him emit a high-pitched, piercing scream, slap Stouffer's hand, and shout, "Nice goin', my man! All riiiiight! And we ain't gonna do nothing but get better!"

A more sobering note was being struck across the room from Stouffer, where Brian Bosworth was struggling into his clothes. Already determined to dress as slowly as possible in the hopes that reporters would be forced by deadlines to leave before interviewing him, Bosworth was further slowed by the lack of maneuvering room his tormentors had left him and by the pain in his shoulder. His left arm hung inert by his side as he writhed and contorted, dressing himself one-handed. By now he knew he wasn't gonna do nothing but get worse—and the season was only six games old.

He turned, fixed his gaze just overhead, and pronounced himself ready for questions. "How does your shoulder feel today?" he was asked. "I don't want to talk about my shoulder," he answered. Then, mechanically, he answered four more questions, his answers coming back each time to the same refrain: "... make the plays when we need to make the plays ... we made the plays when we had to make the plays ... we came up to play and we made the plays ... Enough?"

He was led then to the door and asked to stand still for a minute. Seahawk minions grabbed a few reporters and photographers and arranged them around Bosworth, cautioned everyone to be careful, then opened the door. The aperture was filled with grotesque faces, most of them painted, all of them dimmed by drink. In the center of the arrangement was an immense, fat, witless face, painted orange, with a white stripe flanked by two brown stripes running down the middle. It was a human face disguised as a Cleveland Browns football helmet.

There were a few seconds of stunned silence as Bosworth and his fans regarded one another. Then the tableau suddenly erupted, and Bosworth started inching forward. With flashbulbs erupting in his face, shouts exploding in his ears, and hands reaching out to touch his hair, he forced his way slowly along the stadium corridor. "Boz!" "Hey! Boz!" Pennants, programs, and copies of his book all were thrust at him. Insensate, he pushed on. When he cleared the first phalanx of worshippers, making it clear that he wouldn't be signing autographs, someone screamed, "Ah, Shit!"—and the crowd's adulation turned instantly to hatred. "Fuck you!" "You're an asshole, Boz!" "Asshoooooole!"

It was, mercifully, a short walk to the bus. Once safely aboard, Bosworth contemplated the nightmare he had been driven into by his carefully calibrated moneymaking machinations, while his teammates contemplated their just-completed victory. The Seahawks had dodged a demon in Cleveland. Outgained 334 yards to 227, earning only 14 first downs to the Browns' 21, averaging one-and-a-half fewer yards per play than their hosts had averaged, and playing in one of the toughest stadiums in the country, the Seahawks had somehow managed to win. Now, like all properly confident athletes, they were regarding the improbable victory as their due. They didn't realize that the win was merely a narrative device, cleverly inserted in their saga to set up the wrenching twist of plot that was looming ever closer.

Stouffer's Gambit

Once the opportunity is offered, all the pieces are thrown into action en masse when necessary; and . . . all the pieces smoothly coordinate their action with machinelike precision. That, at least, is what the ideal middle-game play should be, if it is not so altogether in these examples.

       —J.R. Capablanca, *Chess Fundamentals*

The Brian Bosworth that had emerged from the locker room in Cleveland was a commodity aspiring to be an idol. Expressionless, unwavering, unseeing, it moved stiffly through its throngs of worshippers like a stone statue on wheels.

The Bosworth on the playing field had been an automaton, a superhumanoid package of reflexes, instincts, rage, power, and aggression built to carry out its operator's designs and bear the burden of its spectators' dreams. It was not allowed to have identity crises, a conscience, weaknesses, or feelings of pain. It had the rights, obligations, and simplicity of a machine. If it worked, it worked; if it didn't, it was either repaired or scrapped. "We don't think in terms of resting somebody," its operator, Chuck Knox, said after the Cleveland game. "We think, 'Can you go or can't you go?' "

In between these two manifestations of the Bosworth, I had watched Brian Bosworth—worried and in excruciating pain—hunker down in his locker and try to dress himself one-handed. He looked pretty much like anyone else, only bigger, and in a lot more pain. An undersized soul encased in an oversized body, he was a bundle of nerves and fears and needs and failings and unmet desires. He was a creature being pulled every which way at once by conflicting urges and ethics.

He was, in short, a human being, emerging briefly out from under his celebrity during a costume change. And for some reason, either because of the nature of the Cleveland game or because I had been hanging around the

Seahawks for nearly three months, his teammates began to emerge with him, each developing a human identity of his own.

Dave Wyman, for the moment, was most compelling. His play had steadily worsened game by game, anxiety over his performance serving only to feed anxiety over the slow pace of his football understanding. "It's been hard," he said on Monday. "Once I had one bad game, and the pressure builds and gets worse and worse, and I'm thinking, 'Now I *have* to play well, or else I'm gonna be out.' So not only do you have to learn the mental part and try to get comfortable, but now you have all that pressure."

A good year away from grasping the complexities of the NFL game, he was starting for a team that needed to win now. When he was pulled from the game against Cleveland, he stood on the sidelines and watched the defense play better without him. On the flight home, he despaired. "Man, that game was definitely a low point," he said. "I was scared. I thought, 'Jeez, you know how some people just lose it?' Lose it—like if you're a writer, and suddenly you've lost it, you can't write anymore."

When he came in on Monday for his film review of the Cleveland game, however, his coaches were the first to reassure him. "After looking at the film, I could see that it wasn't as much my fault as I thought," he said. Wyman was firmly reinstalled as the starter, although Knox wouldn't say so publicly. "We were getting pounded and we had to make a change," defensive coordinator Tom Catlin said. "That doesn't mean Dave Wyman is screwing up. He's still starting."

Wyman took to practice like a man possessed. "The attitude I'm going to take," he said, "is as if it were all my fault."

Fear—and the ability, or willingness, to talk about it—had restored Wyman from hero to human. Watching him practice with renewed fervor, I realized that there is something about the excessiveness of athletes' lives— excessive pressure, excessive stakes, excessive pain and suffering—that makes fans incapable of regarding them as fellow human beings. Thinking of them as one of us makes us uneasy, because what they endure for the sake of our bloodlust is unendurable. We need to make them into an *other*, a masculine caricature, a. . .

I was derailed in mid-pseudoinsight by a conversation between two players standing behind me:

"What she needs is a good stiff dick in the ass!"

"I used to do that."

"In the ass?"

Somehow, after that, I couldn't get back on sympathetic track.

Although sporting a 4–2 record—fifth-best in the NFL—the Seahawks were running up statistics almost as odious as that brief exchange. On of-

fense, they were averaging 265 yards per game, while their defense was allowing 354. Opponents were gaining 5.2 yards per play against Seattle,
while giving up only 4.4. The Seahawks had earned 102 first downs to their
opponents' 118, outscored their combined opposition by only 3 points (112
to 109), and fallen off drastically in one of their strongest categories: touchdown passes. After six games, they had thrown only four scoring passes,
and none since Stouffer's broken-nose toss three weeks before. In 1987,
they had thrown 31 in 16 games—five in the first two games alone.

Further, they now were a terrible fourth-quarter team both on offense
and defense, giving up 38 fourth-quarter points while scoring only 13 themselves. Small wonder that they had not won any games after being behind
at the half.

The 4–2 record, then, was a mirage, particularly when factored against
the won-lost record of Seattle's opponents. The Seahawks had played only
one team with a winning record (the San Francisco 49ers, who had beaten
them 38–7), and their four wins had come against teams with a combined
8–15 won-lost record.

Most distressing to Knox was Seattle's performance on third down. In
1987, his team had led the NFL in third-down conversion rate, earning a
first down 48.7 percent of the time. Six games into this season, the rate
had dropped to 35.4 percent. "Third down conversion," Knox said on Wednesday, "makes a tremendous amount of difference in total offensive yardage and point productivity. Right now, we're not very consistent in that
area."

And of course there was the ever-lamentable yards-per-rush average,
which still wallowed at 4.7. Out of 28 NFL teams, Seattle ranked 22nd
against the run and 24th in total defense. None of which discouraged some
New Orleans Saints flack, charged with hyping his team's next opponent,
from gushing in a press release, "The Seahawks defense has long been a
strong point. Anchored by nose tackle Joe Nash and linebacker Brian Bosworth, opposing offenses face a stiff challenge moving the ball."

While the Saints had racked up far better statistics than their combined
opposition, their 5–1 record was even more of an illusion than Seattle's.
Their sole loss had come against San Francisco, the only New Orleans opponent with a winning record. The combined won-lost tally for the teams
New Orleans had beaten was 8–22, a record dismal enough to discredit all
of the Saints statistics and to make one wonder why the NFL even bothered to issue statistical rankings.

On Wednesday, team stats were the furthest thing from Terry Taylor's
mind. Knox informed him that morning that Melvin Jenkins had taken his
starting job away. After missing two games because of a drug-test suspen-

sion, Taylor had returned for the third game to back up behind both Jenkins and Patrick Hunter. Taylor then started the next two games in Hunter's place, Hunter having severely sprained his ankle against the San Diego Chargers. During his second start—against the Atlanta Falcons—Taylor injured his knee, and he sat out the Cleveland game altogether. Now, returned to full health, he found that he could dislodge neither Jenkins, the only cornerback to have started all six games for Seattle, nor Hunter. His original four-game suspension had turned into a permanent demotion.

Knox, however—perhaps because he seemed to be shuffling personnel this season faster than the Seattle Mariners shuffle managers—gave Jenkins a less-than-ringing endorsement. Asked if he had firmly entrenched Jenkins in the starting lineup, Knox answered, "Well, I don't know what you mean by firmly entrenched. You mean in perpetuity or what? Going into this game, he's the starter at this point. You get hurt in practice between now and Sunday, or . . . a lot of things could happen."

To defensive backfield coach Ralph Hawkins, the battle among the three cornerbacks for Seattle's two starting positions had been close from the beginning of the previous season, and with his suspension, Taylor had lost the sliver of advantage he held over Jenkins. "I think it hurt him a little bit," said Hawkins, "in the respect that it put him back in conditioning." Taylor also seemed to his coach to be distracted by his drug controversy. "He's been bothered by it," continued Hawkins. "If it happened to you, and you had to go back in your office, you know, you start to look around, and you say, 'Who's looking at me? What're they thinking?' You walk on the field, I'm sure you'd feel the same way. So, psychologically, I think it hurt him a little."

While the Saints' visit to Seattle would be enormously important to individual players—particularly Jenkins, Taylor, Wyman, and Stouffer—it loomed as the year's most psychologically critical game to the team as a whole. It was coming near the halfway point of the season, when a team's most pronounced strengths and weaknesses begin to emerge. It was Seattle's first game of the season against a championship-contending, injury-free team. The Seahawks needed to legitimize themselves in their own collective mind by beating someone worth taking seriously. And most important, they needed to shake off the specter of the 1985 Seattle team, which had finished 8–8, winning two, losing two all season long. The 1988 Seahawks were on an identical pace: With 1985 lurking in the backs of their minds, a 4–2 record, impressive as it sounded in itself, was no better than being up a service break in tennis.

The New Orleans offensive system was much like Seattle's, relying on a strong running game to set up a controlled short-passing attack. And on film, the Saints had seen the Browns run against the Seahawks on nine of their first 13 plays, for 62 yards. So to no one's surprise, they started out almost exactly as the Browns had—by running inside. To everyone's surprise, though, the Seahawks stopped them cold, the Saints managing only 6 total yards on their first four running plays. Kicking from the Saints' 23 after their first possession, punter Brian Hansen sent the ball along a low, 42-yard trajectory, and when Bobby Joe Edmonds returned it 11 yards, the Seahawks were sitting in excellent field position—at the Seattle 46.

This unexpected turn of events was followed immediately by the expected. The Seahawks pitched to Warner, who ran over right tackle into the arms of the entire New Orleans defense. Then, swinging wide, Warner dropped a backfield pass. Now it was third-and-nine, and the Seattle crowd—having been jump-started by the Seattle defense—relapsed. As the Seahawks came to the line of scrimmage in shotgun formation, there arose in the stadium a long, low, collective grumbling. The Kingdome sounded like a huge hive full of disgruntled bees.

As Stouffer dropped back to pass, Steve Largent slipped past Saint cornerback Reggie Sutton. Turning, Sutton positioned himself on Largent's outside shoulder and followed him downfield. Largent saw safety Gene Atkins waiting at the New Orleans 35 to help double-cover him. His head rigid, his body gyrating, Largent fixed Atkins with a deep stare and stutter-stepped, dipping adroitly to the outside. Atkins moved with the fake, Largent cut crisply inside, and Atkins, flailing, watched from 5 yards away as Stouffer's pass came flying at the speed of light into Largent's arms. Seattle had a 17-yard gain, a first down, a stadium full of frenzy victims on its hands, and a monkey shucked at long last off its back: For the first time in a month, the Seahawks had managed to get a first down on their first offensive drive. Now at the New Orleans 36, they were farther into enemy territory at the start of a game than they had been since September 18 in San Diego.

Five more plays—four runs and a first-down pass—brought the Seahawks to a first down at the Saint 14. There, another first-down Stouffer pass was batted down under a heavy rush. Then Warner, slipping through a tiny crack of daylight inside right tackle, gained 5 yards, and a Saint offside penalty moved the ball to the 5, for third-and-one. There, John L. Williams, trying the middle, was met by the entire New Orleans defense, and Seattle was forced to settle for a field goal.

Encouraging as the drive was, it ended on a discouraging note. For the fourth straight time over four quarters, Seattle ended a scoring drive with a field goal instead of a touchdown.

It could have been worse, however, as New Orleans was quick to demonstrate. After Norm Johnson's kickoff, the Saints needed only seven plays to move from their 23 to the Seahawk 2. Then, on second-and-goal, Saint quarterback Bobby Hebert fumbled the snap, Jacob Green recovered, and Seattle regained the ball without relinquishing the lead.

Five plays and 24 yards later, Stouffer was sacked, and Ruben Rodriquez kicked a weak 34-yard punt, which would have set up a New Orleans scoring drive had not the punt slipped through returner Mel Gray's arms. Seattle center Grant Feasel—inserted as special-teams center in place of Blair Bush, Knox had explained, "because he is a heckuva cover guy"— recovered his second fumbled punt in two games.

It was now two plays into the second quarter, and already the Kingdome felt like a pressure cooker. Both teams had mounted long drives—Seattle for 5:35, New Orleans for 4:33—and each had been turned away at its opponent's goal line. And while New Orleans had closed out the first quarter with slight advantages in yardage (89 total yards to Seattle's 70) and time of possession (7:55 to 7:05), Seattle held a 3–0 lead.

Furthermore, Stouffer was throwing with a confidence and authority he had never before shown, save for occasional glimpses in the fourth quarter against Cleveland. He hit three different receivers on five first-quarter attempts, for 42 yards, and one of the incompletions was well thrown but dropped. To his prodigious strength, he had now added a new, heightened level of accuracy and timing. He also served notice to the Saints that the book on attacking the Seattle offense would have to be rewritten.

New Orleans had come into the game determined to do what nearly every Seattle opponent had done: commit an extra defender to stopping the run. Since Denver had tried it, with considerable success, in the season opener, every Seattle opponent except San Francisco had committed its strong safety exclusively to run defense. Ordinarily, it is a daring ploy, but using it against the Seahawks had posed little risk. Defenses commonly commit the free safety almost entirely to pass defense, and the strong safety commits either to the run or the pass depending upon the situation, the down and distance, and the formation and personnel displayed by the offense. But Seattle's opponents, in offensive tackle Mike Wilson's words, had been "deploying their strong safety to take away our cutback lanes." No matter what the offense did, the strong safety would line up at the line of scrimmage, thereby giving Seattle's seven blockers an eight-man defensive front to contend with. Then the safety, unblocked, would shadow the ball carrier. Both Warner and Williams, being "cutback runners," start out in one direction and cut back against the grain if the hole called for by the play's design is filled. Time and again, they had found the strong safety waiting for them.

In employing that tactic, defenses risk giving up more passing yardage, because the absence of the strong safety from the defensive backfield means that one receiver is always left to a single, unassisted cornerback. "When you have a guy covered one-on-one," Knox says, "you should be able to throw the football. You have to be able to throw in those situations." Most often, Seattle hadn't been able, because of Krieg's inconsistency and Stouffer's inexperience. But now Stouffer had just turned in the Seahawks' most consistent first quarter of passing all season, and the Saints realized that simply stopping Warner and Williams would not be enough to win the game.

Now beginning his 12th quarter as an NFL starting quarterback, Stouffer grew more professional with each snap. He was unflappable under pressure, standing just as tall and poised and concentrated under a heavy rush as he did under no rush at all. He threw without winding up, releasing the ball instantly, and his passes were thrown so hard they fairly whistled. To Seahawk fans, watching Stouffer succeed Krieg as Seattle's leading man was like watching Gregory Peck take over for Don Knotts halfway through a movie.

Now, on first-and-10 at the New Orleans 42, Stouffer faded coolly back to pass. Steve Largent, running a post pattern against cornerback Reggie Sutton, turned at the New Orleans 22 to see Stouffer's pass shooting straight and true right into his breadbasket. It was a perfectly thrown, perfectly timed pass, arriving just after Largent's break, before the cornerback could react from the outside or the free safety break over from the inside. Extending his hands, his eyes locked firmly on the ball, Largent gathered it in—exactly as he had done, by my estimation, a good 100,000 times before.

This is no exaggeration. By the end of the '87 season, Largent had officially caught 752 passes as a professional and 126 as a collegian. And for each official reception, there had easily been 100 or more unofficial catches—at practices, at ball-machine sessions, at family picnics—every one of them looking exactly the same. Whoever, or whatever, was delivering him the ball, and in whatever context, Largent always did the same thing as he caught it: He looked fixedly at it, following it with his eyes as he tucked it in. It was like a tic with him. Had a psychiatrist seen him, as I had, day after day, catching passes in practice, casually playing catch afterward with a fellow receiver, playing catch during training camp with his children . . . performing that same ritual gesture with his head time after time after time, pointlessly and obsessively watching the ball, he would have tried to have Largent institutionalized. At the very least, it was obvious, it would take years of therapy to get him to take his eyes off the ball—even for a second.

Suddenly, miraculously, he was cured. Just before tucking Stouffer's pass securely away, Largent turned his head to look upfield. The ball, shocked, leapt out of his hands, slipping free of his panicked attempts to recover it.

In that three-quarters-of-a-second span between the arrival of the ball at Largent's hands and its departure for the ground, the New Orleans game was miraculously elevated from the profane to the sacred. Begun as a mere entertainment, it now was a moving spiritual spectacle. The field was no longer populated exclusively by players and officials: As the referee retrieved the fallen ball, weird little spirits—public and private demons and demigods—sprang into sight all over the place. Such was the power and the mystery of Largent's lapse.

One of the critters insinuated itself between Stouffer's hands and the ball on the next snap. As Stouffer withdrew, the ball flew free, to be recovered by New Orleans linebacker Sam Mills. The Saints then moved efficiently downfield, coming to rest 10 plays later on the Seahawk 19, where they found themselves facing third-and-15.

Knox sent in a pass-defense call for his defensive backfield to fall back into a three-deep zone, with two cornerbacks and a safety strung along the goal line. All the Seahawks had to do to keep the Saints from scoring a touchdown was hold them to 14 yards. With a yard or more to go on fourth down, they were sure to kick a field goal.

The Saints lined up in shotgun formation, and the Seahawks fanned out in front of them. At the snap, Saint wide receiver Eric Martin, lined up as the inside right receiver, slanted toward the right corner of the end zone. Cornerback Terry Taylor, backpedaling in front of him, was supposed to precede him there. Instead, he stopped at the 10-yard line and stepped forward, covering the short zone. Martin passed Taylor, crossed the goal line alone, and made an uncontested touchdown catch.

Afterward, Chuck Knox would say, "We were supposed to be in a zone there. We were supposed to have a deep outside defender back there waiting for that play. Instead, he stayed up on the line of scrimmage." Although he wouldn't name him, the defender in question was Taylor, who had misunderstood the call in the huddle.

It had taken the Seahawks 4 minutes and 58 seconds to go from the verge of extending their lead to surrendering it altogether. They had been victimized by two mental lapses—Largent's and Taylor's—that were as inexplicable as the bounce of a football. The pattern of the game was set. Having seized an early advantage, the Seahawks now had not only the Saints to contend with, but their own sins as well.

Greedily, Seattle devoured yardage, moving 45 yards in 13 plays to kick another field goal and close to within a point, at 7–6. Four plays later, Taylor, attempting atonement, intercepted an overthrown Hebert pass, giving his team the ball at the Seattle 49. With 2:16 left in the half, the Seahawks were within easy range of the lead. Even should they fall short of scoring a touchdown, they needed only to gain 21 yards in order to be within Norm Johnson's field-goal range.

Off they went, reaching the New Orleans 28 at the 1-minute mark. Then Stouffer, still prone to standing too long in the pocket, did so under the worst possible circumstances. With the Seahawks just within field-goal range, he took them immediately out of it, hanging onto the ball long enough to be sacked for a 14-yard loss. Two plays later, he hit wide-open receiver Tommy Kane on the hands, and the ball bounced lazily off them, sailing into the arms of New Orleans cornerback Milton Mack.

Mack returned the ball to midfield, and the Saints took only 30 seconds to execute a slick, five-play drive to the Seattle 6. There, with 4 seconds remaining, the Saints kicked another field goal, and left the field with a 10–6 lead.

The second half had all of the power of the Cleveland game, and far more of the pathos. Every player, on every play, seemed able to conjure up an extra burst of effort. Bodies and souls flew across the field with reckless abandon, as if each play were the last in a dead-even playoff game.

Yet for Seattle, the pattern would always be the same. Advancing to within sight of the lead, the Seahawks each time would find a way to avoid taking it. Their first drive of the half featured two plays of unsurpassed beauty: Stouffer passes of 11 yards to a hook-sliding Steve Largent and 28 yards to a well-covered Brian Blades streaking down the right sideline. Yet there was also a Curt Warner carry, in which he darted toward right end, then for no apparent reason turned away from the open field to cut back inside, immediately meeting four tacklers. And the drive ended on third-and-seven at the New Orleans 35, when Stouffer took off a second too soon on a quarterback draw, ran into the back of center Blair Bush, and fell down inches short of a first down. For the third time that day, and the sixth time over the last two games, Norm Johnson came on to compensate his teammates for the loss of a touchdown opportunity. At the 11:14 mark of the third quarter, Seattle had pulled back to within 1 point.

The Seahawks held the Saints scoreless on their next drive, resuming possession at the Seattle 12 after New Orleans was compelled to punt. Stouffer, like a pro, immediately took control, leading his team to the New Orleans 19 in seven plays, five of them pass completions totaling 63 yards. With each move forward, the excitement in the Kingdome leapt up another notch. Even when Stouffer, after completing five straight passes, twice unaccountably missed open receivers—throwing behind Blades in the end zone and Paul Skansi in the open field—the crowd remained faithfully, noisily expectant. After kicking field goals of 46 and 47 yards, Johnson came on to take back the lead with a mere 36-yard effort.

The two teams lined up for the field-goal attempt, then froze in place, waiting for the suspense to escalate to intolerable levels. Seconds turned into minutes. Hopes turned into fears. Inane worry turned into profound foreboding. Seattleness was in the air. And still the teams stood there, stock-still, crouched, two armies poised on the brink of battle. Seven-year veteran Seattle linebacker Bruce Scholtz, lined up at left end, regarded the two rushers opposite him and thought . . . thought what? Whatever it was, he would keep it to himself for the rest of his life.

Then back came the ball, perfectly snapped. Holder Jeff Kemp caught it smoothly, placed it at the perfect angle on the perfect spot, and Johnson glided forward, his leg swinging in perfect time. From the sound of his kick, he could tell that he had hit it properly, and that it was as good as good.

Instantly, though, came the sound of the ball colliding with the out-stretched hand of Saint safety Gene Atkins. The ball ricocheted back past Kemp and Johnson, bounced and rolled downfield with New Orleans' Dave Waymer in patient pursuit, then obligingly hopped up into Waymer's hands at the Seattle 42. Waymer waltzed downfield, scoring at the third quarter's 2:13 mark.

Scholtz, who for seven years had been trained to take the inside rusher whenever two men lined up opposite him on the end—the reasoning being that the outside man, even if unblocked, cannot get to the kicker before the ball is safely airborne—had instead taken the outside one. Atkins, heading straight for Johnson, had thus been allowed to breach the line untouched.

There was no earthly explanation for what Scholtz had done. His mysterious move cost his team 10 points—the 3 it didn't score, and the 7 New Orleans did—along with the lead, the Seahawks' chances of winning the game, and whatever faith Seattle fans might have had in the justice, or at least the indifference, of the forces that govern the universe. As Waymer crossed the goal line, the spiritually adept, looking domeward, saw hovering overhead an immense angel, covered all over with eyes, held aloft by 12 wings thrumming gently back and forth. The thing held a huge sword in its hand, pointed directly down at the Seahawk helmet painted in the middle of the field.

Immediately, the Seahawks again flirted with victory. On the first play after the kickoff, Stouffer dropped back to pass, held on to the ball till the last possible second—either to heighten the dramatic effect or to catch his receiver at an opportune moment—then rifled a pass to Blades, crossing left to right. Blades caught the ball on the dead run, and accelerated away from Reggie Sutton. Largent, seeing immediately that Blades had only the other cornerback to beat, positioned himself perfectly to block his man to the inside. Blades cut around behind Largent and set off down the right sideline. It was a classic bit of two-man, improvisational football. Free safety Brett Maxie, possibly the only New Orleans player who was faster than Blades, caught up to him at the Saint 28, took Blades's ferocious stiff-arm to the chin, and just managed to force him out of bounds.

Against all evidence to the contrary, the throngs of Seattle faithful allowed their hopes to be revived. Stouffer, confused, took too long to count out his signals on the next play, and Seattle had to take a delay-of-game penalty. Then Blades, who had already caught seven passes for 142 yards, streaked down the left side into the end zone, Stouffer's perfect throw passing right through his hands as diving cornerback Van Jakes, undetected by the officials, tugged insistently on his right arm. After one more incompletion, on came Johnson, to compensate his teammates for the loss of yet another touchdown opportunity.

Typically, when Seattle finally got a touchdown, it was only after allowing New Orleans another field goal. And the touchdown came too late—only 38 seconds remained in the game. Seattle ended the proceedings then with an onside kick that, true to the game's form, came within inches of succeeding. It was a beautifully designed play, and Norm Johnson's kick—two short hops followed by a high one putting the ball up for grabs—was perfect. But the Saints' Eric Martin came down with it, narrowly beating Terry Taylor's lunge from the sideline.

Next to the pile of bodies on the ball, just across the sideline, stood the play's author, special-teams coach Rusty Tillman. He was bent over double, pushing his fists hard enough into his forehead to leave permanent dents. His jaw was clenched, his body quivering with rage. He was living proof that nothing in football is more agonizing than near-success. After a few seconds, he stood up. Still unable to look at the field, he stared straight up at the angel hovering overhead. "Goddammit!" he muttered, "God... dam ... mit ... "

A few minutes later, trapped in the locker room by a group of reporters, he calmed down. He was being peppered with questions about the blocked field goal. "It was a protection breakdown on the left side," he said. "I don't know how it happened—I'll have to look at the films."

"Well... was there something wrong with the hold ... ?"

"No. There was a protection breakdown on the left side."

"Was the snap OK?"

His eyes flashed. "Look," he said. "The snap was good, the hold was good, the kick was good. *There was a protection breakdown on the left side!"*

In memory, that play would loom as the play that cost Seattle the game. It was a single 10-point swing in a 1-point game. But in losing by 1 point, the Seahawks turned countless unremarkable plays into pivotal ones. "The score's 20–19," said Stouffer, "and my job is to win, that's all there is to it. And there were situations in the first half where we ended up settling for field goals where I missed a couple of open receivers and didn't convert on third-down situations. There were key things here and there. We shouldn't have been on the field kicking a field goal when it got blocked, because there was a third-down situation that I should've converted on. There were a couple times where we just didn't do the right thing at the right time to make the good thing happen."

In a 1-point game, almost every failed play is a gamebreaker. Stouffer's two passes just before the blocked field goal—one to Blades in the end zone, one to Skansi far enough downfield for a first down—were thrown behind open receivers. Before their first field goal, the Seahawks had come up with nothing on third-and-one. Just before halftime, with his team in field-goal range, Stouffer let himself be sacked for a 14-yard loss. On the next play, he threw an interception off receiver Tommy Kane's hands, and New Orleans raced downfield in time to kick a field goal. Kane dropped a deep, third-quarter pass at the Saint 3-yard line midway through the third quarter. Stouffer fell inches short of a first down on third-and-seven, forcing Seattle yet again to settle for a field goal instead of a touchdown.

Seattle's defense had just as many gamebreaking plays break against it. The Saints' first touchdown was a gift from Terry Taylor. That drive also included a key conversion, out of field-goal range, on third-and-11. "And their last field-goal drive," said Moyer, "huh! I sucked. I go in and miss a tackle on Heyward [New Orleans' fullback], and he busts for about 20-something, and who knows? I make that tackle, it takes them out of field-goal range, and there's 3 points again. I mean, when you get to a 1-point game, there's so many things. There's too many key plays, unfortunately."

Measured in terms of symbolic value, the onside kick ending the game was the day's most significant play. Ingenious, executed with near perfection, it nonetheless fell short by inches. "Norm hit it just perfect, onside-kickwise," Steve Largent said. "What you want to do is try to get two short hops and one big one. And that's exactly what he did. But they were in the right place at the right time, and we weren't." For one last time in the game, the Seahawks just didn't do the right thing at the right time to make the good thing happen.

The players were devastated. Seattle's offensive linemen, ordinarily the team's most thoughtful, forthcoming unit, sat in collective dismay, their heads bowed. Tackle Mike Wilson, seeing me approach, shouted, "I ain't got nothin' to say!" Then his voice softened. "I'm sorry, but . . . I'm really sorry. . . ."

Devastated as the players were, it was hard not to think that the Seattle coaches, who had devised and implemented an ingenious game plan, were far more devastated. Executing their design, Seattle players had gained 434 yards, to New Orleans' 318, and yet had come up one point short. There had been so many mistakes by players normally incapable of error that the coaches seemed to have lost not to New Orleans, but to some invisible, unidentifiable adversary. "We'll prepare for a circumstance that might come up—like this week it was recovering an onside kick," Largent would say the next day. "Well, I don't know that if we would've prepared for that every day last week, that we would've done any better. But we certainly had an onside kick team, had a plan, and went with it. And it just didn't work." In his view, Seattle coaches, in fighting the unforeseeable, are fighting a losing battle—yet are coming as close as anyone can to winning it. "I don't think there's a coaching staff in the league that does a better job preparing us for as many different circumstances that could possibly come up," Largent said. "But at the same time, you can't prepare for every circumstance. And maybe you can prepare for every circumstance but you can't do it every week."

Back upstairs in the press box, I ran into Gene Moore, the man assigned by the Los Angeles Raiders to scout Seattle's home games. "I don't know what it is," he said, when I asked him what he had thought of the game. "Call it flash, spark, drive, whatever . . . Seattle just doesn't seem to have it. We always say, in games you're supposed to win, 'make 'em *bleed.*' Seattle just doesn't seem to be able to do that. Teams they should be rolling over, they're barely beating. And they should have won this game. It used to be that they didn't have the athletes—but now they do."

It occurred to him that Seattle's problems posed more a question of philosophy than of athletic prowess or coaching strategy. "In the Raider organization," he said, "you say, 'Make the ball bounce your way.' Here, they seem to be waiting to react to the bounce."

There entered my mind the notion—which I immediately dismissed—that it wasn't what the Seahawks lacked; it was what Seattle had that other teams lacked. We watch football, I thought, hoping to suffer through just this sort of loss. Football is never so sustaining as when it evokes sympathy and a sense of mystery. You can never immerse yourself as deeply in triumph as you can in a certain magic kind of defeat. Winners are bimbos; losers have character and soul. This loss had been an epic representation of the human psyche. Just as life is the gradual, reluctant, often viciously resisted relinquishment of dreams, so this game had been a series of enraged confrontations between men and their own limitations. The Seahawks had struggled futilely not against the strengths of their purported opponent but against themselves. And in facing at the end the futility of their ambitions to be winners, the players and coaches, however unresigned, were offering spectators a powerful, consoling lesson.

Gene Moore was still talking. "They always seem to be able to snatch defeat from the jaws of victory," he said. I thought I detected a hint of admiration in his voice.

Circling the Wagons 12

. . . imagine an incarnation of dissonance—and what is man if not that?. . .

—Friedrich Nietzsche, *The Birth of Tragedy*

Somehow, losing didn't seem to charm Knox the way it did me. On Monday, he was dejected and angry enough to fend off questions about the positive with observations on the negative. "I'm never surprised by things, either way," he said when asked if Stouffer's performance against New Orleans had surprised him. "At whatever happens. 'Expect the unexpected' is no longer a cliché, it's reality in professional football today. I never expected a field goal to be blocked the way it was blocked yesterday. But those things happen."

Unexpected as it had been, the blocked field goal, in retrospect, was a thing of beauty, like Ruben Rodriguez's minus-6-yard punt in the final preseason game against San Francisco. In the steadily unfolding context of this season, which was shaping up as a year of well-wrought designs finding a way to go awry, it seemed to make sense. A complete breakdown in the ordered vision Knox had sought to impose on that game, it nonetheless hinted at a grander, more interesting, as-yet-unseen order. Watching the play as it unfolded reminded me of reading a particularly riveting part of a great novel. While you don't understand the passage, it feels right as you read it. You can sense the presence of meaning in it before you can begin to ferret it out.

The play may have been literature to me, but to Knox it was history. Already he had moved on to new torments, the foremost among them being the ever-worsening condition of Bosworth's shoulder. With each game, Bosworth had been growing more vulnerable. As Knox could see from the films, teams were gaining most of their rushing yardage inside, and most of the inside yardage was gained by running straight at Bosworth. Either he would be taken out of the play by his blocker, who invariably enjoyed a 30- to 40-pound advantage and had two workable arms to Bosworth's one, or

153

he would evade the blocker only to be unable to wrap his arms around the ball carrier. Although he was the team's leading tackler, with 58, the bulk of his tackles had come either on sweeps or, if on plays up the middle, only after the ball carrier had gained 4 or 5 yards. Twice against New Orleans, he had dived over fallen bodies to hit a ball carrier in the backfield; each time, unable to raise his arm, he had glanced off the running back's shoulder like a blunt spear off armor.

How much longer, Knox was asked, could he keep playing Bosworth? "Well," he answered impatiently, "if the next guy's better, we're gonna play him." When would that point come? "When we get the next guy that's better. Or the doctor says that he can't play or that they want to do something with his shoulder, or whatever. But we just put the next-best guy in there."

Late the previous week, aggressive attention to the NFL waiver wire had yielded a "next-best guy" in the form of San Francisco 49er linebacker Darren Comeaux. A seventh-year player, Comeaux had gone to San Francisco the previous season after being released by the Denver Broncos. He started eight games for the 49ers, then hurt his knee during the '88 training camp, and was placed on injured reserve. The 49ers, as would be the case with many NFL teams in the coming weeks, had suffered so many injuries that they were running afoul of a league rule regarding injured-reserve players. Over the course of a season, a team is allowed to bring only five IR players back to active status without having them clear waivers first. A player placed on waivers can be claimed by any other team, that team having only to pay $100 to the team owning the waived player, and he can be reclaimed by his old team only after all other teams have turned him down. Since the 49ers were down to their last free move before the season had even reached its midpoint, they were forced to leave Comeaux unprotected.

Seattle claimed him off of waivers immediately, and Knox now could back up Bosworth with a proven veteran, where before Knox had had only a rookie free agent. Comeaux's arrival gave new meaning to Knox's "When we get the next guy that's better." Evasive as that sounded, it actually was a straightforward announcement that Bosworth was about to be sidelined. And sure enough, Knox would replace him with Comeaux during the third quarter of that coming Sunday's game against the Los Angeles Rams in Anaheim, and Bosworth would undergo arthroscopic shoulder surgery the following week.

The substitution of Comeaux for Bosworth, and Bosworth's subsequent surgery, would be among the season's most chilling sequences of events. In playing an injured athlete and postponing necessary surgery for him until an adequate substitute could be found, Knox was adhering to football's most troubling ethic, which dictates that players are employed or sidelined not out of consideration for their health, but out of consideration for the team's chances of winning. Although no one, from Knox on down, would admit it, it was obvious that if Seattle had acquired Comeaux three weeks earlier, Bosworth would have had surgery three weeks earlier. The injury went untreated not because Bosworth didn't need an operation, but because Knox, lacking linebackers, needed Bosworth more than Bosworth needed to be restored to health.

Kelly Stouffer's performance against New Orleans had been so remarkable that the next day even Bosworth's shoulder took second billing. And Knox, knowing that the press would ask whether Stouffer had progressed enough to remain the starter when Krieg came back, came into Monday's press conference with an answer already prepared. The first reporter to ask was hurriedly interrupted with, "Oh, we'll make that decision at that time. It would be presumptuous at this point. We don't know when he's gonna be fully recovered. We don't know when he'll be back in the throwing groove. And a lot of things can happen between now and then. So we just wait and see."

This was vintage Knox. He was trying to keep both players on edge either with hope (in Stouffer's case) or dread (in Krieg's). He was trying to manufacture what Bill Walsh had been given in San Francisco: the kind of competition between two athletes that brings the play of each up to a higher level.

Now 2–1 as a starter, and with his lone loss coming in spite of a 370-yard passing effort, Stouffer was emerging as a player to be taken seriously. His day against New Orleans had added up to the fifth-best passing numbers in Seahawk history, and the best since Dave Krieg's 405-yard day against the Atlanta Falcons in 1985. Each week, the postgame and postpractice crowd of reporters around Stouffer's locker grew larger.

Still new to the pros, Stouffer had not had time to develop properly professional churlishness. He answered questions cheerfully, at great length, and humbly. He was more eager to berate himself for mistakes than to beat his chest over successes. "The interception right before halftime," he said of the pass that bounced off receiver Tommy Kane's hands, "was a pass that I threw a little bit too hard. Instead of having it down here in the body, it was up here where it could be deflected. The difference just in that foot is the difference between us kicking a field goal and them kicking a field goal. When you lose by one point, those [differences] just become gigantic."

The interview session fell into a pattern: friendly, praising question, self-denigrating answer. The tone of the session and the size of the crowd were testament to Stouffer's status as a rising star. He was at the beginning of a parabolic career path that begins with a rise through huge, adoring crowds of interviewers quizzing you on your gifts. From there, it ascends to a level above the fray, where your superstellar stature and impatience with interviews leads the press to keep itself at a respectful, relatively undemanding distance, contenting itself with ever-shorter question-and-answer sessions. Finally it plummets through huge, accusing crowds of reporters quizzing you on your failings.

Other, far less spectacular career paths, of course, are common in the NFL. And the least spectacular of all is that of the perennial backup quarterback. Understudy for the team's most visible position, he is almost always its least visible player. Even the lowliest substitute—the backup offensive guard or tackle—sees more playing time than he does. In his dreams, he sees himself a glamorous immortal, standing tall and strong and indomitable, flinging lightning bolts with devastating effect. In reality, he is a lowly wretch confined to holding for place kicks—a humiliating role calling for him to go down on bended knee, bow like a servant before an angry master, and balance the ball delicately in place with one finger while around him his teammates assume the postures of warriors ready for hand-to-hand combat.

Jeff Kemp, who in the San Francisco game had gained, and lost, a starting quarterback position for the third time in his career, had reacted with genteel stoicism. In the weeks following, there was no change in his regimen or in his outward manner. He kept his Republican stiff upper lip intact, going about his business, working so energetically that he didn't seem even to have noticed his fall from grace. His was the attitude of the sporting chap, the man's man, the team player who would never let his fellow club members down with an unseemly display of emotion.

Only once, in an unguarded moment, did Kemp allow a glimpse at his true feelings. At the Seahawks' headquarters, Stouffer's locker—which is next to Kemp's—sits halfway along a short wall at one end of the locker room. A few yards away a wide doorway leads to a hall that runs the length of the building. Across the hall is an identical doorway, the entrance to the team's weight-training room. Since that room is off limits to reporters, players often retreat there to wait until the postpractice interview period has ended, emerging only when the press has been sent back upstairs. Sitting unnoticed on an exercise bench the day after the Saints game, looking across the hallway into the locker room, was Kemp. He was watching Stouffer's interview session too intently to be aware of anything else going on around him. He clearly had arrived at an emotional crossroads. His face combined the wistful ambition of a dreamy young boy with the disillusion of a failed, middle-aged man. There was no anger there, and no bitterness, or envy, or even resignation or regret. It was a curiously innocent expression. He appeared to feel only an enormous sense of loss, uncomplicated by rancor. Surreptitiously watching him, I was reminded of something he had said just before training camp opened, when asked how his father felt after losing his bid for the Republican presidential nomination. "He was pretty philosophical," Kemp said, "but really, you can never go into something like that without thinking you can win."

The press was not alone in its adoration of Stouffer. To quarterback coach Ken Meyer, he was the fulfillment of a dream. After 30 years of coaching—19 in the NFL—he had found, in Stouffer, unlimited and untapped potential. Talking about Stouffer after practice one day, he kept breaking into a beatific grin. "He's a little bit different than anybody I've ever had," he said. "I think he's a more *powerful* quarterback than any quarterback I've ever had. In terms of raw power. He's got a big-time arm, a big-league arm. And he's a good student. He has a good feel for the game. He has good field vision, too—he can see a lot of things. I think he's done pretty much everything we've asked of him. He's coming in, in kind of a tough situation, and I think he's played better each game."

Meyer is a short and balding man with a kindly face. Like Yoda in *Star Wars*, he looks very much like a Master to whom an aspiring knight is sent to acquire wisdom and invulnerability. While ticking off Stouffer's mistakes—predictable snap counts, passes thrown too hard, breaking out too early on a quarterback draw—Meyer did so gently, as if he regarded them as natural stages in the quarterback's initiation to greatness. Asked if he ever had coached a quarterback who was a first-round draft choice, he answered, "Yeah, I had Namath—he was a first-rounder. I believe John Brodie was too. But I've never had a rookie first-rounder that I've started with." Then he grinned a grin as wide as the practice field. "It's fun—it's really fun," he said reverently. "It's great, because you can kind of build them in your own image, and they're enthusiastic, and they're eager, and . . ." His voice trailed off, and he stood there dreamily, lost in fantasies of future glory.

Stouffer figured to throw less against the Rams than he had against the Saints. A shortage of defensive linemen and a surfeit of superb linebackers had led Los Angeles to abandon the standard modern defensive front consisting of three linemen and four linebackers, and to adopt instead one consisting of five linebackers and two linemen. To offset their size disadvantage against offensive lines, the Rams had devised complex, shifting pass-rush schemes to take advantage of their players' speed—a tactic that had yielded a league-leading 38 sacks after the season's first seven games.

This was the plus side of their experiment; on the minus side, they had the only defense in the NFL with a worse record against the run than Seattle. They were giving up 4.8 yards per rush, compared with the Seahawks' 4.7. Seattle, struggling with a newcomer at quarterback, couldn't have asked for a better defense to face.

They also couldn't have asked for a better day to play football. Fewer things in life are more pleasant to a visitor from Seattle than a 75-degree day in mid-October. And a welcoming Northwestern haze hung high over Anaheim Stadium, blotting out what would have been a blinding sun. And finally, there were the Anaheim fans: although 57,033 were in attendance, the Southern Californians were so laid back that they effectively removed themselves from the home-field-advantage equation.

The one note of hostility toward Seattle was gently struck by a fan's hand-painted sign, attacking Bosworth with an allusion to then-Vice Presidential candidate Dan Quayle's recent loss of face to his opponent during a debate: "Mr. Bosworth," it read, "I know Dick Butkus. Dick Butkus is a friend of mine. And Mr. Bosworth—you're no Dick Butkus."

To judge from Bosworth's performance that day, he certainly wasn't. By the time the ubiquitous plane with Boz banner in tow flew over the stadium, he had retired to the sidelines, not to be seen in action again until three weeks later, when the Seahawks played the Houston Oilers.

As pleasant a day as it was for football, the Seahawks seemed thrown off by the Rams' field. Anaheim Stadium was built purely for baseball, and the football field looks as if it were dropped carelessly from high overhead and left exactly where it landed. Sitting at a disorienting angle to the stadium, the field makes the rest of the world—to the visitor, at least—seem tilted and out of whack.

Small wonder, then, that it took only 13 seconds for the Seahawks to lose the game. After Randall Morris returned the opening kickoff to the Seattle 20, the ball was marched back 10 yards by the officials, who flagged Paul Moyer for an illegal block. Then on the first play from scrimmage, Curt Warner burst around left end, broke a tackle, and was exploding into the flat on his way to a solid 4-yard gain when the ball came flying out of his arms. The Rams recovered at the Seahawk 14.

"Damn!" muttered Mike McCormack, sitting behind me. From his tone of voice, I could tell that he could tell that the game already was lost.

As Los Angeles parlayed the turnover into a touchdown, I fell to wondering what had happened to Warner. Seconds into '88's eighth game, he had committed his fourth unreasonable fumble of the season. He had opened the campaign with a fumble against the Denver Broncos after breaking into the open field; he had fumbled twice against Cleveland—once at the end of a

29-yard run and once on a sweep around end, virtually in the shadow of the Seattle goalposts—and he fumbled again here, once more in the open field and near his own goal line. His yards-per-carry average, at 3.7, was down dramatically from the previous season's 4.3. And his running instincts had gone awry. Time and again, he cut back from diagrammed openings only to run directly into heavy defensive traffic. He looked slower and more hesitant than he had in seasons past, and there was a joylessness about him this year that I had never seen before.

The previous season, I had asked him how he bore up under a 20-carries-per-game regimen. "I just like the game," he said, "and I like the competition, and I like it fast and I like it hard and I like it aggressive."

If these first eight games were any indication, he no longer liked it so aggressive. Perhaps his love of the game—a game more of instinct than of thought, after all—had always been endangered by the workings of his mind, which is more active than the typical athlete's. His love of the game may have been eroded by the effects of his offseason ankle surgery; his only other poor year (1985, when he averaged 3.8 yards per carry) came after recovery from a knee operation. Perhaps it was the effect of having been his franchise's workhorse since 1983, in a sport where running backs typically wear out after three seasons.

Two plays after the Ram touchdown, Knox was undone by a bounce of the ball just as inexplicable as the bounce out of Warner's arms. Stouffer, fading back to pass, found Steve Largent wide open over the middle. As Stouffer threw, LA linebacker Carl Ekern, up near the line of scrimmage, turned and retreated into the defensive backfield. Ekern was scrambling to recover from a mental mistake à la Terry Taylor: Misunderstanding the call in the huddle, he had come forward instead of fading back into a pass-defense zone. His mistake, though, ended more happily for the Rams than Taylor's had for the Seahawks. Stouffer's pass hit Ekern in the back of the helmet just as he reached Largent, and the ball was deflected crazily sideways. It was caught by Ram linebacker Mel Owens, who returned it to the Seattle 9.

Chaos was reigning so thoroughly down on the cockeyed floor of the stadium that I wondered if the ball had a life of its own. On the Rams' first play from scrimmage after their interception, running back Greg Bell dove into the middle of the line, only to become embroiled in a titanic struggle for a few inches of turf. The players in the pile were too engrossed in their fight to notice the ball had popped out. For several seconds it lay on the ground unobserved, until Paul Moyer, standing off to one side, saw it, picked it up, and lateraled to Patrick Hunter just before being felled. Hunter took off, returning the ball to midfield. Then the Seahawks made a pretext of getting back in the game: Warner ran 19 yards around left end, then carried on three of the next four plays, leading his team down to the Ram 18. Three yards later, the drive stalled, and Norm Johnson came on to miss by inches a 33-yard field-goal attempt.

The series of handoffs to Warner were exactly what Knox had envisioned when he traded Seattle's first three picks in the 1983 draft for the rights to Warner, who had set 41 school records during his Penn State University career and finished as one of the top backs in the country. When his selection was announced, Knox said of Warner, "He's the first step in getting this program turned around. Any time he's out on the field, his presence is going to be felt."

Warner's presence was felt the first time he handled the ball. On the first play from scrimmage in the first game of the 1983 season he took a handoff from quarterback Jim Zorn, darted over left tackle, and ran 60 yards before finally being forced out of bounds.

That was the first step in what was to be a season-long run on the record books. In only 10 games, Warner broke the all-time Seahawk single-season rushing record. He finished his rookie season with 1,449 rushing yards, tops in the American Football Conference, second in the NFL, and fifth-most by a rookie in NFL history. He led the AFC that year in rushing (becoming only the second rookie in AFC history to do so), rushing attempts, and total touchdowns, was voted AFC Offensive Player of the Year, and was named a starter in the Pro Bowl.

At the end of that season it appeared that Seattle was well on its way to building a dynasty, with Warner's legs as its foundation. But next season, in the opener against the Cleveland Browns, Warner, running around right end, planted his foot in the Kingdome's turf to make a cut—and suddenly crumpled. His knee had exploded, its anterior cruciate ligament (the cable holding the joint in place) turned, as his surgeon put it, to "spaghetti."

More often than not, a severe knee injury puts an end to a career. But Warner, enduring rehabilitation sessions more agonizing and determined than anything he had ever done on the field, was running at full strength by the next May's minicamp. The first time he carried the ball, his teammates, watching him accelerate as explosively and cut as emphatically as he had before his injury, shouted out awestruck oohs and ahs. Warner himself, after his first full-speed run that day, wept.

He had wept, he said later, because he had realized that all the joys and glories of the game could be taken away forever, in an instant. "I appreciated the game more when I got back," he said. "But more importantly, I appreciated my God-given talents and abilities, and I realized that at any given time, on any given play, it can be over for me."

His year of recovery had given him ample time to reflect upon the joys of professional football. "The most important thing is the camaraderie," he says. "The working together for a certain cause. Togetherness, friendship—all the things that are important in our daily lives. To be accepted to a certain degree by your peers. Not necessarily the crowd-pleasing type thing, but just to be respected by those you work with. I think that's probably what I'll miss more than anything. You know certain parts of these people that no one will ever know."

There is an intensity to these feelings, Warner believes, that is un-equaled outside of sports. "We see more of it," he observes, "because we're put under that stress—that competitiveness. And the magnitude of the game brings out both the best and the worst in people. You see it both in them and in yourself. Because of this tremendous pressure, you open yourself up to things around you. You put yourself out on a limb just to see how good you really are."

When he returned to full form in 1985, Warner was good enough to win *Sports Illustrated*'s Comeback Player of the Year award and to resume his role as Seattle's premier offensive player. He finished fifth in the conference in rushing, with 1,094 yards. In 1986 he again topped the AFC rushing chart, totaling 1,481 yards, was again a Pro Bowl starter, and again was voted AFC Offensive Player of the Year. In 1987 he was named a Pro Bowl starter for the third time, as well as being named to *Sports Illustrated*'s All-NFL team by Paul Zimmerman, the nation's preeminent pro football critic.

Warner stands out from other athletes as much by virtue of his capacity for insight and speculation as by virtue of his athletic ability. He is the rare athlete who spends at least as much time thinking and brooding about the psychology and spirit of his sport as he does studying its tactics and strategies. He is attracted, he has decided, by the game's extreme danger. Like many players, he is stimulated by life on the edge. "There are big people flying at you," he says, "and they're quick. And they have a nasty attitude at the same time. It's exhilarating and it's exciting and it's fun. It may not seem like fun at the time, but it is. You're aware of everything around you. You're just *wide awake* because you know there's someone over there on the other side who's going to take his best shot at you."

Now, in the waning seconds of the first quarter, with his team down 10–0, Warner took Stouffer's pitchout, started out around left end, then took a sudden stutter-step, turned sideways, and burst laterally through a tiny seam to the inside, cutting back for an 8-yard gain that brought the Seahawks into what they call the "red zone"—the area inside their opponents' 20-yard line.

Unfortunately, for much of the season it had become Seattle's "dead zone," and this drive was to be no exception. The Seahawks stalled. This time, Johnson's field-goal attempt was good, and Seattle was only 7 points down.

Three minutes later, however, the Seahawks fell behind by 14 points when Ram quarterback Jim Everett fired a 37-yard scoring toss to reserve running back Robert Delpino over the flapping hand of Paul Moyer. Seattle worked its way patiently downfield again, with Warner absorbing Los Angeles' best shots easily enough to pick up 29 of his team's 68 yards. Then, on third-and-four at the Ram 8, Stouffer tried to finesse a pass to John L. Williams in the left flat. Covered on the inside by a linebacker, Williams broke to the sideline, looking over his left shoulder. But Stouffer had thrown downfield, as if he expected Williams to break that way. Reacting, Williams did something only someone with his prodigious talent could have done. He instantaneously changed direction, contorted, stretched, and almost managed to catch the ball with one hand. The ball flipped, fishlike, off his hand and back over his head, to be snared at the LA 3 by Ram strong safety Michael Stewart. Had Williams just let the ball drop, there would have been no interception, no 43-yard runback, no Ram touchdown 2 minutes later, and no 24–3 Los Angeles lead at the half.

That was pretty much the end of Warner's day—the score dictating that Seattle pass on nearly every down the rest of the way—and he was to carry only two times during the second half. Were it not, however, for Seattle penalties (five first-half fouls for 63 yards) and errant bounces of the ball— out of Warner's arms, off Ekern's helmet, off Norm Johnson's foot, and off Williams's hand—the Seahawks could have stayed close enough to the Rams to keep attacking their weakness (run defense) with Seattle's strength. Except for his fumble, Warner's first-half numbers were fantastic: 14 carries for 75 yards, for a 5.36 yards-per-carry average. At that rate, the Seahawks could have kept the Rams' Everett off the field for most of the day—which is what they would have had to do to stop him. Everett ended up completing 20 of 27 passes, for 311 yards and three touchdowns. The way the Seahawk defense was playing, Warner was the only effective anti-Everett weapon Knox had.

For Warner, a game, with its constant psychological movement, is in many ways a private emotional maelstrom. "There are plateaus in a game, and momentum shifts," he says. "You probably go through more emotions during a football game than you go through for three or four months of living. You go through a lot, I'll tell you. You're not only physically drained, but you're emotionally drained, too."

As much as he loves the game, Warner feels occasional shivers of wonder and fear. It is as if, in order to stay out on the field, he has to deny the reality of what is happening around him. "It's a violent game," he says. "I mean, I'm sitting on the sidelines and I'm going,'*Why* are we out here? *Why* are we doing this?' I'm asking myself that in the middle of a time-out sometimes. 'What are we doing out here? Are we crazy?' Then the time-out's over and it's back in the huddle and you forget. Time to get it on again. But I find myself laughing sometimes. Why are we out here? Well, because we're dumb."

Not so dumb, though, that they can't articulate the joys of playing professional football. Football to Warner is an art form, and as he explains his approach to offense, I wonder how Knox, the consummate scientist who breaks the game down into percentages and forces and vectors and split-second timing, can tolerate Warner's freewheeling mind. "I like being in control," Warner says. "I like analyzing the situation. But at the same time, I like having the freedom to express myself, to do what I like to do. There is a grace to the way the plays and formations are strictly orchestrated. It's very technical, very rehearsed. Yet within that design you have the ability to create and maneuver." For him, football is high-percentage improvisation, enjoyed within the rigid constraints of his coaches' system. "I never know what I'm going to do. The play is called, and it's designed, we've drawn it up on a chalkboard, but it may go from here all the way back across the field—anything can happen. I love the uncertainty of it, the unknown, the mystique behind it. You don't know what's going to happen. When you get the football, you just kind of take the script and write it. It's like I give you a word, and that's it: You take it and do what you want with it. You might want to write a composition or a long narrative story, or a short story . . . And sometimes there's a happy ending and sometimes there isn't."

And sometimes the unhappy ending comes so early there's no point in going on with the story. Less than 3 minutes into the third quarter, the Rams were leading 31–3.

Warner's withdrawal from the action seemed as much a symbolic bow to the pattern of football history as it did a real bow to the pattern of the game's scoring. For Seattle, in taking to the air, was taking the ball from its running back and handing it to its quarterback, as if to acknowledge that the future of the game belongs to passers. As I spent the second half watching Stouffer and Everett, and watching the complex pass patterns and defensive formations unfold in front of them, I thought about how far football had traveled since its inception well over 100 years ago. Once entirely a ground game, it now was entering its space age. Stouffer and Everett were prototypical modern quarterbacks—tall, strong catapults for launching the ball downfield. They represented an evolutionary advance at their position that matched the advances in the game itself, which has gradually gone airborne over the last 82 years or so.

The game took its first giant step toward flight in 1876, when a young Yale student named Walter Camp turned out for a game, called "football," that had first been played seven years before. The game in those days was a cross between soccer and rugby, employing a rugby ball and played on a field 30 percent larger than today's gridiron. It was in essence a riot, played according to rugby rules, with scoring managed only by kicks, as in soccer—although the kick had to sail over a crossbar rather than under it.

Camp, like Knox, loathed disorder, and he began to tinker with football until he more or less fathered the modern game. In 1880 he orchestrated it in order to make it more a game of strategy and less a game of simple running around. He established a line of scrimmage, at which two teams would line up facing one another, the team with the ball in a formation—called a "T-formation" by Camp—that resembled the modern T in every respect except the placement of the quarterback, set back from the line of scrimmage rather than directly behind the center. The center on offense would then kick the ball back to his quarterback, and the offense would try to move forward against the defense.

Unfortunately, since Camp didn't introduce a rule forcing teams to give the ball up voluntarily when they failed to move it a certain distance, weak teams could simply hang onto the ball the whole game long, playing for a tie against stronger teams. Princeton did just that during the 1880 season, playing Camp's Yale team to a 0–0 tie by getting through the whole game without ever fumbling or kicking the ball.

So in 1881 Camp came up with the notion that teams needed to move a certain distance in a certain number of plays or else turn the ball over. A team had to move either 5 yards forward or 10 yards backward in three downs in order get another first down. By 1912, bit by bit, the game had been refined into essentially the game it is today: two teams, of 11 players each, competing on a 100-yard field, getting 6 points for a touchdown, 3 points for a field goal, having to gain 10 yards in four downs, and having the legal option of either running or passing.

Princeton's stalling tactics, and Camp's subsequent rule changes, set in motion a chain of action-and-reaction that continues to the present day. "The handicaps placed on football players—both attackers and defenders—have evolved along with the game over many years," write Bob Carroll, Pete Palmer, and John Thorn in *The Hidden Game of Football*. "Usually someone's new rule was meant to solve a problem that had gotten out of hand. A few rules were tossed in apparently because someone thought they might make things more interesting. Rare is the rule change that did only what it was meant to do and nothing more. Many rules have been added just to contain the carnage caused by earlier rule changes."

For example, the authors go on to explain, the 1906 legalization of the forward pass came about because of an 1887 legalization of tackling below the knees. The 1887 rule sent defenders slanting into offensive backfields and undercutting running backs before the quarterback's pitch could reach them. To counteract that, offenses gathered their troops around the ball carrier and surged forward, tanklike, in what was euphemistically called the "flying wedge." By 1906, the wedge had become a public-image problem for football, as it injured defenders and sedated spectators at an alarming rate. Among the manifold rule changes introduced that year to discourage use of the wedge was one designed to make the game more wide-open: the legalization of the forward pass.

In the early days of the NFL—which was founded in 1920 in a Canton, Ohio, Hupmobile showroom—the pass was largely a gimmick, employed almost exclusively by weak teams against stronger teams. Then, in 1934, the rules were changed to allow a quarterback to pass from anywhere behind the line of scrimmage, rather than at least 5 yards behind it, and the pass became a more legitimate part of the mainstream offense. Gradually, over the remainder of the 1930s, the ball was tapered more and more, making it easier to throw and harder to kick.

The next big change in football came during World War II, when the two-platoon game was instituted. Immediately, linemen—now allowed to rest half the game—started getting bigger, evolving from the pre-1950 210-pound tackle to today's 300-pounder. Quarterbacks also changed from all-around athletes—strong runners who could also block, pass, and tackle—to one-dimensional players, slow of foot, frail of body, and strong of arm. With little else but the forward pass to work on, quarterbacks turned it into a fast-moving, high-scoring mechanism of such popularity with spectators that the custodians of the pro game kept changing the rules to make the pass more prominent—which in turn would give the game more appeal and bring in more money.

Gradually the pass grew in stature. During the 1950s pro teams passed approximately 36 percent of the time. In 1959 the American Football League was founded, and it emphasized the passing game in order to draw fans away from the stodgier NFL. In 1966 the two leagues merged, and by the 1970s pro teams were passing 40 percent of the time and running 60 percent of the time, while scoring 60 percent of their touchdowns by air, 40 percent by ground. In 1977, by which time defenses had grown more brutal and more sophisticated, the rulemakers allowed offensive linemen to pass-block with their hands and prohibited linebackers and defensive backs from making contact with receivers more than 5 yards past the line of scrimmage. In 1982, for the first time, the NFL passed more than it ran.

While my mind wandered back in time from the thoroughly modern game being endured down on the field, Ken Meyer's mind raced ahead in time. For him, the game had become a scrimmage between Stouffer present and Stouffer future. The resemblance between the day's two quarterbacks was uncanny. Both were tall and rangy, with strong arms and quick releases. Both were straight dropback passers who stood calmly in the pocket. Both wore number 11. Except for their uniforms and their statistics, they were virtual mirror images of one another.

The big difference was in performance (Everett's 311 yards to Stouffer's 143, three touchdowns to none, and no interceptions, compared with four), which could be attributed partly to the difference in quality between the Rams' and the Seahawks' cornerbacks and between the two teams' pass rushes. Ram cornerbacks Jerry Gray and LeRoy Irvin, able to cover receivers one-on-one, left Los Angeles with the option of employing as many as eight pass rushers, with the result that Stouffer threw under pressure all day. The Seahawks, already crippled at cornerback by Patrick Hunter's ankle and Terry Taylor's mind, were further hindered when Taylor retired with injuries before halftime and Melvin Jenkins decided to have the worst game of his life. Early in the third quarter, Knox pulled Jenkins for deep reserve Dwayne Harper. To make matters worse, Seattle's defensive line never once put pressure on Everett, who said afterward that he'd never felt so little physical pain after a game.

But the most meaningful difference was in experience. Everett was in his third season, and Stouffer his fifth game. Everett picked apart Seattle's defense all day long, constantly hitting the receiver isolated one-on-one with a defender, reading defenses perfectly, and unloading the ball quickly. His judgment and timing were impeccable. On one play, a flea-flicker perfectly defended by Seattle, Everett saw that his deep receiver was covered, and hit his secondary receiver, Henry Ellard, for a 16-yard completion, even though Ellard was surrounded by three defenders. Everett put the game completely out of reach on the third and fourth plays of the third quarter, with two straight passes over Melvin Jenkins—one for 51 yards, the other a touchdown pass for 32 yards. For the day, he averaged an awe-inspiring 15 yards per completion.

Stouffer, on the other hand, was hesitant, confused by Ram defensive shifts, and prone to forcing passes into good coverage. But afterward, both Everett and Ram coach John Robinson were quick to point out that Stouffer would have his share of Everett-like days. "I can sympathize with him," said Everett. "When I look back over the past two years, I realize all the things I have seen, noticed, and picked up. It's like a guy trying to learn something step by step, compared to somebody who can react on instinct." Said Robinson, "Kelly Stouffer will be Seattle's quarterback into the next century."

Knox, poor man, still had this century to get through. At the end of his 31–10 loss, standing outside his team's locker room, he didn't even wait for questions. "We had opportunities to make the plays in the football game and we didn't make 'em," he said. "If you don't make 'em, you're gonna get beat. We had defenders back there, we couldn't bat the pass down, or intercept it, they made the catches. We moved the ball well in the first half in our running game, which we wanted to do, to take some pressure off our young quarterback, but then we fell behind 24–3, then 31–3, and we had to put the ball up more than we would like to have done. But we just didn't make the plays that we had chances to make. We didn't make 'em, they made 'em, that's the difference in the football game."

His use of the first person plural pronoun notwithstanding, Knox was unequivocally laying the blame for this loss on his players. Gone was his customary postgame circumspection. "If you have one defender back there with one receiver," he went on, "he's *got to make that play*. If he doesn't make it, he doesn't make it. We have a guy, by design, open, then we've gotta try to at least throw the ball to him."

In the locker room, players were dressing and leaving in record time. Surprisingly, one of the players who stayed longest and answered questions most patiently was the player with the greatest reason for sneaking out early, Melvin Jenkins. "This game—I would call it a nightmare," he said. "I don't know . . . I know I didn't play too well . . . "

When he was asked about the defenses deployed against the Rams' big pass plays, he kept reiterating that Seattle had been in zone, as opposed to man-to-man, formations all afternoon. "We were in a lot of zone, you know . . . mostly zone . . . a lot of zone . . . A lot of those big catches were against our zone. You can't really make a lot of adjustments. The ball would be in the air before the receiver would turn—before he would come out to break. And you know, you can't really do much about that."

Cornerbacks always prefer to play man-to-man defense rather than zone. In man, a cornerback simply lines up opposite one player and follows him wherever he goes. The corner knows that the free safety, watching the quarterback, will help out if the ball comes his way. Zones are more complicated. A player fades back at the snap of the ball, watching the flow of receivers, drifts into his zone, and must pick up whatever opponent comes running into it. Instead of watching a single opponent, he must watch for any one of four or five receivers, anticipate their pass routes, and try to take them out of the play. Against Seattle zones, which are bend-but-not-break deployments designed to give up yardage in front of the defense without yielding big plays, the Rams began the game by having receivers run out-patterns from 8 to 18 yards deep. As the game wore on and the score mounted, Seattle's cornerbacks had to come up and play the out more aggressively—in order to try for a gamebreaking turnover instead of patiently containing the offense—and Everett then went over the top of the defense.

Jenkins, while conceding that he had played poorly, seemed bent on subtly blaming the coaches rather than the players for much of what happened. After mentioning, ad infinitum, that the Rams' big plays had come against zone defenses, he said, "The coaches make their decisions and I can't argue with the coaches. They make their decisions and I have to play it. They make the calls." Finally, asked point-blank if he would rather play man-to-man than zone, Jenkins looked searchingly at his questioner and answered, "I can't comment on that."

I realized then that for all the advances football had made over the last century, two things remained constant. When teams start losing, players and coaches divide into separate camps, circle their wagons, and start firing at one another. Coaches fire directly and players obliquely, because from the beginning of football time, players have been afraid of the absolute power wielded over their lives by their coaches.

Reporters kept coming, each new wave forcing Jenkins to replay the same disasters over again. At one point he found himself invoking Seattle's most oft-invoked muse: "The thing is, you've gotta have adversity to be able to bounce back. So if I'm in there next week, whatever, I'll . . . I sure will be a lot better than I played today. So I just have to prove myself after a loss like this, that just makes me dig down, get a lot more hungry . . . "

As he began describing for the fourth time Everett's last touchdown pass against him, a guttural voice came rumbling out from under a pile of towels in the next locker:

"Just say 'what the fuck' . . . "

It was Patrick Hunter, swaddled and sorrowful, uttering his only intelligible comment of the entire season.

I drifted over to Bosworth's locker, where I was treated to a journalistic display even more repellent than the athletic display Seattle had mounted on the field. Just out of the shower, Bosworth was chastely covered with a towel. The customary crowd of male reporters closed around him like shy sharks. A few feet behind them stood a female reporter. Clearly uncomfortable, she stood alone, eyes fixed firmly on the floor, and waited for

Seahawk public-relations people to bring her the player she needed to interview. In a voice deliberately raised just enough for her to hear, Bosworth growled, "Women in the locker room, women all over the place, bunch of swinging dicks in here . . . "

His listeners, fellow men to the core, laughed heartily.

On the Bubble

It was now midweek in midseason, exactly halfway through Seattle's 1988 schedule, and the Seahawks were a middling 4–4 on the year. Their 12½ seasons of struggle had brought them 91 wins and 97 losses in regular-season play. Standing on the threshold of the team's Kirkland locker room, I watched players and reporters go about their business in exactly the same way they had done from the earliest days of the franchise. In many ways, very little in Seahawk history had changed. From the dawn of Seahawk time, players have gone through the same ritual rhythm (game, recovery, practice, game . . .) and fought for the same goal (the Super Bowl) with the same result (maybe next year). In 1976, Seattle fans welcomed their new franchise with dreams of future pro football championships, and now, 13 years later, they were still dreaming. Only twice in all that time had their team finished with better than the 9–7 record it achieved in the third and fourth years of its history.

When you think of how eagerly cities now pant after NFL franchises, it seems impossible to believe that Seattle, courted by the NFL, was at first cool. As early as 1959, Bert Bell, who was then the league's commissioner, listed Seattle among his top choices for expansion—if, Bell said, the city would build itself a stadium.

But Seattle had little use for major-league status of any kind. In the mid-1950s, Dewey Soriano, general manager of the Pacific Coast League's Seattle Rainiers, first floated the notion that Seattle should build a domed stadium to attract professional sports to the Northwest. For this, he was roundly hooted, until Houston, with the opening of its Astrodome, proved in 1965 that Soriano's vision was technologically feasible. Not so feasible, though, was interesting Seattleites in big-time sports. Twice in the 1960s, proposals for open-air stadium bond issues were voted down, and not until 1968, when voters approved a domed-stadium bond issue, did Soriano's vision begin to be realized.

At that time, the notion behind the stadium was the impending arrival of major-league baseball in the form of the Seattle Pilots, who were to begin play in 1969 in Sicks Stadium, then move to the domed field when it was ready. (Instead, they moved to Milwaukee—but that's sort of another story.)

In 1971, Minneapolis businessman Wayne Field formed the Seattle Kings, an organization dedicated to landing an NFL franchise in Seattle. A year later, a rival group, Seattle Professional Football, was founded by local developers Herman Sarkowsky and David Skinner. The two recruited developer Howard S. Wright, Pay 'n Save's M. Lamont Bean, Western International Hotels' Lynn P. Himmelman, and Longacres' Morrie Alhadeff as fellow prospective owners, and signed former Mariners and Golden State Warriors general manager Dick Vertleib as an adviser. In the early going, Alhadeff dropped out—fearing future conflict of interest between his race track and the football team. Sarkowsky then signed clothing retailer Lloyd Nordstrom to replace Alhadeff as the sixth partner.

The Sarkowsky group had the inside track over Field's group by virtue of its being local—practically an ironclad requirement for entry into the league. Not so clear, however, was the meeting of a second requirement— that there be a single majority owner. The group originally had taken on six partners with the idea that each would own one-sixth of the team—in order, Sarkowsky says now, "to spread the risk" of such a large investment—but the NFL required that one person own at least 51 percent of the franchise. Sarkowsky, without naming the future majority owner, assured the league that one of the group would meet the requirement.

In January 1973, NFL Commissioner Pete Rozelle announced that the league's owners had agreed in principle to expansion and that Seattle topped the list of cities considered worthy of an NFL franchise, largely because it had a domed stadium already under construction. The target year for expansion was moved back from 1974 to 1975, with the league deferring the decision whether to expand by two or by four teams.

Rozelle then shocked Seattle Professional Football by setting the price of an expansion franchise at $16 million, far more than the $8 million to $12 million that Sarkowsky and his group had expected. Since none of the group was willing to put in some $8 million of his own money, Lloyd Nordstrom persuaded seven of his relatives to join the group, with the Nordstroms pooling their resources to serve as the franchise's majority owner.

That the Sarkowsky/Nordstrom alliance continued to stand a chance with the league was due largely to there being no competing applicants who met the NFL ideal—a locally based owner. While the Nordstroms would own 51 percent of the franchise, the league didn't regard them as a single owner, because there would be eight Nordstroms with a voice in ownership decisions. The league was further troubled by Sarkowsky's ownership of 40 percent of the NBA's Portland Trailblazers and by his and several Nordstrom family members' ownership of small percentages of North American Soccer League franchises.

For a few months, those appeared to be the least of Seattle's problems. In April of 1974, Rozelle took Seattle completely by surprise with the announcement that the NFL owners had chosen Tampa for its next franchise and had postponed its choice of a second city. The problem with Seattle, according to oone anonymous NFL owner, was the proposed Kingdome lease, which would have granted the county by far the biggest cut granted by any stadium contract in the country. The lease called for the county to take 20 percent of football's gate. It also required the new franchise to spend over $1 million to finish the football press box, locker rooms, and a stadium club, to pay 10 percent of the annual maintenance costs of the stadium, and to pay its heating and cooling bills. By June, however, the problems apparently were ironed out. The league granted a franchise to Seattle and announced that 1976 would be its expansion year.

Turning its attention to selecting a new owner, the league agreed to accept Seattle Professional Football's ownership structure if Sarkowsky would be named the new team's managing general partner. This meant that, although owner of only 10 percent of the team, he would be invested with primary decision-making responsibilities, a plan that sat well with the league because of Sarkowsky's past success with the Portland Trailblazers. Further, Sarkowsky promised to divest himself, in stages, of his Trailblazers interest, thereby conforming to the league's prohibition against cross-ownership of sports franchises.

The owners forged an agreement among themselves, called a "supermajority" agreement, which gave each of the five minority partners one vote in franchise decisions, and the Nordstroms two votes. Four votes were required to approve any decision, although no decisions could be voted through without the two Nordstrom votes. The minority owners also had a right of first refusal should the Nordstroms decide to sell their majority interest. That part of the agreement stipulated that if the Nordstroms reached agreement with a prospective buyer, the minority partners had one year either to buy the Nordstroms' share at the agreed-upon terms or to find another buyer who would.

In March of 1975, the group signed John Thompson, of the NFL Management Council, as the team-to-be's new general manager. Thompson brought instant expertise to the Seahawks. He had been the assistant general manager of the Minnesota Vikings. He had also served as assistant to the legendary George Halas, one of the NFL's founders, and to Commissioner Pete Rozelle. As head of the management council, he had bargained extensively with the NFL Players' Union. He was one of the country's leading experts both on the business side of football and on the acquisition of talent. His only flaw, as would be seen some seven years later, lay in his wholehearted endorsement of the Management Council's hard-line stance against the players union.

In January 1976, Thompson hired Minnesota defensive line coach Jack Patera as Seattle's new head coach, and the Seahawks prepared for their first season of play.

In their early years, the Seahawks were largely a Sarkowsky-built and Sarkowsky-run team. Having helped build the Portland Trailblazers from an expansion team into a perennial NBA championship contender, Sarkowsky was the only member of the Seattle ownership group with extensive sports experience. He developed Seattle instantly into a well-run, profitable franchise. Not content with building slowly, the Seahawks set out to win as much as possible as soon as possible, and enjoyed unprecedented success on the field. In 1977, Seattle became the first NFL expansion franchise ever to win five games in its second season. In 1978, the Seahawks went 9–7, thus becoming the first expansion franchise ever, in any sport, to have a winning record in its third season. They went 9–7 again in 1979, winning eight out of their last 11 games and beating the Oakland Raiders, 29–24, in the season finale—partly by means of two fake field goals.

The fake field goals were typical Seattle plays of that era. The Seahawk attack was built around the gimmick and the improvised pass play, this last made possible by the phenomenal scrambling ability of quarterback Jim Zorn. In a league known for uniform, often dreary, high-percentage offenses, the Seahawks were a breath of fresh air. Seattle became synonymous with weird, wide-open, anything-goes football, employing quick kicks, fake punts and field goals, passes to place-kickers, fake time-outs, tackle-eligible passes, onside kicks in the middle of games, and bombs, bombs, and more bombs to score by stealth rather than by strength.

Crowds and television commentators loved it. Win or lose, the Seahawks were entertaining, and spectators never knew what to expect when Seattle lined up on offense. And since they won more often than they were supposed to, their unorthodoxy seemed all the more wonderful.

Unfortunately, parity, percentages, and physical decline caught up with them. Since draft order and difficulty of schedule are the two means by which the NFL weakens winning teams and strengthens losing ones, the Seahawks' two 9–7 seasons dropped them lower in the draft and earned them gradually tougher season schedules. By their fifth year, they were an expansion team, with an expansion team's talent-poor roster, drafting and

On the Bubble **175**

playing from the position of an established, winning, talent-rich team. They were further weakened by better preparation, on the part of their opponents, for their tricks. And their passing offense, which relied almost exclusively on Zorn's ability to buy extra time, was weakened when Zorn fractured an ankle in 1981—after that, he was never able to scramble as effectively.

After plummeting to a 4–12 record in 1980, the Seahawks returned to action in 1981 and heard, for the first time, rumblings of discontent from their public. Patera's image as a mild-mannered man of few words, with a mile-wide zany streak, changed to that of a temperamental, eccentric, tyrannical drill sergeant whose coaching methods were hopelessly behind the times. The Seahawks went 6–10 that year, the low point of the season being a 32–31 loss to the Raiders in which Oakland scored 29 straight points and Seattle had a 59-yard trick pass to running back Eric Lane disallowed. Seattle lined up in punt formation with only 10 players on that play, then sent Lane on a pass route from out of the group of players standing on the sideline. Clever as it was, the play was a flagrant violation of the rules. Everybody—referees included—objected, and the play, which once would have been regarded as exciting and irreverent, became a shameful symbol of Seattle's chronic weakness.

Two straight losing seasons had Seattle fans clamoring for change. Some disgruntled fans even went so far as to mutilate and return their Nordstrom credit cards. In February of 1982, change came. The Nordstroms, leery of bad publicity, voted 5–3 to sell out to their minority partners, and reached a sales agreement. At the last second, two family members changed their votes. The minority shareholders then offered to sell out to the Nordstroms, but the family declined that offer as well. Instead, they opted to exert more of their own influence on team operations. Sarkowsky resigned as managing general partner, and Elmer Nordstrom—then head of the extended family—took over his role, saying, "I don't think it'll take much to turn things around. We're doing some things that should make a difference."

The first thing the realigned ownership did was bring in Mike McCormack as director of football operations. McCormack served in that capacity for only a few months. The 1982 season began with the threat of a player strike, and when Seattle players joined their opponents in a union solidarity handshake just before a preseason game, Patera stunned the league by fining them half a week's pay. Patera's popularity, already all but destroyed by his team's two losing seasons, was ruined by his rigid anti-union stance. When the Seahawks released well-liked, productive wide receiver Sam McCullum, the team's union representative, the move was widely cited as proof of Patera's inherent meanness. With his players grow-ing more openly discontented and the public increasingly tying the team's image to Patera's, the Seahawk owners fired him—and with him, Thomp-son, the team's general manager—during the 1982 players strike. McCormack finished out the season as head coach.

With the firing of Patera and Thompson, McCormack's subsequent elevation to general manager, and McCormack's hiring of Knox, the Seahawks became a genuine Nordstrom enterprise. Knox installed a sys-tematic, high-percentage attack that relied on the steady gaining of ad-vantage rather than the hit-or-miss big play, and a team once known for its insanity became known for its good sense.

The Seahawks became an athletic expression of the Nordstrom psyche, its irreverence and what-the-hellism replaced by probity, prudence, and stolidity—the hallmarks of Chuck Knox football. Knox, in fact, is himself temperamentally and tactically so much like the Nordstroms that he could almost be mistaken for a member of the family. Under him, the Seahawks came to resemble the immensely successful Nordstrom retail operation. Under the Nordstroms, there were two things—aside from Brian Bosworth—that set the Seahawks distinctly apart from almost all other NFL franchises: the team's positive image in the mind of the public and the unflagging loyalty of its players. The Nordstroms' success at building the Seahawk image was the envy of the NFL, and observers often pointed to the number of Seahawks who have made their permanent homes in the Northwest as a sign not only of the devotion of the players to the franchise but also as a significant factor in the team's image making.

Knox most resembles the Nordstroms in his obsessive impenetrability. The Nordstroms are shrouded in thick mists of self-imposed secrecy. In spite of their obvious ambition, they often seem to have ascended to the heights of wealth, prominence, and achievement almost against their will. They eschew interviews, refuse to be photographed, and assiduously avoid attention directed at them rather than at their commercial enterprises. Even when the sale of the Seahawks to Kenneth Behring was announced, there were no Nordstroms in attendance. Would-be interviewers are al-ways told the same thing, that family publicity is detrimental to the esprit of the company as a whole.

Sportswriters and players alike credit Knox, known throughout the league as a "player's coach," for inspiring unusual dedication in the team's athletes, but it is clear that the Nordstrom touch is at work there as well. Everything the owners have done, from building a new state-of-the-art headquarters to making their head coach the second-highest-paid in the NFL to retiring a Seahawk jersey in honor of their fans, has shown the

Nordstroms' characteristic concern for class and quality.

You learn a surprising amount about the magic of the Seahawk enterprise during the Nordstrom years by looking at the Nordstrom retail operation. In many ways, their chain of stores is run like a sports franchise.

Nordstrom has become the country's, if not the world's, largest independent fashion-specialty retailer. The *New York Times*, citing marketing and retailing analysts, calls it "one of the best-managed retailers in the country." When the Nordstroms bought into Seattle Professional Football, there were 30 Nordstrom stores, all in the Northwest. Now there are 48, in such far-flung ports as southern California, the Washington, D.C., area, Baltimore, and New York, with eight more outlets under construction, and with incursions into the Midwest on the horizon.

There is no end to the list of reasons for the company's continuing success. Experts cite such disparate factors as the Nordstrom policy of meeting competitors' prices, a decentralized management policy that allows department managers, rather than a central personnel department, to hire their own salespeople, a "hire from within" policy that requires all managers to be recruited from the store's sales force, a purchasing system that is directed from below—with each department helping stock its own shelves—rather than from above, and Nordstrom's inventory per square foot, which is nearly double that in other department stores.

Probably the single most oft-cited factor in Nordstrom success is the company's ability to motivate its employees, particularly when it comes to Nordstrom's vaunted attention to customer service. Nordstrom salespeople are cajoled and goaded into superlative sales and service performance in much the same way athletes are, and they take an athlete's pride in the overall performance of the Nordstrom "team".

A Nordstrom salesperson is powered by meetings, skits, goals, awards, folklore, commissions, and profit sharing—all fueled with motivational speeches, seminars, and positive-thinking literature. New employees are given a handbook, view an inspirational videotape (*The Nordstrom Story*, which details the enterprise's history, beginning with John W. Nordstrom's migration from Sweden through Alaska to Seattle, where he opened his first shoe store in 1901 with money made from the sale of his Klondike gold claim), and are initiated into the Nordstrom system.

The system is an inspired mix of hardheaded, sound business practices with a folksy, cornball psychology of the workplace. An old-fashioned brand of employee loyalty to the store is forged from a combination of rigid discipline with praise, rewards, and a semiformal, family feel to the store organization. "We're like a family, all the stores," says a saleswoman who works in the downtown Seattle Nordstrom. "I really can't describe it, it just happens. It's like the Nordstroms are my uncles or something."

On the hardheaded business side, salespeople are paid either a base salary or a commission on their sales, whichever is greater. And those who do not regularly surpass their base salary with sales commissions ("make their draw," or "make their book," in employee parlance) are fired, often very abruptly.

Nordstrom employees work in a highly charged atmosphere of relentless purpose, dedication, reward, and praise. Salespeople work toward such an array of personal, departmental, and store goals that one goal or another is in their minds almost constantly. Employees who make their yearly personal sales goals are admitted to Nordstrom's "Pacesetter's Club." Pacesetters are given a certificate, a new business card with "Pacesetter" emblazoned on it, a 33 percent discount on Nordstrom merchandise for a year (the standard employee discount is 20 percent), and a lavish evening out on the town.

More important, from the motivational standpoint, is a certain air of theatricality accompanying the whole topic of goals at Nordstrom. This ongoing goal drama is remarkable enough to figure prominently in a 1979 Harvard Business School study of Nordstrom prepared by Harvard Associate Fellow Manu Parpia. In dry, academic prose that nonetheless betrays a certain breathless fascination with what appears to be a distinctly exotic way of doing business ("The Nordstroms did not even have an organization chart"), Parpia describes the Nordstrom enterprise in the manner of an anthropologist who has stumbled onto some hitherto unknown tribe. He is particularly taken with the structure of a Nordstrom motivational meeting for managers and buyers: "Goal setting was achieved through means of peer pressure. Every year a meeting attended by all the regional buyers and the store managers was held at each region's headquarters. The regional manager or, in the case of Washington state, the Nordstroms, would call on each individual manager (or buyer, as the case may be) in turn to present his or her sales target for the year. As the figures were called out, the regional manager wrote the amounts against the individual's name on a large chart. Next to the figure in turn was a space on which the regional manager had written his target for each manager. That target figure was kept covered during the initial part of the meeting in which the managers gave their target figures for the year. Then, amidst great excitement and suspense, the regional manager tore off the slip of paper which covered his target for each individual manager. If the sales target of the manager was under that of the regional manager, the assembly would boo the unfortunate manager. However, if the manager's target was above that of the regional manager, then the group of persons would break out into cheers. One manager described the scene as being similar to that of a class-room before an exam, or perhaps during an exam, with all the store managers and buyers doing feverish calculations as they heard what their peers were setting as targets and were tempted to revise their own targets."

Say what you will about the Nordstrom method, it works. It is also remarkably similar to Chuck Knox's Seahawk method. Both are un-compromising. In both cases, employers demand, and get, superlative performances out of their employees. Both Knox and the Nordstroms present their demands in a relentlessly positive way, working hard to create a working environment in which almost everything that happens is beneficial. Both are adept at convincing their charges that they can improve them-selves, their fates, their abilities, their performance, their workplace, and their lives through the power of positive thinking. Both are generous with praise and reward, without robbing them of their value. Both cleverly man-age to mix a feeling of solidarity and purpose, of teamwork, with intrateam competition. Just as the Seahawk player who has lost his starting position to a teammate will praise his conqueror, so Nordstrom employees compete with one another, measure their performances against their fellow work-ers', and yet still retain a sense of shared purpose.

It was prudence and purpose that led the Nordstroms finally to sell their football franchise. The more their retailing empire grew, the less time they had to spend on football. And however important football may seem to fans, to the Nordstroms it always came second after the family store. Late in 1986, having competed successfully against their peers in the NFL, having realized—given the game's rapidly changing economics—as much football profit as they ever would, and finding their attention increasingly absorbed by their stores' rapid growth, the Nordstroms put their share of the team on the market.

It was a move that effectively drove their co-owners out of football, for the franchise's tremendous increase in value had changed the meaning of the game for owners. Once custodians of a small, $1.6 million investment, Seahawk minority partners now found themselves co-holders of property worth $100 million. "We tried to be good citizens when we owned the team," Herman Sarkowsky says now. "The bottom line was important, but it was not the thing that drove us. But it becomes a different asset for people who buy at $100 million." At that price, an owner cannot afford simply to turn it over to football people and let it run itself, as Sarkowsky and the Nordstroms had done. "You'd have to spend full time on football," Sarkowsky says.

The high price tag made it no less different an asset for someone buying at $51 million, for no prospective owner would be willing to pay that much money without getting full control of a franchise. The supermajority agreement, along with the minority owners' first-refusal rights to hold a sale up for at least a year, if not forever, made the Nordstroms' share, in itself, all but unsalable.

From the time they first decided to sell, the Nordstroms' only real options were either to sell their share to their partners or to buy the remaining 49 percent and sell the entire franchise. While selling to their partners had been an option in 1982, it no longer was in 1988. "We looked at it again," says Sarkowsky, "and we just didn't have anyone willing to take it over." David Skinner was ill and would soon pass away; Wright was ill; the five members of Himmelman's group, four of whom were retired, wanted to get a return on their investment based on the present-day value of the franchise, and the only way they could do that was by selling; and Sarkowsky himself was bored with football. "It's the starting up of a franchise that I enjoy," he says. "And my son didn't want it, so . . . " So finally, in mid-1988, the Nordstroms bought out their partners for $35 million, then sold the entire franchise to Kenneth Behring for nearly $100 million —$80 million in purchase price and $19 million in assumed debt.

They had found Behring through athletes' agent Mike Blatt, who brought the Nordstroms and Behring together after learning, during the negotiation of Kelly Stouffer's contract, that the team was for sale.

Football fans soon discovered that the departure of the Nordstroms and the arrival of Behring signaled a new era in Seattle professional football. No longer was the Seahawk franchise a $12 million enterprise that easily turned a profit; in good years, the team came out $4 million in the black. Now it was a $100 million enterprise whose owner, according to Sarkowsky, would have to find ways to generate $3 million to $5 million more in income per year in order to recoup his investment. Despite Behring's protestations to the contrary at his inaugural press conference, he eventually would be looking for ways to raise prices and cut costs.

The arrival of Behring also marked the end of the aloof, hands-off owner with no interest in publicity or attention. Behring proved as ostentatious and as visible as the Nordstroms had been self-effacing. Pictures of his face, along with long articles on his life and lifestyle, shone prominently from the pages of Northwest newspapers as the season began. And he has made a habit of showing up at Seahawk games on the sidelines, in the locker room, among the Sea Gals . . . Fans saw and learned more about him in the first eight weeks of the season than they did about the Nordstroms in 13 years of franchise ownership.

Behring does, though, share one trait in common with the Nordstroms:

He spent half a season fending off interview requests from me and began avoiding nearly all the Seattle media as soon as his inaugural press conference ended.

Behring was born in 1928, in Monroe, Wisconsin. In 1952, he bought a Lincoln-Mercury franchise, and by 1955 had made his first million. From there, he moved to Florida and broke into the real estate business, building 30,000 homes around Fort Lauderdale, and 10 golf-course communities around the state, from the late 1950s until 1972. In 1972, he bought 4,000 acres of land near California's Mount Diablo, buying another 1,000 two years later. There he built Blackhawk, a 5,000-acre community of homes ranging in cost from $400,000 to $5 million, with the community's crown jewel being Behring's own $12 million estate. Now sporting a net worth between $600 million and $1 billion, Behring also owns a Lear jet; the $112 million Behring Museum which showcases his collection of 250 antique cars; and, finally, an NFL franchise.

Still standing on the threshold of the Seahawk locker room, I wondered if I would ever see any visible signs in this room of Behring's impact upon the franchise. There seemed something immutable, imperturbable, about football's pace and rhythm and the pattern of a franchise's life on the field. While upstairs, over 13 years, coaches and general managers and owners had come and gone, downstairs life seemed unchanged. The team had started out struggling to win, was struggling to win when the Nordstroms took control and Patera was fired, and has been struggling to win through five seasons under Knox and McCormack. It occurred to me that you could walk into any locker room in the league on any Wednesday and see more or less the same scene I was witnessing now. The game played on, regardless; teams struggled on, regardless; and with the exception of only one team, teams finished each season dissatisfied, restless, intent on doing better, and limited by the league's parity system from making dramatic improvements. I walked across the room to Steve Largent, sole surviving Seahawk from the franchise's first days, and asked for his assessment of Seattle's season thus far. "There's a lot of excuses that I could make," he answered, "but we just haven't performed up to the expectations that we have of ourselves. Hopefully, that will happen soon, but . . . you know, I feel right now that we're a team that's kind of on the bubble, trying to decide whether we're going to go ahead and be a playoff-caliber team or if we're just going to fall by the wayside with a lot of other football teams. So we'll see what happens."

It was an answer he could have given nearly any midweek in all but a few of Seattle's 13 seasons. While the faces of the players and coaches have changed, and the owner has changed, and the value of the franchise has changed, the nature of the team has not. Through all the years, from the 4–12 one to the 12–4 one and all the ones in between, Seattle has been a team on the bubble: always an unsuccessful play or two worse, or a successful play or two better, than a .500 team.

Night of the Living
Grover Klemmer

One strange thing troubled him. A surprising creature of nebulous features ran out from somewhere—a small, gray lively nedotykomka. *It laughed, quivered, and whirled around Peredonov. When he stretched out his hand towards it, it quickly flashed by and hid behind the door or under the cupboard—only to reappear in a minute and quiver and tease—the gray, formless sprite . . . Peredonov became chilled and depressed. "Why is there all this uncleanness in the world?" he thought.*

—Fyodor Sologub, *The Petty Demon*

The Seahawks were falling apart. Everywhere they looked, they saw trouble, weakness, and ghosts of failings past. There was a dawning sense at team headquarters that too many games—wins and losses alike—had been out of Seattle's control. Whenever the Seahawks seemed on the verge of pulling ahead, something—an injury, an uncharacteristic mental lapse, a freak bounce of the ball—would intervene to set them back. And whenever they seemed on the verge of going under, something—an official's call, another team's injuries, a freak bounce of the ball—would intervene to push them ahead. After getting off to a 2–0 start, they had enjoyed a one-game lead over Denver and Los Angeles in the AFC West, and had stayed atop the standings mostly because the Raiders kept losing and the Broncos kept matching the Seahawks, win for win, loss for loss.

Now at the midway point of the season, Denver has managed to pull even and Los Angeles was still only one game back. Seattle still had a share of first place, but as they prepared to host the San Diego Chargers, Seattle players were unhappy with the way they had earned—or, rather, not earned—their position. "Well, you know," Bosworth said after losing to the Rams, "we're still on top, you gotta take that with a grain of salt, I guess, anytime you're in first place, you want to be in first place by yourself, and I guess you could say we're somewhat lucky, but I'd rather be at this point good than lucky." Paul Moyer was more direct. "I'm getting tired of losing

183

and still being in first place," he said. "I want to start building a lead instead of just hanging on.' "

That was a matter of forcing themselves to play consistent football. Good teams differ from lucky teams in the way they take control of games, not so much taking on opponents as dictating the terms of their surrender.

Even though the Chargers, now 2–6, had beaten the Seahawks five weeks before, their chances of doing so again, especially in the Kingdome, were virtually nonexistent. Still, Seattle was trying its best to reduce its chances of winning. The team emerged from the Rams game in its worst shape yet. Bosworth underwent surgery on Monday, and Bruce Scholtz's foot—in and out of a walking cast all season long—had finally declined to the point where it looked as if he would have to be held out of a game. On offense, two starting linemen—guard Bryan Millard, the team's best blocker, and tackle Ron Mattes—had rib injuries serious enough to postpone a decision on their playing status until the morning of the Charger game. In addition, center Blair Bush was still hampered by an ankle sprain, and backup guard Alvin Powell, after a mysterious disappearance, had checked himself into a substance-abuse clinic. On defense, Knox might be forced to start one journeyman linebacker (newcomer Darren Comeaux) and one rookie linebacker (M.L. Johnson); on offense, he was down to Grant Feasel at center, possibly Stan Eisenhooth at tackle, and Chris Godfrey—a veteran offensive guard released by the New York Giants six weeks before and signed by Seattle a month later—at guard. And there was no telling when Dave Krieg would be back.

Injuries loomed large in Knox's midseason evaluation. "Well," he said on Wednesday, "I think a midyear assessment would be reflected in a 4–4 record. Which is about .500, which is average. And I think that would be a very candid appraisal in all three areas. And I would temper that a little bit by being cognizant of the injury factor. We've gone with a rookie quarterback, we have a starting linebacker in his second year who will not play this week, we've had injuries on the corner, and—you know, we had a lot of changes here. So I think that has hurt us some."

Realizing that he was violating an unspoken code of conduct for coaches (analogous to the code prohibiting an athlete from admitting that he is in too much pain to play, this code prohibits coaches from attributing losses to injury), Knox quickly redeemed himself with a curt, "But I don't think that can ever be an excuse for not winning."

Statistically, his team didn't look good enough even to be 4–4. Over the last three weeks, the Seahawks had managed only two touchdowns from inside their opponents' 20-yard line, while giving up six. After scoring 24.7 points per game in 1987, the Seahawks were down to 17.8, only 22nd in the league. They were gaining 4.6 yards per play, nearly a full yard short of their goal of 5.4. Third-down conversions were down from a league-leading 48.7 percent in '87 to 35.8 percent—this despite average gains on first and second down that were the best Seattle had managed in six years.

Most telling was Seattle's touchdown-to-interception ratio. Last season, in 12 nonstrike games, Seattle had 23 touchdown passes—they led the league, in fact, in touchdowns per pass attempt—and 15 interceptions. After eight games this season, it was touchdowns 5, interceptions 14. A statistician could mix numbers forever and not come up with anything uglier than that.

Except, perhaps, if the numbers being mixed were Seattle's defensive ones. The Seahawks had given up 160 points in eight games, while scoring 141. Opponents had netted 2,907 yards against the Seahawks, for an average of 5.5 per play, and had converted 45.4 percent of their third downs. The Seahawk front line had managed only one sack over the last three games.

With the NFL's 23rd-ranked offense and 26th-ranked defense, Seattle managed to stay at .500 almost solely by dint of a plus-five turnover ratio (tops in the AFC), having taken the ball away an AFC-leading 25 times, while coughing it up 20 times. Turnovers loomed as the critical factor in all eight games: 16 of the Seahawks' 20 turnovers had come in their four losses.

For some reason, the mounting numbers against Knox only seemed to make him more energetic, more alive. Coming off a crushing loss, faced with a lengthening list of injuries, and staring at statistics that were bleak indications of more losses to come, he was . . . zestful. He came into his midweek press conference in a combative mood.

Jacob Green had only one sack over the last six games, that one coming against the Atlanta Falcons a month before. When asked about that, Knox painstakingly explained that often there were three defensive linemen rushing against five offensive linemen on pass plays. "But five guys cannot double three people, can they?" he asked. "That's mathematically impossible, isn't it? That means that one guy's got one-on-one, doesn't it? Does that make sense to you? Then one guy ought to get there once in a while. Shouldn't he? Well, that's how simple that equation is."

Simple as the equation was, it didn't answer the question, and Knox devoted most of the press conference to similar retreats into the fog. The NFL office had announced during the week that next season it would include anabolic steroids among the forbidden drugs it tested players for, and Knox, asked to comment, answered, "I don't think there's any place for steroid use or drug use, and . . . uh . . . how are they going to implement it?

Are they going to come around and test everybody? How do you determine who to test—because a guy's big? I mean, I don't understand how it's gonna be implemented. So are you saying they're gonna wait until July 21 or July 20 next year to test for it? Is that what you're saying? Is that 'cracking down' on steroid use? I don't know anything about it—I'm just asking these questions. These are questions you people ought to be asking."

We the people were more interested in asking about the condition of his team, though, and reporters went through the list of injured players, asking what each one's chances were of playing that coming Sunday. After four questions on four players, Knox started playing around again, until finally he got down to what really was on his mind—inconsistent play from all three of his team's units. The Seahawks' lack of athletic talent, he said, forced Seattle coaches to be better than more advantaged coaches by coming up with more brilliant schemes. Seattle players could only compete with their athletic betters by executing their assignments flawlessly, playing with more emotion, and making fewer mistakes than their opponents. "If we play as a team, and play team defense," Knox said, "we can get some people out, force them to go long field, we can reduce their scoring. You see, in Denver, in the Kansas City win, in the Cleveland win, and in the Atlanta win—that's the way we won the game. Good special teams, sound offense that did not commit major errors and turnovers, and a defense that bent a little bit but didn't break. And we won four games. The four losses, we turned the ball over offensively, we've given up easy plays defensively, and our special teams have not played well."

Mention of special teams recalled to Knox's mind the New Orleans game, and he grew more animated. "See, we had a chance to win a big football game against a good team, and we had a blocked field goal run back for a touchdown. How you can have everybody else going hard as they can go, you have one guy that's supposed to block inside, get a bump on him, it's not a great play—and for some reason we didn't make it. And a guy blocks it. Now the whole thing looks like all the wheels are coming off. See? Yet we lost a game by 1 point to a team that's 7-and-1."

His coachly facade fell away then, and he seemed to grow in depth and stature. The memory of Scholtz's mistake caused him to let his guard down for a moment, and the face of the one-dimensional man Knox strives so mightily to present to the public gave way to the genuinely troubled face of a full-fledged human being.

Before our very eyes, Bronco Nagurski was turning into King Lear.

"Coaches," Knox said softly, "go to their grave asking themselves, you see, with the last gasp of air that they have, 'Why didn't that guy just step inside and get his hand on that guy?' OK? When it's a veteran player who's been told that umpteen thousand times."

The room erupted in laughter, and Knox smiled the most natural smile I'd ever seen grace his face. "But that's how fragile the difference is between winning and losing if you do not have a dominant football team," he continued.

This proved to be one of my favorite moments of the season. I could see that Knox preferred the challenge of trying to win with a nondescript team to the easy task of winning with a dominant one. For a fleeting second, I saw that his question, intended to be rhetorical, had an answer too telling for him to dare being aware of what it was. And just as I was about to grasp the answer, it slipped out of mental reach. All I managed was the intuitive sense that it hinted at crippling weakness. From then on, my sojourn with the Seahawks became not so much a chronicling of their season as a search for tantalizing truth.

Once Knox's little consciousness-raising exercise was over, the week resumed its normal football course. For the first time in six weeks, Dave Krieg started practicing with the team again, taking a few snaps from center, lightly tossing a football, then retiring immediately to the training room for treatment. Bush and Mattes improved, and while Millard didn't, he spent the week insisting that he would be able to play on Sunday.

As things turned out, he wasn't able to play, but it was just as well. From the start, the game was a dud. On Norm Johnson's opening kickoff, Charger returner Anthony Miller was graciously ushered out to the San Diego 39 when the Seahawk defense opted against covering the left half of the field. However, a "5-yard" offensive facemask penalty moved the ball back to the Charger 25. The officials (who, it is worth mentioning, missed at least three illegal blocks on the play) never explained who committed the infraction, or how 39 minus 5 can equal 25. The opening play, featuring failings by offense, defense, and officials, set the tone for the day.

By the first quarter's 6:48 mark, there had been three fumbles. First came a third-down fumbled snap by San Diego quarterback Mark Malone, ending with a Charger recovery for a first down. Next came a third-down fumbled shotgun snap by Kelly Stouffer. The ball fell out of his hands and landed at his feet. When he bent to pick it up, it rocketed out of his hands again, disappearing among the battling bodies in front of him. Suddenly it came shooting back out of the mess, landing in the backfield. Grant Feasel—who now had more recovered fumbles on the season than Steve Largent had pass receptions—finally fell on it. Ruben Rodriguez then booted a 52-yard punt. And on first down, San Diego running back Gary

Anderson went happily charging into the line of scrimmage without bothering to bring the ball along. Since Malone didn't want it either, it was surrendered, by default, to a diving Jeff Bryant.

From there, it took only eight plays and 44 yards for the officials to join the fumbling in earnest.

Perhaps someone told them that Seattle cannot score touchdowns, particularly from inside their opponents' 20-yard line, and they understood the statement to mean that Seattle was not to be allowed to score touchdowns. Or perhaps they were discombobulated by a personnel move Knox had secretly made the day before.

In any event, after a first-and-10 pitchout play to John L. Williams netted 15 yards, Williams plowing his way through three would-be tacklers down to the Charger 6, Stouffer messed up his snap count, the team jumped offsides, and the Seahawks faced a first-and-goal at the San Diego 11. Once again, it seemed, the red zone ghosts were rising up to haunt them. As Seattle came to the line of scrimmage in shotgun formation, wide receiver Louis Clark, who had been on injured reserve from the start of the season, was lined up on the far right—the shotgun spot formerly occupied by Tommy Kane. Knox, disenchanted by Kane's stone-handed performance against New Orleans two weeks before, had diagnosed a "nagging groin injury" in Kane the day before the San Diego game and quietly put him on injured reserve, activating Clark. Now, at the snap, Stouffer took two quick steps and threw a soft timing pattern to the deep right corner of the end zone. Clark ran a fade route under it, turned, caught the ball, expertly touched both heels in bona fide payturf before falling out of bounds— and looked up in dismay to see field judge Don Hakes disallowing his touchdown.

There followed the obligatory interminable delay while video replay official Grover Klemmer stared blankly at his monitor before letting the call stand, albeit with one inexplicable difference: where Hakes had signaled that Clark caught the ball out of bounds, Klemmer ruled that he was in bounds, but that "possession had not been established." When that call was made, Largent broke into a St. Vitus' dance-like exercise, the purpose of which seemed to be the removal of his own head.

Two plays later, as they had six times in the last three games, the Seahawks settled for a field-goal attempt—which they made—and the teams then embarked upon a tiresome series of exchanges of possession, lasting 15 minutes, 24 seconds, and including four punts, one failed field-goal attempt, and all of five first downs. Finally, on second-and-eight at the Charger 23, Stouffer tried to beat the dead-zone jinx by scoring from outside the 20. Sending Brian Blades into the right corner of the end zone, he hit him with a breathtaking pass. Blades caught it, came down on the seat of his pants, slid out of bounds—and looked up in dismay...

Realizing that sideline patterns would get his team nowhere, Stouffer came back on the next play to throw another touchdown pass to Blades, this time with Blades breaking toward the goalpost. The referees, flummoxed, were forced to grant Seattle a touchdown.

Six plays later, the Chargers' Malone closed out the half by running over the line of scrimmage and throwing an interception. Thus the half closed with a penalty and a turnover on the same play, and some unforgettable statistics: one interception, five fumbles, nine penalties, six punts, one sack, and two phantom touchdowns.

The teams spent the second half showcasing such an array of weaknesses that decency—and possibly libel laws—prevents me from remembering what happened. Most of the watchable action took place midway through the third quarter, in the south end of the Kingdome press box. There, the advance scout for the Dallas Cowboys fell into a deep sleep, face down in his charts, and the scout for the Buffalo Bills—Seattle's next opponent—quietly gathered up his things and left. Watching him exit, Raider scout Gene Moore, chuckling, said, "I guess he didn't see anything that scared him."

The one memorable phase of the second half came midway through the fourth quarter, on a 40-yard Blades sideline catch that, upon further review by the helpless Mr. Klemmer, was deemed an incompletion. Unfortunately, since the referees on the field had ruled the pass complete, ball and chains had been moved downfield and none of the officials remembered where the ball had been. Six minutes and three tries later, they finally found the line of scrimmage from which Stouffer had completed his incompletion. Knox, who had spent most of the game in a state of near-apoplexy, was by then thoroughly resigned. As the Kingdome cameras focused on him, lip-readers watched him saying to Red Cashion, "You fucked up."

Upon further review, Klemmer determined that what Knox actually said was, "With your work today, you have raised the craft of officiating to the level of high art, and I feel privileged to have been here on the same field with you."

Perhaps the willful blindness of the officials was an attempt at injecting an element of suspense into what promised to be a dreadful game. By taking away a few Seattle touchdowns, they must have thought, they could turn a poorly played blowout into a game suspenseful enough to disguise the quality of play. To kick off the fourth quarter, San Diego abetted the officials by covering 52 yards in four sudden plays to score a touchdown, pulling themselves within 3 points of Seattle. Twelve plays after that, the officials nullified Blades's 40-yard catch, thereby keeping the game's outcome in doubt—at least theoretically—a little while longer.

But the officials were misguided in thinking that it is suspense that attracts fans to football. Suffering through the second half of that game, alleviating my boredom and mitigating my outrage by trying to find meaning in football, I decided that Americans are drawn to football because each play is a primitive, accessible, little allegorical representation of their own lives. Every play, whether pass or run, unfolds in the same way. At the snap of the ball, an opening is forced somewhere in the defense, so that the ball can either be thrown or carried through it. The opening, though, is there for only a split second before the defense forces it closed again. It is the mission of the quarterback or running back to see the opening and decide instantly whether he can hit it in time. Under intense pressure, convinced that the right decision will bring glory and the wrong one disaster, he confronts his options, then acts. It is the same little drama we play out thousands of times every day as we race against life's clock, deciding anxiously on everything from what to put on in the morning to when to marry to whether or not to open a new retail store on the East Coast.

Watching the seams in the defense open and instantly close, I thought of a knife wound closing and healing itself the instant the knife is withdrawn. It was a perfect image of the high-stakes nonsense that is football. Each play requires an absurd expenditure of excessive effort and anxiety either to enhance or retard the progress of a tiny leather parcel full of air. The procedure, repeated endlessly every Sunday before the adoring gaze of thousands—sometimes millions—has the same earthshaking-yet-pointless quality of daily human routine.

Down on the field, Curt Warner angled out of the backfield, crossed the goal line, turned, looked back at Stouffer, and raised his hands, forming a little oval before his face. Knox's design was working to perfection: There was no defender following Warner. The ball, perfectly thrown, spiraled into Warner's waiting grip, then bounced out. Exasperated, Warner fell to the turf, lay on his back, looked up at the spectacular roof overhead, and asked himself yet again, "Why are we out here?" And yet again, he answered, "Because we're dumb." Then he struggled back to his feet. Time to get it on again.

Mercifully, the game ended. Seattle had managed a 17–14 win at home against a team sporting the NFL's 27th-ranked offense and 23rd-ranked defense. Small wonder that the Seahawk locker room afterward looked and felt more like an emergency aid station for earthquake survivors than a winning team's locker room. The few players still present when reporters were allowed in had little to say, and what little they said was largely apologetic.

The officials had done Knox one favor, at least. In making a fiasco of the game, they turned him into a sympathetic figure—a victim of bureaucratic bungling—rather than that most unsympathetic of figures, the coach of a bad team. The game's controversial calls were a welcome distraction, for they allowed reporters and coaches alike to forget about the game and concentrate on the crimes of the officials.

Knox and Steve Moore made their feelings cryptically clear. "Well, you see," Knox said, "I've been very much in favor of the instant replay review. And I've championed that. You see? But I don't know who they're putting up there [in the official's replay booth] or what. You know, you're struggling offensively and you don't get those, when you should have them. . . The official on the field made the call, and now you get into whether it's conclusive or not conclusive, those two words, you get into semantics and it really becomes very troubled . . . I could be very funny, but I really don't feel like being funny today."

Apparently, he had an instant change of heart, serving up a comic image to his audience. "You could take a big red glove," he suggested, "with the biggest thumb you ever saw in your life, and you could have a guy holding it up like this, or down like this—either 'up,' it stands as is on the field, or 'down,' it comes back."

Moore opted for a more subtle form of humor, resorting to the overdiplomatic euphemism when asked to evaluate Stouffer's play. "There were four clear touchdowns," he said, "of which we got credit for two. We cannot control plays not counting. The execution allows it to be a touchdown, but for whatever reason it isn't called a touchdown, and so from an evaluation standpoint we have to say that that's on target." Asked outright if he thought the officials blew the touchdown calls, Moore gave his questioners a long, evocative look that set off a round of laughter. "Well, I'm not gonna say that, no," he said at last. "I would just say the same thing, that you evaluate what you saw. What'd you see? I saw the same thing you saw."

The replay official, Moore was told, had ruled that Clark had been juggling the ball on his non-touchdown. "Well, that's the easiest thing in the world to say," Moore answered, then paused again. "Now please don't get me started on those guys!" Then he pointed out something that had gone unnoticed amidst the boredom and the controversy. "If those two touchdowns that Kelly threw and completed that appeared to be touchdowns, if they counted, and if the Blades catch on the sideline . . . you give him a couple of those plays, and his performance looks much better."

Indeed it did. Instead of going 14 for 28, with two touchdowns and 109 yards, Stouffer would have finished 17 for 25, with three touchdowns and 143 yards. He would have been seen to have made impressive progress, to be evolving as a more versatile passer. But Seattle reporters would have had little to write about—except, possibly, speculative pieces on a developing Seattle quarterback controversy. When teams in such sorry shape as these two go head-to-head, it is left to the officials to supply the game's principal entertainment.

But on my way back up to the press box, I realized that the follies had been less entertaining than enlightening. The game was an example of the misguided nature of the NFL's video replay system. The system was inaugurated in 1986, after years of pressure from fans and sportswriters who saw, week after week, television replays showing that officials on the field had made drastic mistakes. Reasoning that up-to-date technological advances could reduce the effect of human error on the game, thereby presenting fans with a purer product, the NFL finally caved in to public pressure, inaugurating a one-year experiment with video replay review.

The system was to be limited to ball and line calls only (whether a ball was caught or trapped, whether or not a receiver came down with both feet in bounds, whether a runner's knee was down before he fumbled), leaving judgment calls (personal fouls, pass interference, offsides, and so on) to the field officials. Ideally, reviews would be called for only by the replay official when he thought he saw an obvious error made on the field—although field officials could also ask for review of a call they had doubts about.

Extended through the 1988 season after its first year, the system has created far more controversy than it has resolved. Week after week, fans see television replays showing that the video replay official has either made a drastic mistake of his own or compounded one made by the field officials. All video review has done is show the limitations of technology. Often two video views of the same play, taken from different angles, appear to show different results. Often, video replays show nothing conclusive. And just as often, they appear to everyone but the replay official to reverse a bad call. Even worse, they frequently confirm a good call, only to allow the replay official to misinterpret it—thereby introducing an error into a situation where none would have existed without him.

And finally, there is the problem of the field official's whistle. Against the Rams, the Seahawks recovered a fumble that the referees did not see. Up it went to the replay booth, where the official decreed that Seattle had indeed recovered a Los Angeles fumble and was entitled to the ball. On came the Seahawk offensive unit and the Ram defensive unit. In came the officials to halt play. Off went the Seahawk offensive unit and Ram defensive unit, and on came their opposite numbers. The explanation: The whistle had blown the play dead before the ball was recovered. This sort of play, with the same absurd result, was staged all over the league during the season.

The NFL issues statistics at the end of each season purporting to show that the system has little impact on the game and that what impact it has is good. According to league figures, there were 35,000 or so plays in 224 regular-season games in 1986. Video officials reviewed 374 controversial calls, and reversed the field officials only 38 times. In 1987, over 210 games, there were 490 calls reviewed, of which 57 were reversed. At the very least, the league reasons, the low number of reversals confirms the competence of the field officials, and the reversals—few as they are— simply make the game better.

But I am convinced that the system has made officials careless and hesitant. Knowing they will be reviewed, they either second-guess themselves or make hastier judgments. This impression is impossible to prove, and NFL officials deny it is true, but the fact remains that reviewable calls jumped from 1.6 per game in 1986 to 2.3 per game in 1987. And if Seattle's season so far was any indication, they would jump even higher in 1988. The course of modern human events being what it is, it won't be too long before every play of every game is being reviewed for one reason or another.

The league also doesn't release the only statistic that really counts in evaluating the system: number of mistakes made by the video replay official. The next Tuesday, when Knox's league-mandated tapes of the game arrived at NFL headquarters, he asked league officers to review the three controversial plays. They called him back the same day, to tell him that all three calls had been wrong. On two of the calls, the field officials had been wrong and the replay official had upheld them. On the third, the field officials had been right and the replay official had overruled them.

What the NFL needs to do is scrap the system. What it will probably do instead is add another review tier . . . then another . . . and another . . . until the league resembles the American court system, with players and coaches taking their case through layer upon layer of appeal.

Author Manqué!
Author Manqué!

All of a sudden this guy sitting in the row in front of me, Edgar Marsalla, laid this terrific fart. It was a very crude thing to do, in chapel and all, but it was also quite amusing. Old Marsalla. He damn near blew the roof off . . . We tried to get old Marsalla to rip off another one, right while old Thurmer was making his speech. but he wasn't in the right mood.

—J.D. Salinger, *The Catcher in the Rye*

I left the Kingdome after the San Diego game trying to make sense of the videocy that had nearly undone Knox's efforts. Somehow, as he moved purposefully through this season, he kept winding up with an exploding cigar in his mouth. His professional life was dedicated to rational thinking and planning, yet weird things kept happening to him—player contract squabbles, injuries, drug suspensions, bad bounces, unexplainable player lapses, fits of official blindness . . . And still he slogged on, convinced, against mounting evidence, that logic and reason would prevail.

I couldn't think of anything in American culture so seriocomically intriguing since Buster Keaton.

The video replays seemed to be just one more proof of the misbegotten nature of Knox's quest. For years he had championed the replay system as a way of making football more rational by reducing the incidence of human error in a game. He pointed out, quite reasonably, that a bad call could cost a player or even a coach his job, that coaches and players who lose get fired, and that more than one game over the years has been lost because of a bad call. Then along comes a game in which three of the worst calls in sporting history—all going against Knox—are made by the video official who owes his very existence to Knox's impassioned efforts.

It had the unmistakable reek of poetic justice. In lobbying for video review, Knox had tried to buck the paradoxical nature of football. It is a game in which men try to control a misshapen ball's irrational, unpredictable bounce by means of a rational, systematic plan of attack.

195

Knox himself, to judge from his two favorite aphorisms, is something of a paradox. On the one hand, he professes to believe that "luck is the residue of design," that through ingenuity, hard work, and careful planning, a coach can control the workings of chance. Like the Raiders, he believes in controlling the bounce of the ball.

Yet his other favorite maxim is the more oft-repeated "play the hand you're dealt." A coach content to play the hand he's dealt concedes ultimate control to the dealer. The saying indicates that Knox would rather be dealt to than seize the dealership.

While I spent the evening mulling this over, the Dealer was further stacking the deck against Knox. Cornerback Patrick Hunter left the Kingdome in his Mercedes Benz 300E and started cruising around town, stopping hither and yon to have a few beers. For some reason, he felt that the failure to lose to San Diego was cause for celebration. Driving home around 1am, Hunter tried to take a corner near Seahawk headquarters too fast, and shot off the road. Still at the wheel, he flew some 20 feet through the air before landing on a steep bank, rolling over, and settling, upright, on railroad tracks. He was now snugly tucked into his seat by the car's inflatable airbag.

Slowly he extricated himself, took stock of his pain, and took a last, loving look at the shapeless $52,000 object that had once been his car. Then, properly conditioned athlete that he was, he simply went home.

Just say, "What the fuck."

The matter didn't end there, however. The car was found at 7:30 that morning, and Hunter, promptly unmasked as its owner, was summoned back to the scene of the accident by Kirkland police. There he met police officer E.A. Rhode, who saw immediately that Hunter was hurt, and called an ambulance.

Meanwhile, at Seahawk headquarters, all anyone knew was that Hunter didn't show up for his 12:30pm meeting. Finally the call came, informing Knox that Hunter was hospitalized and undergoing tests. By the next day, his doctors had diagnosed a lacerated kidney, and decreed that he would miss two or three weeks of play.

After informing the press of Hunter's accident, Knox turned his attention to the officiating of football games, putting forth a typically Knoxian proposal for improving the video monitoring of the game's calls. "Maybe what we need to do," he said, "is go out here and hire some guys that have been watching a lot of TV." His audience started laughing, but he apparently was serious. "Listen to me for a minute now," he insisted, "guys that are interested in football, that want to make the $600 per game, or whatever they're paying those guys, and we'll help unemployment in this country, and get some couch potatoes, guys that watch television . . . and it'll be simpler than we're making it."

He was running through his modest red-mitt proposal again now, and his audience was in stitches. But ludicrous as his couch-potato proposition sounded, it really was no different from a coach's search for any kind of talent. When a coach fills out a roster, after all, it is with specialists. Each player at each position is there because he has traits that meet the unique demands of his position. Some tiny physical or psychological attribute has dictated that he be a cornerback instead of a wide receiver, or a fullback instead of a linebacker, or a place-kicker instead of a quarterback. Just as Knox would search among people who had kicked a lot of footballs when looking for a kicker, so, logically, he would search among people who had watched a lot of television when looking for someone to cross-examine referees by watching video replays of their work.

Even the mitt idea, which Knox was replaying for laughs, made a certain amount of sense. More than one attempt by a replay official to reverse a field judge's call had been stymied by stadium noise. Touchdowns intended by the replay official to be disallowed had been allowed by field officials who misunderstood his pronouncement through their headsets. "See," said Knox, "when it's done, you have no recourse. And it's little comfort the next week when you call the league office, and they say that this was good, or that was a bad call, and it cost you a ball game."

"So they said those calls were bad?" someone asked.

"Well, I'm not allowed to say," Knox answered, "but certainly you could read into . . . " He was interrupted by laughter. "What goes between the league office and our people here is confidential, but I'm just saying that if those completions, which were legal"—more laughter—" . . . that's all I'm gonna say about it."

By now, he had more pressing matters on his mind. His next opponent was the Buffalo Bills, with an NFL-best 8–1 record and the AFC's fourth-ranked total offense and second-ranked total defense. Since Knox's departure from Buffalo for Seattle after the strike-shortened 1982 season, the Bills had gone 8–8, 2–14, 2–14, 4–12, and 7–8. Since those years coincided with talent-deep college drafts, they had added some of football's best athletes to their roster. With the first two picks in the 1985 draft, they selected Bruce Smith, a player blessed with the best combination of speed and strength of any defensive end in the league, and Derrick Burroughs, now one of the league's top cornerbacks. Starting linebacker Shane Conlan and starting right cornerback Nate Odomes had been their first two picks of the 1987 draft. Oklahoma State standout running back Thurman Thomas was their first 1988 draft pick, and linebacker Cornelius Bennett, an outstanding player who had refused to sign with the Indianapolis Colts when drafted two seasons before, had come to Buffalo by way of the complicated Eric Dickerson trade among the Bills, the Colts, and the Los Angeles Rams.

The Bills roster, in short, was packed with talent—a legacy of the NFL's parity system. "You see," said Knox, "they've got a lot of number-one, number-two draft choices, and they've been building it for five years, and they've been in a position in the drafts to get outstanding football players. Sometimes, to get outstanding football players, you have to be 2–14 or something. And when that happens, usually the coach is not around. And they've been through three coaches—they're on their third coach now."

At Seattle, Knox had taken a different tack. Rather than lose to get winning players, he had done too well to be entitled to the draft's top athletes. Each year, he drafted low, then combed the league's waiver list to find players to shore up his roster. "We had specific needs," he said, "and we weren't able to satisfy those needs during the draft or with free agents. So we were able to get some players that have helped us without giving up draft choices for them and mortgaging our future."

Every team has to choose one or the other course, either going from 12–4 to 4–12 and back again—as Buffalo had done for nearly all 28 years of its history—or taking Seattle's course under Knox by consistently finishing in the midrange—8–8, or 9–7, or 10–6—and hope to hit the playoffs when your team's on a roll. In penalizing winners by assigning them lower draft picks, the league allows no other choice. And Knox, ostensibly because he feared being the 2–14 coach who is fired just as the athletes he has won by losing join his team, opted consistently for the harder course—trying to win it all, against daunting odds, every season.

That choice made coaching and acquiring talent a greater challenge. It meant that Knox, because of his opponents' mounting advantages, either had to be more skilled than his peers or had to work harder at finding a way to beat them.

Nothing would highlight the consequences of Knox's approach more than the confrontation in the Buffalo game between Seattle offensive tackle Ron Mattes and Buffalo defensive end Bruce Smith. Both players were drafted in the same year—1985. Mattes was a seventh-round pick, Smith the first player taken. While Mattes had spent his first season on injured reserve, being converted from defensive to offensive lineman, Smith spent his first season tearing up the league, being voted AFC Defensive Rookie of the Year by the NFL Players Association. Now Mattes was a journeyman tackle, the youngest of Seattle's starting offensive linemen, and Smith was a superman. Three of Seattle's first four drives against Buffalo would be ended by Smith. Twice he would sack Stouffer on third down, and the third time, locked in battle with guard Edwin Bailey, he would suddenly crumple when a frustrated Mattes dove at his legs, blocking him just below the back of his knees. The chop-block is potentially career-ending, if not crippling, for its victim, and has been outlawed by the league. The resultant 15-yard penalty would wipe out a 29-yard Stouffer completion to Brian Blades, turning a first-and-10 at the Buffalo 41 into a second-and-15 at the Seattle 15.

Judging from that mismatch, Buffalo coach Marv Levy had the easiest job in the world.

Knox seemed to revel in the challenges posed by fielding lesser athletes. While he professed envy at Levy's depth and breadth of talent, he also seemed happier and more energetic without it. As so often this season, he was far more given to bantering and telling jokes during the pre-Buffalo week than he had been during any of the weeks he had been coming off a great game or preparing for a weak opponent. Every week, either because of what had happened to him the game before or looked about to happen to him in the upcoming game, he always managed to find a way to portray himself as the disadvantaged competitor. And the more successful he was at that, the cheerier he was.

Perhaps that is why he had not seemed particularly upset at the loss of Patrick Hunter. By trying to take flight in his Mercedes, Hunter had merely solidified Knox's hold on the role of underdog.

As Hunter was fading from view, somewhere in the Seattle area a ghost was coming to life. After being cut at the end of preseason, then re-signed by Seattle for the season opener against Denver, then released again after that game, then picked up by the Kansas City Chiefs for two games, then cut again, disappearing for six weeks, David Hollis was back in a Seattle uniform. "It's just the breaks you have to prepare yourself for in this league," he said that week. "I had to put a little pride behind when they wanted me to come back, but I really wanted to come back and play. I'm just glad to be here."

He was pressed into service as backup nickel back and backup kick returner to Randall Morris. And, not entirely for Hollis's benefit alone, he and the rest of the return team put in extra time that week going over the same kickoff return play again and again after each day's practice. Two kickoff returners would stand side by side at the Seattle goal line. When the ball was kicked, four blockers, retreating as the ball sailed back to the receiver, would form a wall 10 yards in front of where the ball was caught, then would surge forward up the hashmarks, splitting into groups of two as they made contact with the onrushing defenders, pushing them to the sides to open a corridor for the ball carrier. Then the returner without the ball would precede the ball carrier through the seam, hitting the second-line defender who had stepped in to fill the gap, and pushing him toward the inside of the field as the ball carrier swept past him on the outside.

It was a simple diagram, notable only because special-teams coach Rusty Tillman had his charges running through it so many times. The number of repetitions meant that Tillman had spotted a weakness on Buffalo's film and was rehearsing a way to exploit it.

When Seattle took the opening kickoff that Sunday, it looked as if Buffalo had decided to follow Tillman's script to the letter. As Randall Morris took the kick at the left hashmark on the Seattle 7-yard line, teammates Ken Clarke, Mike Tice, Chris Godfrey, and Tommy Agee dropped back to the 17, turned, and surged upfield ahead of him. Exactly as scripted, they split off in pairs, each player taking a defender with him. Bobby Joe Edmonds cut across and turned upfield in front of Morris, ran through the seam created by his four teammates, met Buffalo linebacker Don Graham—who had come up to fill the gap—and pushed him toward the inside of the field.

For nearly a full second, everything on the field froze, and there was the same huge hole I had seen opened repeatedly on the practice field. The play had gone so according to plan that watching it was like watching a 22-member drill team flawlessly execute an elaborate slam-dance routine. For the first time, I understood the allure of coaching, in both my head and my heart. The possibility it offered of creating and orchestrating systems of such complexity, tension, and high violence was nothing less than the temptation to be a god. Tillman, I imagined, must have been in near-ecstasy as he watched the play unfold exactly as he had directed.

All this passed through my mind in less time than it takes a seam in football to open and close. For no sooner did the microcosm according to Rusty Tillman take form on the field than Morris, Lucifer-like, turned away from the opening Tillman had so lovingly created for him. As he cut inside, there followed several dire consequences, the most immediate being that Graham, blocked away from where Morris was supposed to have gone, now was being blocked toward him. Graham made an easy, uncontested tackle at the 26.

With that single move, Morris had brought down a universe.

The mismove was your basic omen. The game was to prove winnable—Buffalo played far below the potential its 8–1 record and blue-chip roster indicated—but the Seahawks, managing somehow to stay within striking distance of the Bills until fewer than 3 minutes remained in the game, kept self-destructing. They would have lost the game even with no opponent lined up opposite them.

Still, the day proved to be inspiring. Whenever a play was a fraction of an inch from being success or failure, it would succeed if it were Buffalo's play, and fail if it were Seattle's. Seattle would lose 13–3; convert on only one of 10 third downs, while Buffalo converted on seven of 15; gain 145 yards to Buffalo's 336; and have the ball for 25:15, while Buffalo had it for 34:45, or nearly forever. Yet, strangely, the game felt close almost until the end.

Kelly Stouffer's performance, for example, was both better and worse than his statistics. He completed only 10 of 22 passes, for an average gain per pass of only 2.7 yards, but two long completions—a 29-yard pass to Brian Blades and a 24-yard screen pass to John L. Williams—were nullified by penalties. A third—an 18-yard pass, thrown under pressure as Stouffer ran at breakneck speed away from Buffalo defensive end Art Still, and caught by an airborne Steve Largent as he was being hit by two defenders—came on third-and-19. And yes, the fourth-down quarterback sneak that followed came up inches short.

The nullified screen pass to Williams was a classic example of football alchemy, in which a nanosecond is magically transformed into acres of precious real estate. The play was one of Seattle's myriad versions of its John L. Williams screen play. In this one, Stouffer rolled deep and to his right, with Williams freezing at his backfield position as a blocker. Seattle's three interior linemen, after diving at their defenders as if blocking for a running play, jumped up and ran toward the left sideline, and Williams, after delaying, curled out after them, coming up directly behind center Blair Bush. As Buffalo's rushers closed on him, Stouffer turned and threw back across the field to Williams. Bush turned and took the first defensive back he saw, hitting him almost at the same instant the ball hit Williams's hands. Unfortunately, Bush hit his man just before the ball and Williams made contact, with the result that what would have been a solid block was now pass interference. So instead of first-and-10 at the Buffalo 43, Seattle faced first-and-20 at the Seattle 23.

Meanwhile, Buffalo quarterback Jim Kelly, one of the league's rising stars, was, in Seattle defensive coordinator Tom Catlin's words, "throwing the hell out of the football. Late in the game, Mel Jenkins was right on the coverage, and he practically reached it, and we thought he was gonna knock the ball down, and he didn't get it and the other guy did, and the guy was diving . . . just good throws."

That play came on third-and-five at the Seattle 27. Four plays later, Buffalo's Scott Norwood kicked the field goal that put the game out of Seattle's quasi-reach.

The Bills' final field-goal drive was set up by a botched Buffalo punt that wreaked havoc with another of Tillman's elegant designs. Because punter John Kidd was exceptionally fast this day at getting rid of the ball, Tillman opted to have his return team retreat at the snap and set up downfield in a blocking configuration rather than rush the punter. Punting from the Seattle 48, Kidd flubbed, sending a feeble 33-yard effort downfield. As Bobby Joe Edmonds raced over to try to field it, he yelled "Poison! Poison! Poison!" to Nesby Glasgow, one of the teammates running downfield to set up as a blocker. Glasgow, with his back to the punter and his eyes on the man he was supposed to block, never saw the ball. It hit the ground and his heel at exactly the same time, shooting upfield 18 yards on one perfect hop into the arms of Buffalo linebacker Ray Bentley, and Buffalo had a new first down.

Tillman afterward was as close to speechless as he is capable of getting. "You do everything you can to avoid that situation," he said. "But football's not an exact science. We had a call—Bobby was calling, 'Poison!'—and Nesby heard it, and he looked, and the ball was right there. It was a short punt . . . and we're very aware of those kinds of things. I mean, that's just . . . you know, that's something that happens in football. And Nesby's a smart player, he's a very smart player. It . . . it . . . I mean, he *knows!* And he's the guy that you'd want in that situation, you know what I'm saying? . . . It was the only bad kick the guy had all day . . . "

Lost in the depressing shadow of the final score were some of Seattle's best performances of the season. On Buffalo's last kickoff, Tillman walked over to David Hollis on the sidelines. "Do you remember the return play?" he asked. "I sure do!" Hollis answered. "Are you ready?" "I sure am!" "OK—you're in." Hollis charged onto the field, determined, as he said afterward, "to go out there and try to make something happen. To show that I'm still hungry and I still want to run hard as I can and make something happen and give our offense good field position." The kick sailed back to Hollis at the 13, and he ran up the left hashmark behind his four blockers. At the 25, the wall split into two, and Edmonds, cutting in front of Hollis, took on the linebacker filling the gap. Hollis timed his burst perfectly, darted through the hole, and flew out to the Seattle 43 before being brought down. It was Seattle's best return of the season.

Dave Wyman, whose play had grown steadily better and more emotional since his benching in Cleveland, was everywhere during the game, doing everything. He made two tackles on special teams, five on defense, had four assists, half of Seattle's only sack, forced a fumble (recovered by fumble-recovery specialist Grant Feasel), and broke up a 48-yard pass from Jim Kelly to running back Ronnie Harmon at the Seattle goal line.

That play was a highlight-film classic. It went exactly as Buffalo planned. Kelly rolled right, evading the Seattle rush, and Buffalo's receivers flooded the left side of the field, leaving the speedy Harmon one-on-one with the heavy-footed Wyman along the right sideline. An offense can ask for nothing better than isolating a running back on a linebacker. Harmon had a good three-step lead on Wyman when Wyman realized, to his horror, what was happening. Off he lumbered, catching up just as Harmon went airborne for what would have been a touchdown catch. Somehow, Wyman batted the ball away and earned the day's biggest ovation. "If I'd been Catholic," he said afterward, "I'd have crossed myself. I had no idea how deep we were, I was just running as hard as I could, and looking out of the corner of my eye—sometimes I have trouble looking back and finding the ball. Man, by the time the ball got there, I was so tired, I had about this much vertical leap." He held up his thumb and forefinger, nearly touching. "It looked like somebody nailed my feet to the floor."

It did indeed. But, *Knoxiste* that he was, Wyman found a way to win the play.

The Wyman/Bosworth duo at inside linebacker is the two-headed center-beast of Knox's Seahawk Defense of the Future. Close friends, the two constitute as odd a couple as any Neil Simon could conjure up. Wyman is a second-round draft choice who has to play over his head to survive in the pros. Bosworth, who came out of college the same year as Wyman, was the nation's top defensive player (depending on how you feel about Cornelius Bennett) and had a starting job waiting for him the day he showed up for work in the NFL. Wyman is shy, Bosworth brash. Wyman is humble, Bosworth a braggart. Wyman is a slob, Bosworth is fussy. Wyman is flannel shirts and blue jeans, Bosworth is a fop.

Both began their Seahawk careers in the 1987 training camp, and the two have followed almost exactly opposite career paths. Wyman languished, hurt, at the bottom of Seattle's depth chart, was traded—only to have the trade voided when he failed his physical—then came back to Seattle, was nearly released, and then returned from the injured reserve list to fight his way into a starting position at the beginning of the next season. Bosworth, on the other hand, had so inflated his reputation through carefully contrived outrageousness and shrewd self-promotion in college that by the time he finally arrived in the NFL, anything he could have done on the field would have been a letdown. By struggling, rookielike, at his position, he impressed fans as a bust. The pinnacle of his pro career was the signing of his contract.

Yet for all their differences, the two are constantly drawn to one another. They have been training-camp roommates, and they live next door to one another during the season. Each resorts to the other for consolation during times of stress. On the practice field, they are inseparable, talking football ceaselessly between plays and on the sideline, and lining up side-by-side for sprint drills. During the week, they are often the last two players to leave team headquarters, the two of them lifting weights late into the evening. I often saw Wyman doing something that no one else can get away with: issuing moral instructions to Bosworth on his language, on his appearance, on his comportment during games . . . And not once did I see Bosworth do anything other than accept his admonishments in silence.

These two are a football yin and yang, complements rather than opposites. Only when seen in the light given off by the other can either one be fully understood.

Their respective positions during the Buffalo game served as a telling symbol not only of the difference in status between them, but also of the hybrid nature of the NFL product—a cross between serious athletic competition and Hollywood revue. One was evolving into a solid, competent football player worthy of starting at a key position for a Super Bowl contender. The best you could say about the other was that he was Kahoutek the Barbarian. Down on the field now, I could see the uncelebrated one throwing his body—heart and soul—into every play, emerging as a prime cause of his team's ability to stay nearly even with a superior opponent. Yet he was ignored by the camera, which constantly sought out the other, the celebrity, standing useless on the sideline.

While Wyman, unnoticed, spent the game applying bruises to his body, Bosworth—decked out in trademark Gargoyle shades and typically telegenic, flashy, fashion-forward attire—moved down the sideline, carefully positioning himself far enough away from his teammates to give television cameras an unobstructed view of the Boz. For much of the game, he had the same faded, flickering look of teammates from earlier in the season who eventually had disappeared entirely. The difference, with him, was that occasionally he would effulge without warning, stand there in glorious living color for a few seconds, then fade again. It took me half the game to figure out that his shinings forth were an unconscious response to the focusing of TV cameras on him from various vantage points in the stadium.

I have always been amazed at the disproportionate attention focused on Bosworth at the expense of the Dave Wymans of the world. Never have I known of an athlete celebrated so much off the field while doing so little on it. More than halfway through his second season with Seattle, Bosworth had yet to establish himself as a reliable professional player. Yet even at games in which he didn't play, he drew the most notice. In the *Seattle Times*, for example, the day after this game, one of the two largest pictures on the game would be of Bosworth standing on the sidelines.

Ever since his arrival, the spotlight has been so focused on him that the Seattle franchise has come across as "Brian Bosworth and the Seattle Seahawks" to the rest of the nation. During his rookie season, television's

pregame hype was always Bosworth hype—even thou₁
would go on to have little discernible impact on the g
This theme reached a nadir of sorts on Seattle's first ₁
Football" appearance (a November 9 game against ₁
during which ABC, to the accompaniment of cooing by play-by-play man Aı
Michaels, broadcast boyhood pictures of Bosworth—a particularly pointless
gesture in the midst of the 30–14 drubbing the celebrity and his entourage
were suffering at the time.

Three weeks later, Seattle hosted the Los Angeles Raiders on another
"Monday Night" game. Hypemasters went bananas, billing it as a battle
between "Bo and the Boz"—Bo being Bo Jackson, a powerful outfield-
er/running back who joined the Raiders late in the season after his obligations to baseball's Kansas City Royals were fulfilled. As with much Boz
hype, the actual battle was a bust: Jackson rushed for 221 yards, scored
three touchdowns, and led his team to a 37–14 win. His third touchdown
had been a run up the middle, culminating in an absolute flattening, at the
goal line, of Bosworth. Jackson blasted through the Boz as if he were one of
those paper curtains John Madden runs through in Lite Beer commercials.

Any self-respecting athlete would have been humiliated and would have
disappeared after the game. Bosworth, however, had a face to sell. Knowing that postgame television cameras would be broadcasting Jackson's
image across the nation, Bosworth sought him out on the field. Standing
beside Jackson rather than in front of him, Bosworth leaned over until their
heads were nearly touching. Then, perfectly positioned for the cameras, he
stood there whispering endearments in Jackson's ear.

If photo opportunities were quarterbacks, Seattle would have won two
Super Bowls by now.

It first occurred to me that human lives are directed by something other
than pure chance when Bosworth ended up in Seattle. The Seahawks had
to beat 37–1 odds to win the Boz lottery. Their doing so amounted to the
exile of an inflated, headline-hungry ego to a corner of the country where
people go to disappear rather than to seek fame and fortune. If Dante had
included a circle for egomaniacs in his Inferno, it would have been modeled
after the Pacific Northwest.

Born in Oklahoma City, Oklahoma, in 1965, Bosworth moved with his
family to Irving, Texas, in early childhood. There, playing tight end and
linebacker for Irving High School, he excelled enough at football to attract
college recruiters from all over the country. By his last season at the University of Oklahoma, he was college football's most celebrated player, in
the national sports news almost constantly either for thoroughly laying
waste to an opponent or for saying something offensive. *Sports Illustrated*

established Bosworth's reputation as a sporting wit and bon vivant with a controversial cover story packed full of bizarre remarks and anecdotes, the most memorable of which was Bosworth's statement that he liked to spit "loogies" into opponents' faces. The story made "the Boz" a household name synonymous either with clever irreverence or unspeakable immaturity, depending upon the reader's level of intelligence.

Bosworth's college career ended on a scandalous note. He tested positive for steroid use and was banned from his team's season-ending Orange Bowl appearance. He spent the game in sideline exile, stalking before the cameras in a T-shirt emblazoned, "NCAA: National Communists Against Athletes."

From the beginning of his Seattle career, Bosworth has been an enigma. During his rookie year, in person and out of uniform, he was soft-spoken, civil, and thoughtful. In print and on television, he was bizarre, mercurial, and—to all appearances—barely in control of himself.

Watching him during his rookie season, I decided that his on-field persona was an alter ego. He struck me as masculinity's answer to Olympics runner Florence Griffith-Joyner. Joyner, by means of extremely long, painted fingernails, extravagant hair, and running costumes ranging from colorful, one-legged leotards to transparent, lacy unitards, would transform herself before track meets into an exaggerated cartoon superheroine called Flashy Flo. Bosworth, by means of a similar ritual, would transform himself into a caffeinated superhero called the Boz. He would apply war paint to the shaved sides of his head and fashion the hair on his crown into a mane reminiscent of those worn by Mohawk warriors. Then he would work himself into a ferocious rage, ingesting massive doses of caffeine pills, and take to the battlefield roaring like a bull.

It didn't work for him the way it did for Griffith-Joyner, though, and Bosworth suffered through a relatively nondescript rookie season. He returned for the '88 season a more civilized player. Gone were the war paint and the public pregame posturing. He was garrulous and friendly again with local reporters—for about three weeks. Then, when excerpts from his forthcoming autobiography (*The Boz: Confessions of a Modern Anti-Hero*) started appearing, and reporters came to him for clarification of some of the book's scandalous assertions, Bosworth clammed up again.

For good reason. The book, intended as a combination autobiography, exposé of college football, and outpouring of wisdom, is instead an exposé of Bosworth as a lonely, insecure boy hiding behind a manly facade of bluster and physical prowess. It also exposes him as an unimaginative, greedy good ol' boy whose every move is driven not by superstition, as Bosworth claims, or by ritual, or by the search for power, but by self-promotion. The Boz is not an alter ego; it is a commodity, packaged and promoted like beer or deodorant.

Never have I struggled so hard to get through a book so easy to read. Reading it is like being subjected to a non-stop, three-hour harangue by a spoiled 16-year-old. It can be broken down into three parts: supposed exposé of college corruption, rationalization, and unintended self-portrait.

The "exposé" of the Oklahoma football program is most noticeable. A series of anecdotes (all of them, doubtless, containing a kernel of truth) about illegal alumni largesse, player excesses, drug use, and moral anarchy, much of it is exaggerated for the sole purpose of jacking up book sales. The apparent intent, which eventually was realized beyond even Bosworth's wildest dreams, was for an allegation from the book to hit the papers, causing a scandal and generating reams of free publicity for *The Boz.*

Typical is Bosworth's retelling of an incident in which an Oklahoma running back, angered at being hit with a snowball, stepped out on his balcony and fired a few pistol shots into the air. In Bosworth's colorful version, the pistol shots become "about a hundred and fifty rounds out of an Uzi machine gun."

Makes better copy.

What is most interesting about Bosworth's exposé is its way of consistently setting the author apart from his fellow sinners. While decrying his teammates' taking of lavish gifts from alumni, Bosworth justifies his own receipt of them with the argument that he is an unpaid star bringing in millions to the university. He asserts that virtually everyone on the Oklahoma team is a steroid abuser, while he himself used steroids only once, to recover from an injury. The fact that he was the only player on his team during his senior year to test positive for steroids discredits him somewhat, but Bosworth works around that problem with a long, preposterous alibi involving everything from a shoulder injury to food poisoning.

The single topic that Bosworth fails—unwittingly, I believe—to disfigure is his relationship with his father. And it is here that we see Bosworth for what he really is: a wounded ego, unloved in childhood, still striving in adulthood for the unqualified love and approval he futilely craved from his parents.

"Dad did everything for me growing up," Bosworth writes, "but he was a hard guy to satisfy. Second was never good enough for him. Come to think of it, sometimes first wasn't good enough either." He describes his father as a model Little League dad who "had me in every sport he could find by the time I was six and he was my coach for all of it. He was . . . mean as a drill sergeant." Raised by an alcoholic father, Bosworth's father "didn't have anybody around to be proud of him. That's why I think my dad worked me so hard. He wanted me to have someone to make proud, someone to achieve for. That's a big reason why I didn't want to disappoint him. So that was one thing that made us close."

It was impossible to earn his father's affection without being an exceptional achiever. Young Brian was unworthy, in himself, of his father's love. "He was always trying to get me to do better than the other kids. Like I said, sometimes first wasn't good enough. He taught me there's a difference between being first and being the best . . . If he ever praised me, he didn't dwell on it much."

The family goal, apparently, was to make Brian into something bigger and better than he was. "I was always a little smaller than the other kids and so he had all these schemes to get me bigger . . . They really went overboard trying to get me big . . . Whatever their reason was, they'd buy me special food at the grocery store and put it in the fridge with my name on it. And then, when my two sisters—Robbie and Vickie, both older—would ask for something, they'd get shot down."

Only through football stardom could Bosworth achieve legitimacy in the eyes of his father—a goal he finally realized when Oklahoma won the national championship in 1986. But even then, Bosworth writes, he fell short of his father's dreams by not becoming the first defensive player ever to win the Heisman Trophy. "My only disappointment in not winning the thing is that I would have given it to my dad for all that he did for me. That would have really made him proud."

Young Bosworth grew up knowing that he had to choose between football superstardom and banishment from his father's house. The child in him still craved his father's approval, while the emerging adult in him wanted revenge for his childhood's emotional torture. One of the most heavily recruited high-school athletes in the nation, he settled on one of the nation's most celebrated football schools.

In signing with the University of Oklahoma, he entered the court of a football coach—Barry Switzer—who is known in his domain as "the King." As his stardom grew, Bosworth writes with obvious glee, Switzer grew increasingly unhappy. "What you have to understand to start with is that Barry Switzer is an insecure person . . . He's so insecure that only when he owns the whole kingdom, the whole town, does he feel safe. And that's where he and I started to have problems. I took over his town and he couldn't handle it." Bosworth responded to Switzer's attempts at muzzling him by growing as notorious for his off-field behavior as he was famous for his play on the field. His Oklahoma career, by his own account, is memorable for two things: pleasing his father, on the one hand, and overthrowing the King on the other.

It would be tempting to say that Bosworth completed his psychological fulfillment with the publication of his book, by means of which he did to the Oklahoma football program what Oedipus did to Jocasta. But even for a Freudian biographer, that would be going too far.

Sort of. "The last time I went back to Norman," Bosworth concludes in his chapter on his relationship with the King, "he [Switzer] was very friendly to me . . . You don't think he found out I was writing a book, do you? Naaaaaaah."

At Oklahoma, Bosworth was a man in constant conflict with himself. On the one hand, he was driven to succeed, on the other he was determined to fail. While engineering his triumph on the field, he just as assiduously engineered his downfall off of it. Winning the Dick Butkus Award as the nation's best college defensive player in 1986, he also managed—in what should have been his finest hour—to get himself banished from the final nationally televised game of his college career. It is worth noting that this must have been a difficult feat to pull off: In being the only steroid abuser on his team to find a way to test positive, Bosworth beat almost insuperable odds.

Watching him stand on the sidelines now, midway through his second season in Seattle, I wondered if he might not be working at the same cross-purposes now that he's a professional. He is replaying the same drama he played at Oklahoma, fulfilling the same destiny—only with the particulars reversed. In signing an $11 million contract and in playing the role of celebrity to the hilt, he is an unqualified off-field success. But in playing the brash, supremely confident athlete who expects to dominate the professional game, he establishes impossible expectations in the minds of fans (thereby ensuring that someday they will turn against him) and fierce resentment in the minds of opponents (ensuring that they will play against him with heightened fervor). On top of that, he postpones surgery on an injured shoulder and plays hurt—thereby setting himself on an almost certain course of self-destruction. And he is falling disastrously short of his own and others' expectations. Is Knox—whose nickname in college was "Daddy-O"—the next father-figure object of Bosworth's rage?

Call me Tiresias.

The prison fashioned for Bosworth by his childhood is an endless adolescence. Like any tormented teen, he goes out of his way to antagonize the same people from whom he craves adoration—a conflict that is constantly played out in his relationship with the local press.

In the locker room after the Buffalo game, he sat pink and immaculate and ignored at his locker, while reporters sought out his battle-scarred teammates. Knox was saying, "We just made too many mistakes today to beat a good football team like the Buffalo Bills. We had opportunities, but we couldn't get anything going offensively, we made a lot of mistakes, careless penalties . . . We had two center-quarterback exchange fumbles, ball kicked around out there and we're looking at second-and-14. We didn't have a chance."

Stouffer felt compelled to take the brunt of the blame not only for the loss, but also for the bad breaks his team had been getting. "It's a matter of having a rookie in there," he said, "and everyone having to learn along with the rookie. So I'll take the responsibility for a lot of that stuff, because everyone is learning along with me, right now. It seems that a team that is having a tough time doing things right makes their own bad breaks. And you seem to be put in situations where those bad breaks tend to happen."

As I turned away, I saw Rusty Tillman holding forth angrily to a group of sympathetic reporters. "David Hollis," he was saying, "is a heckuva return guy. We weren't getting what we wanted on the kickoff returns, so I decided to make a change, and David Hollis came up with a big play. You'll see David Hollis in there again."

I remembered then that Tillman had been author of the day's most dramatic design-gone-wrong, and began a question: "On that first kickoff, it looked like there was a hole . . . "

"There was!" Tillman snapped, suddenly furious. "A *big* hole." Then he turned and walked off.

The next day, Randall Morris was cut.

In the 16 Bubble

...and what I relate was going on everywhere, either on a small scale or a larger scale, but the same thing everywhere, because it was all chaos and all meaningless.

—Henry Miller, *Tropic of Capricorn*

If you walk from the Seahawks' building to the far end of their practice-field complex in Kirkland, you come to what looks like a gigantic white butterfly pupa. It is an inflated dome—a bubble—that covers the third practice field during much of the season. When the weather is inclement or the two uncovered fields too wet, the team crawls into the bubble to practice unhindered by the elements.

It is an eerie place. The bubble is translucent, the ground is artificial, the residents are dressed in costumes that look like space suits, and the sounds of voices and collisions, echoing through dead air, sound electronically altered. In this manufactured environment, the game is undisturbed by winds, rain, unruly spectators, meddling owners . . . Here, football is boiled down to its essentials: designs and disciplined humans. Everything is calm, quiet, and focused.

Well, almost everything. Watching one day, I saw wide receiver Paul Skansi run a deep out-pattern around defensive back Vernon Dean. When Skansi made his cut, Dean turned opposite from the way Skansi expected him to. Skansi—caught by surprise when Dean surfaced in the wrong part of his pattern—stumbled slightly, and the pass intended for him landed just out of reach. The stumble, throwing the pattern's timing off by less than a second, was just enough to sever the connection.

It was one more reminder of how tiny is the margin for error in football. And as the ball caromed off the turf, Skansi floundering after it, I noticed one other peculiarity of the bubble—a powerful odor of dirty socks. The plastic surface of the dome, exposed to moisture all winter and folded up all summer, reeked of rot. Even in here, sheltered from the world of unmanageable variables, Knox found himself besieged by the one inescapable

211

characteristic shared by every creature and every thing in the universe: the tendency to fall apart.

On Wednesday, Knox was still preoccupied with breakdowns. "There's nothing mysterious about this game," he said. "But mistakes are the things that are gonna kill you." Particularly maddening for Knox had been two fumbled center-quarterback exchanges against Buffalo. The first one came at an especially critical moment. After the Bills punted from their 16 early in the second quarter, the Seahawks started out from their own 46, in excellent field position. On the first play, Stouffer fumbled, leaving his team with second-and-15. "Those are the things that just put you out," said Knox. "And then, if you fall behind, that compounds it."

The AFC West division title race was becoming compounded by coincidence. Ten games into the season, the Seahawks, Broncos, and Raiders all were tied for the division lead. Over the last two weeks, Seattle had won and then lost, Denver had lost and then won, and Los Angeles had won twice. It looked as if Seattle, inconsistencies and all, would be locked in a division race down to the wire.

The three-way tie this late in the season lent particular importance to the upcoming game, against the 7–3 Houston Oilers in the Kingdome. The Seahawks could ill afford another loss, particularly at home. With upcoming trips to Kansas City, where they had yet to win under Knox, and to New England, where the Patriots, although a 5–5 team, were 4–1 at home, and to the LA Coliseum to face the Raiders, the Seahawks were all but guaranteed at least two losses. A third would likely put them out of the title race.

The Oilers were formidable. Like Cleveland, they had three powerful running backs (Mike Rozier, Alonzo Highsmith, and Allen Pinkett) who figured to run more or less at will through the Seattle defense, particularly since the Oiler front line averaged 293 pounds per man. They combined the AFC's number-one defense against the rush with the conference's number-two rushing offense—as deadly a combination as Seattle could fear to face.

Still, the mood on the Seattle practice field was upbeat. Drills were cheerful and crisp, accompanied by the kind of spontaneous horseplay that you see only on winning teams.

The good cheer may have been due to the team's return to relative health. The Seahawks were in better shape than they had been since the season opener. Bosworth was already practicing, and expected to play Sunday. Bruce Scholtz's foot was out of its cast for the first time in weeks. Ray Butler was back. Bryan Millard—the heart, soul, and most of the muscle of the team's offensive line—would be able to play for the first time in three weeks. And Dave Krieg, sporting a set of oversized shoulder pads, was back, radiating intensity and eagerness.

Steve Moore, near the end of Wednesday's practice, took the quarterbacks and receivers off to one corner of the field to practice touchdown passes. Receivers lined up and took turns running fade routes and crossing routes as Krieg, Stouffer, and Kemp took turns throwing. The purpose of the drill was not so much to help the team recover its scoring touch as to recover its scoring state of mind. Whenever a receiver caught a ball, Moore forced him to spike it. "C'mon!" he screamed at Paul Skansi, when Skansi caught a pass and started back toward the receivers line. "C'mon—you gotta spike it!" One by one, players caught the ball and—at first tentatively, then with increasing flair—spiked it. Spiking practice!

High point of the drill came when Krieg threw a completion to Steve Largent. After making his catch, Largent started running off and was brought up short by a stare from Moore. For possibly the first time in his career, Largent looked awkward on a football field. He stood still, hesitating, trying to do something that came as unnaturally to him as public drunkenness or sexual assault. He looked at the ball, he looked around. . . the suspense was building . . . and then he slammed it to the ground, puffed out his chest, and crossed his arms—the Amigo salute!

Low point of the drill came every time it was Kemp's turn to throw. The poor guy had not completed a pass, even in practice, since the San Francisco game six weeks before. Now his tosses either flew over or behind his intended targets, or bounced off their hands, the ball landing every time in some shrubbery planted off in the distance. Throughout the drill, there was always at least one receiver prowling through those bushes, like a helmeted golfer, looking for his lost ball.

There was no question that Krieg would resume his starting role. Stouffer's inexperience had proven too much of a handicap for his prodigious arm to overcome. Because of his indecisiveness, defenses—particularly on third down—were reacting to openings faster than he could, and his inability to change speeds on his passes all but sealed off the end zone to him. The decision on Krieg, even given Stouffer's performance against New Orleans, had never been whether, but when. And Knox's refusal to commit publicly to the return of Krieg had been nothing more than a motivational ploy.

"He threw very well today," Ken Meyer said of Krieg on Wednesday. "He had great leadership, and he handled the team extremely well. And overall, his timing was excellent—in all his patterns."

Stouffer, he said, had more than exceeded his coaches' expectations. "He made great strides and did a lot for us," Meyer said, "but it was just a matter of an experienced man who's been there, who's been in championship games, who's been in playoff games, as opposed to a rookie.

From a coaching point of view, you've got to go with a proven starter."

Krieg had proven sound as well. "He's got good motion, he's not pushing the ball, the ball's coming off his hand good. He threw the ball long today, he threw the ball intermediate, he threw the ball short. We tried to give him all different patterns today, to get a good look at him."

The coaches liked what they saw enough not only to reinstate Krieg, but to reinstate the full Seattle offense as well. "I think," Meyer said as he walked away, "that you'll see different things on the offense."

In the locker room, the players shouted, whooped, threw trash at one another, and generally carried on like winners. It was the workplace not of a .500 team but of a first-place team. I hadn't seen this cheerful a locker room since the Seahawks' 12–4 year, 1984. It was like a day-care center for huge, hyperactive boys—Big Boys' Town.

One of the first players showered and dressed was also one of the last to leave. Thrice-cut David Hollis was back after six weeks of anxious waiting and hoping and refusing to believe that his career could be over. He stood in front of his locker, a baseball cap pushed jauntily back on his head, one foot up on a stool, looking around the room with a disbelieving, joyful expression. Reveling in the camaraderie, he looked like he was afraid to leave, for fear his dream would evaporate yet again.

For every cool, commanding star we see blasting balletically across our television screens on football Sundays—for every Terry Taylor or Kenny Easley or Brian Bosworth—there are hundreds of David Hollises waiting somewhere for their telephone to ring. The established player has about him a certain hauteur, an air declaring his conviction that he belongs at the pinnacle of his profession. The marginal player, who claws his way onto a low-echelon roster spot only because someone else has faltered or been injured, has about him the air of a kid who sneaked into the locker room and was allowed to stay.

Hollis was born with a worried-man's forehead, covered with millions of tiny furrow-muscles the rest of us don't have, and with eyes that flash with a puppy's eagerness to please. As a result, his face sends out a mixed message to potential benefactors: Danger! This man will thank you to death!

An intelligent player, with good speed and good reflexes, Hollis was enough of an athlete to merit pro football's attention, but not quite good enough or big enough to sustain it. He was one of McCormack's "3s," a player lacking some tiny, vital ingredient that sets professional-caliber athletes apart from the nondescript legions of mere college greats.

After graduation from the University of Nevada at Las Vegas in 1987, Hollis went undrafted, was signed as a free agent by the Seahawks, and stuck with the squad through that season, appearing in 11 games. Then, near the end of the 1988 training camp, he saw that his days were numbered when Seattle picked up free-agent defensive backs Vernon Dean and Nesby Glasgow, both established veterans. "I kind of figured it was over when they brought those two guys in," Hollis said, "but I tried not to think about it, I just tried to learn my timing, do the best I could. And when I looked in the mirror, it wasn't like I was disappointed in myself. Because I knew that I gave it my all and did the best that I could."

When he was cut by Kansas City in the season's fourth week—after being twice cut by Seattle—Hollis began to wonder if his playing days might be over for good. He convinced himself that "something would materialize sooner or later. Melvin Jenkins is my best friend, and he kept me going. And my agent called me and said people called him, so it was kind of encouraging that people were still calling and asking about me."

Still, as the weeks went by, Hollis's hopes began to waver. He and his wife had one daughter, and another baby on the way. "It was pretty rough," he said, "but I had to keep good spirits about it. I was preparing myself for somebody to call me, but I wasn't going to wait around until the end of December . . . " Such was his desire to play, though, that he wasn't going to give up after six weeks, either. And when Seattle called him the day after Hunter's accident, Hollis didn't hesitate. "It was very tempting to be angry at the coaches here, but you can't take it personally. I had to look at it through their eyes. They have a job to do, and they have to go with what they felt was best."

Determined as he sounded, and happy as he was to be back with Seattle, his voice and gaze dropped dramatically when he recalled his six-week layoff. He had come face-to-face, for the first time, with the real possibility that he would never again have the chance to do the only thing he had ever wanted to do—play football against the best. With each passing day he had to shed a few more of his illusions. In spite of his protestations, he gave every impression that he would have waited by the phone far past the end of December. "It's just always been a dream of mine to play up here," he said. "I always felt like I was an NFL-caliber football player. I wasn't intimidated by anybody. That's always been my nature."

Behind me, Melvin Jenkins and some other defensive backs were standing over at the locker-room exit, yelling and laughing and shrieking at Hollis. "I just had a little boy this morning," he explained apologetically, "and everybody's trying to get me going." "What are you doing here?" I asked. "Well . . . it's a job!" he answered. "And like any other job, you still have to go to work . . . and afterwards you can go deal with your family." So marginal was his status that he didn't dare miss a day's work—for anything.

Judging from the way the game began, the Seahawks' status in the league was no less marginal. The Oilers, starting out from their own 10-yard line, ran four straight running plays, covering 21 yards. Eleven of the yards came straight up the middle, with tackler Eugene Robinson the last man between Mike Rozier and the Seattle end zone. Three plays later, facing second-and-seven at the Houston 43, the Oilers lined up in shotgun formation, sending wide receiver Drew Hill deep on the left side. Downfield, behind the Seattle secondary, Hill broke inside and Houston quarterback Warren Moon threw outside. As the ball skidded downfield, everybody—Seattle defenders and Houston attackers alike—stood stock-still, stunned. They all saw that Hill had somehow traveled downfield unnoticed, and that if he had caught the ball, he would have scored easily. On the next play, Houston came out in the same formation, and sent Hill deep again, on a post pattern. He was the only one of four Oiler receivers to be double-covered, but, as Vernon Dean said afterward, "We blew the coverage." Moon hit him on the dead run for a 57-yard touchdown. Eugene Robinson had broken briefly in the direction of the other receiver, and Dean, thinking Robinson was covering Hill deep, had broken off short.

To the sound of 60,446 people silently contemplating suicide, Dave Krieg came onto the field with the Seattle offense. The Seahawks lined up with two tight ends, and with Steve Largent, the lone wide receiver, on the right. Warner went in motion wide right as John L. Williams took the hand-off and carried for 3 yards over left tackle. On the next play, Warner, lined up behind Williams, came forward as Krieg began his snap count, crossed in front of Williams, and went in motion all the way across to the left sideline, breaking at the snap into the secondary as Krieg dropped back to pass and connected with tight end John Spagnola 16 yards downfield.

The stadium erupted. Already, fans could see that the scaled-down Seahawk offense of the last six weeks had been replaced by something far more complex. Only two plays into Seattle's first series, and already they had seen more shifting and sending of players in motion than they had seen in total over the past six weeks. Warner darted around left end behind textbook blocking for an 11-yard gain on the next play. Then Largent burst downfield toward the goalposts and curled outside around befuddled cornerback Steve Brown as Krieg lofted a perfectly timed pass his way. It went right through Largent's hands, for his third inexplicable drop of the season—three more, by my count, than he had had over his entire career.

Undaunted, Krieg rolled out on the next play, finding tight end Mike Tice 13 yards downfield. Five plays later, throwing a quick timing pattern over the head of blitzing safety Keith Bostic, he hit Brian Blades for a 23-yard touchdown.

The Seattle offense was back. The Seahawks had scored only one offensive touchdown in their last 12 quarters under Stouffer, and now it had taken Krieg only 5 minutes to direct a 75-yard scoring drive.

But even more amazing was the dazzling look of the drive. For the 10 plays, Seattle had employed five different formations, six different ball carriers and receivers (seven, if you count the incompletion to Largent), seven different player combinations, and—by shifting players or sending a different one in motion on each play—10 different looks. The Seahawks had run only four times and thrown six times, with three of the passes coming on first down. Fans could be forgiven for not recognizing their representatives on the battlefield.

Houston came back immediately, moving 46 yards in 10 plays. With third-and-eight on the Seattle 34, Moon tried to hit wide receiver Curtis Duncan, but Paul Moyer, crossing in front of Duncan, almost intercepted. Had Moyer managed to hang onto the ball, Houston kicker Luis Zendejas would not have been able to come on next to give his team a three-point lead.

Zendejas's kick looked like the beginning of the end for Seattle. On the Seahawks' first play from scrimmage, guard Edwin Bailey was flagged for holding, and Seattle moved back to its 10-yard line. There, Krieg's pass on the next play was deflected straight up in the air by nose tackle Richard Byrd, who turned, waited, and intercepted the ball. The Oilers came out with first-and-goal at the Seahawk 9 and gained an immediate 5 yards. But then, on the verge of scoring, Houston was penalized 10 yards for holding. And on the next play, Oiler receiver Drew Hill broke past Melvin Jenkins into the end zone, and Moon drilled a perfect pass right at him. Moyer, breaking just before the ball was thrown, picked it off on the dead run, returning it to the Seattle 29.

Both Moyer's near-interception and his interception had come about because of his close study of Houston film. He had noticed that when Moon dropped back to pass, he always dropped either slightly to the left or slightly to the right of center. Invariably he would turn then and throw back across to the opposite side—if he dropped right, he would throw left, and vice versa. It was one of those unconscious tendencies players fall into, which opponents pick up only after hours of careful film study. Moyer, remembering the tendency as he dropped into coverage, broke both times for the receiver moving into the area where Moon tended to throw. Moyer's homework allowed him to anticipate rather than react to Moon's passes. Both times, his anticipation enabled him to get to a ball he otherwise would not have reached.

Ten Seattle offensive plays later (five runs and five passes to four different receivers), Houston nearly returned the favor. Safety Jeff Donaldson, crossing in the opposite direction from Largent, caught, then dropped, a Krieg pass. With the ball at the Houston 22, on came Norm Johnson to attempt to tie the game.

With the return of Krieg, Stouffer had been moved to backup quarterback. Since Seattle couldn't afford to keep three quarterbacks on the active roster, Jeff Kemp had been moved to the inactive list—an unspectacular move, except that it meant that Johnson would have to work with a new holder. Although Johnson was a reliable kicker, and outwardly an even-tempered one, kickers have such notoriously fragile psyches that any change in their routines can have disastrous consequences. So as Seattle lined up now for the field-goal attempt, fans prepared themselves for the worst. The snap-hold-and-kick sequence, appearing to go smoothly enough, allayed everyone's fears for a moment, but then the ball headed off to a point far to the right of the goalposts, and the fans—as if the game's outcome were riding on the kick—gasped in dismay.

The ball seemed to slow down in midair, then hang suspended in its misdirected course, waiting while I remembered something Johnson had said to me about field goals earlier in the season. "People always talk about soccer-style kickers hooking the ball," he said. "It shouldn't really hook, it should go straight. When I'm kicking well, my ball goes very straight. If anything, it'll have just a slight, what you might call a draw. Just a little bit of a draw. Just a hair, usually from right to left. But actually, when you're kicking it well and everything is proper, it goes straight as an arrow. It goes up, the ball's straight up and down, it doesn't lie sideways, it just goes straight." As this ball reached its apex, a little zephyr—grayish white, barely visible, with comic red highlights airbrushed on its exaggerated cheeks—materialized to the right of the ball, blowing frantically at it. As ball and zephyr, side by side, traveled toward the upright, the ball slowly, gradually, began to hoo ... er, to *draw*, or to be blown, almost unnoticeably leftward. Minutes passed—surely this must have been the slowest-moving kicked ball in Seattle football history—and then, right in front of the goalpost, the ball suddenly sped up and took a hard left turn. It glanced off the inside of the upright and passed through, good.

Yow!

Oblivious to the pandemonium around him, Johnson trotted over impassively to the sideline, picked up a kicking tee, and came back out to set up for his kickoff.

The combatants, as if trying to collect their wits after Johnson's caress of the goalposts, exchanged punts, after which the Oilers started out from their own 20 with 4:02 remaining in the half. Attacking on the ground, they gained 5 yards, then 7, on Mike Rozier's legs. Then Alonzo Highsmith, sweeping right, found that linebacker Bruce Scholtz had rushed around end and sealed off that side of the field. He reversed, cut back along the line of scrimmage, and burst downfield, gaining 42 yards. Allen Pinkett gained 11 more over right tackle, and with 2 minutes left, Houston, with a first down on the Seattle 15, had a near-certain guarantee of taking the lead before the half.

When Pinkett tried sweeping right on the next play, however, Jacob Green, who had slipped untouched inside his blocker, tackled him for a 4-yard loss. Tight end Jamie Williams, wide open in the right flat on the next play, dropped Moon's pass, and on the play after that, Moon sent three receivers deep into the left side of the end zone, then waited for receiver Curtis Duncan to discreetly slip into the flat on the right sideline. When Duncan caught the ball, Terry Taylor, Dwayne Harper, and Eugene Robinson came flying up from the end zone, racing Duncan to the first-down marker. They collided spectacularly with Duncan, stopping him less than a yard short of a first down.

Houston coach Jerry Glanville, who prides himself on being a football maverick, then made what proved to be a fateful decision. Rather than kicking a surefire field goal, he opted to try for a first down. Moon handed off to Mike Rozier, and defensive end Jeff Bryant, slipping inside of his blocker exactly as Green had done a few plays before, filled the gap Rozier was headed for. As the running back hesitated and began to turn outside, Tony Woods and Ken Clarke smothered him for a loss.

Glanville's misguided decision and Bryant's slant move thus preserved the first half's symmetry. Both teams had scored passing touchdowns on their first possessions, both teams had been intercepted once, and both had scored field goals—each field goal coming on a play following a dropped interception. Although the score was tied, the Seahawks, given their inherent disadvantage and all the question marks they had carried into the game, were far ahead of the Oilers on the psychological scoreboard, simply by virtue of having stayed even—particularly since the Seahawks were only two plays (Moyer's interception in the Seattle end zone and Houston's failed fourth down gamble) from being down 21–7.

For me, the most impressive moment in the first half belonged to Norm Johnson, who reacted to his near-miss with trademark nonchalance. Johnson has been a steady star for Seattle since he signed in 1982, taking over for beloved Seahawk place-kicker Efren Herrera. Six seasons later, Johnson held virtually every team kicking record, and entered the 1988 season as the team's second-leading career scorer, his 531 points trailing only Steve Largent's 577. Aided by the Seahawks' touchdown drought—a condition that had him kicking field goals almost constantly—he passed

Largent seven weeks into the '88 season, when his fourth field goal during the loss to New Orleans pushed his career-point total to 578. Now, midway through the Oiler game, his team-leading total stood at 594.

Seattle special teams coach Rusty Tillman says that equanimity is the key to longevity for kickers in the NFL. "That's what separates the guys who play this game for a long time from the guys who don't," he says. "There are a lot of people who can kick. But the ones who can handle it mentally and be able to shrug it off, so to speak, are the guys who are successful in the long run." In Johnson, he had found a kicker with an almost superhuman capacity for calm. "Kickers are different," Tillman says, "because what they do is different. It makes them more analytical. They can't be rah-rah type guys. I've seen some kickers around the league who are real emotional-type guys, but I've never seen one make it over a long period of time that's really that way."

While rage and competitiveness are de rigueur at every other position—often, extremes of emotion will carry a football player through stressful times—in kickers, high emotion is a detriment. On a team of temperamental artists, Johnson is the lone dispassionate scientist. (To a lesser degree, this is also true of Ruben Rodriguez, although Rodriguez, far less consistent than Johnson, is a moodier player.) A place-kicker is like a surgeon brought in to perform a delicate operation in the middle of a fierce battle. With tension and pressure building around him, with tens of thousands of voices raised in mindless animalsong so loud it drowns out even the sound of the voice inside his head, he must come onto the field, calmly take his measurements, then perform a geometrical miracle: Swinging his leg in a half-circle, he must kick an oval-shaped object squarely enough to launch it along a curvilinear path that will take it straight through a narrow, rectangular opening off in the distance. It reminds me of baseball great Frank Howard's classic line on the impossibility of hitting: "They give you a round bat and a round ball," Howard likes to say, "and tell you to hit it square!"

Johnson likes to compare kicking in football to hitting in baseball. "It's like a baseball player trying to hit a home run," he says. "When he *tries*, he usually doesn't. It's when he gets back there and hits it smooth and slow and easy that the balls go out. That's because everything's flowing: His hips and everything, his shoulders come around, his wrists are breaking, everything is at the proper moment. That's what a kicker wants to do, too: Make it look as easy as he can. You want to be real easy, and the ball should really go. And when your timing is there, that's what happens."

Timing, he explains, is twofold. "There is timing working with the holders and snappers. But that's not as difficult as getting the timing with myself. When my foot contacts the ball, there's got to be a whole lot of forces and movements that come together at that one particular point. If any one of them is off, my body lean or my hips are back or my knee isn't locked at the proper time—all those things—if they're not all coming together at the same time, you're not going to have any power, and everything's going to be off, you're not going to feel right with the kick."

Kickers live in a world apart from other football players. They work harder at maintaining their equilibrium than they do at staying in playing shape. Seattle's kickers, while watched and advised by their coach, are left more or less to their own devices. "I know what the perfect kick in my head should look like," says Johnson. "Getting me to do that on the field takes a long time. I watch myself on film, and try to correct little things. When I'm kicking very well, I'll take that film and put it on a reel that I'll watch all the time when things aren't going well."

When things are going well, Johnson works less, for fear of kicking himself out of sync. "If I'm in a groove, I just go out and kick for a few minutes at the beginning of practice, and if I stay in the groove, then I stop. Most of all, I don't kick when I'm tired. Because then you start getting in bad habits, certain muscles get sore, you compensate with other muscles once those get fatigued, and when you start compensating, that's when muscles get pulled."

Like a pitcher fostering his arm, the kicker fosters his leg. On the practice field, kickers walk around at a leisurely pace, working according to their own shifting mental schedule, while their teammates grunt and grind to the point of exhaustion every day. It is a regimen that often creates resentment in position players—although on Seattle's team, the resentment is curbed both because Johnson and Rodriguez played legitimate positions in their youth (Rodriguez was a quarterback, Johnson a tight end), and because Seattle coaches insist that the two find ways to help their teammates during practice. "I think some players understand kickers and some don't," Johnson observes. "It's funny—it's a job everybody wants to have during the week, but nobody wants it on game day. Everybody wants to be a kicker until crunch time, when it comes down to the kick. Then nobody wants it. Then I think they appreciate us and they say, 'Gee, I'm glad I don't have to do that.' But then, during the week, we don't have to do as much as those guys, and they think that we got a cake job, and they wish they were kickers, and they can't believe us. I'm sure some resent the fact that we don't have to work as hard as they do, but I think when you really look at it, when it comes down to it, I think most of them respect most kickers. I say *most* kickers. I mean, there's kickers *I* don't respect. It's not their job so much, it's that I don't respect *them*, the way they go about it. But I like to feel that I'm an athlete, I can go out there and throw for the running backs, and I make tackles and do things that I think kickers should do, but I see a lot of them that don't do it. That's when I lose respect for a kicker—when he's not gonna make an attempt to make a tackle, when he doesn't feel he has to practice. Some of those guys just go out and kick and go home. That would never work around here. Chuck and Rusty don't believe in it."

Tillman concurs, as only Tillman can. "We make a big deal out of having them help in practice," he says, "so they can feel a part of the football team. Because I've been on some teams where the kicker was really kind of an outcast, and the only time anybody really recognized him was when he made a field goal that won the ball game. But it's really up to them. That's what I sell to them: Make yourself part of the football team. You know, a lot of kickers are called flakes—it's because they are! They act like flakes. Really! If you act like a goddamn flake, and you stay to yourself all the time, you don't try to be part of the team, that's the way you'll be treated!"

Johnson believes that kickers must be precise, focused people. The key to consistent precision, Johnson believes, lies in being as methodical with your mind and heart as you are with your body. "There is an optimal amount of anxiety that you want to have," he explains. "I try to keep that level the same, whether it's an extra point the first quarter, an extra point to win the game, a field goal at the beginning of the game, or a field goal to win the game. I tell myself that this one's no different than any other kick. I think it would be foolish to think anything else. Why should I go in and put more importance on one than on the other? That's putting more stress on myself. If I try really hard to make this one and think it's extra special, then chances are I'm going to screw up somewhere, because my muscles are going to tense up or something."

In an effort to keep himself on an even keel, Johnson refuses to react to his kicks, whether they're inconsequential ones, key misses, or gamewinners. By way of example, he cites a preseason kick he had made against the Detroit Lions, to win in overtime. "If you watched me after that kick," he said, "I didn't get all excited and jump up and down and get real emotional about it, because of the way I was trying so hard to approach it. I wanted to say, 'This is a regular kick,' it could be first quarter, whatever—just go in and kick it."

Johnson moves through the world slowly and calmly, like a man dedicated to the religious observance of leisure. In practice, in the locker room, on an exercycle, on the field, or on the sideline, he wears the same impassive expression. Yet his jaw looks permanently clenched, and his eyes— oddly vacant most of the time—light up whenever he talks or thinks about kicking. He is fascinated by the anatomy of a kick, and by the confluence of physical and psychological forces that make one work. Kickers, he explains, do not kick sideways, with their instep, as is widely believed. "When we kick, the knee should more or less be pointing toward where we want the ball to go," he says. "It's not pointing out to the side—that's when you get in trouble, when you start using your groin instead of the big quadricep muscle up here. You almost kick it with the inside of the quad and a little bit of the groin. But if you open your leg too much, that's when you really put stress on your groin. And we don't kick with the side of the foot, we kick with the top of it."

Whether the ball is placed in the center of the field, or on a right or left hashmark, Johnson goes through the same careful pre-place-kick ritual. He lines the ball up with the center of the uprights—much like a golfer lining up a putt—then steps carefully backward along that imagined line, so that he, the ball, and the target are all in perfect order. Then he steps sideways at a perfect right angle to the line. "I line up the same angle to the goalpost every time," he says. "Extra point, 43-yarder, 15-yarder from the right hash, 15-yarder from the left hash. . . And that right angle is always toward the center of the uprights. So I should be coming into the ball at the exact same angle every time." Once he has lined up and moved over to his starting position, he leans forward slightly, sets himself, and focuses on the spot where the ball will be placed. "I should be able to line up and go over and not have to look again at where it's gonna go. I should know that all I have to do is kick the ball normally and it should go straight. And after I hit it, without even looking up, I'll usually know if I did something wrong. I've been doing this long enough that I pretty much know what I did wrong. I know my style, and how it feels to hit a good kick."

Perhaps. But after he had kicked the game-tying field goal against the Oilers, he stood and watched with understated anxiety until it squeezed through. Scientific and precise as he is, he had to wait with everyone else to see if it was fated to be good.

Seattle started out the second half by running three plays for 9 yards, then punting. Houston, just as in the first half, devoured huge servings of turf with rushing plays. Six plays netted them 60 yards—39 of them on two runs—and brought them to first-and-10 on the Seattle 13. The Oilers had come out in the second half in a peculiar alignment called the "Pro-4," a four-wide-receiver, one-running-back arrangement, with Moon up over center rather than back in the shotgun position. It called for the Seahawks to deploy their nickel defense, with six defensive backs and one linebacker. Then Houston would run a "rag draw," sending a lone running back up the middle, against Seattle's lone linebacker. If Seattle responded by taking out its nickel and putting in its four-linebacker defense, the Oilers would isolate a speedy wide receiver on a leaden linebacker—a match-up guaranteed to deliver them a touchdown.

At the 13, then, Houston came out again in the Pro-4, spread over nearly the whole width of the field. Seattle's four down linemen spread themselves so thinly there was no one lined up opposite Houston center Jay Pennison. Moon came up to Pennison, tapped him on the leg, took a surreptitious snap, and followed Pennison down to the Seattle 2, where finally Eugene Robinson wrestled him down. Two plays later, Pinkett carried the ball around right end for a touchdown.

On the ensuing kickoff, David Hollis showed the world why he had been picked up and put in Morris's place. Taking the kick 1 yard deep in the end zone, he started up the left hashmarks, dodged the lead tackler, then abruptly exploded toward the sideline, cutting up through an almost invisible seam between battling bodies and sideline. He was brought down, finally, at the Seattle 34. Curt Warner was whistled for holding on the next play, then was overthrown by Krieg on the next. Now Seattle faced third and 20 at its 24, was down by 7 points, and was staring a host of Seahawk demons in the face. If they failed to earn a first down here, the game would be lost.

Seattle came out with three wide receivers on the left. Paul Skansi, the middle receiver, went in motion across the line of scrimmage, then angled at the snap back over the middle. Krieg's pass to him was thrown high, Skansi stretched, caught it, and was brutally cracked in the back by nickel back Domingo Bryant. Somehow, he hung onto the ball, and came down just past the first-down marker.

The play served notice that—for this game, at least—Krieg had been resurrected without the self-destructive tendencies that in games past had often led him singlehandedly to orchestrate disaster. His completion to Skansi so inspired his teammates that they quickly committed penalties on two of the next three snaps of the ball, giving Krieg a second-and-27 opportunity to showcase his prowess again. Obligingly, he threw a hanging pass 30 yards downfield to where Largent, blanketed on the inside shoulder by safety Jeff Donaldson, overran the ball, stopped, slipped inside of the stumbling Donaldson with a swim move, and caught the ball on the Houston 42. The spectators, brought to life, ushered their team to the line of scrimmage with an energizing roar, then fell into attentive silence as John L. Williams cut back through a gigantic hole at the line of scrimmage, stepped through a corridor swept clean of linebackers by Ron Mattes and Edwin Bailey, and took on two defensive backs, dragging them 10 yards downfield to the Oiler

22. Three plays later, Seattle found itself facing fourth-and-one at the Houston 13.

Steve Moore sent in Seattle's short-yardage offense, along with a play called "25-Lead." In their schemes, the Seahawks divide the line of scrimmage into numbered "holes," starting beside the center and moving outward, with even numbers on the left, odd numbers on the right. Between center and left guard, then, is the "0-hole," between center and right guard the "1-hole," and so on. The "25-Lead" called for Williams to lead the way for Curt Warner (the "2-back" in the Seattle scheme) through the "5-hole" (the space occupied by the right tackle). Krieg called the play in the huddle, then brought his team to the line of scrimmage. At the snap, Williams dived into the 5-hole, Krieg extended the ball to the trailing Warner, then took it back. "He doesn't tell us he's going to do that," said Ron Mattes afterward, "because we'd give it away by not blocking right. We have to think we're blocking for Curt." Oiler linebacker Walter Johnson, charging unblocked around left end, took one step toward Warner, then recovered too late, reaching out helplessly as Krieg took off outside of him. Racing to the sideline, Krieg stepped out of bounds just past the first-down marker. Safety Keith Bostic, flying at him from behind, reached out and delivered a gratuitous roundhouse punch to Krieg's injured shoulder.

For that breach of decorum, Bostic was roundly booed and flagged for a personal-foul penalty that moved the ball down to the Oiler 5. Two plays later, behind pulling guards Bailey and Bryan Millard, Warner swept around the right side for a touchdown. Millard had cleared the last obstacle for Warner by flattening Houston cornerback Steve Brown. Once the two were safely in the end zone, Warner ceremoniously presented Millard with the ball. Millard delivered what Bailey later would call "the ugliest spike I've ever seen." For that breach of decorum—or possibly of aesthetics— Millard was penalized, the yardage to be assessed on the kickoff.

Norm Johnson, who describes kickoffs as "aggressive kicks," proceeded to deliver one of the most aggressive of his career, hanging the ball in the air for a good 4.4 seconds, until it came down right at the Houston goal line. "If I had my perfect kick," Rusty Tillman likes to say, "it would be right to the goal line, maybe 1 yard deep, with a 4.5 hang time. We'd get 'em inside the 10 every time if we did that." Seahawk linebacker Rufus Porter, slipping unblocked through the Oiler wedge, flattened returner Leonard Harris at the 11.

It was ordained, though, that the game would be too exciting for a third-quarter kickoff to put an end to the exchange of touchdowns. Houston, out of the same Pro-4 set, took 12 plays to score another touchdown, this one coming at the 11:47 mark in the fourth quarter. One kickoff and five plays later, Seattle came to the line of scrimmage on first-and-10 at the Oiler 44, about to demonstrate the importance of every player's assignment—however inconsequential it looks when drawn up.

The play, 44-weak, called for tight end Mike Tice to line up on the right—making that the "strong" side of the offensive line—and for John L. Williams, following Warner, to take the ball, start toward left tackle—the "4-hole"—then cut back toward the right side of the line of scrimmage, the right-side linemen having pushed their men leftward.

On running plays, the wide receiver's responsibility is simply to run down and out, taking the opposing cornerback with him, then to seal him off from the play. Largent, lined up on the right, broke at the snap toward the sideline, taking cornerback Steve Brown with him. He turned upfield, keeping himself between Brown and the hole Williams was running through. Ordinarily, that is all a wide receiver is called upon to do; the play ends after the running back picks up 5 yards or so. But Houston over-reacted to Williams's and Warner's initial surge toward the left side, and when Williams cut back to the right, there was no one save Brown between him and the end zone. As Williams shot by on the inside of Largent, Brown turned to pursue, and Largent, diving, took Brown's feet out from under him. His block turned a 20-yard gain into a 44-yard touchdown run—the score effected only because Largent was conscientious enough to have stayed with his man for a few extra seconds.

With 8:07 remaining and the score tied, the Oilers started out from their own 16. They had scored on all but three of their possessions, and had not been stopped by the Seahawk defense since their ill-fated fourth-down failure at the end of the second quarter. Now it took them only five plays to move 42 yards, to third-and-two on the Seahawk 42. Safety Vernon Dean, blitzing at the snap on the next play, ran right into running back Alonzo Highsmith, wrestling him to the ground for a 4-yard loss. Houston was forced to punt for only the second time all day.

The Seahawks went into their clock-killing offense, taking nine plays to move 47 yards. Playing for the game-winning field goal, they were content—and confident enough in Johnson—to gain yardage in short bursts, moving just into kicking range. At the 1:12 mark, Curt Warner ran straight ahead, gaining 2 yards. Letting the clock run, Seattle waited until 40 seconds remained before sending Williams over right guard for 5 more.

That play ended with the ball on the Houston 28, the score 24–24, and the clock at the 37-second mark. Incredibly, everything but the clock stopped. Seattle players just stood there, as if taking an unrehearsed break, and Krieg sauntered over to one of the officials, then stood casually beside him as the two looked up at the scoreboard clock. Everyone waited while the clock ticked down, until, at the 5-second mark, Krieg called time.

Such was Knox's confidence in his place-kicker that he preferred taking a chance on Johnson's ability to kick a 46-yard field goal to risking disaster for the sake of moving the ball a little closer to the goalposts. He chose to have Johnson kick on third down rather than use that down to give Johnson a shorter, fourth-down kick. "Now, I'm sure a lot of people," Knox said after the game, "will say, 'Well, why did you go for a field goal on third down?' Well, the reason that you do that, is because you don't know what's going to happen on third down. You throw one more in the end zone, you get a holding penalty called against you, you're out! You throw an interception, you're out. You run with the ball, and a fumble, you're out." In football, he was saying, you fly into the face of the odds on every play. The chances of something going wrong are far greater than the chances of everything going right. So he went with the highest-percentage play he had, a Norm Johnson field goal, as soon as the ball was within the outer limits of Johnson's range. Empowered, perhaps, by Knox's confidence in him, Johnson kicked the ball so high and straight and dead-center that it would have been good from 60 yards away.

Once the wild postgame celebration—including a rush onto the field by Seahawk owner Ken Behring—had ended, Johnson's gamewinning kick was forgotten not only by his teammates but by himself. In the locker room, dressing quietly, he was accosted by a television reporter who wanted him for a live postgame interview. "Why?" he asked, genuinely surprised. And when told it was because he was the game's star, he shook his head, irritated. Why should he put more importance on that kick than on any other?

Around the locker room, Krieg was the toast of his team. I could see now that the Seahawks' midweek giddiness had been borne of the understanding of what Krieg's return meant to them all. They had only to glance at the game plans given to them Wednesday morning to see that their days of travail were over. Having managed to go 3–3 without Krieg, they realized, had been an amazing feat. Now, with him at the helm for the season's stretch run, they had it made. For the first time since their season-opening win over Denver, they would be competing from a position of advantage.

A comic theme soon surfaced in the locker room. Reporters would try to initiate conversations with players on all manner of purportedly game-turning topics—the running of John L. Williams, the blocking of the Seattle offensive line, the kicking of Norm Johnson, the wide-open playcalling of Steve Moore—and players and coaches would insist on talking only about Krieg. For Moore, the return of Krieg meant the return to Seattle's standard, deception-rich attack. "We did today what we normally would do with David Krieg," he said. "Which is what we call formationing. A combination of personnel groups and backfield sets and motions."

The Mudbone offense? By reputation, Knox's offense is supposed to be stolid, boring, and predictable. After this game, it looked built on glitz and surprises. "We were mixing it up," said Curt Warner, "throwing some different formations at them, and were able to kind of back them up there for a while. We kept Houston off balance." They were able to do that, he said, because Krieg was back. "He's a great football player, he's a guy that likes to lead, and I think a lot of guys respond to him. It's just good to have him back out there."

Seattle's offensive linemen acted as though Krieg had brought them back from the dead. "Everyone was looking for that little spark that would put us over the edge," said Ron Mattes, "that little rallying point, and Dave coming back . . . it was the old Mudbone back there. He had a little twinkle in his eye, and he knows how to control our offense. He knows what gets us fired up. He yells at us certain times, to get us going, we know that if we miss a block or an assignment that he'll get on our case, we respect that. Because he knows what we're capable of doing, and he knows that if we go on all cylinders, we can win the whole game, and if there's one guy screwing up, it's gonna hurt the whole system."

By the time Krieg emerged from the treatment room, the press was apparently persuaded. Every reporter in the place crowded around him, stopping him cold in the middle of the locker room, showering him with questions.

Krieg resolutely refused to take any credit for winning the game. He dished out terse accolades to everyone from Curt Warner to some anonymous "character of our football team." He was aggressively deadpan, saying far more with his facial expression than with his words. It was his way of reminding everyone of how much they had vilified him in the past, and that after years of being booed by fans, second-guessed by sportswriters, and being denied the unqualified endorsement of his coaches, he was not about to let anyone jump on his bandwagon. It is an old code in pro sports: An athlete never forgives a slight, and never rewards a critic with colorful copy.

Finally, someone asked him about the deliberate attempt by Bostic to remaim him. "I think he took his arm and tried to hit me in the shoulder or the head or something, and I just wasn't fast enough to beat him over there to the sideline," Krieg answered with studied nonchalance. "Whatever he did, I couldn't see it on the replay or anything, but I guess he took a swing at me or something."

To those who had seen it, Bostic's punch—like Mattes's chop-block of Bruce Smith the week before—was an act of unspeakable savagery. Yet Bostic's blow had glanced harmlessly off Krieg's shoulder pad, and certainly had been far less violent than the legitimate collisions and blows that are routinely struck during the course of a football game.

At first I thought that fans' and reporters' gut reactions to the blow had been typical of home-team followers. They were simply reacting to some perceived moral lapse on the part of a visitor. But the referees had reacted similarly, and Bostic's teammates had done little to defend him against the revenge-bent charge of the entire Seahawk offense. Even Houston, which prides itself on its dirty play (the Oilers are the most-penalized team by far in the NFL), seemed embarrassed.

Their embarrassment, like the crowd reaction, stemmed from the double-edged nature of football. It is bestial ballet, a miraculous melding of violence and decorum. The elegance of the game stems not so much from the bold and intricate play, as I had thought, but from its ritualization of rage. If the diagram of a play is an attempt to create a controllable, predictable, sensible world of cause and effect, punishment and reward, then the rules of the game are an attempt to control the far more volatile and unpredictable human propensity for violence. No other game combines such pain and havoc with such exquisite sportsmanship. Players collide, at full speed, attempting to incapacitate one another in a few-holds-barred encounter. Then, time and again, both assaulters and victims rise, calm and courtly, often congratulating one another or helping one another to their feet. They walk quietly back to their respective sides of the battle lines, gather their strength, and have at each other again. It is a spectacle not of the dark side of human nature but of its bright side; not of vulgarity, but of gentility; not of despair and disgust, but of possibility and transcendence. I saw the game then as a bold American experiment, an attempt to harness violence rather than to suppress it. And I understood that if anxious, energetic young men can comport themselves with such civility in the midst of such extreme pain and anger and danger, then there is hope for us all.

Portrait of the Head Coach as a Winning Loser

I'd like to tell you there's something mysterious and deep and intellectual and strategic involved and all this type of thing, but there isn't.

—Chuck Knox, November 16, 1988

Down on the field at the end of the Houston game, I saw a remarkable exchange of roles between Steve Moore and Rusty Tillman. As the two came off the field, Tillman—Seattle's most outwardly emotional coach—was trotting along with his face set in the inexpressive mask of a place-kicker. Moore—Seattle's most urbane, outwardly even-tempered coach—caught up to Tillman, grabbed him, and shrieked in his ear. Tillman gave him a look of confused distaste.

A few minutes later, I asked Moore if the game had been fun.

"Fun?!" he exclaimed. "You gotta be kidding me! That was the greatest! We have been going through some real growing pains around here, and to have our people all rally around and stay in there, keep battling, not giving up, competing the way they did, was very rewarding—absolutely."

He had seen his detailed, diagrammed dream come alive. Seattle had turned in a virtually flawless offensive day, acting according to Moore's designs time and again. Seattle had averaged 6.8 yards per play, up from 4.4 per play over the first 10 games. The Seahawk attack had been perfectly balanced: 26 pass plays, 33 rushes, 10 first downs passing and 10 first downs rushing, 177 rushing yards, and 188 passing yards. And the mix of run and pass on first down, leaving out the game's final clock-killing, ball-protecting drive, had been what Moore regards as ideal: 13 running plays, nine passes. By staying even with Houston, and by performing so well on offense, Moore's players allowed him the luxury of multiple attacks, almost identical to the ones he had played out beforehand in his imagination.

To all appearances, Moore is a phlegmatic man. On the practice field, he almost never raises his voice; he has a vaguely professorial manner and comes across as more a teacher than a coach, even when talking with a re-

231

porter. He wears a permanent frown of concentration, which combines with his detached manner to make him seem interested in football more as an intellectual exercise than as an emotional and physical struggle for power.

Yet Moore is intensely competitive, as obsessive as any professional coach, a confirmed workaholic, and every bit as thin-skinned and contemptuous of the media as Knox is.

Two things that set him apart from his peers, though, are his courtliness and his quirky sense of humor. He conveys a certain respect to writers that few other coaches ever show. He gives long, thoughtful answers to questions. And while he is guarded, he is guarded in a disarming way, rather than in the customary abrasive manner of his peers. After the Denver game, I asked him why his team had problems running against the Broncos, and he said, "I have an impression, but I'd rather not comment. I'll have to look at the films—it was a complicated game out there." Two weeks later, I asked him again, reminding him what he'd said. "Uh, let me evade it another way," he answered. Then he claimed not to remember. It was his way of keeping something secret—as coaches are sworn to do—but at the same time offering an indirect apology for his paranoia.

The Houston game had turned Moore into an instant genius, after months of being regarded as a dullard by Seattle fans and writers who felt that the Seahawk offense was predictable and outdated. He was to make no secret during the latter half of this season of his skepticism over the new-found regard reporters felt toward him. "I never read the papers here," he said after the game. "You don't dare, if you want to keep your self-esteem."

From the day Knox and his staff first arrived in Seattle six seasons ago, Moore has struck me as an anomaly. Of the six coaches Knox brought with him from Buffalo in 1983, Moore, at age 35, was by far the youngest. While the rest of Knox's men were stolid Midwesterners and Southerners, Moore was, of all things, a Californian. His longish blond hair and relaxed, loose posture stood out in marked contrast to his fellow assistants' short hair, stern faces, and military bearing.

Now 41, Moore graduated from Glendale High in Glendale, California, in 1965, and graduated from the University of California at Santa Barbara in 1970, where he was an All-Coast selection at wide receiver. After spending two years with that football team as a graduate assistant, he moved on to Temple, Texas, to serve as assistant football coach and head track coach of the town's high school. From there he moved to Mesa Verde High in 1973, where he coached for one season, before going to West Point to serve as quarterbacks and receivers coach in 1975. After one season there, he held the same position at Rice University before signing on with Buffalo's new head coach, Chuck Knox, in 1978. Now in his 11th season with Knox, he had been working for him in the NFL longer than anyone else on the staff, save for defensive coordinator Tom Catlin, who was in his 16th Knox-governed season.

Growing up, Moore was obsessed with football strategy. In childhood, his favorite activity was drawing up plays in the dirt during neighborhood games. From fifth grade on, he says, he knew he was going to be a coach. Beginning in his high-school years, every summer he attended as many coaching clinics as he could. He rose with remarkable speed through the coaching ranks, spending only two years at the high-school level and three at the college level before breaking into the pros. Under Knox, he started out as special-assignments and special-teams coach, became wide receivers coach when Knox and his staff came to Seattle, and after the 1985 season was promoted to offensive coordinator. During the subsequent offseason, he says, he first realized how many years of round-the-clock work he had devoted to football. "I was rewriting our playbook that offseason," he recalls, "and I looked up late one night and saw my reflection in the window. It was dark outside, around 3 in the morning or so, and I said, 'Man, you have got to be crazy! To be doing this at this time of night at this time of the year!' But that's the kind of effort it takes to compete at this level."

Offensive game-planning is tedious work, with long hours spent poring over computer printouts, staring at film, compiling lists and charts, and studying statistics. The first step, each week, is information-gathering—both on the upcoming opponent and on the Seahawks themselves. Next comes a sifting through of Seattle's arsenal of plays, looking for those most effective against the particular defense the team will face that week. "The first thing we do," Moore explains, "is say, 'Now what is best against their defense?' For play and for motion, backfield sets, personnel groupings. Then we say, 'What are our people really good at doing?' And then finally, we ask, 'How many of these plays can we have game-ready?' And so we'll arrive at a certain number, and we'll rank our plays and rank the things and say, 'OK, we can handle this much.' So that's the weeding process."

Sorting the plays into a plan of attack means "trying to account for every conceivable situation. For instance, if we have just three plays to go, and we need 7 points to win, we know which three plays we would call. If we come up with a third-and-15, we know what play we would call by game day. Even third-and-25, we know what we're going to call." The idea is to make game decisions under low-pressure conditions, when a coach has time and resources at his command and is in a calm, more analytical state of mind. "There's lots of advantages to making decisions in midweek. When you have access to computer reports and film, and so on. As opposed to a 5- or 10-second period on the sidelines. We have all the time in the world on a weeknight. We can discuss it, talk about it, make the decision."

Following a prewritten plan of attack is based on accurately predicting a team's defensive tendencies—which, according to Moore, is fairly easy. He knows days in advance that if his team comes to the line of scrimmage with a third-and-five at midfield in the third quarter of a 4-point game, he will see a particular defensive alignment. Defenses tend to deploy and react the same way week to week. "If I've done my homework," he says of his own playcalling, "I know exactly, going in, what's going to be called. And so long as defenses are coming down track, doing what they tend to do, playing the way they've been playing over time, then we basically can come down track with the things we have preplanned."

The preplanning against Houston had been most accurate in predicting that the Oilers would play aggressive defense. Moore's plan called for more play-action passing (passing after faking a handoff), more subterfuge, and more cutback running. The intent was to take advantage of Houston's tendency to charge, en masse and unthinking, toward where the ball first appears to be headed. Two critical plays—John L. Williams's cutback run for 44 yards and a touchdown, and Dave Krieg's fourth-down run—succeeded because Oiler defenders overreacted to the play's initial flow.

Mentally, Moore "plays" an upcoming game over and over during the week. It is a way to memorize his new plan and to build his confidence in the plays and in his ability to call them at the proper time. "I go over the game plan maybe five times, and I visualize the play happening, and seeing it be successful, the way I want it to come out. Otherwise, some of these things you'd have trouble calling—like that triple pass [a flea-flicker, called during the Houston game, in which Krieg pitched to Warner, Warner handed off to Largent, Largent pitched back to Krieg, and Krieg threw downfield to Mike Tice]. You know, that's a high-risk play. Unless you feel good about calling it, you're not going to call it. So I spend a lot of time doing that. Then on game day, I should be like this"—he snaps his fingers.

Moore goes into a typical game with a 65-play repertoire—25 run plays and 40 pass plays—in place. With each play, there are several formations, casts of characters, blocking schemes, shifts, uses of men in motion, and combinations of pass patterns to choose from. It seems an almost infinite set of possibilities, yet Moore has it all so firmly stored in his mind that his playcalling during a game is a matter of reflex. "Now, some days I'm not as hot as others," he says. "Just like you have days that aren't quite as good. But generally, on game day, I'm highly activated, and when I am, and I'm *walking,* I'm *moving . . .* because it's *stored* and I've visualized it. Ask me what's a first-and-10, second, first-and-10, third . . . what's a first, second, second-and-10 pass play, and it's like that!" He snaps his fingers again. "What's a second goal-line play? Zap! Because I've been through it. I've visualized it. I've already done it—I've already played the game four or five times."

Seattle's record in Moore-imagined games, I would imagine, is perfect—with the possible exception of one game each year. However susceptible football in general may be to scientific analysis and data-driven projection, the particular game Seattle faces whenever it travels to Kansas City—as the Seahawks were to do this week—defies rational understanding. Seattle had last won in Arrowhead Stadium in 1980, and since then had lost six straight games there by a combined score of 187–67, throwing 15 interceptions and losing seven fumbles.

Two of the losses had been particularly costly. The previous season, when they traveled to Kansas City to face the 3–11 Chiefs, the Seahawks could have guaranteed themselves the home-field advantage in the wild card round of the playoffs with a win; instead, they lost, 41–20. In 1984, with a chance to clinch at least a tie for the first division championship in franchise history, the Seahawks—12–2 at the time—lost to the 6–8 Chiefs, 34–7. Now, at 6–5, tied with Denver and Los Angeles for the AFC West lead, they were off to Kansas City to play a 2–8–1 Chief team that seemed to be resurging: The week before, the Chiefs had knocked off the 8–2 Cincinnati Bengals, 31–28, on a last-second field goal.

Knox, while insisting that he didn't believe in jinxes, nevertheless resorted to superstition when it came to Kansas City. "This'll be the sixth time we've gone over there," he said on Wednesday. "We've gone over on Friday for a Sunday game, we've gone on Saturday the last couple of years, we've stayed in three different hotels—we've about run out of hotels over there—and it didn't make any difference." Out of despair, then, he resorted to the only remaining options: proper planning and attitude and play. "So the thing is, we're gonna go back in there, we're going back to where we started. We came to the conclusion that it doesn't make any difference where you stay and when you leave. None of that has anything to do with winning. Because none of those factors block, tackle, catch the ball, throw the ball, defend, or any of those things." It was not so much a philosophy as it was a desperate grasping at tangibles.

Knox, having beaten a legitimate team in Houston, and having looked good doing it, had reverted to his old combative, cliché-spouting self. When recovering from failure, he is more searching and forthcoming in his answers to questions. But when things are going well for him, he finds something wrong with every question he's asked. And this week, reporters' questions were met with cutting remarks and non-answers.

Every coach, on every team, at every level, eventually gets around to reminding writers that they are ignorant. That sportswriters are incapable of understanding the complexities of football is the most widely held conviction in the NFL. What coaches never acknowledge, of course, is that part of their job is to keep writers that way. Beat writers, asking a coach about the most mundane of matters, always come away feeling like they've been trying to pry military secrets out of a career colonel. Everything from how a play is supposed to unfold to the details of player trades is classified information. (In one of Seattle's more notorious examples, the Seahawks had written into a 1987 trade agreement with the Green Bay Packers that the Packer draft pick given Seattle for defensive back Dave Brown was not to be revealed to the media.)

Paul Zimmerman, writing in *The New Thinking Man's Guide to Pro Football*, offers a stirring defense of writers as he attacks the NFL's obsessive secrecy. "We are at a great disadvantage, not being allowed to see the films the coaches see," Zimmerman writes. "I wonder how many of them could come up with a coherent story about a game, based on only one look, as we have to . . . So players and coaches bitch about the dumb writers who don't really know what's going on out there, and yet the farthest thing from their minds is trying to educate those dumb writers."

Kansas City's Arrowhead Stadium is the weirdest structure in the Milky Way Galaxy. A real estate ad for this place would describe it as "moderne." Dedicated in 1972, it seats 78,097, and is built exclusively for football. To judge from the stadium's sightlines, the architect knew what he was doing. But to judge from its unsightliness, he must have been a Saturday morning cartoon addict: Arrowhead is a stage set lifted out of "The Jetsons." From the air, it looks like what was left of a football after someone cut the ends off of it, then sliced it lengthwise. From the press box, you look across the field at a self-consciously futuristic sweep, along the top of the stadium wall, that apparently is intended to give a space-age look to the place. Everything looks lightweight, plastic, and fake. It was the week before Thanksgiving, crisp and sun-drenched in Kansas City on the day of the game, and the natural setting (snow, blue sky, bright winter light) only served to highlight the stadium's alien look.

Seattle's last four visits to Arrowhead had been unmitigated disasters from the outset, so it was bracing to see the Seahawks open the game by getting a first down on their first drive. Even though their next three plays netted them only 1 yard, forcing them to punt, they at least managed not to turn the ball over.

The Chiefs, though, started out from their 19-yard line with 11 minutes remaining in the quarter, and proceeded to stroll stubbornly downfield, using nearly the entire quarter to work their way into the Seattle end zone, for their first first-quarter touchdown of the season. Running 15 plays—four passes and 11 runs—they exploited Seattle's two greatest defensive weaknesses, the run inside and the sideline pass. Three of Kansas City quarterback Steve DeBerg's four completions on the drive were out-passes—two for 7 yards, one for 10 yards—each one completed in front of a retreating Seattle cornerback. The Seahawk corners, vulnerable to the long bomb, give opposing receivers such a big cushion that every opponent this season had started out the game with frequent 7- to 10-yard sideline completions.

All but one of the passes came either on first or second down, and passes and runs alike were so successful that Kansas City faced only three third downs on the drive: third-and-two twice, and third-and-seven once—that one coming only after Kansas City false-started on third-and-two. Eight of the Chiefs' 11 rushes were into the middle, for 44 yards. On the Kansas City touchdown—a 2-yard James Saxon romp through a huge hole over right guard—Chief guard Mark Addickes had cleared the way by effortlessly pushing Bosworth halfway through the end zone. If the Chiefs continued to attack that way, the Seahawks—particularly Bosworth—were in for a long afternoon.

Still, if that quarter was any indication, this game was fated to follow a saner course than had any of the last four Seattle visits to Arrowhead. This time, at least, Seattle made it through the quarter without turning over the ball.

After Bobby Joe Edmonds returned Kansas City's kickoff to the Seattle 27, NBC called a TV time-out. As Seattle's offense stood loosely huddled on the field, waiting, Mike Tice solemnly walked around the huddle, ceremoniously butting heads with each offensive lineman. It was a formal call to arms, a defiant refusal to accede to the demons of Arrowhead Stadium.

The Seahawks then commenced a punishing, determined drive that established once and for all their primacy over the Chiefs. Covering 66 yards in 12 plays, they threw six passes—only one of them incomplete—to four receivers, and ran six times, gaining 27 yards on the ground, 29 in the air. They mixed plays so well, and executed them with such ease, that the confused Kansas City defense began to cave in. The drive amounted to a sustained Seahawk declaration: "You can't beat us unless we beat ourselves." And the Chiefs, back on their heels, acknowledged that they believed it.

It was first-and-10 for Seattle now, at the Kansas City 15. Mike Tice,

lined up as right tight end, went in motion left, and broke into the short secondary, crossing over the middle. Kansas City's linebackers had dropped
deep at the snap and Tice was left completely free. Krieg hit him
immediately—it was his third pass of the drive to Tice—and Tice turned upfield, bulling his way straight up the middle toward the Kansas City goal
line. Chief linebacker Dino Hackett, closing from Tice's left, dove, and Tice
carefully tucked the ball under his right arm. As Hackett hit his legs, Tice
dove forward just as another linebacker, Jack Del Rio, slammed into his
right, punching blindly at Tice's underside.

The ball popped free. And as it looped past astounded rookie defensive
back Kevin Porter, I was seized with the urge to avert my eyes from the
field. Since only 33,000 fans had shown up to cheer their 2–8–1 heroes on,
the stadium was less than half full. Yet when I looked up this time, the place
was packed, the 45,000 previously empty seats now occupied by 45,000
Chuck Knoxes—each wearing the same stunned, mirthless smile, and
gazing numbly heavenward. I blinked my eyes, disbelieving, and looked
again: The seats were empty, Kansas City's offense was on the field—
Porter having recovered enough of his composure to pounce on the ball—
and Tice, disgusted and confused, was already standing by himself over on
the sidelines. Knox, unsurprised, was watching his defense take the field.

Disastrous as Tice's fumble was, Seattle had Kansas City in such poor
field position that the fumble could be taken by the nonbeliever for a delay,
rather than an outright denial, of Seattle's first touchdown. And for six of
the next nine plays, the Seahawks played like determined optimists.

On the three other plays, though, they were men dispossessed. Ken
Clarke started things off by jumping offsides, turning a first-and-10 at the 2-
yard line into a first-and-five at the 7. After holding the Chiefs to 9 yards
over the next three plays, the Seahawks had the upper hand. The Chiefs
faced third-and-nine on their own 14—a difficult down-and-distance in a part
of the field where they dared not take chances. At which point Terry Taylor
took a lunch break, allowing journeyman quarterback Steve DeBerg to
complete a 19-yard pass to Stephone Paige. Again the Seahawks stiffened,
and the Chiefs were forced to punt from their 41. Punter Kelly Goodburne
got off an awful, sidelong kick that bounced at the Seattle 20. Bobby Joe
Edmonds came running casually up to it, then stopped, frozen momentarily
by the ball's bounce. It sailed by him on the right, hopping and rolling happily down to the Seattle 5. Nine plays and 3½ minutes after having the
Chiefs backed up against their own goal line, the Seahawks had fiercely surrendered 93 yards in field position.

Immediately, Seattle's offense, now terrified of the turnover in a way
they would not be in any other stadium, tried three running plays for 3 total

yards. Ruben Rodriguez, fielding a low snap, managed a good, 40-yard kick just over the outstretched hands of an onrushing Stephone Paige, and Kansas City took over at the Chief 49.

Melvin Jenkins, for one, was tired of giving up out-pattern yardage to the Kansas City receivers. Determined to show the Chiefs who was in charge of the airways, he lined up in Stephone Paige's face. When Paige angled for the left sideline, Jenkins stayed with him, ready to break to the outside in step with the receiver.

Paige faked toward the sideline, then burst downfield, leaving the leaning Jenkins three steps behind. DeBerg, throwing with all his strength, threw poorly, but Jenkins was so far out of the play that Paige was able to slow down, reach out, and grab the ball, tumbling to the turf at the Seattle 4. Two plays later, fullback Christian Okoye, slanting off right tackle, nonchalantly took a Bosworth blast to the thigh and sauntered into the end zone. The Chiefs, who had managed only two rushing touchdowns through 11 games, now had two more in the first half alone.

With 4:16 left in the half, the Seahawks now trailed 14–0, and were well on their way to another 34–, 28–, or 27–7 drubbing. But then Krieg, for some reason, decided to show how savvy and accurate he can be, completing six of eight passes as his team covered 75 yards in 3 minutes, 15 seconds, to score a touchdown with 1:06 remaining. Looking deep, making quick, wise decisions, deftly hitting secondary receivers, and gaining 8 yards himself on a quarterback draw, Krieg looked unstoppable. His receivers—particularly Blades, who twice slipped tacklers after making catches, turning short completions into 17- and 14-yard gains—suddenly were world-class. Krieg's touchdown pass was thrown through the eye of a needle: Ray Butler, with a 4-inch height advantage over cornerback J.C. Pearson, curled in from the right sideline, leapt, stretched to the limit of his reach, snared Krieg's pass—which came in inches over Pearson's outstretched fingers—and came down with his feet millimeters inside the end line. It was a pass for which there had been no margin of error at all, and Krieg had hit it perfectly.

Kansas City came back after the halftime intermission looking enthusiastically for a way to lose the game. On the Chiefs' second play from scrimmage, DeBerg misread the Seattle defense. Thinking Seahawk cornerbacks were covering Chief receivers man-to-man, he sent his wide receivers deep, then had running back Herman Heard slant into the right flat. Terry Taylor, though, had dropped into a short zone, and waited, salivating, for the pass he saw coming. He intercepted at the 28-yard line, on the dead run, and scored a lonely, astonishing touchdown.

With the score tied, the Chiefs were reeling. Norm Johnson's kickoff, hitting at the 12-yard line, was left untouched by three Kansas City receivers locked in heated debate over whose turn it was to handle the ball. Finally, after it had rolled to the 2, returner Kenny Gamble fell on it, just before half the Seattle team fell on him.

In only eight plays the Chiefs gave the ball up again, and Seattle, in control now, started out to take the lead from their own 39. Two runs each by Warner and Williams brought Seattle to the Kansas City 43, where Krieg and his troops came to the line of scrimmage facing third-and-three. Looking over the defense, Krieg saw a quarterback's dream situation: Steve Largent covered by a rookie cornerback, J.C. Pearson. Largent broke slightly to the inside, ran 10 yards downfield, then curled to the outside. Pearson, unimpressed by Largent's fake inward, stayed on his outside shoulder. Krieg, after taking a good look at Pearson, threw the ball to Largent's outside anyway—afterward, he would not be able to explain why he did—and Pearson made an easy interception.

From a coach's viewpoint, a play is one of two things: a success or a failure. It has no meaning beyond that. From a fan's viewpoint, however, every play is telling, and key plays are downright symbolic. This one, as Tice's fumble had been, was both. It was not some simple quarterback mistake, committed and then forgotten. It was a sign from the football cosmos that the Seahawks, no matter what they did, no matter how many yards they totaled, no matter how well they played, were not going to win this game. It was a matter not of blocking and tackling and throwing and catching and of players making plays, but of fate, or karma, or destiny, or whatever other euphemism for mystery fans like to employ. The schedule may have called for another 22 minutes, 15 seconds of play, but everyone not in a Seahawk uniform knew that the game was over.

Krieg went off to soliloquize, crudely, on the sidelines. Knox went about his business, although he did take a few expressive seconds to share some insights with Krieg. And the Chiefs, having rediscovered their offense, made their way down to the Seattle 16, from where they settled for a field goal and a 17–14 lead.

Before proceeding to the next demonic item in the program, it is worth noting that Seattle came within less than a yard, on third-and-three, of not having to send its punting unit in. It is also worth noting that the punt team was escorted onto the field by an air of anticipation unequaled in richness since Kathleen Turner first came steaming onscreen in *Body Heat*. The stadium crowd knew that *this was the play*.

The snap came back to Rodriguez so low that he had to step forward and bend to the ground just to get his hands on it. It slipped through his fingers a hair's-breadth above the turf, bounced off his instep, then hid on the ground behind him. He looked around, saw it, picked it up, and ran a slow semicircle away from two hulking Kansas City rushers, who mercilessly slammed him down at the Seattle 19. The Chiefs' subsequent four-play touchdown drive was interrupted twice—once by the end of the third quarter, once by the replay official, who determined that DeBerg's 14-yard quarterback draw for a touchdown was actually a 13¾-yard quarterback draw for a near-touchdown. On the next play, DeBerg bootlegged his way into the end zone, and the crowd was informed that the Chiefs had totaled three rushing touchdowns in a game for the first time in 58 games. Kansas City kicked off again, and, with 14:30 remaining in the game, down by 10 points, Seattle once again, out of perversity (or, more likely, because finally they were sufficiently inspired by adversity), reverted to greatness.

Krieg, Williams, and Tice combined to cover 60 yards in only five plays: a 9-yard completion to Tice, a 7-yard run by Williams, two 9-yard completions to Williams, and a 26-yard pass to Tice. Then, under pressure at the Kansas City 15, Krieg side-armed a weak pass to John Spagnola, for no gain. On the next play, Spagnola, wide open at the 4, dropped a pass that hit him right in the hands. Instead of first-and-goal at the 4, Seattle faced third-and-10 at the 15, and the Kansas City rush on the next down forced Krieg to hurry a pass to Williams. It fell yards short, and the Seahawks settled for a field goal.

For the first time in the entire game, Seattle held Kansas City to four downs, and after the Chiefs punted, the Seahawks had the ball at their own 41 with 7:29 to play. Again, Seattle was indomitable, covering the 59 yards in 3 minutes, Krieg connecting with Blades three times, for 16 and 18 yards to start out the drive, and for 14 and a game-tying touchdown to end it.

Kevin Porter, returning the ensuing kickoff to the Chief 27, fumbled. The ball sat on the ground, between Seahawk Dwayne Harper's legs, waiting for the Seahawks to recover it—and along with it the victory—while Harper and his teammates lost themselves in one-on-one battles with their blockers. The only Seahawk who seemed to notice the ball was kicker Norm Johnson, who came sliding in just in time to see the fallen Porter's arm come slithering across the turf and pull the ball in.

Hard as it is to believe, Kansas City tried three more times not to win the game. At the 1:55 mark, DeBerg threw a pass into Dave Wyman's hands, only to have it bounce out. At 1:46, with the ball still at the Seattle 45, the Chiefs faced their first third-and-10 situation of the entire game. Terry Taylor, playing off of receiver Kitrick Taylor as if he expected Kansas City to throw deep for a touchdown, surrendered a 16-yard completion. Accordingly, with 51 seconds remaining, Nick Lowery kicked his second game-winning field goal in two weeks, putting the Chiefs up 27–24.

Seattle's demons, however, couldn't resist giving the Seahawks one final, teasing glimpse at a scoring opportunity. Kicking off, Lowery squibbed a line drive that took one hop into Mike Tice's arms. Bulling straight ahead, Tice returned it to the Seattle 41. With 41 seconds remaining, Seattle had only to move 29 yards to be well within Johnson's field-goal range. Krieg's first pass attempt was knocked down at the line of scrimmage by defensive end Leonard Griffin. Then Brian Blades, lined up on the far right, took cornerback Greg Hill 20 yards downfield, dipped his shoulders inward, then broke to the sideline. Hill, trying to react, twisted his ankle, and Blades was left completely uncovered. Krieg's throw was short, but Blades got a good break on the ball. He reached out for it at the Chief 40, fully aware that a catch would give his team a first down within 10 yards of sure field-goal range, with time to run four more plays. But the ball hit his fingers and the ground at the same time, and bounced free. After seven completions for 89 yards and a touchdown, the Krieg–Blades connection came up one inch short.

After Griffin knocked down another Krieg pass, he knocked the ball out of Krieg's hand on fourth down, and Kansas City took over on downs at the Seattle 25. As players from both teams piled up on the ball, I saw, 10 yards upfield, one of the season's most affecting sights: Krieg, sprawled full length and face down, furiously pounding the turf with his fist.

Knox, his midweek bluster gone, greeted the press in the subterranean hallway outside a door leading to his team's locker room. After ticking off the mistakes his players had made, Knox said resignedly, "It just went that way all afternoon. We had the effort, we were intense, we battled back, we were down 10 points, we came back to tie it. I can't fault anybody for lack of effort. We just didn't make the plays. We were a little off here, and a little off there, and that's what happens to you."

Inevitably, he was asked about his persistent problems at Arrowhead Stadium. His questioners were offering him a chance to confess his faith in intangibles, in spirits, in fate—to confess, in short, that there were forces in the universe he could never bring under his control. "The stadium didn't have anything to do with it," he snapped. "*We* dropped the ball, *we* didn't make a good snap on the punt. We can't blame anybody but ourselves. We have no excuses. We just got beat! OK?"

The door to the locker room opened, and I stepped into a scene of indescribable psychological carnage. Players sat sprawled against their locker walls, their eyes staring blankly at nothing, or leaned forward, heads bowed, as they ferociously ripped tape from their limbs. I felt crass and out of place. Reporters picked their way through the room, silently looking for signs from some player, somewhere, that he might be willing to talk. I tried my luck with Ron Mattes, the player I got along best with. "You feel some-times like there's just nothing more you can do, I guess," I ventured. "Sometimes," he muttered, without looking up. "There's nothing you can say, either. Fuck it!"

Ashamed, insight-starved, I tiptoed through the locker room. Grant Feasel, who had delivered the low snap to Rodriguez, was facing his locker, muttering over his shoulder to the crowd of reporters behind him. Eugene Robinson, oblivious to the microphone someone had thrust in front of his face, stared silently straight ahead.

Finally, Krieg came walking through, arrived at his locker, and turned to face the sea of reporters closing in around him. "They gave us some chances, and we didn't take advantage of them," he said. "We gave them some chances, and they did take advantage of them."

This was the sort of unintended brilliance that Krieg always proffered af-ter losses. Today, he proved once again that the more bitter the loss, the better the postgame interview.

As he talked on, enumerating again and again the critical errors his team had committed, I realized that advantage was exactly what this game had been about. Disadvantaged, the Seahawks had played brilliantly. Given the chance to seize the advantage, they had folded. And at the end of the game, with the loss firmly in their grasp, they had played like a team to whom losing was a good and natural thing. I was convinced they had reverted, on their last defensive and offensive series, to the players they felt themselves in their hearts to be. "But we did come back! We kept coming back!" Krieg blurted out. "And . . . I don't know what to say, because, shoot, we did al-most all we could, but there were still some things we could've done ob-viously better."

"Don't you ever feel," he was asked, "that it's just out of your hands?"

"No!" he insisted. "It's always in our hands! We gotta be the ones that score the points. I don't care what else happens. We have to go out there and score points, however many it takes. And we kept coming back today, but we just ran out of time at the end."

On his way out of the locker room, Mike Tice, pausing to discuss his fumble, delivered himself of a poignant monologue. "I looked up, and I saw the end zone, and I thought I had a chance of maybe getting in and scoring, so I was running as fast as my slow legs could carry me, and I saw one of the fellas, and I didn't realize until someone just told me here, that two guys hit me, I saw one of the fellas coming, and I thought I protected the ball from him, but I must've turned into the other guy. It happened so fast and you're so intense! I thought it was just one guy. That's why I was be-wildered . . . I was trying, I was trying to do my best! I was trying to get some yardage. When I caught the ball, I was trying to make that one of my improvements—to get some yardage. Maybe I fought a little bit too hard on that particular one. Maybe for once I should've fell down . . . "

That, to borrow Knox's phrase, is the way it went all afternoon. That excess of effort had been as harmful to Seattle's chances against Kansas City as lack of effort had been in other games. And in the final analysis, the Seahawks' level of effort or even their level of competence would have been irrelevant. Because for whatever reason, and by the grace of whomever, they were not ordained to win this game. "All is not lost, believe it or not," Tice muttered as he left the room. "Six and six . . . unbelievable."

It became more unbelievable later in the day, when the New Orleans Saints and Atlanta Falcons conspired to keep Denver and Los Angeles even with Seattle. The Saints beat the Broncos, 42–0, while Atlanta, playing in Los Angeles, beat the Raiders 12–6. The three-way tie for first in the AFC West was now held by teams with 6–6 won-lost records. Seattle, fighting for its first-ever division title, was locked in a down-to-the-wire wheelchair race.

On the flight home, out of a sense of duty, I reluctantly picked up *Hard Knox: The Life of an NFL Coach*, by Chuck Knox and Bill Plaschke, and started reading it. Having already suffered through Bosworth's blather, I couldn't imagine reading another jockography, but it was an unavoidable task, and my flight was a long one.

By the third page, I could see that I was in for something unexpected from a sports professional: humility, first of all, and beyond that a sense that one's own successes and failures are inexplicable. *Hard Knox* is not the book of a self-professed legend. It is the book of a human being picked by chance to lead a remarkable life, and it is filled with a sense of awe not at oneself, but at the irresolvable mystery at the center of existence. "I'm not a superstar," Knox writes. "I'm not a hero. I don't glitter. I survive. . . Even when I've won, I've just survived. I've coached in four conference championship games, but you know how many of those games I've won, how many Super Bowls I've coached in? None. A big-game loser, that's what the critics called me. A guy who loses when it counts. I used to think they were right. For much of my early life, if there existed a definition of *winning*, I sure as hell didn't know where to look it up."

Knox was born on April 27, 1932, in the Pennsylvania steel-mill town of Sewickley. His family was extremely poor, and he grew up determined to escape the grinding life of poverty and hard drinking that awaited him in Sewickley. When he left, over the strenuous objections of his father, to attend Juniata College in Huntingdon, Pennsylvania, he was in effect running

PHOTOGRAPHS BY ROD MAR

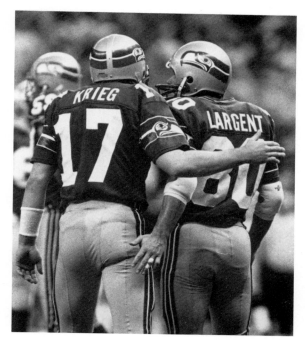

Above, Dave Krieg congratulates Steve Largent; *below*, at the April press conference announcing Seattle's signing of quarterback Kelly Stouffer, everyone's mind is on Kenny Easley's just-discovered life-threatening illness.

Above, Steve Largent in repose, during preseason training camp (photo by Curt Warner); *left*, two unknowns fight for survival in the opening days of preseason.

Above left, Fredd Young, in training camp, tries to explain his on-again, off-again holdout; *above right*, Chuck Knox leads the Boz off field during preseason practice; *below left*, offensive coordinator Steve Moore oversees stretching exercises at training camp; *below right*, Mike McCormack and bored Seahawk managing general partner John Nordstrom watch a preseason scrimmage from the sidelines.

Above, Brian Bosworth obliges his fans during preseason; *below left*, free safety Eugene Robinson, the brains of the Seattle secondary; *below right*, Terry Taylor takes a break during training camp.

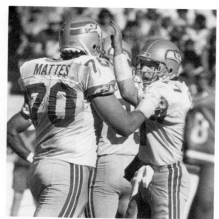

Above left, Brian Bosworth in midroar during preseason home opener with Phoenix; *above right*, quarterback coach Ken Meyer talks things over with Dave Krieg on the practice field; *below left*, Chuck Knox signs copies of his autobiography, *Hard Knox*; *below right*, Dave Krieg thanks Ron Mattes for his protection after a touchdown against the Broncos.

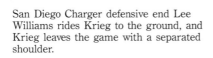

San Diego Charger defensive end Lee Williams rides Krieg to the ground, and Krieg leaves the game with a separated shoulder.

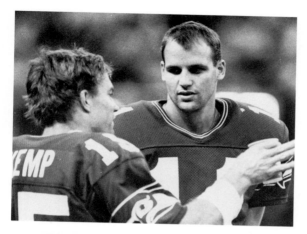

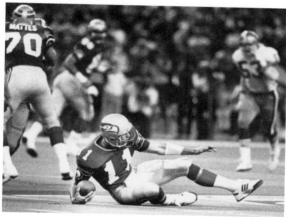

Above, Jeff Kemp and Kelly Stouffer confer during Seattle's disastrous loss to the San Francisco 49ers; *middle and below*, Kelly Stouffer, his nose newly broken, leaps to his feet and throws a touchdown pass against the 49ers.

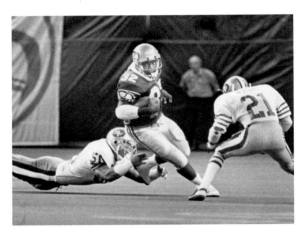

Above, John L. Williams slips through the San Francisco 49er secondary; *middle*, Curt Warner finds nowhere to go on a carry against the Atlanta Falcons; *below*, John L. Williams cuts upfield against Atlanta.

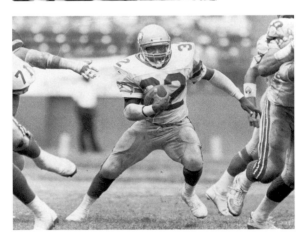

THE BOZ
AT BOOK STORES NOW

Above, Brian Bosworth and Vernon Dean break up a pass to Atlanta Falcon Jesse Hester; *middle*, airplane with Boz banner in tow, as seen in Atlanta, Cleveland, Los Angeles, and Seattle; *below*, Curt Warner has an outstanding day against the Cleveland Browns.

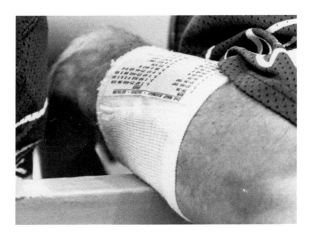

Above, Kelly Stouffer's cue card, used to help him decipher signals mimed in by assistant coach Chick Harris; *middle*, Los Angeles Rams receivers Henry Ellard and Aaron Cox celebrate a Ram touchdown, as humiliated cornerback Melvin Jenkins retires to the sideline; *below*, Seattle defensive backs Patrick Hunter, Paul Moyer (21), and Eugene Robinson (41), with linebacker Dave Wyman during Seattle's defeat by the Los Angeles Rams.

Above, Chuck Knox faces the media after being slaughtered by the Rams; *middle,* Curt Warner in the Kingdome against the Chargers; *below,* Kelly Stouffer fumbles yet another snap against the Buffalo Bills.

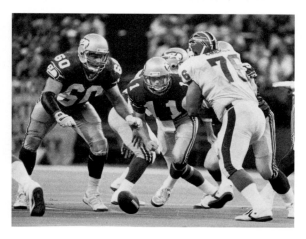

Above, Brian Bosworth, recuperating from shoulder surgery, talks with Darren Comeaux on the sideline during game against the Houston Oilers; *middle*, Curt Warner, after scoring a touchdown against the Oilers, is congratulated by team owner Ken Behring; *below left*, Chuck Knox objects to replay officials' calls during game with San Diego Chargers; *below right*, referee Jerry Markbreit confers with replay official George Sladky after blowing a call during the Chargers game.

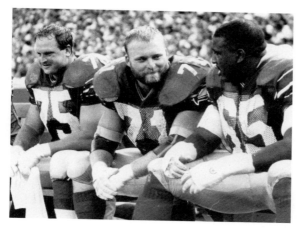

Above, Seahawk offensive
linemen (*left to right*) Mike
Wilson, Bryan Millard, and
Edwin Bailey relax on the
Kingdome bench during the
Raider game in November
(the disembodied shoulder
belongs to Ron Mattes);
middle left, running back
John Stephens commiserates
with Curt Warner after New
England's win over Seattle;
middle right, Curt Warner is
stopped cold by the New
England defense; *below,* Patriot
running back John Stephens
runs through a gaping hole
in the Seattle defense.

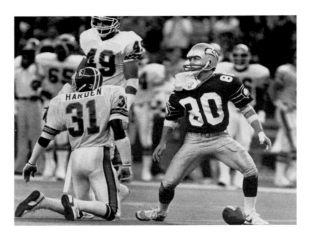

Above, Steve Largent after making a catch against the Denver Broncos; *middle*, Norm Johnson kicks an extra point after one of Seattle's six touchdowns against the Denver Broncos in the Kingdome; *below*, Brian Blades hauls in a touchdown pass in the season-ending win over the Los Angeles Raiders.

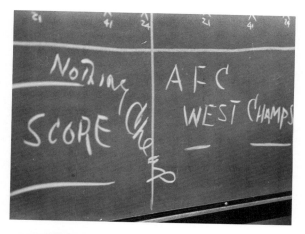

Above, Knox's final halftime message to his troops during the last Raider game; *middle*, Raider quarterback Jay Schroeder's last-ditch attempt against the Seahawks falls incomplete in the end zone. Players pictured are Nesby Glasgow (22), Patrick Hunter (23), Paul Moyer, and Raiders Mervyn Fernandez and Willie Gault (83); *below*, Joe Nash suffers a mysterious knee injury during the playoff game against the Cincinnati Bengals.

Ken Behring poses for a postgame shot
with the Seattle Sea Gals in the Kingdome.

away from home, so strong was the tradition that sons of millworkers must themselves enter the mill. After lettering for four years as a tackle at Juniata, and graduating from there with a degree in history, Knox—already determined that he was going to find a way to become a professional football coach—served as assistant coach for one year at Juniata before taking a coaching job at Tyrone, Pennsylvania, High School. A year later, he moved on to Ellwood City (Pennsylvania) High, where he coached three years before becoming an assistant at Wake Forest University. After two years there, Knox spent two years as an assistant at the University of Kentucky, then broke into the pros in 1963 as an assistant coach for the AFL's New York Jets. Four seasons later, he moved into the legitimate professional league—the NFL—as an assistant with the Detroit Lions. Then, in 1973, 19 years after he started out on his quest, the Los Angeles Rams hired him as their head coach.

He was greeted in Los Angeles, he remembers, by confusion and skepticism. After Knox was introduced to the local media, *Los Angeles Times* columnist Jim Murray wrote, "A press conference was called yesterday to announce the new head coach of the Rams. A limo pulled up, the passenger door was opened, and nobody got out."

Recalling that day, Knox writes, "At first it hurt, but then like most things that hurt, it just made sense. Why should anybody know me? What had I done? Where had I come from? But really now, isn't it better when nobody knows you? On the streets, you can always sneak up on somebody better that way. That's eighth-grade Sewickley."

That term—"eighth-grade Sewickley"—is Knox's synonym for street smarts. It represents the survival instinct of the fighter who can find a way to overcome adversity, whether it be in the form of poverty, or prejudice, or self-loathing, or a superior opponent. It signifies strength of will that will not be denied, however much conventional wisdom might dictate that it should be.

The Rams had finished 1972 with a 6–7–1 record, and Knox led them to a 12–2 finish and a division championship in his first season. It was the first of five division championships he would win there, before being forced out of his job and moving on to the 3–11 Buffalo Bills in 1978. He suffered through two losing seasons there (5–11 and 7–9), before winning the division championship in 1980 with an 11–5 record. He took the Bills to the playoffs the next season, going 10–6, before sliding to 4–5 in 1982—a strike year—and slipping out of town shortly thereafter to come to Seattle, where the Seahawks had also finished 4–5.

By the time he arrived in Seattle, Knox had a solid reputation as a coach who could turn losing teams around, and one who could get more wins out of lesser-talented athletes than any man alive. He also had a reputation as a coach who always fell short of the top. In Los Angeles, he had made the NFC Conference Championship game three times, and lost all three. "Let's face it," ex-Ram player Tom Mack says in *Hard Knox*. "I have to hold the record for the most playoff appearances without going to the Super Bowl. Twelve games. I counted . . . The bad thing about it was, we were physically beating teams in the playoffs, really beating up on Minnesota twice. Yet we could never get over the top . . . Like I said, a record. And yeah, it makes you mad. It makes you wonder. Nobody would ever blame Chuck, but I still could never figure out what was wrong."

His first loss, in 1974, stemmed from a late-in-the-game false-start call against Mack—a call that Knox, to this day, insists was wrong. The call moved the ball 5 yards back from the opponents' 6-inch line, and the Rams, with three downs to manage it, couldn't get into the end zone, and lost 14–10. The next season, facing the Dallas Cowboys in the Championship game, Knox and his Rams were soundly beaten, 37–7. Back again the next year, facing the Minnesota Vikings, the Rams tried a wide receiver reverse on third-and-two from the Viking 2, and came up inches short, the officials ruling that the ball carrier bounced, rather than dove, into the end zone—a call that Knox, to this day . . . Knox called for a field goal, and the Vikings blocked it and returned it the length of the field for a touchdown. It was a 10-point swing in a game Knox wound up losing, 24–13. "And now everybody is asking," Knox recalls, "How come you didn't go for the touchdown? I answer, How was I supposed to know the kick would be blocked? How did I know that a little mistake would occur? I went for the field goal because earlier that year in Minnesota, we went for a touchdown on fourth-and-one from the one-yard line and did not make it . . . Like I've said before, I live a lot by history."

History, in his life, had a way of repeating itself. "In both Los Angeles and Buffalo," he writes, "I won but I couldn't win. I was a loser in the big games and in earning the big money from the owner, and finally in Buffalo I wound up losing almost all faith in a system that had failed me twice. So I left—but only to take over yet another neglected child, the Seattle Seahawks."

It is no accident that Knox employs the neglected-child metaphor in describing floundering football franchises. Knox himself survived a horrendous childhood. He was a victim of severe child abuse. Had he grown up in this era, he would have been taken away from his parents.

The Knoxes were so poor that they lived in a four-room, unheated apartment that often had broken windows left unrepaired for months at a time.

Knox's father was an alcoholic who constantly beat his two sons. "He would hit us for coming home 15 minutes late," Knox writes. "He would hit us for coming home, period. He would chase us underneath the bed and pull us out by the legs and hit us . . . I can honestly say some of my best weekends were spent when my father was locked up by the cops on Friday for being drunk, and my mother wouldn't go down to get him until it was time for work on Monday."

His childhood forged in Knox a ceaseless anger and a determination to show his father he was worth something. The anger manifested itself in almost constant fighting and in fierce and unsportsmanlike play on the football field. "All the kids at school," recalls Knox's high-school teammate, Tom Sanders, "tried to stay away from him during one-on-one football drills. He was flat-out dirty." Knox agrees, with pride. "More than anything else, I was known for playing dirty. I was never great, but I worked hard and did anything to win."

From beginning to end, Knox's book is a paean of praise to the underdog. He depicts himself as an underdog from birth, a virtually homeless boy who fled "a town and a father that doesn't want or need" him and went on, against impossible odds, to reach the pinnacle of the coaching profession. "People wonder why I succeed with what they consider less-gifted players, and win championships with less-gifted teams," Knox writes. "Well, this is why. I wasn't gifted with anything. I learned everything. I learned what it took to win because if I didn't, I would be living twenty-three steps up from Walnut Street this day . . . I have a soft spot for players and teams who physically don't have what it takes." Later, writing about his first year with the down-and-out New York Jets, he says, "I love all teams like that, teams that kind of remind me of me. We went 5–8–1 in each of my first three years there, but we were competitive when we shouldn't have been. I loved that." And when he broke into the NFL with the Detroit Lions, what he would come to remember most about those days is his lowly status. "This Lions team had produced two NFL championships and twelve NFL Hall-of-Famers . . . Most everyone else on the staff had either played or coached in the NFL. And then there was me. Once again, the new kid. The outsider."

In both Los Angeles and Buffalo, Knox ascended in status from habitué of the bottom of the standings to Super Bowl contender. Then, history repeating itself from childhood, he found a way to have to start over again from the bottom. In both cities, he had fallings-out with team owners, and looked elsewhere in the league for work. His last move, from Buffalo to Seattle in 1983, was decided upon after the 1981 season, when he took the

Bills to the division playoffs after a 10–6 year, then was offered a new contract without a raise. "I decided . . . that after the 1982 season I would be gone."

His reasons for settling on Seattle are telling. From the way he describes his expectations, Seattle was made for him. "I had heard about Seattle's rain, its gray, its dreariness. I had read about it being so far from the rest of civilization that back in the 1800s businessmen on the East Coast would ship women out there by boat so the lumberjacks would have someone to talk to . . . This was a program that in the previous three years had gone 14–27. In the seven years of the franchise there had been only two winning seasons, and no playoff appearances. The way things were run, it seemed they hated the idea of succeeding. Most certainly, my kind of team."

Once again, Knox, in a renewed search for inspiration, had reached out and seized disadvantage for himself. It was the only thing that had ever worked for him.

His first season in Seattle was his best. For the first time in their history, the Seahawks made the playoffs. Against all expectations, Knox led them to the AFC division championship, losing to the eventual Super Bowl champion Los Angeles Raiders, 30–14.

Seen in the light of his past, it makes sense that Knox's Seattle years have been consistent in one glaring respect. He does best with his worst teams, and worst with his best teams. And in every Seattle season, just as in every season past, he looks back and finds an agonizing pattern to his struggle: He has been denied unqualified success because, in his words, he has been "haunted by more tiny mistakes."

It was nearly midnight as my plane came down in Seattle, from Kansas City by way of Chicago. It was windy and raining—the kind of night that is portrayed in the movies as portentous. The next day, I would hear Knox say, "We're only two plays from being 8–4." Having discovered his life and career through his memoirs, I saw innumerable echoes of both in the current season. I saw the New Orleans game, lost by a blocked field goal that caused a 10-point swing in the score. I saw interceptions in the San Diego and Kansas City games, thrown by a quarterback who knew as he wound up to throw the ball that it was the wrong thing to do and then afterward couldn't explain why he had done it. I saw again Tice's fumble at the Kansas City goal line in that day's 3-point loss, and again I saw the fateful low snap coming back to Rodriguez, whose fumble would set up Kansas City's last touchdown. I saw games won that should have been lost, and games lost that should have been won. I saw a man struggling less with physical shortcomings than with psychological ones. And I saw demons haunting not a city, not a franchise, not a team, but a single man.

"I just can't rid myself of Sewickley," Knox writes. He means that his roots in poverty have made him unreasonably thrifty and anxious in wealthy adulthood. He also means he is still a street-fighter. But unconsciously he is still fighting the struggle he fought as a child in Sewickley. It was drummed into him there that he was worthless, that he would never amount to anything, and that if he tried to escape his millworker's destiny he would fail. He grew up knowing that nothing he ever did or became would earn him his father's love. He was an outsider, a kid born to lose. In escaping his fate there, he had to rely on the only skill he's ever completely mastered: the ability to win an uphill struggle. Take away his plight, and you take away his inspiration. In not being able to rid himself of Sewickley, Knox is shackled by the Sewickley-borne sense that he doesn't deserve prosperity. Give him star billing and star athletes, and he is lost. *That*, more than anything else, is eighth-grade Sewickley.

I saw him as a man who lives for the luxurious, melancholy feeling of not quite making it. He fights heroically, he does better than anyone ever thought he could, but ultimately he falls short of winning it all—because deep down inside, he neither wants it nor feels he deserves it.

That state of mind is evidenced most strongly in his own motivational techniques, described by ex-Lion offensive lineman Bob Kowalkowski. "Knox would always talk ... about the great and decorated players," Kowalkowski recalls in *Hard Knox*. "Because he always felt like an underdog, he made us play like underdogs, too."

Where do you go from underdog? To top dog? Or back again to underdog? "This is where my coaching philosophy was generated," Knox writes of his boyhood. "I realized that everything I had learned while trying to survive on the Sewickley streets was applicable to my survival here. I'm not going to get into a big thing about how football mirrors life and all that stuff, but when you think about it, the struggle is the same."

Consciously, the pinnacle of Knox's life is the Super Bowl Championship. But unconsciously, he may already have reached the pinnacle. Writing of his 1986 season with Seattle, Knox recalls, "One of the craziest things of all was that we missed the playoffs that year by one game, which meant we missed them by one play in one of our losses, depending on how you looked at it. I was too frustrated to figure it out. I took it hard, probably harder than most close calls in my career ... At that year's Super Bowl—we were the only team to have beaten both competitors that year—I took it even worse. I looked down at the Rose Bowl field and watched the Giants' Bill Parcells and Denver's Dan Reeves and thought, What wouldn't I give to be there. I'd been so close to being there. I had coached several teams good enough to be there. And yet I was up in the stands for the fourteenth straight season. That day I discovered tears in my eyes and resolved that if such a moment were ever mine, I would never let it go."

It is the book's most eloquent passage. It represents the hidden attainment of Knox's secret life's goal. In a profession where coaches are supposed to want to be Zeus, Knox would rather be Sisyphus. He prefers the constant, futile, uphill battle to the kingly defense of privilege against the assaults of the underprivileged. He is a coach who lives to find an impossible way to win. There is no challenge in having a way to win handed to you in the form of a star-studded roster or a can't-lose game. Knox is a man who wins by losing. He is not so much an underdog as a *chronic* underdog—a man who knows, however unconsciously, that he has to be coming off a loss in order to do his best work. Small wonder that he always seems so much more a man after losses than after wins.

Yeah, Daddy

18

"My whole family—my mother, my father, my brother—we all were great basketball fans and football fans. And I was a great fan of the game before I met Edwin. Matter of fact, I was kind of a snob: offensive lineman!"

"Who wants to go out with a LINEMAN? I wanna go out with the quarterback!"

—Cherise Bailey and Connie Millard,
adoring wives of Seattle offensive linemen

Perhaps because he was entering the season's stretch run, Knox withdrew into a contemplative cocoon. He lost interest in lecturing reporters and in offering unsolicited observations. For all of the trouble he had been through this season, he was tied for the division lead, and three of his last four games would be against the other two co-leaders. In the standings, he had his best shot at a division championship since 1984, when he let it slip away with two season-ending losses—the first of which had been to Kansas City in Arrowhead Stadium. As was the case at the end of that season, his team's destiny this season—as his players would never tire of saying over the next four weeks—was in its own hands. To earn the division title, Knox would not have to rely on victories by other teams over his rivals.

Knox, then, was a general gathering his strength for the final battle of a long, exhausting war.

But I think it was something more than that. The Kansas City game had shaken Knox. It had been an illusion-shattering defeat, and it left him preoccupied by the nemesis—the tiny, untimely mistake—that had dogged him throughout his life. "Going into Kansas City, we had the best week of practice we've ever had," he said two days after the loss. "Why those things [mistakes] happen, I don't know. You'd like to be a good enough coach to overcome them."

He saw that once again, with the chance of emerging on the inside track to the division championship, he had entered a late-season game against a

251

weak opponent and had somehow found a way to lose both the game and the advantage he could have had over the other division leaders. When he pointed out to reporters that the Seahawks were only two plays from being 8–4, he was pointing out the agony of being persistently on the wrong side of the close call. He was also showing how huge the difference can be between a play nearly made and a play barely made. Those two plays (the field goal blocked by New Orleans and, against Kansas City, Feasel's bad snap to Rodriguez) made up the difference between being the fifth-best team in the NFL and being ranked a dismal 14th. An 8–4 Seahawk record would not have inspired Seattle papers to begin running "What's wrong with the Seahawks?" stories, speculating on everything from ineffective pass rush, poor game planning, and fading offensive line, to declining running back and thin linebacking corps. And with an 8–4 team atop the AFC West standings, newspapers in Seattle and elsewhere would not have begun printing "AFC Worst" stories, along the lines of a *Seattle Post-Intelligencer* story that ran the day after the Kansas City loss. "Doesn't anybody want to win this thing?" the story asked. "In the AFC West, apparently not."

An 8–4 team also has a far happier, less visible owner than does a 6–6 team, particularly when the owner in question is a football enthusiast, with a fan's understanding of the game, who has bought himself a pro franchise and likes to spend game days down on the sidelines. After weeks of public silence, Ken Behring surfaced on KOMO television a few days after he had run onto the field at the end of Seattle's last-second win over Houston, saying, among other things, "I think last Sunday [against Houston] we were a pretty exciting team. It was the most exciting team I've seen play all year here. I was really proud of them, and I was proud of him [Knox]. I mean, we had some innovative plays."

Presumably, had Bruce Scholtz not blocked the wrong rusher on his team's ill-fated field-goal attempt against New Orleans, Behring would have seen "innovative" plays all through that game, too.

The next weekend, interviewed on television in Kansas City, Behring was given an opportunity to clarify his remarks, and happenstance afforded viewers a perfect illustration of one of Knox's most oft-stated principles. After Seattle's tying touchdown at the 4:20 mark of the fourth quarter, Behring's comments ran long, so NBC kept the audio of the interview running while switching the camera to the ensuing kickoff. As viewers heard Behring say of Knox, "I thought he did a great job last week," they saw Kansas City fumble the kickoff and recover the ball before Seattle players could track it down. The words "last week" gave Behring away. He was incapable of seeing innovation in Seahawk losses. And there on the screen, the players were illustrating the sliver of difference between innovation and dullness, between great coaching and lousy coaching: Had the Seahawks recovered that fumble, they would have had the ball on the Chief 27—already in field-goal range—with 4 minutes, 10 seconds left to play in a tie game. Instead, Kansas City recovered the fumble and marched downfield on its way to a game-winning kick.

Frequently throughout the season, Knox had lamented—and would continue to lament—that, "When you win, you're innovative and creative; when you lose, you're predictable." Until watching a replay of the Kansas City game, I thought Knox was directing his remarks at the press. Now I realized he was directing them through the press at the team's owner.

With Knox off confronting his private and public demons, I focused my attention on the group of players that had emerged as the heart of the Seattle team: the offensive line. I had been watching that group with particular interest ever since the Atlanta game, when Kelly Stouffer labeled it his team's emotional center. "Our offensive line was pushing and grunting and groaning and all of them were flying around!" Stouffer said that day. "It was fantastic to see it! When they play like that, it just lifts everyone."

An offensive lineman is the only player in all of pro sports not to have a statistic measuring his performance. His work goes unnoticed by fans and writers and cameramen alike unless he lets a defensive lineman through to sack his quarterback. The rest of the time, action at the line of scrimmage is so furious and confused and complex that spectators cannot tell whether an offensive lineman is playing poorly or well or decently or indifferently.

When Knox arrived in 1983, his most pressing order of business was the rebuilding of the Seahawk offensive line. He immediately traded his 1985 first-round draft choice to the Cincinnati Bengals for center Blair Bush. He brought offensive guard Reggie McKenzie from Buffalo that same season. In 1984, he signed free agent Bryan Millard, who had spent the previous two seasons in the short-lived United States Football League. In 1985, McKenzie retired, and Knox replaced him with Edwin Bailey, a guard drafted by Seattle in 1981 who had spent two years being refitted to take McKenzie's place. Knox also acquired defensive end Ron Mattes in the seventh round of that year's draft, and put him on injured reserve, where Mattes learned to play offensive tackle. In 1986, Knox completed his rebuilding effort with the acquisition of tackle Mike Wilson from Cincinnati. He also picked up two centers-of-the-future (rookie free agent Stan Eisenhooth in 1986, and veteran free agent Grant Feasel in 1987) as insurance against Bush's age, the veteran having been in the NFL since 1978.

Bush and Wilson stepped right into starting positions for Seattle. Millard bounced around, backing up in 1984, starting nine games at three different positions in '85, then settling in at right guard, next to Wilson, in 1986, the same year that Mattes settled in at left tackle.

Nowhere else is there required such a powerful combination of strength, quickness, savvy, patience, and ability to take punishment as is required of offensive linemen. So complex are the choices made in the offensive line and so intricate the technical skills employed, that the position is known as "the thinking man's position." The offensive lineman must be quick enough to get off the line of scrimmage instantly, engaging a lineman or linebacker before the defender can react to the flow of a play. He must be aggressive enough to blast a defender away from the line of scrimmage on straight-ahead runs, fast enough to pull and run wide on sweeps, blocking defenders on the dead run, and calm enough to retreat coolly on pass plays, enduring insults and injuries from onrushing defensive linemen without losing his composure. One minute, linemen are commanded to be snarling attackers; the next, quick-witted punching bags.

Seattle's offensive line is a cohesive unit, bound by a finely tuned appreciation for sophomoric humor. Off the field, they are big, amiable guys, given to group antics. After practices they almost always stay behind on the field, either working together on certain techniques or moves or sitting quietly together, talking football. In the locker room after practices and games, they sit in front of their lockers, all in a row, contemplating the team arrayed around the room. In hotels on the road, I often saw them walking in a group, as if clearing a path for their quarterback through the lobby. I could never manage to interview just one offensive lineman; whenever I engaged one in conversation, at least two others would chime in. They were sort of a mandatory package deal: You want one, you have to buy the whole lot.

My interview notes with linemen are filled with mocking interruptions. "Come on, you guys, I'm on my soapbox here," Bryan Millard pleaded to his fellows after one game, when they wouldn't let him deliver a serious answer to my questions. Another time, it was Millard's turn to ridicule a teammate. "It's a quick screen to Curt," Ron Mattes tried to explain to me, describing a play in which he had thrown a key block for a Curt Warner touchdown. Before he could continue, Millard shouted, "Big deal! He fell in front of somebody!" Then the two started screaming at each other, and I had to go off in search of another interview.

"The linemen are a very tight group," says Connie Millard. "If you really want to touch home with Bryan, you just even think about saying something about another lineman." She notes, laughing, that "They all sit on the same end of the bench during games, and they always sit in the same order, and if one of them's gone, like if Mike gets up, Ron won't sit down by

Bryan. They won't—because that's Mike's place." During the offseason, she says, when *Sports Illustrated* came to do a profile of Millard, he insisted that his fellow linemen pose with him for photographs. When the story finally appeared in November, there was a picture of all five, playing darts together. Thrilled as he was at having his work noted by a national magazine, he had not wanted to be singled out from his fellow linemen.

I had the weird feeling throughout the season that it never mattered which one of these gentlemen I interviewed. They all seemed to think the same thoughts at the same times, share identical reactions to wins and losses, and shift moods not individually, but as a group.

Theirs strikes me as football's hardest position to master. "The whole game—but especially the line play," says Mattes, "is technique. Technique wins 90 percent of the time. If you learn the proper technique, you can play this game 10 years, 12 years."

While football is strength and speed and power, those attributes are less important, relative to technical skill, at the professional than at the college level. "Strength is good to a certain point," Mattes says. "But you're not gonna overpower a guy at this level. The guy you're playing against is 280, 290, 300 pounds also. And you have to have a good combination of speed and strength. You can't get too strong and lose your speed, and you can't have all the speed in the world and no strength."

Most linemen love run-blocking and hate pass-blocking. "The run game is basically the same, week in and week out. You just have to go and blow a hole in the line. But pass-blocking changes every week. The guy you're playing against is different every week. That phase of the game you have to work at every week, refine the particular skill you need for that week."

When an offensive unit lines up at the line of scrimmage, the linemen exchange signals among themselves as the quarterback calls out the snap count. The guard-and-tackle duo on each side of the center is responsible for deciding between themselves how best to attack the defensive end and linebacker lined up opposite them. They decide which of the two of them will take which of the two defensive players, and what type of blocking technique and blocking combination they will employ. "It's two on two," Mattes explains, "and the different techniques, the different blocks that we use, both of us [in his case, he and Bailey] have to get both of them [the end and linebacker], and it's up to us to use whatever technique that we want." Told in the huddle which hole to open, and in which direction, they decide at the line of scrimmage how best to attack the defense that forms in front of them.

The longer two players work together, the easier that communication becomes. "We have basic calls on the line," says Mattes. "Different defenses that we face, we make a different call, for a different blocking scheme. A grace call, a tag call, a U call—there's various calls." As with all teams, the longer Seattle's offensive linemen play together, the more efficient they become. "Playing next to Bailey, I call him 'Daddy,' I go, 'Yeah, Daddy,' and he knows what block I'm gonna throw at these players just by me saying, 'Yeah.' Because we've seen the defensive front so many times, and we know what each other's going to do in that front, in that situation, he knows what block I want."

The biggest problem with pass-blocking, according to Mattes, is that it calls for a player to act against his own instincts. Pass-blockers retreat, forming a protective pocket around the quarterback, and defend against attack, whereas run-blockers attack from the line of scrimmage. "Every offensive lineman is more temperamentally suited to run-blocking. The passing phase of the game is probably the hardest to master. But it's 50–60 percent of the game in the pros. It's your bread and butter, so you have to learn to do it. I find myself fighting the tendency to be overly aggressive, every day."

Aggression hurts the pass-blocker because he must be balanced and ready to react to any number of sudden moves. As the defensive player advances upon him, the blocker must be set firmly enough in his position to resist a direct hit, yet light enough on his feet to leap instantly to either side. "You have to be more passive than aggressive. You take the brunt of a hit without being overaggressive and extending yourself and losing your position. That's what martial artists work on all the time: trying to use their opponents' force against them. And if you're off balance, that defensive lineman will use that against you. For me, it's been hell trying to learn that. I was a defensive lineman in college, and when I came up, everything for me was still . . . 'Aggressive! Aggressive!' The first couple of times I saw the guy coming I'd brace up and try to hit him, and he'd just give me a quick move as soon as I tried. I still find myself now wanting to punch more than be passive."

Basically, there are three types of pass-rushers: "bull" rushers (who try to run right through a blocker), "speed" rushers (who employ quickness and finesse to sneak around a blocker), and "the guy who can bull you *and* who is quick enough on his feet to get around you," says Mattes. "Those guys are the hardest ones, because you can't get down and firm up your pass set and set back on your heels, because he'll beat you with his speed. And if you get too light on your feet, he'll just bull you."

A few weeks after telling me these things, Mattes would have a miserable day trying to block Buffalo's Bruce Smith, the consummate all-around defensive end. And when I walked up to Mattes in the locker room after his humiliating afternoon, he looked up at me with a gaze as murderous as it was devastated. I never could determine, after that, whether I decided against asking him questions that day out of regard for his feelings or out of fear for my safety.

Given the rigor of Mattes's self-criticism, his film review of that game must have been brutal. "When I watch film," he says, "when I do my job I give myself a zero. And when I screw up I give myself a minus, because I didn't get the job done. Then I go back and ask, 'Why did I get a minus on this one play? Was it my technique? Were my hands in the wrong place?' We can get 10 yards on a play and if my guy has slipped off on the inside or something, I still give myself a minus. Or say our quarterback just gets the ball off, my guy beats me or something, the quarterback just gets the ball off and gets walloped after the play, then I didn't do my job on that play, my quarterback's getting up off the turf, so I get a minus even if we get a touchdown. It's not the end result—it's the individual battles."

There being little glory and no celebrity at their position, linemen play—crass as it sounds—for pride and for money. Late in the season, I asked Edwin Bailey what kept him going through the weeks of work and pain, and Mike Wilson answered for him: "WINNIIIIIING!" "And gettin' paid, baby," Bailey continued. "Winnin' and gettin' paid. Those are the two most important things. Because the more you win, the more you get paid."

Bryan Millard chimed in with "The more you win, the more chances to get in the playoffs, the chances to get you one of those big rings that have 'World Champion' written on 'em."

Bailey: "The more chances to get paid. You keep winnin'—if we win the next seven games, we get a Super Bowl ring, and we get paid!"

Millard: "Seven? Seven!? It's six!"

Bailey: "Five, then."

Millard: "Seven? It's somethin'—but I know it isn't seven!"

Bailey, growling: "FIVE games, man!"

Millard: "Yeah... "

Mattes: What the fuck you guys playin'? Round robin elimination there, or what?"

Bailey: "I know we got somethin' like that. But it's winnin' and gettin' paid, that's the bottom line. If anybody tells you anything different, they're tellin' you a bald-faced lie."

Wilson: "I'm doin' it for the hell of it. I'm donatin' all my money to the wife and boys. HAHAHAHAHA!"

Bailey: "You do whatever it takes, you know. You better yourself as a ballplayer, you go out and work out in the offseason, you concentrate on what you have to do, so you can go out there and WIN and get paid. Just winnin' and gettin' paid seems kind of shallow, but there's a whole lot that goes with it. You have a winnin' atmosphere, and you have the camaraderie that goes with it. You know, I'm 29 years old now, and I been playin' football for 19 years. And all my football friends are still there. You get a team that's real closeknit, you go out there, you prepare yourselves like a good team should, there's no way you shouldn't win a lot of games. And like I say, always after you win, you get paid!"

Lest I should think that Bailey has a one-track mind, he started talking about other pleasures in football. "I like to be on the scoring part. I never myself scored a touchdown, but I've been a part of a lot of scores. I like to see the offense clicking. I've felt that way on every level of football I've played, and I've always been an offensive lineman, from midget league right up until this point. I like the fact that I've had the stayin' power—that I've been there for the better half of 17 years. I like the work that goes with being an offensive lineman. The concentration. The idea that you can make decisions while you're on the run. A lot of people can't do that."

Bailey relishes the status of being part of an exceptionally talented class of people. "I like the idea of being a professional," he said. "I heard Sammy Davis, Jr., on TV a couple of days ago, and they asked him what he liked most about being an entertainer. And he said that he was a quality professional. That he was a *professional* at what he does, and that every time he steps on the stage he goes out to perform at his best. So you see, he's a professional's professional. And I like the idea that I'm a professional football player. Because that means that I've put forth an effort and I've sacrificed to be in the position I am in now. And it's good—it feels good. I'd like to play as long as Mike Wilson's played. . . "

"You can be an ol' fuck, too!" Wilson interjected.

The Seahawks' first game of the season against the Raiders, in the Kingdome on the 13th week of their 13th season, was critical not only because it was against a fierce rival, but because it was on Monday night. To be showcased on "Monday Night Football" was to be showcased to your peers all over the country, since 26 of the NFL's 28 teams have the night off. On Monday nights, players are literally professionals' professionals—they are playing in front of nearly every NFL coach and player in the nation.

Pro football on Monday nights first debuted in 1970, when CBS ran a few experimental broadcasts. Although the programs were successful, the network didn't want to preempt "The Lucy Show," so CBS declined to make Monday night football a regular feature. NBC, not wanting to move its popular "Laugh-In," also declined, so the broadcasts went to ABC by default. ABC, a floundering network at the time, leapt at the chance at prime-time sports broadcasting, and used "Monday Night Football" as a means of turning itself into a major sports network.

"Monday Night Football" was undisputed Los Angeles Raider territory. The Raiders entered 1988 with an all-time 25–5–1 record on Monday nights, far and away best in the league. Seventh-best was Seattle, with a 7–5 Monday night record (2–2 against Los Angeles). In 1986 the Seahawks humiliated the Raiders, 37–0, at their Monday meeting, and in 1987 the Raiders returned the favor, beating the Seahawks 37–4. Raider running back Bo Jackson ran roughshod over the Seahawk defense that night, carrying 18 times for 221 yards, 91 of them on a single touchdown run, on his way to a three-touchdown night. It was the first—and, by the 13th week of 1988, the only—over-100-yards rushing night of Jackson's pro career.

This game would be different in one particular. Hypesters hoping for a rematch between "Bo and the Boz" were to be disappointed. Bosworth, his shoulder ailing again, did not suit up to play, and in fact did not even come to the stadium. His absence, along with the continued absence of Patrick Hunter, threatened to further undermine the already weak Seahawk defense. The only thing in the stadium potentially weaker—with the exception of the beer sold by the Kingdome concessionaire—was the Raider offense, which had scored only one touchdown in its last 14 quarters.

Ordinarily, the game would have been regarded as a tepid match between two 6–6 teams with nowhere to go. But because the NFL is divided into six divisions, there were six separate title races in progress, each race involving either four or five teams. And since the AFC West was in a down cycle, its three top teams sported identical 6–6 records, turning what should have been a dreary year for the division into a suspenseful race to the wire for its championship, and a shot—however unrealistic—at getting into the Super Bowl. Throw in the longstanding ferocity of the Seahawk-Raider rivalry and the added intensity players brought to Monday night games, and you had the makings of a game compelling enough to make fans ignore the poor athletic quality of the product.

As fate would have it, the game turned out to be one of the most exciting ever played, anywhere, at any level. It was a vivid demonstration of the value of such meretricious devices as suspense and plot twists. If football games were novels, this one would have been *Princess Daisy* rather than *Madame Bovary*.

For me, though, the game was almost entirely lacking in suspense, for by kickoff time I had stumbled upon the Coin Toss Factor in Seahawk football. Once the Raiders won the opening toss, I knew Seattle had the game won. Already, through 12 Seattle games, the Factor held a 9–3 edge: Nine times, the team winning the coin toss lost the game.

Los Angeles quarterback Steve Beuerlein was such a poor passer that Seattle was able to devote all its defensive attention to stopping Bo Jackson. After weeks of seeing teams stack eight-man fronts against their offense, Seattle was at last able to turn the tables. The Seahawks were challenging the Raiders to beat them with the passing game.

For the Raiders, this was unthinkable. They tried Bo Jackson cutting back over left guard, but he was held to a 2-yard gain. Next, they tried a wide receiver reverse into the middle of the line, but ball carrier Tim Brown was tackled by Joe Nash after a 3-yard gain. Then, with the Raiders lined up in the shotgun, the Seattle crowd unleashed its loudest roar of the season, forcing LA tackle Don Mosebar to jump offsides. Beuerlein's eventual third-and-10 pass was batted down by Jeff Bryant.

Starting from their own 37, the Seahawks moved at a deliberate, clock-killing pace downfield. Averaging 6.8 yards per play, they took 6½ minutes to score their first touchdown, running five times with John L. Williams, once with Warner, and completing passes to Tice, Williams, and—for the touchdown—Largent. Earning four first downs on the drive, Seattle faced only two third-down situations: third-and-two at the Raider 42, and third-and-seven at the Raider 15. If that drive was any indication, the Seahawks would be able to run and pass at will against the Raiders all day long.

The 15-yard touchdown pass to Largent—his first touchdown of the season—offered dramatic proof of the value of an experienced quarterback to a franchise. Lined up in the shotgun as the inside right receiver, Largent burst downfield at the snap, with cornerback Lionel Washington glued to his outside shoulder. At the 10-yard line, Largent gave Washington an almost imperceptible outside move, and Washington bought just enough of it to give Largent a quarter-step advantage to the inside. Krieg, seeing Largent's fake, threw the ball immediately, lobbing it into the end zone. Largent turned at the goal line, extended his arms, saw the ball at his fingertips, and pulled it in. It was a masterpiece of timing, possible only between a receiver and quarterback who had worked together for years and knew one another's moves—and opposing defenses—inside out. "I threw it a little bit before he broke," Krieg said afterward, "because I knew that Steve knew what the defense was. Steve knows what's going on, so I don't have to worry about that. I can just throw it." The Raiders had not had a safety playing deep, so once Largent stepped past Washington, there was no second defender to pick him up. "There wasn't nobody back there. I knew he was making an out move, so the guy has to go with that a little bit, so I threw it way before he even made his break to where he was gonna be. It was a short pass, so there wasn't much—there was a lot of margin for error. I mean, I just lobbed it out there and he just ran underneath it."

Simple as Krieg made it sound, the key to the completion was what had been missing from the Seattle offense while Krieg was out with his injury: the confidence, at quarterback, to throw a pass, in a pressure situation, into the void, believing—*knowing*—that by the time the ball arrived, the void would be filled. It is a rare and valuable thing, and all the athletic ability in the world can't compensate for its absence.

The Raiders, with Tim Brown receiving, brought Seattle's kickoff back up the right sideline to the Los Angeles 42, from where they moved to the Seattle 24 in only three plays. Then, engulfed by deafening crowd noise, they committed five straight illegal-motion and false-start penalties, the last one coming as Beuerlein, gesticulating madly, begged his oblivious center for the ball, while various jittery teammates jumped offsides. Forced out of field-goal range by Seattle fans' enthusiasm, the Raiders punted beautifully, forcing the Seahawks to start from their own 3-yard line.

After two short-yardage-offense runs brought the ball out to the 8, Seattle came out in shotgun formation. Raider lineman Bill Pickel, lined up at left end, curled around behind two teammates lined up over center, and came tearing up the middle untouched. Center Blair Bush moved to his left, helping out Edwin Bailey, and Mike Wilson, who lined up opposite Pickel, was unable to get around Bryan Millard in time to pick Pickel up. Williams, the lone back, tried futilely to block him, but bounced off. Krieg was so focused downfield that he didn't even see Pickel loom into view until he was crunched. He fumbled, and the ball took a perfect hop into Raider lineman Greg Townsend's arms, for a Los Angeles touchdown.

There descended then a Great Silence over the Kingdome field, as fans came to grips with Seattle's distaste for easy wins and early leads. Three plays later, their disquietude deepened. Before their eyes, there unfolded the kind of strange, telling play—so typical in Seahawk losses—that leaves fans convinced that nothing in football, bounce of the ball included, happens purely by chance. On third-and-six from the Seattle 33, Largent broke to the left sideline, curled around Washington, turned upfield, and caught a perfect Krieg pass on the run. Not quite managing a firm grip on the ball, he pinned it against his hip and was running and trying to gather it in when Washington hit him from behind, slapping at the ball. Down the two went as the ball popped loose, and Largent tried frantically to slither forward after it, with Washington crawling up his back. The ball took one lazy bounce, floating toward the sideline, then came down right on its point, less than an inch from the boundary. Had it gone out of bounds, Seattle would have retained possession, since the pass was ruled complete. Instead, it bounced straight up. Raider safety Vann McElroy came flying over, reached down, and swatted the ball inward as he flew out of bounds. It was recovered by nickelback Stefon Adams, and the Raiders had the ball at the Seattle 49.

It was time now for an interminable video replaying of the episode for purblind replay official George Sladky, during which various Seattle coaches and players vociferously lobbied the field officials. Watching the replay from various angles on the press-box monitors, I fell into heated debate with myself, the fan in me taking on the reporter in me. The fan insisted that the ball had touched the sideline, or that, at the very least, McElroy had stepped out of bounds before batting the ball back in. In either case, reasoned the fan, the ball should be Seattle's. My reportorial eye, though, forced me to concede the incredible: Laws of physics to the contrary, the ball and McElroy had managed to stay in bounds, and the officials had made the correct call. Close as it was, it was not a difficult call to make. Watching the Seahawks argue, I began to wonder if they really believed the officials had called it wrong, or if the closeness of that call, in a season marked by close calls and close plays and ill-timed bad bounces of balls and minds and bodies, was simply one bad bounce too many. It seemed to me that they were hoping not that the replay official would overrule his fellow arbiters, but that he would overrule fortune.

Raider teams are renowned for their assassins' instincts, and this year's team was no exception. LA struck immediately. Tim Brown, lined up opposite Melvin Jenkins, came straight downfield and faked to the outside convincingly enough to make Jenkins stumble. Then he burst by Jenkins, got a good five-step lead on him, and waited patiently at the 2-yard line for Beuerlein's late and underthrown pass to arrive. Gathering it in, Brown stepped daintily across the goal line to give the Raiders a 14–7 lead.

The quarter came to an end with the Seahawks committing a foul on the next kickoff and being moved back to the Seattle 14. Having dominated the Raiders in time of possession (9:04 to 5:56) and—subtracting the 49 yards Los Angeles gained on the last play of the quarter—in total yards (79 to 39), they were behind by a touchdown, having twice turned over the ball.

Undaunted, the Seahawks again mounted a classic ball-control drive. Thirteen plays taking nearly 6 minutes brought them even with the Raiders when the drive culminated in a 6-yard touchdown pass to Blades, who was running a post pattern from the right side. Blades slanted directly toward the goalpost, and Krieg, checking off receivers with confident, veteran speed, looked at Largent, saw he was double-covered, then threw instantly to Blades, burying a bullet too low in his gut for cornerback Ron Fellows to reach it from behind. "Steve was the guy I was looking at first," Krieg said later, "and if they're doubling him, then I go to Brian. They can only double one of the two guys."

The next 7 minutes were taken up by a long Los Angeles drive to a field goal, a short Seattle drive to a punt, and a long Los Angeles drive to the Seattle 13, where the Raiders came to the line of scrimmage at the half's 1:54 mark to face third-and-10. Under pressure, Beuerlein scrambled and was caught from behind by linebacker Tony Woods, who knocked the ball from his hand as he embraced him. As Beuerlein went down, the ball bounced up, slithered between his arm and torso, and came out on top of his back, where it was recovered by Woods. Referee Jerry Markbreit came charging in, signaling that Beuerlein had been sacked. Seattle players objected yet again, and Sladky was called in for consultation. Since one of the television cameras had been on the sideline looking directly across at Beuerlein, Sladky could see clearly that the ball was knocked loose by Woods well before he had tackled the quarterback, and he accordingly reversed Markbreit's call. On came the Seattle offense and the Los Angeles defense, to the ear-splitting approval of the home crowd.

Play, though, was not resumed. Markbreit went first to a sideline telephone, then to Knox, to explain that, because he had been standing behind the quarterback, he had not seen the fumble and had blown the play dead before the ball had been recovered. His error would have to stand, as even legitimate fumbles cannot be recovered after the whistle. On came the Seattle and Los Angeles field-goal units, off boomed Raider Chris Bahr's kick, up went the Raider lead to 6 points, and down plummeted Seattle fans' hopes that the Seahawks would quit finding ways to lose football games they should easily win.

But then the Seahawks came soaring back like a championship team. Krieg gained 13 yards on a quarterback draw, then completed a 9-yard swing pass to Williams. After taking two plays and 10 seconds to gain 1 more yard and a first down, they covered the remaining 53 yards in three passes, the last being an 11-yard touchdown pass to Paul Skansi, who was running a post pattern from the right with the unfortunate Ron Fellows on his back. Norm Johnson, kicking at :29, recaptured the lead for Seattle.

By this time, the fans were on their feet, their celebration in full roar as Johnson set up, then kicked off. Tim Brown caught the ball at the 2-yard line and headed up the left sideline. His team blocking perfectly for him, he shot straight up to the 30, then, seeing the way closed, suddenly burst across the center of the field.

The Seahawks, in their zeal to end things on a dramatic note, had overreacted when Brown started up the sideline. Now, as he cut back against the grain, there was no one there to greet him. He crossed, turned upfield, and took off, unobstructed, for the Seattle end zone.

The crowd was traumatized. Melvin Jenkins, angling across the deepening silence, was able to catch up to Brown at the Seattle 20, but Brown, tall and long-limbed, stiff-armed Jenkins to the turf and kept going. Then, chasing him from behind, Dwayne Harper jumped on Brown's back at the 7, dragging him down at the 3. In the space of 22 seconds, Seahawk fans went from elation to despair to desperate hope to disappointment to one last faint hope that somehow, after an entire half of Seattle gifts to Los Angeles, the Raiders would finally fail to take advantage of a Seahawk mistake.

Immediately their hopes were dashed. Bo Jackson, a decided non-factor for the entire half, burst through right tackle for a touchdown.

Just as immediately, their hopes were revived. Raider tight end Trey Junkin was flagged for holding, the Raider touchdown was nullified, and the ball moved back 10 yards. Los Angeles called time, then brought out its field-goal unit, and grateful fans resigned themselves to being down by only 2 points at the half.

Then Bahr missed the field goal.

Finally the half came to a merciful close. As fans babbled incoherently in the stands, somewhere in the back of their minds a dim understanding of the symbolic importance of Bahr's missed kick began to take form. The Seahawks had lost every game in which they had trailed at the half. In kicking wide of the goalposts—if omens counted for anything in football—Bahr had given Seattle the game.

Only this Seattle team, in this season, could have racked up such strange statistics by halftime. Outgaining the Raiders 267 yards to 137, earning 16 first downs to LA's eight, converting on six of nine third downs while the Raiders converted on only one of five, allowing only three Raider pass completions, and keeping the ball for 19 minutes compared with Los Angeles' 11, Seattle managed only by the grace of chaos to eke out a 1-point halftime lead.

Exhausted by the first half's tension, the two teams played quietly for the first 9 minutes of the third quarter, each team punting twice. Then, on third-and-two at the Seattle 36, John L. Williams, in the backfield with Krieg in shotgun formation, went in motion to the right, then broke into the flat at the snap, curling into the open behind linebacker Reggie McKenzie. Krieg, indecisive, threw weak and short, and McKenzie picked off the pass, returning it 26 yards down the sideline to the Seattle 17. It took Los Angeles four plays—one a 16-yard completion under pressure on third-and-13—to score a touchdown.

As if rejuvenated by that unfortunate turn of events, Seattle struck back, Bobby Joe Edmonds returning Bahr's kickoff to the Seattle 41, and Krieg hitting Blades down the right sideline for a 38-yard completion. Then Ray

Butler, angling into the left corner of the end zone with Lionel Washington giving chase, was pushed in the back by Washington as the ball came down toward him. The ball bounced off Butler's helmet into Washington's grasp, and was ruled—over the strenuous objections of Steve Moore—a legitimate interception.

By this time, Seattle fans had visions dancing in their heads of the early-season game against San Diego, in which Krieg had killed his team's chances with untimely interceptions. By the end of the third quarter, Seattle increased its total yardage advantage to 385–175, its time-of-possession advantage to 26:36–16:24, and turned its 1-point advantage into a 6-point disadvantage.

Seattle ended the third quarter with a sudden 26-yard run off left tackle by Curt Warner, followed by two John L. Williams rushes that brought the ball down to the LA 26. Staying on the ground as the fourth quarter began, the Seahawks pushed their way down to the Raider 7, where, on third-and-six, they came out in shotgun formation, with Curt Warner—for the first time all season—in place of John L. Williams as the lone running back. Lined up to the right of Krieg, Warner crossed in front of him at the snap, as if receiving a handoff. Krieg kept the ball, though, then looked into the end zone as Warner looped wide into the left flat. Ron Mattes, having no rusher to block, broke left along the line of scrimmage. Krieg lobbed the ball to Warner, Warner caught it and came up behind Mattes, and Mattes pushed safety Eddie Anderson to the outside as Warner cut inside for a touchdown.

Although nothing is more fragile than a 1-point Seahawk lead with nearly a full quarter left to play, that touchdown signaled the end to the Raiders' pretensions. Having stayed in the game more by virtue of Seattle-dictated misbounces of the ball than by their own ingenuity, the Raiders grew desperate and started overreaching. A holding penalty on Seattle's kickoff moved the ball back to the Los Angeles 7, where Marcus Allen was smothered for a 1-yard loss on first down, and Beuerlein, unable to decipher Seattle's six-back defense, threw wildly incomplete on second down. Then, on third-and-11, Beuerlein overthrew a crossing Tim Brown, and the pass was picked off at the Raider 15 by—and here the story line of the game and of the season takes a wildly poetic turn—David Hollis.

Late in the second quarter, Terry Taylor had tackled Bo Jackson, and suffered a concussion for his trouble. Dwayne Harper had taken over Taylor's cornerback spot, and Hollis had taken over Harper's nickelback spot. Playing on national television, Hollis, in picking off Beuerlein's errant pass, completed a dizzying, four-week ascension from unemployed marginal player to professional's professional. Had Curt Warner not fumbled at the Los Angeles 2-yard line three plays later, Hollis's interception, in setting up Seattle's final touchdown, would have been the play that iced the game.

As it was, it gave the Seahawks enough of a field-position advantage to give them the ball, five plays and a punt later, on the Raider 36. And 2 minutes after that, Krieg put the game out of reach with a 20-yard touchdown pass—his fifth TD pass of the game—to wide receiver Louis Clark.

On their next series, the Raiders brought in cannon-armed Jay Schroeder at quarterback, and Schroeder guided his team from the Los Angeles 19 to the Seattle 23 in six plays. There Hollis, retreating as receiver James Lofton angled into the middle in front of him, broke instinctively for the ball before Schroeder released it, cut in front of Lofton, and picked off another pass. It was a solid play by a competent pro who had done his homework. To the adoring screams of nearly 63,000 fans, Hollis floated dreamily off the field, committing the moment indelibly to memory.

Moments later, the game ended, and Hollis, heading for the locker room, was pumping both arms in the air and screaming like a man who had just won the world championship.

Knox, afterward, was considerably less jubilant. While pleased with the win and acknowledging that it had been among the most critical games of the season, he also called it—in an uncomplimentary tone of voice—"entertaining."

By that, he meant that it had been a game filled with mistakes, pratfalls, disasters, and almost insurmountable weaknesses. It had been a comedy of errors instead of a championship display of strength, as he would have preferred. It had been a matter of pitting weakness against weakness, both teams suffering through the down cycles that are the inevitable lot of every successful NFL franchise.

The game was redeemed by the closeness of its score, the number of touchdowns, the plot twists afforded in the form of turnovers, the scoring pattern (fans were treated to 10 scoring plays and seven lead changes), and by the context established by a tight division-title race. Take away any of those elements, and you have one crummy game between two hurting franchises.

Once the thrill was gone, the game struck me as a fraud, an indictment of the NFL parity system. The suspense had been a thin disguise, a sugar-coating of contrived, high-stakes excitement applied to a lackluster product. Yet, clear-eyed as I tried to be, I couldn't forget how wrapped up I had been in the game, how I had been perched as tensely on the edge of my seat as I was the first time I saw Hitchcock's *Psycho*. It made me wonder, yet again, at why we follow football with such fascination. All the things that should make it a great game—great athletic ability, great resourcefulness in players and coaches, great organization, brilliant strategy, flawless execution of assignments—are all but imperceptible. The basic level of athleticism at the professional level is so high that the distinctions between indifferent pro athletes and superb pro athletes are lost on all but the most expert of observers.

So, for that matter, are the so-called finer points of the game. Americans, I decided, watch football simply to be entertained. And, just as in movies and novels and plays and television shows, nothing is more entertaining than suspense, high emotion, and an elaborate plot. Football struck me then as little more than a primitive art form, a shallow amusement that offers the spectator distraction rather than sustenance.

This momentary fit of snobbery, however, was not enough to keep me from going into the locker room to revel vicariously in the postgame bliss.

Hollis, trying to maintain a professional demeanor amid the crush of reporters surrounding his locker, looked instead like a child granted an impossible wish by his fairy godmother. "I was thinking 'protect the ball,' making sure I had it," he was saying with studied nonchalance, "not give them another chance to put it in the end zone . . . "

His locker was flanked by those of Nesby Glasgow and Vernon Dean, who couldn't resist chiming in. "Look who's got all the reporters," Dean shouted. "They don't want to talk to nobody else but *David Hollis!*" "Tell 'em, Hot Lips!" Glasgow shrieked exuberantly. "Talk to 'em, Hot Lips! Talk to 'em . . . "

Hollis, beaming now, continued, patiently recounting his interceptions time and again for succeeding waves of reporters. Then, after most of them had moved on, he reflected quietly on his moment in the spotlight. "It may never come again," he said. "Ah, I'm just glad. I feel great! I feel great! Right now, I'm on top of the world! Monday night, the Raiders . . . used to be my favorite team when I was a kid . . . But ever since last year, they been one of my worst-hated teams. To play that well against them . . . " He couldn't get over the twists of fate that had brought him almost overnight from nowhere into the national spotlight. "I had to make the most of my opportunity. If Terry wouldn't have gotten hurt, he would've been the hero today. So I just had to make the most of it. Especially the way it was—to come back and play on *Monday night,* my mother here . . . my family watching . . . I never imagined anything like this. I just have to make the best of my opportunities, that's what I try to do . . . I never played too much on TV in college . . . we played New Mexico State on ESPN once, and I went 92 yards and you know, it's just something about TV, that I just . . . kind of ironic that I play, you know, in this big game . . . " He was rambling, lost in a dream, letting himself be unreservedly boyish . . . and then he seemed to remember that he was supposed to be a *professional*. He drew himself up, adopted a stern expression, and tried his hand at a few clichés. "I'm just happy to help the team win today, it was a big win for us, and we're just one step closer to our goal—which is the division championship."

Hollis was living proof, in reverse, of the tenuousness of an NFL career. Professional football is so dangerous, and the competition for its few jobs so fierce, that players can ascend just as precipitously as they can descend. It is the David Hollises of sport, rather than the Steve Largents or the Curt Warners, who keep marginal athletes' hopes alive, for what happened to Hollis could happen to any of them. For every heartbreaking story of the decline of an athlete, there is an uplifting story of someone's rise. "That's the nature of this game," Hollis said. "No one's very secure in this league. You have to be prepared for whenever your number's called." At the same time, you have to be prepared for it all to end instantly. "The adversity of the game sometimes, you're in the league, you could be here today and out tomorrow. Whenever you get a chance to go out there and play, you have to go out there and prove that you are NFL-caliber. I just go out there, I try not to think about it no more, just go out there and work hard, prepare myself, and whatever happens happens. You hope for the best, prepare for the worst. That's what I've been doing. I've been through almost everything you could possibly be in as far as the NFL is concerned."

However hard he tried to cultivate his resignation, though, his incredulous happiness kept shining through. "I'm just happy it worked out so well," he said. "Especially on Monday night. My mother used to tell me, 'There's something about it, when you're put in the spotlight, you seem to respond.' I guess she's right. Mother knows best! And the good thing about it, after the game, the camera was there, and I got a chance to wave to her . . . "

A few lockers away, at the far end of the NFL spectrum from Hollis, stood Steve Largent, patiently answering questions. "I told Dave on the sideline," he said, "that I'd never seen him throw with such confidence and accuracy as he did tonight. It was fun to watch him play, fun to be out there with him. I think more than anything, Dave was just the trigger guy tonight—he was on. And I think over the course of the game it was obvious to everybody."

Even Krieg couldn't help but be in an expansive, talkative mood after this dramatic a win. "I'm emotionally drained," he said. "I'm just so happy for our football team, the way we played . . . I don't know, in the second half, we got out there and I threw an interception, and another interception, and I just started feeling, 'Well, darn it!' I never thought we were gonna lose, though. I just felt that we were gonna find a way to win this football game—and we did."

He recounted, one by one, his five touchdown passes, his two interceptions, and his fumble. Then, intending to praise his teammates for fighting through the setbacks they had encountered throughout the game—in the form of turnovers and bad breaks from the officials—he found himself citing adversity as a plus. "There was so much adversity, and we still refused to lose," he said. "I think winning this game goes to the intangibles. Like, how much is it really worth for us to go out here and win this football game tonight? And the sacrifices a lot of people have made, and a lot of adversity on this team. You look at your background, how you got here and how hard you worked to get here, and a lot of people never get the opportunity to win a divisional championship, and we got some guys on this team who never won a championship in high school or college. And who didn't get drafted—free agents. Guys who are playing out here—Joe Nash, myself—I mean, you could go on and on down the list. I mean, you know, Dwayne Harper's running down there chasing a Heisman Trophy winner, a high draft pick, and Mel Jenkins, you get him out of Canada . . . look at Dave Wyman out there: We try to get rid of him, send him to San Francisco, and he's back . . . David Hollis—cut him, cut him again, bring him back, he makes a big interception for us. Paul Skansi, he only gets to play on third downs . . . Darren Comeaux, look at him . . . I mean, it's just amazing. Those are the kind of guys that are . . . unheralded I guess is the word . . . they come out there and give you a little bit extra . . . "

Krieg is declaiming the Gospel According to Chuck Knox now. It is the notion that only when you feel that your opponent is blessed with more ability, and favored by fate and the establishment and the referees and by all those forces and influential people who are determined to control your destiny—only then can you make a winner out of yourself.

Two days later, talking to Warner, I realized that he too is one of Knox's underdogs. Highly touted as he was throughout his college career, he had always been eclipsed by running backs from higher-profile college programs. He had never achieved the superstardom that was his due—he had never, for example, come close to winning the Heisman Trophy—yet he quietly went about his business in college, racking up records while getting relatively little ink. And to those on the Seattle team who know him well—running back coach Chick Harris, for one—the lack of recognition seemed only to have inflamed the conviction in his heart that he was the *best*.

Warner carried 27 times in the Raider game and gained 130 yards, for his season's best performance. "The difference between winning and losing," he said, "is fractional. I mean, it's a weird game. Sometimes mentally you'll have the edge and you'll know what to do and things'll fall into the right place for you, and then sometimes when you don't have that mental frame of mind, that mental edge, you can very easily lose a football game, too." He thought, as Krieg did, that bad breaks had finally driven his team to realize its potential. Recalling the inexplicable bounce the football had taken to stay in bounds after Largent fumbled it, Warner said, "Oh, man! That's just the kind of year that it's been for the most part, and when things are going like that, you just have to say, 'No, this is just not gonna happen. We're not gonna get beat because of this today. They're gonna have to beat us legitimately, for them to win.' And either you can get mad about it, and say you'll do something about it, and suck it up and go back out there and get the ball back down the field, or we can quit and say, 'What the heck—what's the use of being out here, because thing's aren't going our way.' "

This team, under this coach, is driven—or inspired—by the bad break. "I don't know," Warner sighed. "We need someone to just kind of slap us a little bit, and get us mad . . . "

He stopped for a moment, distracted by wads of tape bouncing off his head. "These guys," he said, pointing toward the offensive linemen's lockers, two lockers away from his, "they throw stuff at me all the time down here . . . and then we go out and say, 'Hey! You're not gonna lose this game like this' . . . Leave me alone! Can't you guys see I'm doing an interview! Jeeminy Christmas! . . . " He was yelling at the entire offensive line now, a group of ponderous pranksters, looming up en massive masse, gleefully bombarding him with garbage.

The Boys Behind the Bus

The NFL schedule called for the Seahawks to follow their win over the Raiders with a trip to Foxboro, Massachusetts, to play the New England Patriots. Leaving a Monday-night game on the West Coast for a game the following Sunday on the East Coast made for a week so short that I felt as if I left the Kingdome and proceeded immediately to the team hotel in Boston, slept a few hours, and ambled down to the lobby the next morning to cadge a ride to the stadium.

The trip taught me how easy it is for a reporter to miss a wintertime football game. Seattle-Tacoma airport was fogged in on Saturday, and Seattle media spent the day scrambling to make travel rearrangements. I finally arrived at my Boston hotel at 2am, and when I descended to the lobby later that morning, it was to discover that many of my fellow choristers, having traveled all night by way of Washington, D.C., were just arriving.

The media go through the same routine at all Seahawk road games. Three hours before game time, they gather in the lobby of the team's hotel, get stadium passes from Seahawk public relations people, then either pick up their rental cars or catch rides with those who have them, and head for the stadium. In some cities, reporters in their cars follow the team bus, which is escorted by local police to the stadium. In others, where the route from hotel to stadium is short and easily decipherable, reporters get there on their own.

Foxboro's Sullivan Stadium was some 30 convoluted miles away from downtown Boston's Westin Copley Circle Hotel, so the Seattle press contingent piled into four cars and lined up behind the Seahawk charter bus, which was preceded by a motorcycle state trooper. Seahawk public relations director Gary Wright came back to our car, leaned in the window, and said, "Follow the bus. If he speeds—you speed. If he goes through a red light—you go through a red light." The *Times'* Gil Lyons, who was driving our car—the other passenger was *P-I* columnist John Owen—blanched visibly. "And *I'm not responsible!*", Wright intoned, laughing sadistically as he walked on to the next car.

271

We no sooner turned out of the hotel drive than two or three Boston drivers insinuated their cars between ours and the bus. And the bus no sooner hit the freeway (or throughway, or beltway, or expressway, or whatever the hell they call it back there), than bus and trooper, accelerating like rockets off a launching pad, took off. With varying degrees of success, the four media cars tried to follow suit. But it was immediately clear that drivers acclimated to Seattle traffic are no match for their over-adrenalized eastern counterparts. Looking over Lyons's shoulder, I noticed that our speedometer was inching toward 80. Looking out the window, I saw that ours was the slowest car on the road, and that the bus was pulling away.

Lyons was doing his best, but cars were diving and darting in front of us like barn swallows. Every time Lyons tried to get around one, he would find the other lane suddenly blocked by a zealous lane-switcher. He is a reserved and courtly older man, but now I could see that the back of his neck was knotted even more tightly than one of Dave Wyman's biceps.

Inexorably the bus-cum-escort grew more distant. And the four-car caravan of reporters and photographers grew ever more scattered. Then I noticed that we hit a patch where it seemed that every mile or so brought a conjunction of freeways.

"Which one did he take?" Lyons shouted. I looked out just in time to see the bus disappear over the top of a distant hill as it shot off on a ramp heading right. We were in the far left lane.

"He went off on that ramp!"

"Oh shit. Oh shit. Oh shit," muttered Lyons. Then he executed a four-lane, 90-degree turn onto another freeway. There again, half a mile or so distant, was the bus. Lyons, a patch of open road in front of him, floored the accelerator. I kept my eyes on the bus. We were still losing ground. I looked at the speedometer. The needle had reached the top number—85—and was banging against an invisible barrier. *Zoot*—we changed lanes. I looked out the window. *Zoot*—we changed lanes again. Traffic was keeping pace with us—*zoot-zoot*—but I could no longer see any of the other Seattle cars.

Zoot. Zoot-zoot-zoot. The landscape around Boston is a peculiar, desolate place. It is eerily flat—all soft, rolling hills covered with short grass, spindly trees, and freeways. It looks like the meeting-point for all the freeway systems in the world, an impression enhanced by the road signs, each one directing the driver to a different state. The jumble of roads and signs added considerably to our driver's panic. One wrong turn would send him off not only in the wrong direction, but on an irreversible path into the wrong state.

I noticed that no two cars bore the same state's license plate. You've got a friend in Pennsylvania . . . the Garden State . . . Live Free or Die . . . Keep Up with that Bus or Die . . . "You still see it up there?" I heard Lyons bleat. "Straight ahead, Gil, straight ahead!" The bus disappeared over another little rise in the road.

"Oh shit. Oh shit. Oh shit."

Traffic was getting thicker, the bus farther away. Occasionally pausing to shout out freeway-change instructions to Lyons, Owen and I distracted ourselves from terror by swapping Seahawks-beat stories. Because the team is so secretive with the press, the most innocent events take on an aura of mystery and significance. Official Seahawk explanations for everything, unless they hint at earth-shattering possibilities, are always dismissed at first as part of a coverup.

The Mysterious Story of the Week centered around Bosworth's not having been on the sidelines for the Raider game. Everyone wanted to know where he was, and why he wasn't there. Knox tried to explain that the NFL had sent out directives telling teams that players not in uniform were not allowed on the sidelines, but reporters weren't buying it. When they pressed Knox, he took refuge in humor. "I'm surprised you didn't ask about Roland Barbay or Robert Tyler," he said with a smile on Wednesday. "Remember those guys? Alvin Powell? Why would you pick this guy out? Hm? Remember those guys? They're on injured reserve. I wasn't asked one question about Roland Barbay. You didn't ask where he was or how's he doing or anything."

"How's he doing?" someone asked.

"He's doing fine."

Zoot. "Where'd it go? Where'd it go?" "Straight ahead, Gil . . . "

I was telling Owen about the latest twist in the Boz saga—a phone call last Tuesday from my mother, who lives in Bellingham. "Do you know where *the Boz* is?" she asked. "In Kirkland, I imagine," I answered. "Noooooo!" she answered gleefully, then asked, "Why wasn't he at the game on Monday?" I tried Knox's explanation on her, but she laughed. "He's been seen at a substance-abuse clinic outside Bellingham!" she exclaimed.

Stop the presses!

Owen laughed. The *Post-Intelligencer*, it turned out, had received calls telling them that Bosworth was in substance-abuse clinics in the Seattle area. And the Everett *Herald*'s Todd Fredrickson had been called several times by readers who knew, absolutely, that Bosworth was building a condominium complex in Lake Stevens.

Boz sightings! Having arrived in the Northwest touted like the Second

Coming of Christ, he had degenerated into the second coming of Sasquatch.

Zoot. We shot off the freeway, and the roadsides around us now were filled with people dressed in heavy parkas, scarves, and thick woolen caps. We were within walking distance, obviously, of a football stadium.

Suddenly we were there. Lyons, his hands shaking, brandished his parking pass in the general direction of a uniformed attendant.

"Awright! Just drive along the gawdrail theah," the attendant said, "and you'll come ta yuh pawking spot. Just fawllah the gawdrail."

As we pulled into our pawking spot, I saw the team bus, 30 yards ahead, disgorging its players. Some of them were looking back at our little media fleet and snickering. What a perfectly symbolic situation, I thought, for the relationship between this franchise and its chroniclers. The Seahawks so insulate themselves that Seattle reporters are always, in one way or another, struggling to keep up with the team bus. And the team is just helpful enough to allow them, through strenuous effort, to barely manage to keep the bus in sight.

Behind me, I heard a New Englander ask where his "pawking spot" was. I couldn't get over the coarse, barely intelligible English people speak back there.

"What's a gawdrail?" I asked.

"It's where you go to thank Gawd you made it to the stadium," Owen answered.

Play the Coin You're Tossed

The horror-worn eyes linger abject on all they have beseeched so long, in a last prayer, the true prayer at last, the one that asks for nothing. And it is then a little breath of fulfillment revives the dead longings and a murmur is born in the silent world, reproaching you affectionately with having despaired too late.

—Samuel Beckett, *Malone Dies*

Seated in the Sullivan Stadium press box, warming myself against the brutal New England winter with massive doses of crummy hot coffee, I marveled at the following: one, my fellow sports historians, who were making history, rather than writing it, by reading something other than sports pages; and two, the fact that this game between two crippled, 7–6 teams was about to be broadcast, via television, to 75 percent of the nation.

The first matter was resolved by a quick look over the shoulder of a rapt reader nearby. The Boston papers consisted almost entirely of long, lurid stories on the troubled marriage of Arnold Schwarzenegger and Maria Shriver. The two, it had just been revealed, were undergoing treatment by. . . a sex therapist! The trouble, apparently (as I learned as soon as I was able to borrow a paper from a spent reader), was that Arnold was an old-world kind of guy, to whom, as one of his anonymous friends put it, the most important word in the marriage contract was "obey."

Hot news, indeed—well worth the long trip east. But duty called, and I turned my attention to the second marvel: the nearly nationwide broadcast of the game.

Every year, NFL marketing strategy turns such nondescript contests as this one into struggles of national significance by extending the contention for playoff spots to as many teams as possible as far into the season as possible. By dividing the league into two conferences—the National Football Conference and the American Football Conference—and by dividing each conference into three divisions, the league turned the football season into a protracted, three-stage race, beginning with six simultaneous division title

275

races, followed by a tournament among the title-winners to determine a champion in each conference, followed in turn by the season's third stage: the Super Bowl championship game between the AFC and NFC conference champions. Further drama was lent the regular season by adding two play-off spots in each conference—called "wild card" berths—which afford two non-title teams from each conference the right to play one another in a "wild card" round, the winner becoming the fourth team in the conference tournament. What all this boiled down to was that in each 14-team confer-ence, no fewer than five teams (three division champions and two wild-card teams) would make the playoffs. It was an arrangement that made the maximum possible number of teams, late in the season, appear to have a fighting chance at the Super Bowl. So now, in the 14th week of a 16-week season, 19 of the league's 28 teams were still in playoff contention, with only two teams having clinched postseason berths. Thus, virtually every late-season game had at least one contender playing in it, which meant that each game had some kind of division-title or wild-card berth implications—a circumstance that made many of them seem falsely pivotal and dramatic.

The Seattle–New England game was a classic example of how the stra-tegy worked. The opponents, even though they each had won only one more game than they had lost, stood good chances of qualifying for the playoffs. This meant that, 7–6 record and all, they were Super Bowl con-tenders rather than mere .538 teams playing out the string. Consequently, the stadium was sold out and television advertisers could be persuaded to use this game between purported Super Bowl contenders as a vehicle from which to hawk their products nationwide.

Sitting in the stadium press box, waiting for the game to begin, I found myself privately fulminating at the fiction that so thoroughly dupes not only fans, but sportswriters as well. At this time of year, every sports page in the country has at least two stories a week on the complexities of the play-off system. The stories are all in the same vein. Certain teams have to beat certain other teams by a certain number of points in order for such-and-such a team to make its conference's final wild-card berth . . . Reams of free publicity accrue to the league over this matter, all of it in one way or an-other triggered by the release, at the end of November, of a directive entitled "NFL Procedures to Break Ties in Standings and Determine Play-off Sites." This byzantine three-page document defies description. "Note," it reads at one point. "If one team wins multiple-team tiebreaker to advance to playoff round, remaining teams revert to step 1 of applicable two-club format, i.e., either in division tiebreaker or Wild Card tiebreaker. If two teams in a multiple-team tie possess superior marks in a tiebreaking step, this pair of teams advance [sic] to the top of the applicable two-club format to break tie. One team advances to playoff round, while other returns to original group and step 1 of applicable tiebreaker."

The more I looked ahead to this game, the more fed up I got. These two teams were both crippled and falsely strengthened by league policy. The NFL's parity doctrine dictated that all teams help finance a scouting combine that dispenses the same information on graduating college talent to everyone, that all teams share television revenue and gate receipts, that the best teams each season pick lowest in the succeeding player draft, that the best teams each season play the toughest schedules the next season, and that the price (its number-one picks in the next two player drafts) a team pays for signing another team's "free agent" player be so high as to make free agency nonexistent. The effect of the policy was to blur distinctions in quality among teams. Each season, there might be one or two exceptionally good teams, one or two exceptionally bad teams, and 24 or 26 unexceptional teams.

Both New England and Seattle, by having done reasonably well over the previous several seasons, were now diminished at so many critical positions that they had degenerated into average teams. Formerly terrible teams (Buffalo, Cincinnati, New Orleans) had risen above the fray, while formerly great teams (Miami, Pittsburgh, Dallas) had sunk into the abyss. The main reason for the constant changing of the NFL guard was the parity-dictated tying of the hands of team front-office personnel. While players and coaches still competed freely on the field, general managers and player-personnel directors were forbidden from competing freely off of it.

The only remedy, I decided, would be total free agency and the elimination of the player draft. Front offices would then have to compete for talent just as fiercely as players did for touchdowns. Some teams would become perennial powerhouses, perhaps, and others perennial patsies, but fans at least would see the level of front-office competence and effort reflected on the field, and the whole league would be a showcase for unfettered, free competition. The present system made no more sense than one in which a 12–4 team in 1987 would have to play its 1988 games with a scoring handicap—against a team that went 4–12 in 1987, for instance, it would have to start out the game two touchdowns behind. This system imposed a phony order. Franchises should have to compete in an off-field arena that was at least as chaotic as real life.

Maybe I was just cranky because the press box was so damned cold. Or because the season is just as long and draining for writers as it is for players and coaches. Even allowing for all of that, though, I still was convinced that

I was about to watch two Super Bowl pretenders play a bad football game made "interesting" by slick league packaging. Through parity and playoff hypenotism, the NFL was making suckers of us all.

Down on the field, players were enduring pregame workouts in bleak, brutal conditions. The temperature was 31 degrees, but 18–33-mile-per-hour winds, gusting hard enough to make the goalposts sway, made for a windchill factor near zero. And the sun was blinding; time and again, Seattle players lost the ball in the sunlight.

The teams completed their pregame warmups and retreated to the warmth of their locker rooms. Incredibly, the stands were packed, and the fans were boisterous. I saw one of them, directly below me, climbing over the rail and slipping down onto the field. Through my binoculars, I recognized him immediately. It was the zephyr that I had seen blowing Johnson's first place kick against Houston just far enough over to squeak between the uprights. Today he was disguised as a fan. Dressed in heavy overcoat, scarf, gloves, and hat, he skimmed along the ground to the far end of the stadium floor, and disappeared through a door behind the goalposts.

For Seattle, there was a certain inconsequence to this game. Since the Seahawks would close out the season with games against the Broncos and the Raiders, their shot at a division title would not be hurt by a loss to the Patriots, and helped only slightly by a win. This must have been the main reason that Knox opted not to bring Bosworth along. He left him back in Seattle to work at rehabilitating his shoulder. And, at the last minute, Knox decided to put Largent on the inactive list. Largent had injured both a foot and a hand against the Raiders, and it made more sense to have him sit out this game—in which wind conditions made passing nearly impossible, and which had no bearing on the division title race—than to risk having him unavailable for the pivotal season-ending games.

New England, on the other hand, needed to win in order to keep its playoff hopes alive. And fans there were enchanted by the team's quarterback, local hero Doug Flutie, a diminutive (5'9") player who had replaced injured starter Tony Eason six games into the season, and who had a genuine mystique in the form of a lifetime 8–0 record (5–0 with the Patriots, and 3–0 with Boston College) in Sullivan Stadium. When Flutie took over at quarterback, his team was 2–4 and coming off a 45–3 loss to the lowly Green Bay Packers. Now, after going 5–2 under Flutie, the Patriots had vaulted into playoff contention.

Flutie, of course, was being given credit for the resurgence, even though his job consisted almost solely of handing the ball off to running back John Stephens. The Patriots virtually never passed the ball. Over the last seven games, Flutie completed only 68 passes—fewer than 10 per game—and handed off to Stephens 162 times. This rather unfashionable run-pass ratio was the result of Patriot coach Raymond Berry's study of the strengths and weaknesses of his team. Berry opted to have it do the only thing it could do—run—and the 5–2 result conferred upon him the title of genius. Running the football—especially straight ahead, the way New England did—may be hopelessly passé, but as long as it kept working, no one would be calling the regressive Berry dull or predictable.

However low the stakes may have been for Knox, he made it clear that he was determined to win the game. As was his custom, he left as little as possible to chance. Whatever he could control, he would—and whatever he couldn't, he would try to find a way to control. He started fighting right from the coin toss. When fate turned up the side of the coin he had called, he decided against the winner's customary choice of taking the ball, electing instead the loser's customary choice of which end of the field to defend. Excited, I thought at first that finally he had abandoned his beloved tangibles and percentages and opted for the mysterious world of superstition. He must have come to believe in the Coin Toss Factor, I reasoned, when he realized that 10 of the last 13 Seahawk games had been won by the team that started out on defense. By refusing to choose the ball, he was refusing, in effect, to win the toss.

This redeemed him, in my eyes. Irrational superstition is a commendable virtue in one who has made a vice of rationality. By the game's fifth play, though, I realized, to my immense disappointment, that Knox had started off the game relentlessly true to rational form. The fifth play was a run up the middle by Patriot fullback Robert Perryman, who fumbled at the New England 29, where Seattle's Dave Wyman recovered. Three minutes into the game, the Seahawks already had the ball within field-goal range, with a strong wind at their backs. There was nothing superstitious at all about Knox's refusal to take the ball. He simply played the percentages, deferring the choice between offense and defense to New England, taking instead the choice between starting out with or against the wind. By starting with the wind, he left the Patriots with a choice between two evils: taking the ball against the wind or giving it to the Seahawks, who had the wind at their backs. Knox's decision was an ingenious tactical move. In taking the ball, then turning it over, the Patriots made him look brilliant.

He looked brilliant for exactly four plays, at which point Norm Johnson missed a field-goal attempt, kicking the ball on a perfectly straight line to the right of the goalposts. The Patriots then ran eight straight times, trying a shovel pass on third-and-11 at the Seattle 46, gaining only 7 yards, and punting. Seattle then ran three plays, moving out to the Seahawk 18, from where Ruben Rodriguez kicked a wind-aided 40-yard punt, returned 8 yards by Irving Fryar to the 50-yard line. Four plays and 27 yards later, the quarter ended. As the Seahawks turned to face the wind, they also had to face the fact that they had cast aside the advantage Knox and Perryman procured for them at the start of the game. Four plays into the second quarter, they gave up a 34-yard field goal to the Patriots. Four plays after that, the Seahawks strengthened their hold on disadvantage even further. Krieg, back to pass on third down, dropped the ball as he wound up to throw, and New England recovered at the Seahawk 6. Against a belatedly aroused Seattle defense, New England managed in three plays to move only 1 yard closer to the Seahawk goal line, so in came place-kicker Jason Staurovsky again. Again his kick was good, and the Patriots, 6 minutes into the second quarter, had a seemingly insurmountable 6–0 lead.

By this time it was clear that the game was a health hazard, exposing spectators to toxic doses of tedium. There wasn't a team in the NFL that could have passed against the wind that day, let alone two teams that would have had trouble passing under ideal conditions. The Patriots simply had no pass offense, and what pass offense the Seahawks had was more or less eliminated on Seattle's third play from scrimmage, a quarterback draw in which Krieg was leveled by defensive end Garin Veris for a 4-yard loss. Veris's hit left Krieg woozy for the rest of the game, with the vision in his left eye blurred. Krieg was so impaired that Knox wrestled for most of the game with the idea of removing him for Kelly Stouffer.

New England, perhaps out of a feeling of obligation, did try eight first-half passes, completing four, for 42 yards. Flutie's last pass of the half, though, was intercepted by Darren Comeaux and returned to the Patriot 34 with 1:50 remaining in the half. There, Krieg completed an 11-yard pass to John L. Williams for Seattle's only first down of the half. Three plays later, having sandwiched an incompletion between a 6-yard loss and a 6-yard completion, Seattle closed out the half with a missed 41-yard field-goal attempt.

The second half opened, again, with Seattle opting for the wind rather than the ball. And again New England fumbled, and again Seattle recovered, this time at the Patriot 27. John L. Williams ran straight ahead for 4 yards, then caught a pass from Krieg for a 4-yard loss. Then an incredible thing happened. Ray Butler, running a post pattern, turned in front of his defender, sealing him off to the outside, and caught New England without a safety in the middle. Krieg threw a short, wobbling pass, Butler slid into the end zone on his hip, and—in the referee's view, at least—caught the ball for a touchdown. After a long, thoughtful review by replay official Ralph Morcroft, the touchdown was upheld, and Norm Johnson entered to give Seattle a 1-point lead.

The New England fans, who had been enjoying themselves immensely, now began to brood. They revived somewhat when Johnson's kickoff was returned 34 yards, to the Patriot 43, but then lapsed into silence again when New England lost 3 yards on first down. Then Flutie, scrambling out of a broken pass play, ran out of bounds after a 5-yard gain. As he stepped daintily out of bounds, the fans, with their team facing third-and-eight—a longer third down than any they had managed to convert in the entire game, save for one third-and-13 play in the first quarter—saw disaster looming. But suddenly salvation came flying Flutie's way. Seattle line-backer Tony Woods, trying to "make something happen," hit Flutie well out of bounds, well after the referee's whistle, with the result that the Patriots were given an additional 15 yards, and a first down at the Seattle 40. Six running plays later, at the 8:44 mark of the third quarter, the Patriots concluded the day's scoring with a game-winning touchdown.

The game's single exciting play came on the ensuing kickoff. Bobby Joe Edmonds, catching the ball at the Seattle 5, ran straight up the right hashmarks, slipping through a seam to the inside at the 20, then breaking upfield. With one burst, he had breached New England's entire coverage team, and he took off at full speed, unobstructed, from the Seattle 40. New England kicker Teddy Garcia, falling backward and flailing, reached out as he hit the ground and just managed to grab Edmonds's toe, tripping him at the 48. Edmonds had come within half a toe's length of scoring a touchdown.

The Seahawks closed the third quarter with their longest sustained drive of the game: a 25-yard march backward, employing a holding penalty, a fumble 10 yards deep in the backfield, and a delay-of-game penalty to move from the Seattle 43 back to the 18.

Two hours and 42 minutes after the opening kickoff, this gruesome spectacle came to an end. It had been the longest of games, the shortest of games. Left in its wake were Seattle statistics that made the numbers racked up by Grenada in its celebrated war game with the U.S. military look awesome by comparison. The Seahawks totaled—*totaled*—two first downs, to the Patriots' 16. Seattle converted one of 13 third downs, while the Patriots converted five of 14. Total net yards: Seattle 65, New England 212. The Seahawk juggernaut averaged 1.1 yards per rushing play, 2 yards per pass completion. New England had a time-of-possession total of 41:05, compared with Seattle's 18:55. The only statistical category in which Seattle outscored New England was in net yards passing: Seattle 45, New England 35.

The Patriots won the game simply by running... and running... and running. They ran 54 times, and threw 10 passes—only two in the second half. Stories about this game should have been headlined "Doug Flutie Gives Good Handoff."

Never, I thought, had so many traveled so far to see so little. Yet the fans clearly loved every minute of it. They stayed well after the end of the game, screaming and reveling as if they had won a championship. Cold as it was, they lingered, gathering in the aisles over the door through which the Seahawks exited to their locker room, taunting them mercilessly. Why weren't they bored? How could they have sat through such a game, in such weather, and stayed engaged enough not to leave at halftime? Does football have such a powerful hold on the American mind that there is no way to make it boring?

I was standing down on the field as the Seahawks, heads bowed, exited. The wind was fierce and cold, the sky was growing dark, and the artificial turf looked and felt like tundra. It was one of the most desolate places I had ever been. Why any human would be there by choice, I couldn't imagine. Trying to reconcile the fans' fierce joy with the quality of the game that inspired it had me replumbing, yet again, the mystery of football's popularity. Catching a fan's eye, I shouted up at him: "What did you like about this game?"

"AAAAAAAAUUUUUUUUGH!" he answered.

I turned away then, to see one of Behring's right-hand men standing next to me. It was John Loar, director of special projects for Behring's Blackhawk Corporation. He had watched the game from the sidelines. Flapping his arms for warmth, smiling coldly, he said—in a voice heavy with sarcasm—"Great coaching, huh?"

This was just one more in a quickening series of danger signals flashing around the Seahawks. Loar, Mike Blatt, Behring, and minority owner Ken Hofmann were growing more visible with each Seattle game. Behring spent home games—and some road games—on the sidelines, sometimes in the company of Blatt and Loar. Sometime in November, Blatt, as first reported by John Clayton in Tacoma's *Morning News Tribune*, had divested himself of his sports agency and put in escrow the purchase price of 5 percent of the Seahawk franchise, in preparation for becoming a minority partner. Clayton's story elicited a furious denial from Loar, who branded it as a "ridiculous rumor."

Still, Blatt was taking on an increasingly important role in the changing Seahawks picture. He, Loar, and Blackhawk executive Steve Beinke were studying Seahawk business practices carefully, going over everything from player contracts to the Seahawk phone system. And more and more, it looked as if Behring's group was forcing Mike McCormack out. The day after the New England game, it would be revealed that they had been talking at length with University of Miami athletic director Sam Jankovich. According to Jankovich, Behring's group asked him if he would be interested in McCormack's job should they make a change. According to Loar, they were simply studying top college and professional sports franchises in order to increase their "knowledge base" about the sports business. According to Clayton, McCormack's peers around the league were already predicting that he would be gone by next season.

And then there were Behring's own occasional disturbing comments. He felt himself a qualified-enough football man to pass judgment on Knox's work, praising him only after wins, and complaining publicly that Seattle needed to play a more wide-open offense. And in an incautious moment one day, talking with McCormack in a room adjacent to the media room at Seahawk headquarters, he was heard saying, "I think we ought to move Bosworth to outside linebacker." McCormack's reply was inaudible— but knowing him, I would guess that even if he said nothing, his face gave him away.

After what seemed an interminable wait, we were led into the funereal Seahawk locker room. Gloomy as it was, there was none of the fury or depression that clouded the team's quarters after the demon-driven loss to Kansas City. This was, after all, a meaningless game, from Seattle's perspective. Mostly the players seemed uninterested, tired, and physically beaten. They looked worn not so much from the game as from the season. The room looked like a warehouse full of wounds.

In one corner, Largent was talking with reporters about the pain in his foot, which had been attributed to a severely bruised arch. "I don't know," he was saying. "It feels more serious than a bruise. But it's in a pretty critical area. When you play wide receiver, when you're cutting on the ball of your foot all the time . . . it just needs some rest, really. It's just been kind of progressive."

Largent was fighting the one battle players fight throughout the season that is more difficult and more draining even than the games: the battle against injury. There is no player on any roster anywhere in the league who does not play at least part of the season when reason dictates that he shouldn't. And there is no problem more vexing to those who worry about the ethics of professional sports than the complex problem of playing with pain. "Every player has an injury during the season," says team trainer Jim Whitesel. "I don't care who it is. And it's a whole new level of pain here. It's like night and day, compared with college. It's crazy. The players expect so much more of themselves." A season, for an athlete, is a war of attrition, with the player warding off the effects of injury for as long as he can, hoping to make it to the offseason before he has to resort to surgery or has to give his body the rest it needs for recuperation.

I just couldn't seem to shake loose of this issue. After watching Bosworth and many of his lesser teammates fight off their injuries, I decided they underwent their sufferings for two principal reasons: a compulsion to play—an inability, really, not to play—and the fear of losing their jobs permanently to the players filling in for them while they are hurt. In both cases, it seemed to me, the players simply lacked the mental or psychological resources to see the sense of resting until they were recovered. "Pro athletes," says Whitesel, "are very aggressive, very intense people who don't like to sit watching. They've always been the ones who have pushed forward. They know how to be intense. But they don't know how to engage their intensity, to focus it with some rest at times."

According to Whitesel, players are constantly trying to distinguish between "pain and injury. If you're injured, you don't play. But if you have little nicks that you have to play with, then you've got to suck it up and go out and play. That's what the game is."

To Whitesel, the two things distinguishing injury from pain are the risk of long-term damage from playing with an affliction, and the inability to play at full strength. Which sounds reasonable enough, until you consider what "full strength" must mean in light of Bosworth's playing entire games without being able to lift one of his arms. And the term "little nicks," from what I have seen, covers such ailments as broken noses, sprained ankles, arthritic shoulders, broken ribs, broken hands, sprained backs . . . "Ultimately," says Whitesel, "the goal I have is the same goal that everybody has—to win, to go to the Super Bowl. To do the best we can to help the coaches and players win."

That goal necessitates ever-more-creative means of taping and "wedging" (supporting or protecting with orthotics) injured limbs and extremities, and injecting players with painkillers to get them through games. And that goal is so all-consuming that players, coaches, and medical technicians alike seldom, if ever, err on the side of caution. It drives them beyond the bounds of common sense when deciding whether an athlete should play with a given "nick." Bosworth's shoulder condition, remember, was a "nick" until the team acquired Darren Comeaux. As soon as Comeaux demonstrated some prowess on defense, Bosworth became "injured." The "goal that everybody has" meant that Bosworth's condition had to be evaluated not in and of itself, but as part of an equation that included the impact on Seattle's fortunes of his being replaced with rookie free agent Darrin Miller. Factor in the difference between the rookie Miller and the veteran Comeaux, and you have factored in the difference between a nick and an injury.

Consistently, the goal of winning comes first, the goal of healing second. This is as obvious as Bosworth's ego problems. Not so obvious is the answer to the moral question posed by that set of priorities. Outside the game, it would be unforgivable; in the world of football, though, it is not only necessary, but—strange as it sounds—it is magnificent.

For most of the season (particularly through the dark, debilitating six weeks stretching between the Atlanta and Buffalo games), I had been tempted to believe that players needed to be protected first of all from themselves, that they were too single-minded and too pressured to keep themselves out of danger, and that coaches took advantage of that failing to coerce them into playing when their bodies were pleading for mercy. Players struck me as football's version of helpless, accused innocents in the hands of the police—at medical proceedings assessing their physical conditions, they needed to have an attorney present.

But the spectacle of a wounded Steve Largent persuaded me that I was wrong. Here was a player with nothing to fear from sitting out games. In the last year of a contract paying him more than $1 million annually, he was financially secure; he was a star of such magnitude that no one—coach, fellow player, general manager, team owner, or fan—would question his courage or will to play. Further, he is an intelligent, level-headed man with relatively balanced priorities, and with enough interests outside the game to curb his competitive obsessions. Yet for all of that, he was determined to play on in the face of a potentially crippling injury—not to his foot, but to his hand.

I had first learned of Largent's hand injury the previous Thursday, when I met with his wife, Terry, and four other wives of Seahawk players (the others being Connie Millard, Gia Robinson, Cherise Bailey, and Sue Krieg) at a Kirkland restaurant. Largent had torn ligaments in his thumb during the Raider game. After consulting with team doctors, he sought a second opinion from a private physician. In Terry's retelling, "Steve said, 'Just pretend like I'm not a football player, and tell me what you would tell somebody.' And the guy said, 'I'm glad you said that, because what I would tell somebody is that I would put them in a cast for eight weeks, and then if it didn't heal up, I would do surgery on it.' " Terry Largent paused here, and all five women laughed heartily. "So," she continued, "Steve said, 'What will happen to me if I play with it, then?' He said, 'Well, it could cause enough damage that you'd have to fuse the bones together, and then you wouldn't have movement in that joint [where the thumb meets the palm of the hand] right there.' He said, 'OK, now tell me—can you fix something to keep my hand from moving and allow me to play?' He said, 'Well, I think so, but I'm not sure—we'll work on it.' So he made a thing and Steve's not sure if he can play or not . . . whether he can catch with this thing wrapped around his thumb. The team doctor wants to just tape it up. The thing that it's not supposed to do is close. It's supposed to stay open. He had it taped like that today, I just saw it, and it looked like it would work, but . . . "

"What's going to keep it from closing if he gets hit?" Connie Millard asked.

"Well," Terry answered, "if he gets hit, that would mess it up. I mean, if it got hit and smashed the thing . . . I don't know . . . I don't know if his foot'll even be well enough to play, anyway."

After missing the New England game, Largent would go on to play out the season with his hand taped and his foot wedged and anesthetized, and when the season ended he would have surgery done on both.

I can think of no other context in which that decision would make sense, but in football it seems not only sensible, but necessary. We are taken with football, at least in part, because it is a simple, uncompromising, cut-and-dried game. Either you win or you lose, and only the strongest survive. While there is much in it that mirrors modern life—it is a game, for example, rich in disappointment, failure, and frustration—it really is a game that hearkens back to simpler times. We live in an age in which all issues and decisions seem colored entirely in cloudy, shifting shades of gray rather than in clear blacks and whites. Football is an escape to a world of simple heroes and villains, of uncomplicated males undergoing grueling tests of strength and will. The goal of everyone in football, from owners to coaches to players, is to win, and all decisions are made with that goal first and foremost in mind. That ethic makes football a game of unrelenting pain and sacrifice, in which there is no room for equivocation. There is no question that players are coerced by that pressure into suffering travails that otherwise they would avoid, but, as Knox often says, "That's the game."

Frequently, there arise calls in the media to protect players from the risks inherent in football by limiting their right to decide for themselves how much risk they are willing to undergo. Like drug testing, it is one more example of the new American way—the urge to protect people from themselves. But to do that is to rob football of much of its glory. We tend to rationalize our love of football by saying that we love it in spite of its violence; really, we love it because of its violence—because its players, as heroes have done forever, undergo unthinkable trials, submit to cruelty of a sort that is no longer permitted in the modern world.

One thing that struck me as particularly noteworthy during this season is the casual attitude players' wives adopt toward the game's dangers. "I don't get emotionally wrapped up about it," Connie Millard said, from what seems to be a typical perspective. Added Terry Largent, "I've watched Steve play since high school, and he has had one knee operation that whole time. I guess when you've played that long, and you don't get hurt badly, you just don't expect it. That time he was knocked out on the field in Denver, I didn't even really think he was knocked out. Even when I saw him lying there on the field, I just thought he kind of got his bell rung. I didn't know he was knocked out for five minutes. I never even guessed that. And I never expect that to be what happens. So when I see Steve get hurt, I don't panic. I don't expect it to be bad. I just expect it to be a little injury."

For Sue Krieg, violence is an aspect of her husband's life made worthwhile by the joy football brings him, and she has learned to keep her fears at bay. "He jumps up right away, usually, after a hit, even if it hurts bad," she said, "because he doesn't want the defense to think that they hurt him. And so, I know if he doesn't jump up right away, something's goofy." She remembered a 1987 game in which Krieg had been "knocked silly" and had to come out of the game. "And even after that game, he walked out of the locker room and looked at me, like, 'Who are you?' It was really weird. That's scary—when you get hit in the head. Then you think, 'Is this game worth it?' Years from now, are you going to worry about brain damage or something? But I think it is worth it. Because *he* does. Because the feeling he gets from playing is unbelievable. The competition and everything—he's such a competitive person. He loves the feeling of the game."

There is just as strong a spirit of camaraderie among Seahawk wives as there is among Seahawk players. Partly, it is borne of the sense that no one can understand a player's wife the way another player's wife can, that football wives live in a world apart, with its own peculiar stresses and rewards. It is also borne of an uprooted feeling, all the wives having been brought to Seattle from far away. "I think we're more of a family," Largent said, "because everybody is transplanted. There's very few players that play in their own city." "That made me feel so good," Millard said, "the first year I came here, everybody was so nice. That's why I go out of my way to make someone feel at home. And I have to say that we have been really good as a group of wives. I mean, there are new people coming in all the time, and we try to watch out for everybody: baby showers, everybody has baby showers, everybody doing this and that for somebody else, in that sense it's very much like a family. You don't have to feel alone here."

The players' wives have a section of seats on the 300 level of the Kingdome, from where they watch their husbands more closely than they watch the game. "I just keep my eyes on Dave the whole time," Krieg said. "I don't watch the game, I watch Dave." "I'll watch Bryan," said Millard, "and his man's slipping around, and his man's inches from Dave, and I'll be like, 'Oh, no! Oh, no!' and all of a sudden, Dave completes a pass to Steve, and he's running 50 yards, and I'm still screaming. And people are saying, 'What's your problem?' " Robinson watches the way a defensive coach would from the press box. "I watch Gene, especially on third-and-long situations," she said. Invariably, as a play unfolds, she sees where he should go before he breaks that way. "You get up there with him and you just want to help him, like try to block someone . . . I get nervous, start yelling, 'Get over! Get over! Get over!' if I see where the quarterback's going with the ball."

For all the pain and insecurity and anxiety that is built into professional football, the worst thing for wives is the insensitivity of fans. Hearing fans talk about their husbands is even worse than reading about them in the newspapers—the more so since fans turn up everywhere. "My first year here, I worked at Microsoft," said Robinson. "And I can remember after a game, if we'd lost, people waiting for me at my office for me to come in, and wanting to know why we lost. They were brutal sometimes: 'Why did your husband do this?' Or, 'What's wrong with that team?' They don't realize that we're part of it, too."

No one suffers the slings and arrows of outraged fans more than Sue Krieg. "You never get used to people criticizing your husband," she said, referring both to fans and sportswriters. "I sometimes feel like people just wait for Dave to do something wrong. Because a lot of times when things go good for him, you don't hear anything about it. And then when things get screwed up, they just pounce on him. I don't know if they have it in for him, or what, but it doesn't seem like they like him too much."

Krieg tries to console herself by taking seriously only her husband's teammates ("The thing that keeps you going is the teammates, the way the guys stick up for him to the end") and by trying to persuade herself that booing is directed not at her husband but at the quarterback position. "Booing's hard," she said, "but I remember when a friend would say to me, 'Always remember that they're booing the position, not the person,' because you can take it too much to heart. You almost wish they would boo you rather than your husband, because someone you love, you'd rather. . . you can take it yourself better than you can take hearing someone you love being booed."

I may never write another critical word about an athlete.

While Dave Krieg claims publicly not to notice fans' booing, it is clear from the things he says to his wife that he is deeply hurt by it. "He said to me last game [the Monday-night win over the Los Angeles Raiders], 'Do you believe they even cheered when I came out during the player introduc- tions?' Because usually he runs out right behind John L. [Williams], right on his tail, while they're still cheering John L. He said, 'That's the first time I ever heard them cheer! They weren't even yelling for anyone else to come in when I threw that interception!' Even I feel now like something's gone wrong if he gets cheered. I get nervous. You hear the criticism all the time, but I don't know—what can you do? He's heard it his whole career here, and he's still going strong."

All five women feel a sense of estrangement not only from the public, but from their husbands' employers as well. Time and again, they see their husbands turning aghast at management's approach to football. "I think the players have a harder time seeing football as a business," said Largent, "because it is kind of like a family, I think, among the team members. But they're not in it in a business way, the way the guys a little further up are." She believes that the esprit among the players will prove the hardest thing for her husband to do without once he retires. "Steve was just thinking about it last night. He said, 'I'm just trying to decide if I'm really going to miss the camaraderie or not.' I said, 'Well, are you?' He said, 'Yeah, I really am. I'm just trying to picture all those guys in the locker room with- out me there.' "

The wives seem acutely aware that the Seahawk world is strictly stratified. "As far as management goes," said Millard, "I can walk upstairs and they're kind to me, they're very nice. But yet everybody seems to still stay very separate. There is management, there are players, there are coaches, and everybody seems to know where their place in all this is." The divisions seem stricter in the wake of the 1987 players strike. Largent has observed "a different atmosphere this year—and you know, it could be related to the strike." Bailey has noticed that many of the social functions held for players and their families by management no longer take place. "There's a lot of things that we used to do but we don't anymore because of the strike," she said. Even game days are different. "The owners used to invite us up to their box before game time—but we didn't do that last year, and we haven't this year either."

Millard has noticed a change not only in the attitude of management to- ward players, but of players toward their teammates as well. "That strike," she said, "created a lot of hostility between those players that wanted to cross the picket line and those who didn't, and everybody had their opin- ions, and everybody knew where everybody else stood, and that doesn't make anybody right or wrong, but it was dissension about what to do. When to go back and when not to go back. Even the date to go back. So there was dissension the whole way, in that particular year. Because of the issue." The bitterness of the strike even carried over to relationships among the wives. "I mean, I never saw these ladies, we didn't have the games to go to together, and it was hard to think about coming together when so much else was going on outside anyway."

Largent feels that, strike or no strike, the ownership change has brought tremendous pressure on Knox and his staff to win, and that pressure has filtered down to the players. "I feel like from this year just from the things that Steve has told me that our coaching staff has been under a lot of pressure themselves, and that it all gets passed down," she said. It is not, she added, as if the players needed any more pressure from Knox. According to her, he strikes his players as a man obsessed by mistakes—particularly by mistakes that lose ball games—and that once a player errs critically, Knox is incapable of forgetting the mistake. "This is the kind of mentality that Knox has," she said. "This player"—naming a retired player whom Knox has often praised publicly when recalling glorious moments in the Seahawks' past, she also enjoined me from repeating it—"came back to watch a game, and he went in to see Chuck, and the first thing that Chuck said to him was, 'Oh, we have that old such-and-such play, you know, that one that you messed up so many years ago?' And, you know, he wasn't joking! It was something that this guy had done wrong—I don't know if we lost that game, probably we did, because I think that's what I've understood before, that those are the plays that Chuck remembers, those plays that lost a game for us. And that is what he remembers about a player. And I know Steve said that if he had messed up—he messed up in some game recently—he said, 'Man, I'm glad we didn't lose that game. Chuck would've remembered me like that!' So that's kind of where the hostile things come from. I guess it's really frustrating to Chuck to have a player mess up and him feel like that's the cause of the loss."

Amen.

My conversation with these women was punctuated with laughter and humorous asides, the women playing off one another's comments with jokes and exaggerated, playacted examples of scenes from players' lives. One moment that particularly struck me, and that seemed to capture perfectly the fear players feel toward the organization that employs them, came during Largent's description of her husband's injuries. When Steve Largent wanted a second opinion, she said, he went to see "a real hand specialist, who's not a Seahawk puppet doctor—you know, who doesn't say what the coaches tell him to say." The women all laughed then, and they laughed again when Millard, pretending to be one of the "puppet doctors," picked up an imaginary phone and exclaimed, "Let me make a phone call, and see what I better tell you!"

I was remembering that moment in particular as I stood in the locker room in Foxboro, listening to Knox—his horror-worn eyes gazing out at nothing—talk about the 89th loss of his career. He was obliquely blaming his players. "We didn't execute," he was saying. "We didn't throw the ball, we didn't catch it. And if you don't execute, that's what happens. We didn't block—you know, we couldn't make the short-yardage situations, and that's very frustrating."

In his eyes, the game was one of mistakes and shortcomings on the part of his players. In the eyes of one of his owner's men, it was a game of mistakes and shortcomings on the part of Knox. Everyone in football, it seemed, was the prey of someone else. On the field, opposing players preyed upon one another. Off the field, teammates preyed upon one another, struggling for roster spots. Always, coaches were preying upon their players, constantly looking for better replacements. General managers preyed upon coaches, and owners upon general managers. Football struck me then as a little Darwinian world, a constant struggle for survival, in which every creature is trying to devour some other creature, while trying at the same time to avoid being devoured in turn. And the whole closed system was devouring money at a phenomenal rate, money pumped into it—like feed into a fatted calf—by fans with inexhaustible, ravening dream-appetites.

Dr. Jekyll and Mr. Largent

I began to perceive more deeply than it has ever yet been stated, the trembling immateriality, the mist-like transience, of this seemingly so solid body in which we walk attired . . . I not only recognised my natural body for the mere aura and effulgence of certain of the powers that made up my spirit, but managed to compound a drug by which these powers should be dethroned from their supremacy, and a second form and countenance substituted, none the less natural to me because they were the expression, and bore the stamp of lower elements in my soul.
—Robert Louis Stevenson, *Dr. Jekyll and Mr. Hyde*

We thus arrive at the image of a world-mosaic or cosmic kaleidoscope, which, in spite of constant shufflings and rearrangements, also takes care of bringing like and like together.
—Paul Kammerer, quoted by Arthur Koestler in
The Case of the Midwife Toad

As fate would have it, the Raiders beat the Broncos, 21–20, immediately after Seattle had perished in the fire and brimstone delivered by the puritanical New England offense. Thus did a great unease settle over the AFC West, as its sore and troubled teams contemplated the three-way tie that once again obtained at the top of their standings. And as the National Football League approached the final two sabbaths of its 16-week pilgrimage to the postseason, there arose great wailing and gnashing of coaches in Denver and Los Angeles, while in Seattle there was tremendous girding of expectations.

Incredibly, the Seahawks emerged from 14 weeks of travail to find themselves, at 7-7, both with their worst 14-week record since 1983 and closer to a division championship than ever before.

The latter circumstance was due to a combination of the remaining schedule and the weakened conditions of the Raiders and Broncos. The

Seahawks, hosting the Broncos for their 15th game, then closing out the regular season with a trip to Los Angeles to take on the Raiders, had only to win both games to capture the division crown.

Of the three teams, only the Seahawks enjoyed the unbridled support of their fans, while in the other two cities, cynicism and contempt prevailed. In Seattle, fans were lining up to reserve playoff tickets. In Los Angeles and Denver, where fans were accustomed to watching Super Bowl–caliber football, the season had already been written off. Raider linebacker Matt Millen, embarrassed that 7–7 teams could be considered contenders for anything, called the division race a contest "to see who stinks least." And where, in years past, the Denver trip to Seattle had always been preceded by visits from at least two Colorado newspapers and all three Denver network-television affiliates, this year there were no Denver reporters at all in Seattle during the week before the game.

Seattle, though, was in the grip of playoff fever. Seahawk practices were jaunty proceedings with loud ventings of emotion after every play. On the field and in the locker room, Seattle players exuded such a festive, purposeful air that it was impossible to believe they had lost so grimly the Sunday before.

The team's mood was all the more improbable in light of the persistent indications that Ken Behring was soon to fire McCormack, and that significant player trades might be in the offing. In spite of Behring's denials in the press, credible Blackhawk sources, consistently funneling reports through the *News Tribune*'s John Clayton, kept alive the news that McCormack's days were numbered. Behring himself had said two weeks before that no Seattle player was untradable, and now a sense dawned among the players that their once-solid franchise was beginning to crumble.

To those who remembered Behring's first public appearance in Seattle, there was an ironic twist to the timing of his machinations. Just before the season opener against the Broncos, at the press conference announcing his acquisition of the team, Behring had piously stated that he wanted the sale to be completed before the season started, so as not to serve as a distraction to Seattle players. Now, as they headed into the season-closing stretch with a second game against Denver and with their championship hopes on the line, he was serving up new, troubling distractions every day.

However distracted his players may have been, Knox was too taken with the loss to New England to be diverted from his lifelong preoccupations. The loss had re-energized him, and he attacked the press with renewed combativeness. After decrying his team's performance against the Patriots, he took off on a long, digressive journey through his Wednesday press conference, taking on press and players alike. "You're playing for first place in the division, stay alive with a chance to win a division, ensure an opportunity in the playoffs . . . but to win, we have to make some plays. See, when you make some plays, like we did in the Raider game, then everything's imaginative, everything looks very good. But if you don't catch the ball, you don't throw it, or like last week, we win the toss and we elect to defend the goal, so we have the wind at our backs. We couldn't have had any better scenario for what happened: We kick, we control 'em, we force a turnover, we get the ball right there, OK? That could've been a *master piece of strategy*. OK? And given you something to write about—if we had won the football game. We didn't score a touchdown and we missed a field goal. Now if that had been the decisive point in the game, everybody would've said, 'Boy, that was brilliant! What really enabled you to do that?' And I would've explained that in great detail. But I have not been asked that question once . . . "

By the time he was finished with this meandering line of thought, Knox had covered some 20 years of football history, and his audience had scarcely enough energy left to ask any more questions. Reporters did manage, though, to elicit from Knox the news that Patrick Hunter would be back on the practice field for the first time in five weeks. Knox would wait until Saturday before activating Hunter, making room for him on the roster by putting Bosworth on injured reserve. Until then, David Hollis—whose return to the NFL had been effected by Hunter's injury—would be practicing on tenterhooks, as he waited to see if he would be the player cut to make room for Hunter. So focused on his fate was the talkative Hollis during the week that he retreated into near-silence, answering every question on every topic with the same, "I'm doin' fine—just fine."

During his midweek press conference, Knox touched on emotion as a critical factor in the upcoming Bronco game. And the honing and heightening of emotion marked his team's practice sessions and meetings all week long. Pass completions in practice were ferociously cheered, and assistant coaches regaled reporters daily with discourses on the pivotal role emotion plays in winning. It was as if, having tried every tactical and strategic move they could devise, to little avail, they had turned at last to motivation.

Running back coach Chick Harris, whose use of italics in speech escalates dramatically week by week during football season, was determined to work his charges into a homicidal rage by kickoff time against Denver. Asking him for a scientific analysis of his team's running game—particularly his players' inability to run as well as they had in seasons past—I was treated to a textbook display of artistic temperament in full rant. "We've gotta just go ahead and *bite down* on it and start *attacking* people with our running," he shrieked. "And when there's nothing there, we have got to find a way to get something when it's not there. And that's it. And it's gotta be a *street-fight alley brawl* to get yards. We talked about blocking *through* people and running *through* people . . . You can analyze it and analyze it, but the thing is, is that going out there, *every* opportunity that you have, you just gotta go and get after it. *Attack* people!"

I tried asking about defensive deployments, but Harris had too much heart on his mind to talk tactics. "It all stems from *heart*," he said. "When you run well, you've got a back with a *lot of heart to get it done*. Squirm, fight, *claw* for every bit of it. *Hungry*. That's important. *Every* time—not some of the time, but *every* time. When you line up and you're the starter, you can't be a ham-and-egger now! You've got to be a money man! And sometimes you have to be an *angry* runner. Because when you're angry and *pissed off*, you *can* run. Because you take your *anger* out on the defense. And you make them miss tackles. You run through them, *over* them . . . *around* them . . . you don't give a shit! Because you want it!"

It took nearly the entire Seattle defense to keep me from strapping on a helmet.

Harris, apparently impressed at how easily he had infected me with his intensity virus ("HA! I got you fired up! I can tell!"), restored me to health with an injection of reasoned analysis. In the Seattle ground attack, he explained, "everything is choreographed—you know, the line blocking, the designation of where the point of attack should be." But built into the attack is the running back's right to improvise, either by cutting back inside or darting to the outside if the designated hole is filled by a defender. "You use the great vision of a running back," Harris continued, "to be able to find where the seams are." Seattle employs what Harris calls a "run-to-color" offense, in which Seahawk running backs are trained to react instinctively to the color of an opponent's jersey. "When our running back comes into the hole, sometimes if a color flashes in front of him, he will automatically cut back or bounce it to the outside. That's basic run-to-daylight football. Somebody's voiding an area, so now we're going back to the spot where they came from."

Defenses had adjusted to the Seahawks' run-to-daylight attack by committing their strong safety almost entirely to the run. The safety, playing up close to the line of scrimmage, would shadow the play, knowing that the ball carrier would cut back inside almost every time, and would fill the cutback lane. The tactic worked so well for opposing teams, Harris said, because Seahawk runners had been cutting back too often, either because they gave up on the designated hole too soon or because they cut back when they should have broken outside. Often, they would cut back to avoid a tackler just as a teammate was coming up to block him, thereby running away from a hole before giving it a chance to open.

Warner concurred, adding that he had become a runner of such predictable tendencies that teams could anticipate rather than react to his moves. "I have a tendency of cutting back all the time," he said. "There's nothing wrong with cutting back, but what you have to do is try to stay front side a little bit longer, so that they will pursue. Then if you make that cut-back move, it's there. If I go back against the grain all the time, they see it, they anticipate it, and they try to set for it."

By Sunday, Knox had worked his players into an emotional lather. The Seattle locker room in the minutes before the game looked like an institution whose inmates had been extravagantly padded and helmeted for their own protection. Players' eyes bulged unnaturally. Conversation was infrequent and muted, everyone focused inward. Standing over in the offensive lineman's corner, Ron Mattes had donned his helmet, stood, and was calmly butting his head against the wall. Next to him, Edwin Bailey was trying to keep a fidgeting Bryan Millard calm. "What time is it?" Millard would ask, every 30 seconds or so. "What time is it? Time to go out there yet?" "He was just itchin' to go out on the field," Bailey said later. "He wanted to go! Just like a big ol' bull during ruttin' season. He was just over there snortin', and I'm sayin', 'Hey! We are ready to go!' "

So was the Seattle crowd. The combination of Seattle's place in the standings and the Seattleite's reflexive hysteria at the very mention of the word "Denver" had created an air of furious, foaming expectation far out of proportion to the likely quality of the game. Denver was hurting. Its midweek injury report had listed 13 players, including Elway, as either questionable or probable, and while all but one of them (Gerald Willhite, the Broncos' best running back) eventually suited up to play, none were playing at full strength. The most obviously crippled player was standout defensive end/linebacker Karl Mecklenberg, who played with a cumbersome cast extending down from his elbow to completely encase his hand, robbing him of the use of his fingers.

Seattle, to everyone's relief, lost the coin toss—a significant development, since the week before, Knox had proven that it is the loss of the toss, rather than simply starting out without the ball, that guarantees a team the game. Norm Johnson kicked 5 yards deep into the Denver end zone, the Broncos downed the ball there, and it was brought out to the 20-yard line, from where—to the ecstatic screams of 63,000—Denver fired the first shot.

An Elway pass to wide-open tight end Clarence Kay, it was thrown behind the receiver—another significant development, for it signaled that El-way was not at his best. Even though he went on from there to lead the Broncos on a brief, 35-yard, five-play march, everyone in the stands knew that without a flawless performance from him, the Broncos were doomed. And sure enough, the drive stalled at the Seattle 45 when, on second-and-six, Elway overthrew wide receiver Mark Jackson, who had beaten Terry Taylor downfield by a good two steps only to watch the ball drop just out of reach on the threshold of the end zone. Two plays later, Elway, whom Knox extols as one of football's few legitimate triple-threat backs, pulled off his neatest trick of the day: He quick-kicked a masterpiece that was downed at the Seahawk 3.

Denver thus opened with a near-perfect drive that had come within a hand's-breadth of scoring, then ended with the next-best thing, a daunting field-position advantage and the chance to force Seattle—as the Raiders had done two weeks before when they caused Krieg to fumble in his own end zone—into committing a fatal error.

Seattle came out with its short-yardage offense, and Curt Warner bulled straight ahead for 1 predictable yard. Next, Seattle lined up in its standard I formation, with tight end Mike Tice on the right. Krieg faked a handoff to Warner, who stepped just across the line of scrimmage, found no one to block, and turned back to face Krieg as the Denver defense fanned out into deep coverage. Krieg flipped Warner the ball, Warner turned, and ran straight ahead for a 12-yard gain.

In a day that would prove rich in memorable plays, that was probably the play of the game. Krieg, under pressure, had run through his inventory of receivers so quickly, and seen the defense so well, that he had found his open receiver before even the heaviest of rushes could reach him. He looked as on now as Elway had looked off when he missed Kay. And the Denver defense clearly would pose little threat. In dropping deep, it had left the running back—the one receiver Seattle is most prone to employ when backed up against its own goal line—completely undefended.

Four plays later, on third-and-13 at the Seattle 37, the Broncos committed another error. Safety Mike Harden, covering Steve Largent, allowed him such a wide berth that Largent, curling in 19 yards downfield, made a sliding catch with Harden 10 yards behind him.

The Seahawks didn't face another third down until six plays later, when Krieg, on third-and-10 at the Bronco 14, dropped back, looked downfield, then threw a little swing pass in the backfield to John L. Williams, so ignored by the Denver defense that he was able to angle untouched into the end zone. On their first possession, the Seahawks traveled 97 yards in 12 plays, to take a 7–0 lead and establish, once and for all, control of the game.

The drive was a Seattle coach's dream. The Seahawks gained 24 yards on the ground, 53 in the air, and 18 on a pass-interference penalty. Krieg threw to four different receivers, averaging 11.5 yards per pass. Running wide, running inside, and throwing short- and medium-range high-percentage passes, the Seahawks consumed 6 minutes, 47 seconds—nearly half a quarter—scored a touchdown, and saw that they could gain yardage with just about anything they tried. It was classic Seattle ball-control offense, and it worked almost exactly as diagrammed.

The Seattle crowd and the Seattle team were locked in a frenzied symbiosis, each feeding off the emotions of the other. The Seahawk kickoff team smothered returner Ken Bell at the Bronco 14, and a holding penalty moved the ball back to the 7. Elway immediately hit tight end Orson Mobley for a 7-yard gain, then the Broncos ran straight ahead on a draw play, to gain 4 more, get a first down at the 18, and move out of apparent danger. Seattle broke through on the next play, though, and linebacker Tony Woods sacked Elway for a 5-yard loss. Flushed out of the pocket by Jacob Green on second-and-15, then, Elway scrambled to his right, angling backward . . . backward . . . as nose tackle Ken Clarke methodically maneuvered him into the corner formed by the sideline and the Denver goal line. Elway tried to throw deep downfield while still moving backward, and the ball flipped out of his hand, to be recovered at the 3 by Denver when it took a perfect hop into the arms of Bronco center Billy Bryan. Dropping into the end zone now on third-and-25, Elway saw Clarke rushing in at him, threw wildly, then turned his back, waiting for the blow. Clarke flattened him, and the pass fell incomplete.

After Denver punted, Seattle started out on offense from the Bronco 48. On first down, John L. Williams went in motion to the right, breaking into a deep pass pattern at the snap. As Williams, Blades, and Largent ran deep, tight end Mike Tice angled into the middle, catching a Krieg pass for 12 yards. After Warner swept right end, running out of bounds for a 2-yard gain, he stayed off the field, and Seattle clandestinely sent in its four-wide-receiver shotgun personnel and lined up without a huddle. Denver, caught without its nickel defenders on the field, lined up haphazardly as Krieg began his snap count. Suddenly the officials jumped in and stopped the game. As Denver hurriedly substituted its nickel backs for linebackers, the referees decreed that the game clock was off by 3 seconds and needed to be reset.

On the sideline, Knox was apoplectic. The officials, as Steve Moore succinctly explained later, "had taken a touchdown away from us." Knox had outmaneuvered the Broncos, only to be robbed by chance of a carefully designed mismatch. Now, as he vented his spleen at referee Gordon

McCarter, Moore quietly reinstated Seattle's standard offense, and the Seahawks lined up against Denver's nickel package with two running backs, a tight end, and two wide receivers. Having been denied one mismatch, Seattle still managed to create another. Warner, cutting back over left tackle into a middle protected by one linebacker instead of two, gained 13 yards.

Warner tried right guard on the next play, squirming and clawing for 2 yards, then Krieg, out of the shotgun formation, passed to John L. Williams, who had delayed coming out of the backfield, for 11 more yards. The quarter ended as Warner, darting right, then darting left, then lowering his head and charging straight ahead, made his way down to the Denver 3.

As the players moved to the opposite end of the field, the crowd filled the Kingdome with a gradually swelling roar. Seattle lined up on the 5-yard line, second-and-goal, and John L. Williams, legs churning furiously, carried up the middle, took on three defenders at the line of scrimmage, and pushed them 5 yards back, coming to rest with the ball just across the goal line. The referees, impressed, awarded him a touchdown. But as the teams lined up for the extra-point attempt, in jumped the officials again. Edwin Bailey, standing up and retreating, waved his arms in disgust. The officials huddled around an earphone connecting them with replay official Chuck Heberling, then reversed the touchdown call. Harder to please, Heberling had decreed that Williams's knee touched down before the ball crossed the plane of the goal line, and he insisted that the ball be placed at the half-yard line.

In games past, Seattle players would have reacted with bitter protests. But this reversal was less a setback than it was a witty allusion to reversals from earlier in the season. The Seahawks acted almost as if they had expected the call, lined up nonchalantly, and sent Warner, escorted by Bryan Millard, on a sweep to the right. The touchdown was so uncontested that Warner paused on his way into the end zone to watch diminutive cornerback Jeremiah Castille attempt to deal with the ministrations of the massive Millard, who with one flick of his meaty arms flipped the hapless defender to a far corner of the Kingdome.

Denver is known for nothing so much as scoring quickly, and in only five plays the Broncos traveled 80 yards into the Seattle end zone. The touchdown play, however—a 15-yard Elway pass to wide receiver Mark Jackson—was comically marred by fellow receiver Ricky Nattiel, who was flagged after the whistle for a personal foul. The Broncos, having managed to take a big step forward by closing to within 14–7, now took a bigger one backward by having to kick off from their 20-yard line, instead of their 35. A delighted Seahawk offense, then, started its next drive from near midfield, at the Seattle 45.

There now followed an unforgettable series, beginning with four plays which, as they unfolded, struck me as strangely and disproportionately exciting. Warner, trying left end, gained only 1 yard. Then when the Seahawks tried another no-huddle play, Millard jumped offsides. With second-and-14, the Seahawks came out in their bread-and-butter I-right formation, rather than the shotgun they ordinarily employ on second-and-long plays, and snapped the ball as soon as they were set, without taking a snap count from Krieg. Warner, taking the handoff, slipped into the line of scrimmage at left guard, ran straight through a tackle, and gained 12 yards. Now, with third-and-two at the Denver 47, Seattle came out in the shotgun. At the snap, John L. Williams, like someone out on a Sunday stroll, walked forward just past the line of scrimmage, then, suddenly accelerating, curled outside in front of linebacker Jim Ryan. Krieg fired to Williams, Williams caught the ball, stiff-armed the diving Ryan in the helmet, and took off, gaining 17 yards. When safety Mike Harden finally wedged Williams across the sideline, the fullback—to the delight of the partisans in the stands—felled him with a stiff-arm to the chin.

The ball now rested at the Denver 30, and Seattle had another first down. The Broncos were reeling. As the teams huddled, the crowd howled for blood, and when Seattle came to the line of scrimmage, an expectant, hungry hush settled over the stadium. Steve Largent, running a fade route deep, couldn't quite shake his way open, and Krieg dumped off to Williams again for a 4-yard gain. Seattle lined up next with Brian Blades aligned on the left, opposite cornerback Jeremiah Castille. Blades ran 10 yards downfield, keeping Castille to the outside, as Krieg handed off to Warner. Castille, seeing the handoff, broke inward, back toward the line of scrimmage, and Blades felled him with a textbook block to the legs.

Castille, enraged, landed on Blades, jumped up, picked him up by the shoulder pads, then locked Blades's head under one arm while working over his face with the other hand. Blades, in a superhuman effort at self-control, simply stood there, bent over, his hands on his thighs, taking Castille's punishment. Around them, the game degenerated into a disordered mess as officials and teammates came running. Finally Blades and Castille toppled over, taking one of the officials with them.

There is an unspoken understanding of sorts between NFL cornerbacks and wide receivers that receivers will not block their defenders below the waist, even though such a block is legal. On nearly all running plays, cornerback and wide receiver run together away from the play, then stop and dance at one another ineffectually, occasionally swatting each other's shoulder pads, until the whistle is blown. Cornerbacks are hysterical about knee injuries, and regard it as a serious breach of trust for receivers to cut them low. This is not so much a gentleman's agreement, however, as an understanding among receivers that if they do cut a cornerback, they will have to suffer the consequences. Castille, already frustrated by Krieg's superb day—Krieg so far had completed nine of nine passes—and still raging over his abject humiliation by Millard on Seattle's previous touchdown, had boiled over at Blades's breach of trust, and lost all control.

Incredibly, field judge Bob Wortman ruled that Castille's personal foul had been offset by Blades's "retaliation" and that, since the penalties canceled each other out, Castille's infraction would go unpunished. As Wortman's decision was announced by referee Gordon McCarter over the loudspeaker system, McCarter was interrupted by an explosive outburst from . . . Steve Largent?

Largent's voice was unrecognizable. It was the voice of a linebacker, of a man-turned-monster. He was in a murderous rage. "He said it *wasn't* retaliation!" Largent thundered, pointing furiously at one of the other officials. McCarter, thunderstruck, stumbled through the rest of his announcement, then went back to his position.

I barely had time to begin to take in the meaning of Largent's transformation before the Seahawks, to outraged accompaniment from the stands, came to the line of scrimmage. Blades lined up opposite Castille again, and I had the ominous feeling that the referees were about to let the game slip out of control.

At the snap, Castille jumped in front of Blades, grabbed his helmet, and hung on as Blades tried to break inside. Letting go, he then grabbed Blades around the hips and hung on again as Blades tried to make his way downfield. Seven yards farther on, he released his quarry, and Blades, open now, turned to look for the ball. Unfortunately (or, as things would soon turn out, fortunately), Krieg, seeing at the snap that free safety Mike Harden was shaded toward Largent, on the opposite side of the formation, had thrown the ball to Blades's destination in the end zone almost as soon as Blades broke from the line of scrimmage. It was one of those timing passes that are thrown out of whack by the slightest deviation from the design. And Castille's holding of Blades had thrown the timing of his pattern off by just enough to make the pass unreachable.

Because Blades was detained, the ball sailed right through the dotted outline of a human form—drawn in the air at the goal line to indicate where the receiver was supposed to be—into Harden's arms. An excited Harden, swept out of the end zone by fans' cries of dismay, took off upfield, and the careful arrangement of Broncos and Seahawks, frozen for a second in the postures to which Seattle's just-completed play had directed them, dissolved instantly into chaos.

Players were running every which way, trying to figure out which direction Harden was headed. Coming straight out of the end zone up the right sideline, he cut inside at the 10-yard line, angling across the field until he crossed the left hashmarks at the 17. There he turned upfield again, and saw, 10 yards distant, Curt Warner waiting for him. Just to the outside of Warner stood Denver nose tackle Greg Kragen, and behind Warner stood nothing but open field. Harden paused, stutter-stepped, then turned toward the sideline as Kragen turned to block Warner inward. At the 22 Harden turned a little more to the outside, when suddenly a flash of blue came shooting upward right into his chops...

I like to think that Harden, in the microsecond before impact, saw that something was about to hit his face with terrible force. Undoubtedly, his whole past flashed before his eyes, with the great moments in his career highlighted. And what he remembered most vividly was the moment midway through the third quarter of his team's season opener against Seattle some 14 weeks before, when Steve Largent, crossing, had reached high overhead, caught Krieg's pass, and sailed helplessly on as Harden, running full speed in the opposite direction, had launched himself right into Largent's face, obliterating the defenseless receiver's facemask and consciousness with one savage, satisfying blow.

Now the bolt made contact, there was a deafening explosion, and Harden crumpled, his feet flying out from under him as he plummeted to earth 4 yards from where he had been blasted. As he hit the ground, the ball came flying out of his grasp, and the bolt of blue, still flying in the air overhead, slowed and materialized into . . . Steve Largent! The stands erupted in explosive, gleeful surprise, and Largent landed lightly on one toe, next to Harden's throbbing head. As his arms and shoulders followed through from the blow he had delivered, Largent looked down at Harden, taunting him as the ball bounced away. So absorbed was he in his vengeance that he didn't notice the fumble. Blair Bush, coming up behind Largent, shouted that the ball was loose, and gave him a shove. Largent, recovering his sense of responsibility, looked, leapt, and pounced. The fans, their voices rising in stages, screamed their approval as he jumped up, still shouting at Harden, while three officials tried futilely to wrest the ball from him. Strutting like a cornerback, Largent headed back to his huddle, his eyes blazing, as Harden struggled to his feet, took two steps, and fell against a teammate.

Referee McCarter seized center stage then, to announce that the play was nullified because of Castille's holding of Blades, and that Seattle had a new first down at the Denver 16. Four plays later, Curt Warner, bursting toward left tackle, then breaking outside, faked his way around a stumbling Castille to score, untouched, and slam the ball groundward with such force that the resulting bounce would set a new record for vertical distance traveled by a spiked football.

Finally, with the game out of the shaken Denver team's reach, the crowd could relax and reflect upon a coincidence so compelling it seemed to negate the very meaning of the word. The series of events leading to Largent's opportunity for revenge was so improbable that even the most nihilistic of minds could not accept it as accidental. Because Blades had cut Castille, Castille lost his temper, and because the officials bungled the adjudication of the subsequent mugging, Largent lost his. Because Castille lost his temper, he grabbed at Blades on the next play. Because Castille grabbed at him, Blades was late getting to the ball Krieg threw. Because Blades was late getting to the ball, Harden intercepted it. Because Harden tried to run the ball all the way back for a touchdown, Largent was in a position to fell him. And because Largent was still angry, he was able to do so with particularly powerful force.

Of all the soap-operatic events of this season, this hit, echoing so poetically the hit delivered by Harden to Largent in the last meeting between these two teams 14 weeks before, seemed the most scripted. Scripted by what, or by whom, and for what reason, who could tell? It was the kind of moment you could build a theory of the universe around. The more I replayed it in memory, the more I saw the chaos that Knox had devoted his life to fighting as an order so vast and complex, so grand, as to be beyond human understanding. What I had taken for randomness now appeared instead to be a subtle, imperceptible design, and I looked ahead to the rest of the season not the way one looks ahead to next week, wondering idly what chance has in store, but the way one looks forward to reading on in a gripping book.

The violence of the hit, and the way the hitter reveled in it, revived my years-long obsession with the riddle of Steve Largent. And since the hit on Harden opened the floodgates of the Seattle offense (the Seahawks led 28–7 at the half, 42–7 by the end of the third quarter, and won 42–14), I lost interest in the game. By halftime the Seahawks were just beating a dead Bronco.

With the possible exception of ex-Mariner Roy Thomas's pitching motion, Largent is the greatest enigma in all of professional sport. Everything about him seems to contradict everything else. Polite, soft-spoken, and self-effacing off the field, he is fierce, aggressive, and uncompromising on it. In uniform, he is driven; out of uniform, he exudes a disturbing calm. He is gracious and thoughtful with reporters, answering questions at length and never losing his temper. Yet you always come away with the feeling that his civility is a mask, a means of keeping people at bay. His even temper off the field seems curiously programmed, particularly when you contrast it with the emotion-wracked player you see on the field. He is also fiercely private, and for all of his apparent accessibility, he is most notably remote and guarded.

Terry Largent feels that the real Steve Largent stays behind in Tulsa, Oklahoma, when the family comes north to work at football. Even to his own family, there are two of him. "He's a different person in the offseason than he is during the season," she says. "In the offseason, he's a real goofy, fun-loving guy, and—it's not that he isn't fun-loving during the season, but he's so exhausted and experiences so much stress, having a job where all of Seattle and whoever else is watching, knowing the mistakes that you make—I just think that there is a lot of tension and stress involved with it, and he becomes more serious than he is in the offseason."

Largent himself agrees. "During the season, I become a lot more preoccupied with my job," he says. "I really have tunnel vision. I'm always thinking, 'How do my legs feel? How was practice? How am I catching the ball?' "

What is most true to form about the Largent reporters encounter is that he never fails to say the right thing, the morally correct thing, the sportsheroic thing, whatever the occasion. He is as predictable with his moral pronouncements as Knox is with his clichés. You never catch Largent reacting spontaneously to anything off the field. In his public conversations, he is as studied as a politician. You find yourself constantly looking for flaws in Largent, for some sign that he is human.

And constantly you are met with a paragon. After Seattle's devastating loss to San Francisco, he was asked what was wrong with his team, and his answer was characteristically pristine. "I know we have people capable of playing a heckuva lot better than we played today," he said. "In fact, playing at a championship caliber. But it's time to start doing that and quit talking about it. The most important thing is that every guy has to look within himself. The worst thing that can happen right now, and there's definitely a tendency on teams that don't have as much character, is to start pointing the finger at somebody else, trying to take yourself off the hook, and say, 'Well, I know it's not me.' You can't do that. What you've got to do, is say, 'What is it that I have to do to help the football team to win?' And if you've got 11 guys out there trying to do that, you've got to improve."

This answer bothered me for weeks. I kept wondering what Largent would find if he subjected himself to that treatment. Here was a guy who goes all-out on every play. What more could he do?

Three weeks later, I asked him, and he did something I hadn't seen him do once in the six seasons I had been watching and writing about this team. He hesitated, floundering for a moment, before coming up with an answer. "I tell you, the biggest thing for me at that point was just healing up, trying to get well from knee injuries, and... you know, it's my responsibility to get in here and get well as fast as I can." To have answered honestly—by saying, "There's nothing more that I could have done, because I never let up in my effort to improve and to win"—would have been unthinkable for someone who lists humility among his most cherished virtues.

His humility, or clearheadedness about celebrity, leads him to insist, in his private moments, that he is not the perfect man he is perceived to be. "We were at a banquet," recalls Terry Largent, "and people kept saying nice things to him, and he said, 'I was just thinking, as they say all those nice things to me, I just feel like saying, 'Hey, I'm not as great as you think I am. I do things wrong every moment!' "

Every once in a while, for the briefest of seconds, imperfection will flash in his eyes, in the form of fury at the press. Let more than two or three reporters gather around him after practice, and he will snap, "I've got two minutes, guys!" His facial muscles will still be set in their characteristically courteous pose, but his angry eyes and voice give him away: Inwardly, he is seething.

Even on the field, Largent projects contradiction. Regarded as physically nondescript, he is known as an intelligent, determined overachiever. Yet you can pick out any game at random and find a play that says far more, and far different things, about Steve Largent the athlete. His play, it is true, is marked by an overachiever's ceaseless effort, high intelligence, and un-rivaled willingness to do whatever he is asked. Yet it is also marked by gen-uine athletic talent—which for some reason goes unnoticed.

For all of the great catches Largent has made, for all of the touchdowns he has scored and records he has set, the plays from this season that stick most in my mind are all plays in which he was not thrown the ball. In each of them, he exhibited great physical prowess. His block on Karl Mecklenberg in the season opener was a classic example. To throw a high block on a larger opponent with enough force to knock him out of the play, and to dis-guise the move into the block as the beginning of a pass pattern, requires not only self-sacrifice (run-blocking is considered by many receivers to be work below their station), but also hours of hard work and study on block-ing technique, and—most important—the ability to deliver the blow.

In the season's third game, against the San Diego Chargers, Largent furnished an unforgettable example of how fixated he becomes on winning a football game—even in a game's garbage time, when winner and loser are decided well before the clock runs out. With 1½ minutes remaining in that game, Seattle was down 17–6. On third-and-11, Jeff Kemp was flushed out of the pocket and threw an aimless pass downfield as he was hit. Largent broke from his pattern and went after the ball, but before he could get to it, John L. Williams crossed in front of him and caught it. Instantly, Largent turned and looked for someone to block. Throwing a cut-block on cornerback Elvis Patterson, he sprung Williams loose for an 18-yard gain, then left the game with an injured eye that took three weeks to heal. The play had no effect on the final score—the game was out of reach by that time— but from watching Largent, you would have thought the score was tied. "I've been here for eight years," Edwin Bailey said afterward, "and I've seen him do some amazing things. He goes out there and works hard. I mean, if you actually watch Steve Largent play in and play out, you never see a letup. I think his ball-catching ability takes a back seat to his blocking. He's one of the only receivers that'll go in and knock somebody out. I'm talking about defensive tackles, linebackers—you know, he's just a helluva competitor. He's one person that gives his all, every snap."

Two aspects of the "all" that Bailey was talking about surfaced most dramatically in Largent's assault on Harden. One was his physical ability— his athletic power; the other was his capacity for anger, which he prefers to call "zeal."

The two most insidious stereotypes in sport today are those of the gifted black athlete and the unskilled white athlete. One is regarded as a lazy player who is born with such prodigious strength and skill that he doesn't have to work for his success. The other is regarded as a player with indifferent skill who gets the most out of himself by dint of hard work, self-sacrifice, and heroic grit. One is a born athlete, the other self-made. One we envy because he was handed his success, the other we admire because he came by his the old-fashioned way—he *earned* it.

What Largent's felling of Harden proved was that he is as physically gifted as he is emotionally and psychologically gifted, and that he has been no less slighted by racial stereotyping of athletes than some of his black teammates have been. "He is a more gifted receiver physically than people give him credit for," says Knox. Steve Moore, talking with *Inside Sports'* Peter Korn in 1987, described Largent as both perpetrator and victim of the Myth of the White Overachiever. "A lot of people are wrong in that they try to categorize a lot of receivers as being Steve Largent-types that are not," he said. "Every time we're around college guys, they have a receiver that's maybe not the tallest guy, that isn't the fastest guy in the world, that's a white kid, something like that. They are always saying, 'Well, this guy is a Steve Largent.' And they're wrong because Steve Largent is a very great, talented receiver. He has exceptional quickness, his lateral bursting ability is the best I've ever seen. He's a very acrobatic receiver. He is a finely tuned athlete."

Before there was a Steve Largent archetype, there was a Howard Twilley archetype, and when Largent graduated from Tulsa University in 1976, he was constantly being compared to Twilley, who was a white, record-setting receiver preceding Largent out of Tulsa by a few years. The comparison made Largent bristle, and he refuted it whenever it was brought up, if only because, with the ability to run 40 yards in 4.6 seconds (only two-tenths of a second slower, incidentally, than Terry Taylor), he was considerably faster than Twilley.

The slow-white-guy label stuck to Largent, though, and he had to wait until the fourth round of the 1976 draft to be picked by the Houston Oilers. The Oilers gave him the briefest of looks before releasing him, and he was driving back to Tulsa to look for "a real job in the real world" when Seattle picked him up on waivers. Houston reclaimed him then and worked out a trade with Seattle, sending Largent there for the Seahawks' eighth-round pick in the 1977 draft.

Largent was an immediate success, being named to the NFL's first-team All-Rookie Team by both wire services. He was voted his team's Most Valuable Player the next season, and the season after that—1978—was named to the Pro Bowl for the first of seven times. Through 13 seasons, he would be Seattle's most reliable, durable, consistent, and productive player. When he sat out the New England game this season, it was only the fourth nonstrike game he had missed in his entire career. Entering 1988, he held four NFL receiving records: career receptions, with 752; 50-catch seasons, with 10; 1,000-yard seasons, with eight; and he had played 152 straight games with at least one reception. By the second game of the 1988 season, he would add one more, surpassing Charlie Joiner's career-yardage record of 12,146.

In 1983, Largent's 26-year-old brother Doug died of viral meningitis, and soon thereafter Largent began talking of retiring from football. That year, for the first time, he and his family began making their offseason home in Tulsa, and that September, Largent said that he might retire after the 1984 season. "If they still want me," he said then, "I'll decide whether I want to play one additional season." One thing was sure, he continued: "At 10 or 11 or 12 years or so, I couldn't see myself coming in and starting and taking that beating."

So what happened? On this topic, Largent is characteristically guarded, almost as if the thing he least understands in life is his love of football. He views his attachment to the game as a form of addiction. "It's almost like a slot-machine setup," he says. "You get tremendous, immediate ego gratification. There's a game every week, and in three hours' time, you have either a reward or a setback. Very few jobs have that constant, regular kind of feedback."

"I don't know what's kept Steve from retiring," Terry says, in a voice that hints at more than a little exasperation. "He has enjoyed playing the game. This year he's enjoying it less, because he's been hurt most of the season. This season's been hard. He's had a lot of nagging injuries. He's had other seasons that have had them, too, but not this bad . . . I guess because this season he was at such a crossroads point anyway, that these injuries are affecting him and making him think that this could be the last. . . this one really could be . . . he's been saying it for so many years now, this one *really* could be the last . . . "

My own suspicion is that Largent, whether consciously or subconsciously, has been discovering that football is far more important to him than he had ever realized. He had a rootless and traumatic childhood, and the game helped turn him around. When he was 6, his parents divorced, and when he was 9, his mother married a man who turned out to be an alcoholic. The family moved four times in the ensuing two years, Largent remembers, and he grew up without any close friends. He started out his high-school years a troubled kid (his troubles were compounded, he says now, by his being a "nerd") given to minor scrapes with school authorities. His mother, in an effort to straighten him out, persuaded him to turn out for football in his sophomore year. There, Largent found a refuge from the trouble at home, in the form of a coach who worked him to the point of exhaustion every day and—most important—praised him when he did well. Largent was hooked.

Largent came upon football the same year he embraced Christianity and the same year he met Terry. At a critical time during his sophomore year in high school, Largent found, and grasped, what were to become the three focal points of his life. Small wonder that now, leading a life of stability and family cohesiveness in adulthood that he could only dream about in childhood, he finds it so hard to let go of the game that figured so prominently in his redemption.

Not so, Largent says, predictably enough. "Those are the three relationships that have been woven together to create the fabric of my life. But in reality, it's my relationship with Christ that is the foundation. So it doesn't really matter what happens in football."

Still, watching the final minutes of the Denver game, taking in again the barely contained ritualistic fury of the game, I wondered if the opponents Largent constantly outwitted and out-hit and frustrated and enraged were not, in fact, surrogates for the tormentors from his youth. And if the calm that emanates from him off the field might not cease once he is deprived of the outlet football provides for his prodigious temper.

The time allotted for their mugging of the Broncos expired at last, the Seattle players came off the field sporting a whole panoply of moods, from Blair Bush's radiant smile to Dave Krieg's scowl. Krieg looked like he was leaving the field at halftime in a tie game. Entering the locker-room door, he turned to special-assignments coach Joe Vitt and snarled, "We gotta win one more."

Inside, the Seahawks were subdued, happy, and proud. They had eliminated one of their two remaining opponents for the division crown. Already they were looking ahead to the Raider game. "You can't ask for more than to play for the championship in the 16th week of the season," Knox said. "See, if you don't win it next week, then it tarnishes what you did tonight. We have to win it next week—so that's the challenge. OK?"

He was not focused enough on the season-ending game, however, to slacken his ongoing effort to educate the media. Every question—whether about the game plan, the effect of Largent's hit, the success of a fourth-down touchdown pass—brought Knox back to his penultimate obsession: that the interpretation of a coach's work is always colored by the success or the failure of the players who try to carry out his designs. "When players make the kind of plays we made tonight," he said, "it looks like the game plan is pretty good. If you don't make them, then it looks like the game plan is not too good. But we got it done tonight."

Krieg, for one, seemed to agree. He had played an outstanding game, completing his first 14 passes, and ending the day with 19 completions out of 22 attempts, for 220 of his team's 450 total yards. Yet he refused to crow. He turned aside reporters' accolades as if they were insults. He answered questions grudgingly, and was determined to avoid introspection. His expression stony, his voice flat, he gave the impression that he had just been through one of the least memorable experiences of his life.

Largent, on the other hand, was in a trance. Showered and dressed, he lingered in the locker room, dreamily. He was as soft-spoken and reserved and polite as he always is after games, but now he seemed more reflective—or at least more aware of where he was. It occurred to me that this might have been his last game in the Kingdome, and that he was staying longer than is his custom because he was memorizing these final moments. Asked about Harden, he said, "I'd be lying to you if I didn't tell you

I've been thinking of this game since we played in Denver. I don't know. . . it was kind of a Walt Disney-type situation, storybook or whatever you want to call it . . . "

Walt Disney? *Bambo.* Across the locker room, Ron Mattes had a different story in mind. "You know," he said, "after coming off a tough loss last week, an embarrassing loss, two first downs—one rushing—we had something to prove . . . It seems like when we have to stay in first place, we always win. And who knows? Who knows why that's happening? It's kind of tough to figure us out this year. Kind of like Dr. Jekyll and Mr. Hyde—you never know who's gonna play that week."

Kriegschmerz

Not Weltschmerz *but* Kriegschmerz *the weariness of the mercenary.*

—Josiah Thompson, *Gumshoe*

While the rest of the league has gone to glitz and glamour, the Raider franchise has proudly donned the mantle of resentful deprivation. Owner Al Davis obsessively cultivates the image of a delinquent for his entire operation, from himself on down. At 58 years of age, Davis looks like an aging motorcycle hoodlum. His public relations people look—and often act—like thugs. Davis sets himself at odds with the other 27 NFL owners at every opportunity, even going so far as to be the only owner to testify on behalf of the USFL in that fledgling league's pyrrhic antitrust suit against the NFL. He constantly culls the league's rosters for rejects, bringing them to Los Angeles and reshaping them into sullen, oversized adolescents, bent on seeking revenge for all the real and imagined wrongs visited upon their heads by the staid NFL establishment.

I have often wondered why Davis has never hired Knox as his head coach. Constantly, Davis drums into the heads of his players the notion that the whole league is out to get them, that they are hated, disrespected, looked down upon . . . It is the siege mentality of the deprived teenager, the chronic loser who gets back at the winners of life's war by beating up on them whenever he gets the chance.

Raider fans have taken to the attitude with an enthusiasm only the genuinely disenfranchised could muster. In contrast to the trim, white, well-dressed, wine-sipping Ram fans in Anaheim, Raider fans are coarse, overweight, beer-swillers who revel in their vulgarity. Ram fans are upscale Orange County WASPs. Raider fans come from the other side of Southern California's tracks: Chicanos, blacks, lower-middle-class whites— they are the state's poor, huddled masses.

On game days, they come pouring into the stadium across a tired landscape in wave after wave of piratical silver-and-black. When the game is the last game of the regular season, on December 18, with the 8–7 Raiders hosting the 8–7 Seattle Seahawks to see which team will win the AFC West division championship and move on to the playoffs, the hordes descend on the stadium a good two hours early, like Visigoths upon Rome. Walking around outside the Coliseum, I watched, amused, as a timid knot of Seahawk fans made its way toward the stadium entrance. The nearer the group came, the tighter together it drew. In a moment of early-morning bravado, the Seattleites had decided to wear shirts, sweatshirts, and hats festooned with Seahawk logos and colors, and now they regretted their decision. Walking apprehensively through the thickening mob of black-bedecked outlaws around them, the Seahawk fans quickened their pace when they heard, from somewhere close behind, the shout, "The Raiders'll have fuckin' Seahawk for Christmas dinner!"

Real football for real people.

The Coliseum is a vast, Romanesque ruin. A vulgar, out-of-scale, classically American imitation of Classical architecture, it is now in such disrepair that it looks unusable.

There could be no better setting for a battle between two crumbling franchises contesting the championship of a crumbling division. The inevitable, parity-driven decline of the AFC West was in full swing now, with the Raiders and Seahawks emerging as the best of a sorry lot. And as I took measure of the anticipation in the air around me, I couldn't help but admire the NFL strategy of spreading suspense and high stakes to as many cities as possible. The league's playoff/parity formula had elevated a mundane game between two .533 teams to the level of religious (or, in the case of Raider fans, irreligious) experience.

With only minutes to go before the game, the Ambassadors of the West Military Drill Team was putting on a pregame show. As Ken Behring, entourage in tow, made his way through the cramped press box to the staircase leading to the owner's box, he found himself momentarily face-to-face with ex-Raider great George Blanda. "Hi, Coach!" Blanda sneered. Uneasy, Behring edged past.

Excited as those in attendance were, Los Angeles in general wasn't buying the proposition that such lame teams were worth watching. LA fans are too jaded to take 8–7 teams seriously, and the Raiders had had trouble all season selling tickets to their games. Although there were 61,127 in attendance, the crowd looked puny in the 100,000-seat Coliseum.

What the crowd lacked in relative size, though, it more than made up in intensity and volume. The Raiders, in spite of their pretensions to underprivilege, opted to win the game-opening coin toss, and when the

Seahawks kicked off, there arose a roar so loud I could have sworn there was a dome overhead.

Late in the previous Seattle–Los Angeles game three weeks before, Jay Schroeder had replaced Steve Beuerlein at quarterback for the Raiders, and had held the position ever since. Schroeder had a powerful arm, and the Raiders sported unequaled speed at wide receiver, with Willie Gault, Mervyn Fernandez, and Heisman Trophy–winner Tim Brown, three of the fastest receivers in the league. The Seahawks, committed up front to stopping Bo Jackson, would also have to contend with a serious deep-passing threat that the Raiders lacked last time around.

Johnson launched a high, hanging kick to Tim Brown at the 2-yard line, and Brown managed to return it only to the 17. From there the Raiders started out competently, with Schroeder just managing to get off a 5-yard completion to tight end Andy Parker under a heavy Seahawk rush. Next, Bo Jackson bulled over right guard for 5 yards and a first down, then Schroeder did what opposing quarterbacks had done to Seattle early in every game: Making the most of the big cushion afforded by Seahawk cornerbacks, he threw a 16-yard out-pass, this one to seven-time Pro Bowl receiver James Lofton. Running over right tackle, Jackson burst through Jacob Green's attempted tackle, for 10 more yards. Then two Marcus Allen runs netted only 5 yards, and on third-and-three, Schroeder's pass to Lofton was jarred loose by a superb, evil, Melvin Jenkins hit. Punter Jeff Gossett then kicked a work of art, the football rolling out of bounds at the Seahawk 8.

On first down, John L. Williams, trying to cut outside after the hole at left guard closed in front of him, slipped and managed only 3 yards. He had been met, it seemed, by the entire Los Angeles roster.

At their last meeting, Seattle had run roughshod through the Raider defense, with Warner gaining 130 yards, Williams 105. It was the first time two Seattle backs each topped 100 yards in the same game. Two weeks later, against the Broncos, the two repeated the feat, this time gaining 126 and 104 yards, respectively, with Warner scoring four rushing touchdowns. Looking at film of those two games, the Raiders decided to stop the Seattle run at all costs, at times committing as many as nine defenders to the line of scrimmage. If Seattle was going to win the game, it would have to win it in the air.

On second-and-seven, Krieg dropped back to pass. Inside linebacker Jerry Robinson, rushing at the snap rather than dropping back into pass coverage, tried to sneak through to the left of center Blair Bush. Bush, though, picked him up, and the two grappled, drifting over against left guard Edwin Bailey. Then Robinson darted to Bush's right, and Bush, off balance and tangled up with Bailey, couldn't react in time. Krieg had scarcely begun his pass drop when Robinson came steaming right at him. Taking off to his left, Krieg ran with the ball held like a bottle in his right hand, and when he dove at Krieg, Robinson knocked it free, dragging Krieg down as Raider nose tackle Bill Pickel fell on the ball at the Seattle 5.

As Krieg trotted off the field, looking like he wanted to find a third sideline—one without any Seahawk coaches standing along it, waiting to decry his failings—I thought that he had never looked more... Krieg-like. He looked undersized and slightly slumped, and there was a hint of resignation in his bearing. He was moving like a loser, and as I watched him give way to the tall and stalwart Schroeder, I gave up the game as lost. The Raiders, in overplaying the run, were exploiting Seattle's weakness—Krieg—and already the strategy was paying huge dividends.

The Seahawks, though, dug in, and twice Bo Jackson was met by foaming Seattle hordes that stopped him short of the goal line. After those attempts, the Raiders resorted to subterfuge, sending Tim Brown around left end on a wide receiver reverse. Melvin Jenkins, coming up from the end zone, lunged and delivered a devastating helmet-blast to Brown's midsection, knocking him off his feet at the 3, sending him flying backward, and popping the ball loose. Brown came down in the end zone, Jenkins landed on his stomach at the 1-yard line, and the ball landed on the goal line. Miraculously alert, Jenkins reached out and laid his hand on top of the ball. Then, just before he could pull it in, Brown reached out with both hands and took it away, pulling it into his gut for a touchdown.

It was yet another symbolic play. The Seahawks had come as close to stopping that Raider touchdown as they had come to winning their losses against the Saints and the Chiefs and the Patriots. Having come within a hand of keeping the Raiders off the scoreboard, they now were down a touchdown in the home park of a team that makes a habit of winning big games. And on top of all that, from all appearances, they would have to claw their way back on one of Krieg's fabled off days.

The Raider fans were jubilant. Surveying the mob, I thought I was sitting in a vast halfway house for criminal football fans. Never had I seen so many drunks in one place. Screams, roars, gunshots, and the swoooosh! of knives rent the air. Across the stadium, a huge section of fans stood up, and for the first of many times that day, I thought a Wave was breaking out. Instead, it was only fans standing up to watch a fight breaking out in the stands.

The revelry intensified on the kickoff, when Bobby Joe Edmonds crossed in front of Kevin Harmon to take the ball away and run it out poorly, being stopped at the 18. Mingling in the air now with the scents of beer and blood was the definite odor of early Christmas dinner.

Curt Warner, trying left guard, managed to squirm his way through the entire Raider defense, for 3 yards. Seattle next came to the line of scrimmage with Largent and Blades both lined up wide to the left, and tight end Mike Tice on the right. As Krieg began his snap count, Largent went in motion across to the right, breaking downfield just to the outside of Tice at the snap. Tice, a step behind, broke straight downfield with Largent, and John L. Williams angled immediately into the flat behind them, catching Krieg's short pass. The Raiders—who lined up safety Eddie Anderson on the Seahawks' left, sent safety Vann McElroy after Tice, and sent four rushers after Krieg—were unable to cover Williams because their middle linebackers had been sealed off from him by Largent, Tice, and their two defenders. Williams took off, dodging the first Raider to meet him—safety Vann McElroy—20 yards downfield, finally being tackled from behind by cornerback Ron Fellows after gaining 36 yards.

Warner, taking Krieg's pitchout on the next play, tried left tackle, found it closed, then darted outside, bursting around right end for 7 yards. Trying left end on the next play, he gained 1. On third-and-two, at the Los Angeles 35, Seattle came out in shotgun formation, with Largent out near the left sideline. Cornerback Mark Haynes, knowing that Largent's forte—particularly on third-and-short—is the short pass pattern, came up close at the line of scrimmage and stayed close, backpedaling, as Largent ran downfield. Krieg, meanwhile, was dropping back to pass and looking directly at Brian Blades, who was streaking straight down the right sideline. Vann McElroy, playing deep, edged Blades-ward. At the Raider 20, Largent gave a subtle fake outside, and Haynes broke that way as Largent continued downfield alone. It was a stern reminder to Haynes that Largent's greatest skill is the ability to cut, or to fake a cut, without losing speed. Krieg turned and threw so accurately that Largent, reaching out at the 5-yard line, four steps ahead of Haynes, caught the ball without breaking stride and waltzed into the end zone.

The Raider fans fell into sodden silence. In wonderment they watched their homeboys return Norm Johnson's kickoff to the 35, then lose 4 yards on a screen pass, and 2 more on a draw play. On third-and-16 at the 29, Schroeder dropped nearly 15 yards back to pass, and found himself face-to-face with a single-minded Jacob Green. Evading Green, he retreated, pursued by Tony Woods. Off-balance, falling backward, and terrified for his life, Schroeder threw a languid pass upfield, directly at Terry Taylor, who obligingly intercepted. Having scored a touchdown only 2 minutes before, the Seahawks now had a first down at the Raider 23.

Krieg, rolling right on first down, found no one open, tucked the ball in, and gained 4 yards. Williams, stacked up at right tackle, then gained 2 more. Krieg, under heavy pressure from blitzing linebacker Jerry Robinson on the next play, threw almost as soon as he got the ball, to a crossing Blades. Blades caught the ball, ran right through cornerback Ron Fellows's tackle at the 5, and scored.

Only 12 minutes had expired, and already the game had yielded three touchdowns. At this rate, by my feverish calculations, the final score would be 70–35.

Norm Johnson, perhaps tired out from having had to kick five times in 12 minutes, kicked off out of bounds, a lapse that gave the Raiders the ball at their 35. Biting off middling chunks of yardage, they moved down to the Seahawk 35, where Seattle nose tackle Joe Nash closed out the quarter with a grotesque squishing of Schroeder, for an 11-yard sack. As the teams changed ends, fans consoled themselves either by taking note of LA's huge time-of-possession advantage (10:09 to 4:51), or by beating their wives and girlfriends, then sending them out for more beer.

The Raiders started out the second quarter with a false-start penalty, leaving them with third-and-22 at the Los Angeles 49. As they came to the line of scrimmage in shotgun formation, the Seahawks deployed in an umbrellalike configuration, with Eugene Robinson and Paul Moyer playing deep, and four other defensive backs up near the line of scrimmage, each facing off against a receiver. At the snap, the backs retreated to their zones while the Raider receivers fanned out into the secondary. Willie Gault, the inside right receiver, burst straight downfield. Suddenly Robinson found himself alone with one of the fastest men in the universe. He turned and gave chase gamely, only to get a closer view of Gault hauling in a 51-yard touchdown pass.

Before spectators could catch their breaths, Bobby Joe Edmonds took Chris Bahr's kickoff at the 10-yard line, in the middle of the field, and ran straight ahead, right through the middle of the four-man wedge Seattle had set up for him at the 20. For some reason, there were no Raiders there to greet him. Angling to his right, he took off, until cornerback Lionel Washington managed to bring him down from behind at the Los Angeles 25.

I was reminded then of how easily magic can slip away in football. Krieg threw to Mike Tice, lumbering down the middle of the field toward the goal line. Ignored by the Raiders, Tice was all alone at the Los Angeles 10 when Krieg's pass, thrown high and hard, bounced off his hands. The game's scorer ruled the pass a drop rather than an incompletion, but Krieg had thrown it just high enough and just hard enough to make it uncatchable. His first errant toss of the game, it was only imperceptibly off—yet that was all it took to deny his team another touchdown.

Blades, running a fly pattern, beat Ron Fellows by three steps into the end zone, but Krieg's pass was thrown seconds late. Blades had to slow down, and Fellows was able to recover enough to keep Blades from catching the ball. For the second time in a row, Krieg's touchdown touch had deserted him.

It was now third-and-10, and Seattle seemed out of options. Krieg, in shotgun formation, took the snap and retreated to his right as Williams angled to the right side of the line of scrimmage and took on a linebacker there. Suddenly, Krieg was trapped: Two linemen were descending unobstructed upon him. But then Williams turned and ran across to the left, caught Krieg's pass, and turned upfield. Arrayed before him by prearrangement were three Seattle blockers. The play was yet another permutation of the John L. Williams screen pass, and this time it gained 11 yards and a first down at the Los Angeles 14.

There Seattle stalled for good. Warner, trying to sweep around right end, was stopped for no gain, and Krieg was sacked. Then Blades, running the same pattern he had scored on minutes earlier, beat Fellows again, but Krieg's pass was thrown at him rather than in front of him, and Fellows was able to catch up, getting a hand on the ball. It was Krieg's third missed touchdown in fewer than 2 minutes.

In football, you are constantly reminded of the pivotal importance of the insignificant. A pass thrown a tenth of a second too soon can turn a touchdown into an interception. By hitting a hole at a 45- instead of a 46-degree angle, a running back can allow a defender to get a hand on his leg, slowing him down just enough to bring a defensive back a half-step closer to the play, thereby preventing a touchdown.

I was thinking this over—remembering how close the Seahawks had come to preventing the first Raider touchdown, and how close they had come to scoring their third—as Norm Johnson came on to kick a field goal. Largent, holding, took the snap and put the ball down, flawlessly, and Johnson, his form perfect, kicked. The ball sailed right for the center of the uprights, exactly as Johnson aims it every time. Then perversely, it began to slice wide. I have watched thousands of place kicks in my life, and never have I seen one move like that. It kept slicing over . . . over . . . the angle of the curve steadily sharpening . . . over . . . over . . . over . . . then, before the proper dismay could register with any of the Seahawks, the ball hit the upright and bounced through, good by half an inch. His face expressionless, Johnson trotted to the sideline—carefully avoiding the whooping and hollering teammates dissolving in dementia around him—found a kicking tee, and returned to the field to set up for a kickoff.

Trying to keep track of the twists and turns of the game's first 18 minutes and 31 points had left me exhausted and disoriented. Like a kid at a Fourth of July fireworks display, I watched through a fog of awe as the two teams devoted the last 12 minutes of the half to four drives—three of them ending in field goals, one in a punt—then retired to their locker rooms with Seattle ahead, 23–17.

By halftime, Krieg had racked up some phenomenal numbers. He had completed 13 of 20 passes, for 207 yards, hit six different receivers, passed twice for touchdowns, and thrown no interceptions. He had also elicited a phenomenal first-half performance from Mike McCormack, sitting behind me in the press box. Every time Krieg completed a critical pass, McCormack came up with a new way of reacting: He sat stone-faced, his eyes spinning in their sockets; later, the color drained from his face, he stared at the press-box ceiling; another time, watching Williams slip into the flat, McCormack leaned forward, screaming, "There it is!" and Krieg, as if hearing him, connected; and then, as Krieg moved his team into field-goal range in the waning seconds of the first half, a red-faced McCormack, eyes and fists clenched, was frantically reducing his desk to splinters. BOOMBOOMBOOMBOOMBOOMBOOMBOOM.

Both offenses started out the second half desultorily—whether because the aggrieved defenses were tired of being ignored or because the offenses were simply tired, I couldn't tell—and then Krieg came alive with a 15-yard completion to Largent. Williams tried right end then, to no avail, and Krieg missed connections with Warner on a short side-arm attempt under pressure, setting up third-and-10 at the Seattle 49.

Paul Skansi, lined up as the far left receiver in the shotgun, went in motion as Krieg commenced his snap count. Curling back toward Krieg, he crossed in front of him, taking a handoff, then handed off to Largent, running in the opposite direction. Largent pitched the ball back to Krieg, who looked deep downfield.

The ol' triple pass, thrilling as it was to watch unfold, began to break down. Ray Butler, running deep down the middle, was perfectly covered, and unfazed Raider tackle Bill Pickel, all 6'5", 265 pounds of him, was closing quickly on Krieg. Largent, unimpressed with Pickel's size, threw a rolling block at his ankles, and felled him. Krieg, given a few extra seconds, found Blades on the right sideline and drilled a perfect pass to him, for a 21-yard gain. On the next play, Blades beat Fellows for the fifth time, Krieg rifled a pinpoint 30-yard pass to him, inches out of the leaping Fellows's reach, and Blades caught it in full stride. Krieg had completed his third touchdown toss of the game, and Seattle had built its lead to 30–17.

Lest Seattle fans relax, though, in only three plays, the Raiders showed how fragile a 13-point lead can be against a team with a strong-armed quarterback. On second-and-10 at the Raider 44, the Seahawk defense left Bo Jackson, running a deep pattern out of the backfield, uncovered, and Schroeder found him 46 yards downfield, running full tilt toward the end zone. Schroeder threw, the Seattle defense turned to look, and cries of consternation came bursting out of living rooms across the Pacific Northwest. Blown coverage! But, for the moment, no matter—Schroeder overthrew his target.

The chastised defense stiffened, and the Raiders were forced to punt. Jeff Gosset kicked poorly, and an indecisive Bobby Joe Edmonds charged, stopped, then charged again, trying to short-hop the ball. At the last second, seeing that he wasn't going to field the ball, he made an incredible play, leaning backward and avoiding contact with it. The ball had come so close to him, though, that the other players couldn't tell that he hadn't touched it, and Patrick Hunter, thinking he was preventing the Raiders from recovering a Seattle fumble, dove for the ball. It slipped off his hand, and the Raiders recovered at the Seahawk 16. Had Hunter not touched it, the Raider recovery would have been a simple downing of the ball.

Somehow, Seattle held, and Los Angeles had to settle for a field goal. With 7:41 remaining in the third quarter, the score now 30–20, Los Angeles kicked off, Seattle's Kevin Harmon returning to the 25. Taking the snap on first down, Krieg turned and faked a pitch to Warner—who was breaking toward the right sideline—then followed him, rolling out to pass. Largent streaked deep down the right sideline, and Blades, double-covered, flew down the left. Tice, lined up as tight end on the right, ran a slow pattern over the middle, 15 yards downfield, with linebacker Linden King picking him up. Left guard Edwin Bailey, protecting Krieg's flank, dropped back into pass protection, facing off against Raider defensive end Howie Long, who—unaccountably—stopped and stood still rather than pursue Krieg. Right guard Bryan Millard had pulled, leading the way for Krieg. In the middle, center Grant Feasel, right tackle Mike Wilson, and John L. Williams got tangled up trying to block—and fell down. Standing over that pile, doing his best to look thoroughly confused, was tackle Ron Mattes. Three Raider linemen, unobstructed, were closing fast on Krieg, who was looking intently downfield.

Whenever I remember this game, it is that tableau I see, with the 22 players spread out over 35 yards of the field, in various classic football postures of attack and defense.

Then, suddenly, the picture changed. Williams, Feasel, and Wilson untangled, and leapt to their feet. Wilson, with Williams right behind him, ran 5 yards downfield, and hesitated while Williams looked back toward Krieg. Mattes and Feasel broke toward Long, and Krieg tossed the ball in a lazy arc, over the reach of the three rushers closing on him, into the grasp of Williams. Wilson turned back, saw that his companion had the ball, turned upfield, and the two of them took off. Six of the 11 Raider defenders were now out of the play, being too far behind to catch up to Williams, and none of the other five had an unobstructed shot at him. Mattes and Feasel took on Long, who had turned to pursue the ball, Tice knocked King down just as he was about to close on Williams, Blades cut both players covering him, and Williams, running through a diving tackle at the 50, then bursting between two late-closing defensive backs, was gone, on his way to a 75-yard touchdown.

This version of the Williams screen ran so smoothly that the Raiders—including Long, who had dropped out of the pass rush to look for the screen—played it as if they had rehearsed their losing roles as thoroughly as the Seahawk players had rehearsed their winning ones. Every Raider defender either ran himself out of the play or aligned himself with a Seattle blocker. An ingenious design, perfectly rendered, the screen call had a far more dramatic effect on crowd and combatants alike than had any of Schroeder's bombs. A quarterback hitting a receiver for a long touchdown is simply winning, with his arm and the receiver's feet, a two-on-one athletic struggle. A coach pulling off an equally long, far more complicated touchdown—one as remarkable for its deception as for its athletic power—is orchestrating the creation of the world. In giving all 22 players a significant role in the touchdown, Knox and Moore had established their own credentials as the game's gods—as the forces controlling the action and dictating its outcome.

The Raiders, however, were unimpressed enough to return Norm Johnson's kickoff to the Raider 41, from where they commenced the day's only sustained touchdown drive, moving 59 yards in 12 plays, taking 6 minutes, 12 seconds to pull back within 10 points. Then, after their kickoff, Krieg, handing off to Williams, retreated, and Williams, stopping just before diving into the line of scrimmage, pitched the ball back to him. Krieg threw with all his strength to a wide-open Blades, who had to slow down for the ball. Had Krieg not underthrown him, the Seahawks would have had another touchdown. As it was, they settled for a 55-yard gain, leading to Johnson's fourth field goal of the day, three plays into the fourth quarter.

Seattle now led 40–27, for exactly five plays. On first-and-10 at the Raider 46, Mervyn Fernandez took off down the right sideline, with Terry Taylor running with him, stride for stride. At the goal line, the two leapt in tandem, Taylor reaching up in front of Fernandez, nearly touching the ball. Fernandez hung onto it, coming down in the end zone. "A perfectly thrown pass," Mike McCormack would say later, "and I don't care how good the cornerback is, if you're one-on-one, the only way he can stop it is if he has help. Taylor was there, but Schroeder threw that damn ball with such an arc, that it was almost coming straight down. Which you couldn't . . . where that thing . . . oh, boy."

My notes indecipherable, my mind a mess, I looked out over the crowd, which had achieved new levels of frenzy. Across the way, I thought I saw spectators, high up in the stands, performing human sacrifice. Directly in front of me, down on the track surrounding the playing field, I saw a group of Raiderettes—"Football's Fabulous Females," as they are described in Raider promotional literature—engaged not in the customary bumping and grinding and ecstatic high kicking that usually follows Raider touchdowns, but instead in the cryptic, quiet, ritual miming of ancient domestic tasks. One was squatting before an imaginary fire, fussing over invisible food; another was going through the motions of grinding grain with stones; still another waddled clumsily around, cradling an unseen child on her hip; while a fourth faced the field, looking into the distance with a hand shading her eyes, as if trying to spot a familiar ship at sea. Confused, I blinked, and when I looked again, they were dancing with customary modern American pizzazz.

Caught up in the spirit of the shootout, Steve Moore waited only three plays before firing away. Sending Butler deep down the left sideline, Moore watched him leave Lionel Washington awash in his wake. Butler turned at the Raider 25 to look over his outside shoulder, then stumbled, confused. Krieg had thrown the ball over his inside shoulder. Safety Eddie Anderson, breaking late, intercepted, and Butler and Largent brought him down at the Raider 13.

I understood then that the game had been Krieg's from the beginning, to win or lose, and that he had carefully kept himself from putting it out of the Raiders' reach. He began the game with a fumble on the Seattle 3-yard line. Six of his seven first-half incompletions were in the Raider end zone, and four of those six were near-misses of open receivers. Had he managed to connect on two of them, Seattle would have totaled 8 more points, scoring two touchdowns where they settled for field goals, and would have buried the Raiders by halftime, leading by 14 points instead of by 6. Midway through the third quarter, when Williams scored from 75 yards away, their lead would have swelled to 25 points.

Instead, the Williams run put Seattle up by a mere 17 points, and with nearly 13 minutes remaining, the Raiders had pulled back to within 6. Krieg had thrown his interception at the most inopportune time imaginable: right after the Raiders fought their way back into the game, by scoring on their last three possessions. Slowly, subtly, Krieg had maneuvered his team back into a position of disadvantage.

The Raiders, though, seemed directed by their own demons. For the first time since their opening series of the second half, they failed to score. Instead, they ran three plays and punted. Edmonds, catching their punt at the Seattle 30, angled to his right behind a textbook wall of blockers, and found himself 25 yards downfield with only punter Jeff Gossett to beat. Faced with the choice between icing the game and being humiliated by a kicker, thereby prolonging the suspense, Edmonds chose the latter, going down humbly at the Raider 41. He was now 0-for-3 on the season in confrontations with kickers.

After the Seahawks moved 12 yards in two plays—a swing pass to Warner, for 7 yards, and a Williams run straight ahead for 5—Knox sent Blades yet again on a post pattern into the end zone. Yet again Blades beat Fellows badly, and yet again Krieg missed him. Yet again the Seahawks had stopped short of winning the game outright. As Blades headed back to the huddle and Krieg gave himself a quiet tongue-lashing, I remembered something Raider scout Gene Moore had said to me earlier in the season. "Krieg," he said, "has always seemed to me like a guy who can kind of get it done."

Just as they had done against Denver in the season opener and again against Cleveland, Seattle took to the ground, moving 20 yards in four plays to face third-and-one at the Raider 9. There Williams, trying to sweep wide around right end, was drowned in a tidal wave of Raider resentment, washing over him in the form of five apparently forewarned defenders tackling him for a 5-yard loss. Norm Johnson, in kicking his fifth field goal of the day, put the Seahawks up by 9 points, with 5:18 remaining. The lead was just slender enough to keep fans on the edge of their seats until the final gun.

Sure enough, Seattle, in deep zone defense, let Los Angeles throw its way to the Seahawk 6, from where three straight passes to the end zone fell incomplete. After Chris Bahr's field goal and subsequent kickoff, the Seahawks found themselves with the ball, a 6-point lead, and the championship well within reach—all on the Seattle 28, with 2:12 remaining.

Carefully, fiercely, the Seahawks edged forward, with Williams carrying straight ahead for five, then Kevin Harmon—subbing for Warner, who had sprained his ankle on the previous series—carrying straight ahead for 8 more and a critical, clock-killing first down. Harmon carried again, gaining 5, then Williams ran straight ahead for 3 more. Then, on third-and-two, with all 22 players gathered in close in a pawing, snorting pack, defensive end Greg Townsend shifted into the center of the line, standing upright next to nose tackle Bill Pickel. At the snap, he burst through the line of scrimmage, unblocked.

The play, amazingly, was a pass play—a little flat pass to Williams, just long enough to get another first down. Krieg, of course, never had a chance even to cock his arm. Townsend hit him before he had even dropped back into position to throw. Krieg was caught so by surprise that when the 6'5", 250-pound Townsend slammed into him, he was holding the ball away from his body, in one hand. No one, Krieg included, will ever understand how he managed to keep from letting go of it.

That bullet dodged, the Seahawks sent Ruben Rodriguez in to punt the ball away. Rodriguez, with a comic's impeccable sense of timing, kicked a miserable 27-yard punt. With 1:08 to play, the Raiders were within 77 yards—nearly within range of Schroeder's remarkable arm—of the Seattle end zone.

By now, I was down on the field, standing behind the end zone the Raiders were headed for. The fans had completely lost their minds. The Raiderettes, standing at loving attention, had tears streaming down their faces. The players were covered with blood and mud and grime, and their uniforms were in tatters. The Raider bench was glum and anxious, the Seahawk bench simply anxious. Schroeder threw two incompletions, then brought one last flicker of hope to his fans and teammates with a 22-yard completion to Fernandez. His team was now at the Seattle 45, with 33 seconds left.

Three more times Schroeder threw, with one of the passes being a bomb thrown into the end zone, where five players—two Raiders and three Seahawks—leapt for it. Willie Gault, at the back of the pack, came down juggling it, and as he struggled to keep his feet in bounds, the ball eluded him. Two passes later, on fourth down, Schroeder's last throw to the end zone bounced off an airborne Nesby Glasgow's hands. Seattle had the first division championship in its history.

So scrupulously and consistently had the Seahawks snatched suspense from the jaws of boredom throughout the game, that no one could quite manage to believe, at first, that the battle was actually over.

But over it was, and the antagonists hurriedly retreated up a cavernous tunnel to their locker rooms. Among the last players through was Jacob Green. He was a mess. His uniform was torn and muddy and grass-stained. He was walking gingerly, as if his whole body was in pain. And his face, streaked with sweat and grime, was vacant, his eyes wide and unseeing. He looked like a combat-weary soldier emerging, in deep shock, from battle.

Immediately after football games end, I always have to fight off fierce attacks of self-loathing. The game is nothing but excess and vulgarity: excessive violence on the field, excessive importance attached to these games by spectators and sportswriters, excessive money, excessive drinking in the stands, excessive hype, excessive worship, size, strength, time—entire afternoons!—spent watching these affairs... And what are they? Jousting matches between teams of shallow, one-dimensional American males—the sort of men I grew up determined not to become. I always leave the stadium secretly asking myself the same question my wife asks me almost every day: "What do you like about this game?"

Today, the question was particularly pertinent. On its surface, the game seemed a worthwhile afternoon of entertainment because it was suspenseful. But the suspense, upon close examination, was revealed to be a disguise, a gratuitous element introduced into the show by perfectly timed Seattle errors and comings-up-short. Teams and spectators alike—teams through manipulations of the scoring pattern, designed to keep Seattle from bursting out to too big a lead, and spectators through their willing suspension of disbelief—conspired to create an atmosphere of contrived excitement. By making the game seem a down-to-the-wire contest for a championship, we all created an illusory need to be there, spending time and money and heart and mind on an overblown version of professional wrestling. And the more I asked myself why, the more I came up with the answer that we indulge wholeheartedly in these bloated, empty spectacles out of despair. And that our despair is made up partly of nostalgia, and partly of the need to escape from the certainty that all of our purported values—political, religious, cultural, national—are fictions. Citizens of a nation that believes in nothing, we take refuge in this extravagant ritual display of waste, because we see in it the clean clear light of . . .

Suddenly I was caught up in a riotous surge forward, as the Seattle locker room door swung open to allow in the media. As that door opened, some corresponding door in my mind slammed shut, just as I was on the verge of understanding once and for all the appeal of this grand and gruesome game.

My conspiracy theory evaporated as soon as I entered the riotous locker room, where an emotional Knox, pressed against a wall by a pack of reporters, was invoking, one last time, the goad that constantly inspires and destroys him: "You know," he said, "to get it done. That's what it's all about. When you get it done in spite of a lot of adversity, that makes it even nicer." Somewhere among us, I decided, there must be a latter-day Voltaire about to run back up to the press box and write, under deadline, "If adversity didn't exist, Chuck Knox would have to invent it."

I turned away as Knox, keeping alive his favorite adversarial relationship, snarled, "Now I guess I'm innovative and creative and all that stuff."

Steve Moore stood alone off to one side, more visibly thrilled than I have ever seen him. I am so accustomed to his measured, academic manner that, seeing him still in the full flower of football emotion, still *competing*, I hardly recognized him. And caught up in his elation, I felt all my postgame cynicism ebbing away.

I asked him if he had called so many flashy pass plays because Krieg looked to be in for one of his better days. "You don't really know," he answered. "You expect that those plays will work every time. But you know, those are not high-percentage passes, so there's always the risk that it doesn't operate. Fortunately, today they hit." On the one hand, he went on to say, he had never felt secure—even when up by 17 points. "They've got more talent in their offensive unit . . . you know, they've got those three Heisman Trophy winners [Marcus Allen, Bo Jackson, Tim Brown], they've got a guy back there throwing passes that's got a cannon, and so you never really felt secure."

On the other hand, he had come into the game as juiced with adrenaline as any player. "I knew all along that we were gonna win! Our people responded so well this week, and they were so committed, that I didn't see that there was any way possible for them to come down here and not win. There are times when you feel like your people are on a roll, and have the confidence to go get it done and we really had that feeling all week long. It's an energy level, but it goes beyond that. It's just a . . . " Here, I think, Moore realized that he was revealing too much of the inner workings of a football man's heart, and he stumbled to a stop. "I shouldn't even talk about it, because people think that it's just air."

Nevertheless, that confidence in his troops—particularly his sense that Krieg was on—had given him the courage to call for long passes and gimmick plays. "It affects what we're willing to risk in playcalling. If you have a feeling that whatever you do is going to operate, you're gonna go with it."

Everywhere, players were letting themselves savor the victory. "Sweet ride home tonight . . . "; "I don't have any idea what I've been doing, to be honest with you! I've been brain-dead for the last four hours . . . "; "Gonna shoot myself a Christmas goose and enjoy it instead of sulking while we're eating it . . . "

Gradually, the reporters moving through the room devolved toward Krieg's cubicle, and he stood before them, hatred emanating from the mask that was his face. Before the first question was asked, I could tell that platitudes and magnanimity would be the order of the day. "We know that we still have some work to do," Krieg muttered, "but I think everybody is happy and proud of the fact that we won the first-ever AFC West divisional title for the Seattle Seahawks and the city of Seattle. But we do know that there's more to do, left to do in the playoffs, and I think that's a good attitude."

He was asked about the criticism he had taken over the years, but declined to gloat. "I just think that we're very happy to win the AFC West like we did, and as far as all that other stuff goes, that's just part of the game. You guys got a job to do, we got a job to do, we did it today, and that's it."

I have always been mystified by the lack of love Krieg inspires in followers of Seattle football. If ever there were an athlete fans should identify with, it is Krieg. He is the consummate Everyman—the kid who ascended from nowhere, against all the proverbial odds, to establish himself as a winning quarterback on the field and in the record books. He has overcome a sordid pedigree, an unimpressive physique, an arm even he describes as "only 75 percent, even when it's at full strength," the thinly veiled disgust of both his professional head coaches, and his employers' constant attempts, over the full nine years of his career, to dump him. He has managed to endure through six seasons as the starting quarterback for one of the NFL's top franchises without losing any of the unpretentiousness that characterized him when he arrived in Seattle as an unheralded free agent in 1980. The NFL's complicated quarterback-rating system gives Krieg the third-highest ranking of all time, behind San Francisco's Joe Montana and Miami's Dan Marino. He is a master of the touchdown pass: In throwing his 100th scoring toss in his 65th career game, he reached that milestone faster than all but two quarterbacks in NFL history—Dan Marino and Johnny Unitas. In his first five seasons, he totaled more touchdown passes than all other quarterbacks save Marino.

For all of that, though, he is esteemed only by his teammates. The rest of us malign him far out of proportion to his shortcomings.

Krieg grew up in Schofield, Wisconsin, graduating from D.C. Everest High School in 1976 and entering Milton College, a 300-student school that has since closed its doors. A member of the Illini-Badger Conference, Milton was not exactly a breeding ground for professional athletes, although its coach, Rudy Gaddini, had been a running back and quarterback for Michigan State University, had scouted for the San Francisco 49ers, and employed a pro-set offense at Milton that featured a complex passing attack.

For two years, with Krieg as its starting quarterback, Milton ranked eighth in the nation in total offense, but when Krieg graduated in 1980, there were no pro scouts waiting to sign him up. Gaddini, convinced that

Krieg had pro-caliber talent, wrote to the Seahawks, and asked them to give him a look. After studying film of him, the Seahawks signed him to a free-agent contract, and Krieg came to their 1980 camp.

Krieg was one of seven quarterbacks in that camp. Sought out by a feature writer looking for obscure story subjects, he obliged the reporter by beginning what would prove to be a long tradition of curious Krieg quotes. "I'm in the right place," he said, "I'm just not sure it's the right time." Slowly, he worked his way up the depth chart, yet survived the final cut only by a fluke: He would have been released had not quarterback Steve Myer injured his back.

Krieg settled in as a career backup behind starter Jim Zorn, who had been Seattle's starting quarterback from day one of the franchise's history. Zorn was probably the most popular athlete in Seattle history, being the figurehead of the city's first pro football franchise, and being a master of quirky, unpredictable play and improvisation. Further, he played for a team with no running attack, and when the Seahawks did better in their first four years than any expansion team in history, in any sport, it was largely because of Zorn's passing. Until Knox's arrival, Zorn was so firmly entrenched in Seattle's sports pantheon that fans couldn't imagine their team ever having anyone else at quarterback.

So it came as a surprise to everyone when Krieg, called upon to replace the injured Zorn in a 1981 game against the New York Jets, turned in a better performance than Zorn would have. He completed 20 of 26 passes in that game, for 264 yards, throwing two passes for touchdowns, running for a third, and beginning what would prove to be a long tradition of curious Krieg quotes from coaches. "He doesn't always make decisions for the right reasons," head coach Jack Patera said after that game, "but they seem to work out the right way." The Seahawks upset the Jets that day, 27–23, and Krieg, swamped by media, exhibited an engaging, unpretentious boyishness, saying, "It's really been like a Walter Mitty fantasy," and professing astonishment at having the likes of CBS's Brent Musburger asking to talk with him. "Imagine that," he said after being interviewed by Musburger, "I listen to the guy all the time and here I am talking to him on the phone."

Krieg finished out that season as the Seattle starter with a loss against the Denver Broncos and a win over the Cleveland Browns. At the start of the 1982 season, Patera named him his team's permanent starter, to the consternation of more than a few fans. The Seahawks opened with two losses, the NFL players went on strike, Patera was fired, and when the season resumed, Mike McCormack was head coach. McCormack reinstated Zorn in the team's first poststrike game when Krieg injured his thumb, and Krieg did not see action again until the second half of the last game of the year—"so," as McCormack explained later, "we could get him on film." When Knox took over in 1983, he kept Zorn as the starter until halfway through the eighth game of the season, when the Zorn-led Seahawks fell behind the Pittsburgh Steelers, 24–0, and Zorn left the field at halftime to loud booing from the stands. Krieg came on in the second half to lead a furious comeback, throwing three touchdown passes as his team lost 27–21.

Krieg's starting position has been more or less in jeopardy since 1984, when the Seahawks made a highly publicized effort to sign free-agent quarterback Warren Moon, who eventually signed with the Houston Oilers. In 1985, Seattle went after another highly touted free agent, Bobby Hebert, eventually losing him to the New Orleans Saints. In 1986 Krieg was benched for backup Gale Gilbert, then was reinstated two games later when Gilbert proved incapable of winning. And in 1988, they drafted Stouffer, billing him as Seattle's "quarterback of the future," without specifying how distant that future was, and taking care to praise Stouffer for all the attributes he had that Krieg lacked.

Krieg has suffered similar slights from fans and media. There remain present-day followers of Seahawk football who think Zorn should still be Seattle's starting quarterback. Seattle's inconsistency since its unexpected success in 1983 has been blamed almost entirely on Krieg, and one gets the sense that the entire Pacific Northwest is counting the days until he is deposed.

The effect of all this on him has been dramatic. During his first two years as a starter, Krieg gave the impression that nothing delighted him more than talking about football with a reporter. He would discuss failed plays and successful ones with the same passion, dissecting them thoroughly and patiently. From 1984 on, though, he has grown increasingly hard-shelled. Although resolutely refusing to criticize or defend himself against his critics, he exudes bitterness and treats reporters with a combination of politeness and disinterest that seems designed to drive them mad.

The 1984 Krieg was inexhaustibly quotable. "When things don't go well, I tend to get a little frustrated or what-have-you, get down on myself," he told me after a game that year against the Buffalo Bills. "Well, actually, I don't get down on myself, I just get mad at myself. There's a difference. I think some quarterbacks get down on themselves, after throwing a few interceptions, they just go to pieces. And I don't think I'm like that at all. It might look like I'm frantic out there, but I'm not—I'm just mad. Because I think I've got enough capabilities and ability to go back out there and rectify the situation."

He also used to love to describe plays and the pattern of his thoughts as plays unfolded. "What happened there," he said of a near-completion to Seahawk fullback Dan Doornink in that same game, "was that Dan was just supposed to run out to the flat. But from playing with him a few years, I just figured he'd take it up the sidelines. And sure enough, he did. If I could've stood up in the pocket and seen him clear, I could've completed it. But I just kind of threw it where I thought he was going to be. And he almost did make a play on it. So that was something we improvised together on our own. Their rush was a little bit of a factor. Which made me hurry the throw a little. And I couldn't find anybody else open. So I just threw it over there, hoping that he'd be taking it up the sideline. Which is actually what he did. I just threw it a little high for him . . . It was just getting to be that time. So I just said, 'Well! Time to throw it!' "

Football was fun for Krieg in those days. Now he plays with more determination than zest, and he talks as little as possible. "The longer you wait for something," he said, in a monotone, after winning his first division championship, "the better it is when you finally realize it. I wish we didn't have to wait this long . . . it would've been better earlier, too."

According to his wife, Krieg leads the life of a man forced into seclusion by a public that is most often hostile, at best insensitive. "Dave likes to go to a movie right when it's started and he'll leave 10 minutes before it's over," Sue Krieg says, "because he doesn't want to have to deal with people talking about him. We'll be at a restaurant, and somebody at the next table will be saying, 'Yeah, did you see how he did last week?' Or, 'There he is there—we probably could have pulled that game out if we'd had a quarterback.' They don't feel like we can hear them."

Krieg is so incapable of carving out his own identity as a solid starting NFL quarterback that to this day people still confuse him with Jim Zorn, who last played for the Seahawks in 1984. "He'll be walking into the stadium now," says Sue, "and there are still people who say, 'Have a good game, Jim!' We were in Fred Meyer once last year and some lady came up and said, 'Jim! Can I get your autograph?' Then Dave signs it 'Dave Krieg,' and she goes, 'Oh! . . . Ooooh . . . ' "

Krieg, for his part, refuses to talk about his status in the Seattle community, fending off questions about it with the usual platitudes about fans having the right to their opinions. But everything about his bearing and his behavior suggests that he is deeply wounded by it. For some reason, qualities that in most people are admirable do more to hurt than to help Krieg's reputation. It is not so much his alleged inconsistency on the playing field as it is his consistent self-effacement off the field that makes people reflexively denigrate him.

For one thing, Krieg is the embodiment of the common man. He has the face of a peasant and speaks with a noticeably rough, plebian accent. To judge from his syntax, he has never been to grammar school, let alone college. He looks, sounds, and acts the part of an unskilled laborer, and his ascension to a position of such glamour strikes those who meet him as one of life's most hilarious miscastings.

For another thing, he has a Cro-Magnon nickname: "Mudbone." You could sit around for months trying to dream up nicknames that don't fit quarterbacks, and you could never come up with anything as inappropriate as "Mudbone." No matter how you say it, it still sounds like a cruel epithet, something you would call the village idiot: Mudbone. *Mudbone.* MUDBONE. After Krieg, with consummate command, led his team downfield to its winning field goal against the Houston Oilers, Edwin Bailey said, "That was our old Mudbone back there . . . " Even though I know in my heart that he meant it as an accolade, my mind keeps insisting that it was some kind of coded insult.

For yet another, Mudbone's willingness—eagerness, actually—to confess and detail his mistakes is rarely equaled. Talk with Krieg after a loss, and he will tell you everything. Most athletes are voluble after wins, uncommunicative after losses, but Krieg is as graceful in losing as he is graceless in winning. He has taken the blame for every interception he has ever thrown—even some that his coaches have attributed to pass interference. If a receiver makes a mistake in running a pass route, Krieg finds a way to blame himself. Losses are always his fault; wins are always because of something his teammates did. He seems almost to embrace losing, while winning, recollected in tranquility, bores him.

Krieg's efforts at modesty have succeeded beyond his wildest dreams—everyone sees him as he presents himself. He gives the impression that playing professional football is more of a struggle for him than it is for his peers, and that his place among the sporting elite is undeserved. Here again, I thought, is Knox's attitude of the chronic underdog, a psychological tie that binds him to his head coach. Even in this game, Krieg completed touchdown passes whenever his team's lead was in danger, and missed them whenever a completion would put his team definitely out of danger. It was as if he felt undeserving of a dominating role.

Time and again now, reporters tried to prod Krieg into saying something heartfelt about this game, about this championship, about his career, his image, his quest for respectability. And time and again Krieg refused to oblige. With each answer, he sounded more and more like he was reading a speech. He was not so much hostile as tired of the years-long battle with the press for respect and understanding. So consumed had he been by this struggle that it seemed to rob him even of the joy of winning a championship. Now it was more out of that weariness than out of revenge that he was stonewalling his reporters. He just wanted it all to be over.

As I worked my way out of the pack, I saw four commiserating writers at the back, looking at one another in exasperation, ruefully shaking their heads.

I lingered, garnering a few more quotes, then made my way out of the locker room. Out in the tunnel, there was Krieg, sitting in a phone booth, talking with Brent Musburger. A newspaper photographer, reverently down on one knee, was snapping pictures of him. And for the first time, Krieg let his facade slip. He shrugged his shoulders, turning his free hand palm upward, and looked out from the booth, grinning boyishly, wordlessly asking the question: "Can you believe this? *Me?*" He was the Man Who Wouldn't Be Superman. Regarding him, I felt, for a second, a shiver of elusive insight—as if I were on the verge of understanding him.

PART III

POSTSEASON

When War Was Civil

The joy of battle has given place to the conventions of the board-room, the dream of martial glory to the peculiar satisfactions of remote, anonymous, abstract death. The world has for years been moving away from a glamorous notion of war, first to the squat green ugliness of tanks and now toward computerized bombs that go it alone in their eerie search for targets.
—Fred Reed, "Dive, He Said" (Harper's Magazine)

As the Seahawk charter descended into Seattle on the evening of the team's first-ever conference championship, some 3,500 fans gathered at Sea-Tac Airport to hail their conquering heroes. Up in the plane, the players joyously indulged in a titanic pillow fight—making, among other things, for a rocky landing.

The homecoming grew even rockier when the team deplaned directly onto charter buses instead of coming into the terminal. The fans, hoping to celebrate, instead were treated to a few obligatory words from Knox, then watched a few players make their way silently through the crowd and head for their cars.

Whoopee!

Mike McCormack later cited communication problems with the Port Authority, and the Port Authority denied responsibility, but the details really didn't matter. Somehow, the foul-up was a perfect ending to the regular season, which had been filled with weird events, setbacks, and curious moments, on and off the field. Even the division championship was as much a matter of happenstance as it was a measure of the Seahawks' worth. While it was true that they had "done what they had to do," as they would point out repeatedly in the ensuing days, and that they won the championship outright by beating the two other contenders on the last two weekends of the season, it was also true that they won it in the AFC West's worst-ever year. They had three other seasons with identical 9–7 records, and two with better ones (12–4 in 1984, and 10–6 in 1986), and won no title in any of them. Of the 10 teams in the NFL playoffs, they sported the worst record—worse even than the four wild-card teams. So the championship was as much a matter of NFL marketing as it was a matter of Seattle's championship-caliber play.

Still, the Seahawks had been on the other side of the playoff formula coin (in 1986, when they were playing the NFL's best football at the end of the season and were shut out of the playoffs by a tie-breaking formula) and were more than entitled to their designation as division champs. And they had overcome injuries and troubles that only Knox could have overcome. They and their city were entitled to their pride. "It's taken 13 years to win the first division title," McCormack said a week before his team's first-round playoff game against the Cincinnati Bengals, "and I don't care how many asterisks they put on it, that's the division title. We *beat 'em.* We beat the Raiders twice and Denver twice."

He was convinced that his team's 9-7 record was misleading, and that the Seahawks stood a better-than-apparent chance against the 12-4 Bengals. "I think we were soundly beaten three times," he said of the season. "The 49ers, the Rams, and Buffalo. I think Buffalo, the 13-3 game, we had a chance, but again we didn't have a chance. I'm not sure even if David had been in there we could've beaten them that time. I think we're a better football team now . . . So there's those three games, and you look at the other four losses and just kind of shake your head, and say, 'If we had done better, if someone had done something different, we might have had those games. You can drive yourself crazy that way, though . . . "

One thing that had been driving McCormack crazy for years was Krieg. "Remember back when he was benched?" he said, referring to the brief installation, in 1986, of Gale Gilbert in Krieg's place. "He came back, and we had a five-game winning streak. I think a little bit of the same thing happened this time. At that point, we thought it was because his job had never been threatened up till that time. But this time there wasn't that stigma. He wasn't benched because of an inability to play."

Those two periods, as it happens, have been Krieg's most productive as a quarterback. He had come back from his injury to compile a 106.7 quarterback rating over the last six games—a surge that pushed his season rating up to 94.6, leaving him the second-highest-rated quarterback in the NFL, behind Cincinnati's Boomer Esiason, who finished at 97.4.

Quarterbacks are hard to measure, and the NFL's rating system is far from perfect, but it does indicate that Krieg is a better athlete than Seattle fans think he is. First instituted in 1973, the rating is compiled by looking first at four statistical categories (completion percentage, percentage of passes that are intercepted, percentage of touchdown passes, and yards per pass attempt). The NFL provides a chart that allows the compiler to assign a point value to each category's percentage, with the highest possible point attainable in any category being 2.375. The points are added up, with the total divided by 6, then multiplied by 100. At 94.6 on the season, Krieg was near the rating regarded as the measure of true greatness—100—which has been attained only 12 times.

Two things have helped Krieg attain a high quarterback rating. One is the number of touchdown passes he throws (his 1988 numbers extrapolated over 16 games would have included 32 touchdowns—tops in the league), the other is Seattle's passing offense, which is built around the short pass.

As is typical of everything Krieg accomplishes, his high rating, thanks to this second detail, has a gigantic asterisk plastered next to it. Paul Zimmerman, complaining about the quarterback-rating system, points out in *The New Thinking Man's Guide to Pro Football* that "The low-risk, high-percentage, 'dink' quarterbacks are going to be helped in three categories. The more daring guys who throw downfield are going to suffer." Then, in citing an example of how one dink play can dramatically alter a quarterback's rating, he describes a play right out of the pinnacle of Krieg's career. "How important can one completion be in a guy's overall rankings?" Zimmerman asks rhetorically. "Well, look at the 49ers versus the Cowboys in the final 1983 Monday night game. In the first quarter Joe Montana threw a little screen pass to Freddy Solomon. Dennis Thurman got blocked by Bubba Paris, and Solomon raced 77 yards for a TD. Here's what that 77-yard TD pass did for Montana: raised his rating from 93.2 to 94.6 for 1983, raised his lifetime rating from 89.7 to 90.1, making him the only player in history to score over 90, lifetime."

Substitute the Seahawks for the 49ers, the Raiders for the Cowboys, 1988 for 1983, Krieg for Montana, John L. Williams for Solomon, Mike Wilson for Paris, and 75 yards for 77, and you have Zimmerman writing about Krieg and his screen pass to Williams in the season finale. Even the two quarterbacks' final rating—94.6—is the same.

Still, the relative worth of the statistic is beside the point. While it may not be an accurate yardstick for comparing quarterbacks, it is an accurate one for comparing a quarterback to himself, and the number shows that Krieg is never so great as when he is emerging from . . . well, from adversity. The question is, "Why?"

His teammates don't care—about that, or about his numbers. They just flat-out believe in him, for whatever reason, and attribute his image problems to his willful lack of glamour. "I think Dave Krieg is one of the smartest quarterbacks in the NFL today," Mike Tice insisted. "He may not have the arrogance or cockiness of a Boomer Esiason or of a Marino, but he knows how to *lead*."

Everywhere I looked around the Seahawks' complex that week, I saw cockiness and the arrogance of champions. It showed in the form of a visible, relaxed sense that events had finally proven the legitimacy of the players' pretensions throughout the season. They were *playoff-worthy*, a designation that set them apart, that raised them above the pack. No longer anxious about their image, they let their guard down a little, and interviews became more like conversations than interrogations.

Knox, having dispensed with the division championship, now had his team right where he wanted it: in the role of the underdog. The 9–7 Seahawks were seriously impaired—Curt Warner, with a severe ankle sprain, might not be able to play—and the Bengals, at 12–4, were one of three teams tied for the league's best won-lost record. The Bengals were the NFL's top offensive team, had the league's top quarterback in Esiason, the league's top celebrity in running back Ickey Woods—famed for his post-touchdown dance, the "Ickey Shuffle"—and a head coach, Sam Wyche, whose flashy no-huddle offense and complicated defensive sets established him, along with San Francisco's Bill Walsh, as one of 1988's most respected coaches. He was this year's rising star. In addition, Knox would be taking his team, which reputedly played poorly in cold weather and in games back East, to a cold-weather game, east of the Mississippi, against a team that was 8-0 at home.

The Seahawks were thus written off almost immediately, which served only to bring out the fighter in Knox. "Well, see," he said when asked about Cincinnati's cold, "we've kind of made a little joke of the weather, so that we can get it handled mentally. They'll come out with all those big offensive linemen, and it's a psych job, they won't have any sleeves on, they'll have bare skin showin', you know . . . and then the first thing you know, they run off and put two capes on." He paused, then indulged in a little demystification of football. "The weather's not gonna block and tackle . . . we just have to make some plays . . . " Reporters' eyes glazed over at these hackneyed phrases, so he paused, then launched an entertaining assault on his favorite villain—the hydra-headed media. Alluding to a comment made the day before by ESPN talking head Joe Theismann (Theismann had said that the Seahawks can't play east of the Mississippi), Knox started wandering through a forest of assertions: "It's like anything else. You know, somebody says, 'Well, you're playing a game at 4 o'clock—can you win a game at 4 o'clock Saturday?' I said, 'Well, we played 6 o'clock Monday night, and we won. We played 5 o'clock Sunday night and we won. We're playing 4 o'clock Saturday, that's all. What's the difference?' Guy said, 'Well, now you gotta

go east of the Mississippi.' Somebody must have forgotten, we did go to
Atlanta and win, we did go to Cleveland and win . . . I hear these guys on
TV predicting it's gonna be low-scoring, another guy says it's gonna be
high-scoring, and they get up there and all that and then they forget what
they said when it's over with, and the exact reverse of what happened happened. All these so-called experts, and this same guy'll come on there the
next week and say the same thing and be wrong again, and then they lose
track. Of when they were right and when they were wrong. Hey. It's the
daggonedest thing in the world!"

The exact reverse of what happened happened?

Knox was less talkative about the Bengals' no-huddle offense, a
speeded-up attack that makes it difficult, sometimes impossible, for
defenses to make situation substitutions. "We have to contend with it—but
it's part of football," he said. This was his way of saying that he'd already
figured out how to beat it, but wasn't about to tell anybody.

Chick Harris, being a devoted Knoxist, seemed thrilled at the nation's
low regard for his team. "The energy around here," he said one day, "is
that we won the AFC West when we had a lot of things happen to us. When
we lost our quarterback, we were very inconsistent in games, but we
fought and stayed the course and now we're a much better team. The division title—we overcame a lot of adversity to win it. And we played contrary
to what a lot of people said we could do. That's where the energy is—the
energy also is that we have the opportunity to succeed and we're still in the
hunt for the Big One. So we're just gonna take our little ol' guys up there
and see what we can do!"

Krieg, for the first time all season, relaxed completely with reporters
one day. Talking with them almost as if he regarded them as fellow human
beings, he even relished their jibes about his torso, rendered comically
asymmetric by his shoulder separation. "Been kind of a bizarre year, hasn't
it?" he was asked. "There's been some weird things that happened within
the team," he answered, "as far as owners and all that other stuff, but
those things are bound to happen to you eventually." "Just a typical year,
then?" "Well . . . typical as they go!"

This was a classic Krieg Mystery Answer, and I wanted to explore it further, but someone interjected with a question about the press he'd been
getting, which, of late, had taken a dramatic turn for the adulatory. "I
haven't taken so much time to read a whole bunch of junk," he said. "The
only thing I've seen is sometimes on TV. And that was not very much, either, so that didn't make no big difference to me."

"Well, it seems like the LA papers . . . " began another reporter, who
stopped when he saw Krieg mentally turning inward, shutting himself off.

"See, I wouldn't know," he said quietly. "All the nice things are written about people in other cities, I guess . . . "

In Cincinnati, fevered excitement over the playoffs had local reporters writing nice things about everybody—particularly everybody from Seattle. "Knox keeps 'em guessing," read one *Cincinnati Enquirer* headline over a story detailing the variety and unpredictability of the Seattle offense. "Quarterbacks finally get passing marks," trumpeted the *Cincinnati Post*, in a story on the undeserved disrespect both Krieg and Bengal quarterback Boomer Esiason had endured. Other writers fretted that Cincinnati, high draft picks and all, was at a disadvantage because Seattle, although built around "discards," had "been to the playoffs four times in the last six seasons," and therefore had more big-game experience. Cincinnati was further disadvantaged, wrote *Post* columnist Paul Daugherty, because the Bengals had reverted to a "Ground Sam" offensive attack. "Worry about an attack," Daugherty advised fans, "which has gone right-of-Reagan conservative in the last month, leaning too heavily on Ickey Woods at the expense of its versatility . . . Which, if it doesn't rediscover its cut-it-loose heart, could be in big trouble this afternoon."

Either Cincinnati is a far more obsessive football town than Seattle or 12–4 buys you trainloads more ink than 9–7 does. Whatever the cause, the people of Cincinnati seemed to have nothing other than the NFL playoffs on their minds. You couldn't turn anywhere the day before the game without reading or hearing something about it. Seahawks Mike Wilson and Blair Bush—ex-Bengals—were hounded by autograph seekers and newspaper and television interviewers wherever they went. Boomer Esiason had become a civic idol whose legend was growing by the column inch. Both local newspapers contained special playoff sections on the day of the game, and the week's papers were filled with countless feature stories on players, coaches, team histories, player relationships, roster building, parity. . . The media covered everything from week-by-week summaries of both teams' seasons to Krieg's performance in cold weather.

This last article was a case study in how myths are made. Reprinted in the *Post* from the Tacoma *News Tribune*, headlined "Krieg fails when mercury falls," the piece was a detailed airing of *News Tribune* reporter John Clayton's theory that Krieg cannot win games in cold weather. Clayton apparently had attributed the New England loss exclusively to the cold there, rather than to any other factor, or combination of factors, and had decided that Krieg was a bad cold-weather quarterback. Further, Clayton wrote, "Krieg suffered more in that loss. Again, the Seahawks front office was reminded of his weaknesses. It's these bad performances in cold weather that have had the Seahawks management searching for taller and stronger-armed quarterbacks through the years."

When Clayton went to the Seahawk history books to further nail shut the coffin on Krieg's career, however, he ran into a significant problem. In legitimately cold weather—under 40 degrees, say—Krieg's record was 3–3, with one of the losses being in Kansas City, where the Seahawks can't win no matter what the weather is. Further, one of Krieg's best performances under any conditions came in 38-degree weather, with 29-mile-per-hour winds, in a win over the Chicago Bears the previous December. Krieg also had outperformed his opposite number (New England quarterback Doug Flutie) in the most recent loss, managing 62 yards on nine completions, throwing one touchdown and no interceptions, compared to Flutie's 5-for-10, for 47 yards, with no touchdowns and one interception. Well, wrote Clayton, Krieg's performance actually was worse than it looked, for "his only touchdown pass . . . was trapped, Patriots coaches said a day after reviewing tapes of the play." Dare we guess the reason for not reporting Seahawk coaches' views of the play?

Left with the vexing problem of Krieg's thesis-destroying numbers, Clayton carefully redefined his definition of "cold." By raising Krieg's fatal temperature to include 40-degree game days, he was able to add two more losses—one of them, again, in Kansas City. Somehow, though, a 3–5 record didn't quite merit "Krieg fails when mercury falls," so Clayton coaxed three more losses out of history (one of them, yet again, in Kansas City) by turning up the thesis temperature to an apparently frigid 45 degrees (the 45-degree game being a loss to the Denver Broncos in 1981, when Krieg was subbing for an injured Jim Zorn during a 6–10 Seahawk season), and came up, at last, with the stuff of which factors are made. "Cold has been Krieg's Achilles' heel," Clayton thundered. "He's 3–8 in games started in 45-degree-or-lower temperatures." Clayton would have done better with "Midrange temperatures have been Krieg's Achilles' heel. He's 0–5 in games started in 40-to-45-degree weather."

Boomer Esiason, meanwhile, was flawless—a tall, blond, handsome, well-spoken signal caller for a 12–4 team—and his picture was everywhere. A full-color photo of the gorgeous Esiason, his gorgeous wife Cheryl, and their gorgeous grand piano graced the front page of the *Enquirer* the day I arrived in Cincinnati. There seemed to be an Esiason photo and story on every page of every paper. Even his restaurant/nightclub, La Boom, was Cincinnati's hottest night spot.

I went down to Esiason's club one night to study the rewards of celebrity, and came away with a whole new restaurant concept. La Boom is a flashy, state-of-the-art club on the banks of the Ohio River. With pastel neon lighting, tropical decor, and stunning cocktail waitresses strutting in white cutaway coats, bow ties, high heels, and black, high-cut leotards, the place is a veritable Miami-on-the-Ohio.

Hard as I tried, I couldn't imagine Seattle paying homage to Krieg by trooping into this kind of place. I also couldn't imagine what you would call a Krieg-owned nightclub: Somehow, "La 'bone" lacked the requisite trendy tone.

Caught up in the excitement in Cincinnati, I looked for signs that Seattle had a better-than-even chance of winning the game. The Bengals' 12–4 record was supsect. They had started out 6–0, then, just as the Seahawks had done, had gone 6–4 over the last 10 weeks of the season. Against common opponents, Seattle compared favorably with Cincinnati, the Bengals going 5–4 against teams the Seahawks had gone 6–4 against. Cincinnati's 8–0 record in Riverfront Stadium, I decided, meant only that they were overdue for a loss there. If Krieg came into the game with a hot hand—a guarantee, so long as the temperature was either above 45 degrees or below 40—then Seattle would win, and if Houston could somehow manage to get by the Buffalo Bills, who had ended the regular season on the skids, then the AFC Championship game would be played in the Kingdome, against a team Seattle had already beaten, so the Seahawks would win that one easily, and then they would be in the Super. . .

What all this proved was that numbers make for great folklore. Seattle, one Cincinnati writer decreed, didn't stand a chance in Riverfront Stadium, because "the Seahawks are notoriously poor on the road." "Notoriously poor" meant 4–4—the same road record compiled by the purportedly Super Bowl–bound Bengals.

Finally all the numbers and factors and trends and character assessments and analyses of style had been combined in every conceivable way, and there was nothing left to do but play the damned game. On a pleasant, 42-degree day, under sunny skies that eventually would cloud over, the teams convened in their Riverfront Stadium locker rooms some four hours before game time.

Outside, Riverfront was filling up fast with raucous Bengal fans—beasts in a stadium they call "The Jungle." Bundled against the cold, and bearing noisemakers of every description, the fans lent a perfect football-in-the-Midwest look to the proceedings—a remarkable feat, considering the artificial, all-purpose look the stadium has when empty. And when the teams came out to play, the fans lent a perfect championship sound to the game by screaming and blowing horns, nonstop, from the opening coin toss to the final gun.

The timing of the game, 4pm on New Year's Eve, may have had something to do with the fans' noisemaking capacity. Few things could excite an Ohioan more than kicking in the New Year with a pro football playoff game. But Cincinnati so loved its team that Bengal fans would have shown up anywhere, at any time, ready to shriek their troops to victory. These fans were so primed that the most insignificant developments set them off. Even the opening coin toss, which (to my secret relief) the Bengals won, inspired a roar so loud you would have thought Cincinnati had just won the Super Bowl.

It didn't take long for me to see that all of the statistical evidence I had conjured up to prove the Seahawks belonged on the same field as the Bengals was proven ludicrously wrong. The game instantly established the fallacy of the NFL's playoff system. The Seahawks had simply been served up as cannon fodder for the Bengals, so the league would have one more game to sell, and one more city to involve in the Super Bowl chase—even though that city's team stood no chance of advancing beyond its first playoff game. By halftime, Cincinnati led, 21–0, and Seattle had racked up some of the most gruesome numbers I had ever seen outside of New England. The Bengals had 229 total yards—165 rushing, 64 passing—to the Seahawks' 49. Krieg had completed six of 13 passes and been intercepted once. The Bengals averaged 5.34 yards per rush, while the Seahawks totaled all of 0 yards rushing on nine carries.

I felt as if I'd been through hundreds of Seattle games exactly like this. Krieg was cold, the whole offense was flat, the Seattle defense was hopelessly porous against the run, and Knox was out of weapons and devices. Yet the closer I looked at the game, the more closely matched the teams appeared, and the more illusory seemed the one-sided statistics.

Seattle started off with a superb kickoff play, Nesby Glasgow putting a little head fake on his blocker, making him lunge the wrong way, then slipping through Cincinnati's wedge untouched, to level kick returner Ira Hillary at the Bengal 15. On Cincinnati's first play, an Ickey Woods run over left tackle, Darren Comeaux stepped up into Woods's cutback lane and held him to a 2-yard gain. On the next play, Woods dropped Esiason's little dump-off pass, and the Bengals were faced with third-and-eight. Coming immediately to the line of scrimmage, they had to wait while Seattle team doctors tended to a fallen Joe Nash, and Seattle's nickel defense rushed in. When the ball was snapped, Esiason, confused, found no receivers open, scrambled, and was tackled 2 yards short of a first down.

Seattle nose tackle Ken Clarke, however, had jumped offsides, and the Bengals were given one more chance, from 5 yards closer. So instead of punting, Cincinnati tried to pass, and was on the verge of being stopped when a scrambling Esiason found an improvising receiver, Chris Collingsworth, coming across the middle with Dave Wyman lumbering in tow. Esiason lobbed the ball to him, and Collingsworth angled up the field, to be pulled down from behind by Wyman after gaining 30 yards.

In a game that would set a new record for "what ifs," this was the first. Had Clarke not jumped offsides, Cincinnati would have punted rather than passed, and Seattle, rather than Cincinnati, would have had the ball. Given second wind, the Bengals drove downfield, scoring their first touchdown at the 9:11 mark, at the end of a nine-play, 83-yard drive, and establishing their running attack as an unstoppable, punishing force.

To be sure, there would be other problems for the Seahawks, but that single play, heavy with a season's worth of symbolism, so burdened the team that Seattle struggled for the rest of the first half, both on offense and on defense, to get out from under it.

The Bengals attacked with a combination of ruthlessness and deception on defense that rendered Krieg helpless. Shifting their secondary just before the snap, blitzing strong safety David Fulcher from nearly every point along the line of scrimmage, and routinely rushing six men at a time in different combinations, the Bengals kept Krieg under constant pressure, and had him consistently throwing either to no one or to double- and sometimes triple-covered receivers. Shutting down the running game entirely—both because they stacked the line of scrimmage and because Curt Warner was too hindered by his ankle sprain to run or block with authority—the Bengals forced Krieg to throw under pressure from the outset.

The Seahawks did manage two first downs in the first quarter, and the Bengals were kept from scoring through the balance of that stanza, but their dominance was established. High point for the Seahawks was Nash's second injury, which came as the Bengals assembled at the line of scrimmage on third-and-10, at the Cincinnati 41, midway through their second possession.

Cincinnati, coming to the line without huddling, was stopped by the referees when Nash glanced over at the sidelines, then fell gently to the ground. The fans—savvy football folk—began to boo vociferously, and Bengal coach Sam Wyche screamed in outrage at the nearest official—who, in officialdom's finest hour, laughed.

The one-downed-lineman defense was Knox's way of contending with Wyche's no-huddle tactic on third down. Wyche's intent, as he would later admit, was not to get mismatches on the field so much as it was to catch an opponent in midsubstitution, as nickel backs ran onto the field and linebackers off it. The Cincinnati offense, calling its play while standing at the line of scrimmage rather than back in a huddle, would simply snap the ball—

whether or not Esiason's playcalling was complete—as soon as they saw an opponent begin to substitute, thereby getting a 5-yard penalty called on the defense for having too many men on the field. Knox, signaling to Nash to take a fall, sent team doctors and defensive backs rushing onto the field as the officials called a mandatory injury time-out.

Your garden-variety modern coach, seeing what Wyche was doing, would have publicly appealed to the league in the days before the game to curtail the no-huddle tactic—which, in its intent to draw a penalty, was a stretch beyond the bounds of the league's rules. Knox, though, is still what he was in boyhood, a Sewickley street-fighter who solves problems (or, in his parlance, challenges) with his fists rather than with appeals to authority figures. If Wyche was determined to find an advantage by stretching the rules, Knox was determined to negate it by stretching the rules himself. Football to him is more of a fight than a game, and he would rather win it down on the league's mean streets, where he belongs, than in its sterile, alien boardrooms.

In trying to out-street-smart one another, Knox and Wyche were also carrying on football's grandest tradition. In their boundless hunger to win, football's combatants constantly bend and stretch and slide by the rules, looking for some kind of edge over an opponent. From the earliest days of the game, football has evolved by means of rule changes, as opponents introduce tactics and countertactics, and league officials react with new, ever-more-refined edicts. Before the first quarter of this game was over, you knew that the Knox-Wyche confrontation would lead to new rule refinements in the coming winter's owners meetings.

My favorite part of this little battle-within-the-war was the difference in demeanor between Wyche and Knox. Knox used the trick-knee play six times, by my count, and until midway through the fourth quarter, Wyche grew increasingly outraged each time Nash or Clarke went down. After pleading his case the first few times with officials, to no avail, he turned on Knox, screaming epithets across the field at him. "Fuck you! Fuck you!" he screamed at one point, completely out of control. "This is bullshit! Bullshit!" Knox—calm, magisterial, indifferent—simply paced impassively along the sidelines, as if Wyche were far too insignificant to merit the slightest consideration. It was a marvelous, arrogant display of contempt for a lesser man.

Nash's recurring ailment, alas, was the only breakdown that did Seattle any good. Krieg ended Seattle's second possession of the first quarter with an interception, thrown far beyond everyone except Bengal cornerback Eric Thomas, and Cincinnati mounted a 75-yard drive to take a 14-point lead less than 4 minutes into the second quarter. On their next possession, the Seahawks moved from the Seattle 17 to the 25 on one play, back to the 17 on the next, suffered an injury to Steve Largent on the third play, and punted on the fourth. While Largent sat on the sidelines having his foot anesthetized—afterward he said that it had been "bent in half"—Cincinnati ran 55 yards in three running plays, then 1 yard in the next two, to take their 21–0 lead.

By now, I wanted only that the game be over quickly. There is nothing worse than traveling halfway across the country to watch a blowout in football. The effort and the money and the expertise and the risk that go into professional football become the greatest waste of resources in the history of modern civilization, when expended on a game that is 21–0 at its one-third mark. Forcing myself to focus my attention on the players out of a sense of duty, I couldn't help marveling at how hard they kept playing. What kept them going? How could they make themselves keep flinging their bodies around with such reckless abandon?

John L. Williams dived into the middle of the line for no gain, and Largent came up swinging furiously at Bengal linebacker Joe Kelly. Under glowering Midwestern skies, to the tune of thousands of voices chanting, "Who dey?"—the ritual Cincinnati fan cheer—the world as well as the year seemed to be coming to an end.

Krieg's swing pass to Williams gained only 1 yard, and a deep lob to Blades, running step for step with cornerback Eric Thomas, was batted away. And still the Seattle players fought, as if they expected at any moment to break out of their doldrums. It was painful to watch, this refusal to surrender when beaten. Ruben Rodriguez came on, and punted like a man convinced against all evidence that he had a chance to win. A beautiful, high, slow, 54-yard kick, it was easily covered by his teammates, and as it sailed down just behind returner Ira Hillary, Hillary reached back only to have it slip through his hands as he fell. The ball, wriggling dangerously, wouldn't bounce up into Melvin Jenkins's arms—if it had, he would have scored a touchdown—so he fell on it at the Cincinnati 26.

Even the Cincinnati fans were impressed enough to observe a split second of silence. After one run each by Warner and Williams netted 4 yards, Williams slipped into the left flat unobserved by the Bengal defense, caught Krieg's swing pass, and rammed his way down to the Cincinnati 8. With 4 minutes remaining in the half, Seattle had a chance to get back into the game.

The Seahawks ran Williams straight into left tackle, and he hit a huge pile of bodies there, pushing furiously forward, moving the whole stack 2 yards. Still refusing to go down, he kept churning, calling upon heretofore untapped reserves of power, when suddenly the ball, as if greased, slithered out of his grasp. Bengal defensive end Jim Skow, crawling in under the pile, gathered the ball in, and the Seahawk offense, shell-shocked, crept off to the sideline to ask themselves why such a player would make such a mistake at such a moment. Williams is the greatest all-purpose player Seattle has ever seen. Already in this game he had accounted for 35 of his team's 44 total yards. Coming into the '88 season, he had handled the football 313 times, and fumbled only three times. He had gone the entire '88 season, handling the ball 247 times, without once fumbling. However adept Knox may have been at taking on the Bengals, he was helpless against fates that could coax his best player, carrying the ball in the game's most critical situation, into turning it over.

Four plays later, chance, to make things worse, allowed Ken Clarke to force Esiason to fumble at the Cincinnati 20, but the ball bounced the Bengals' way, and tight end Randy Holman recovered just ahead of a sliding Jacob Green. Five plays later, as the half drew to a close, Largent, slipping behind the Cincinnati defense, was overthrown. As he reached for the ball, it sailed just past his fingertips, and he came down clutching the small of his back. He walked over to the sideline, then slowly collapsed. It was a freak football accident. Making a routine move, making contact with no one, Largent had sprained his back.

As the players retired at the half, the fans turned up the noise a notch— already savoring the win. I couldn't remember ever having felt so luxuriously sorrowful in such a joyous setting. Where only minutes before I had thought I was watching something utterly banal, I now felt I was watching something profound.

Outside the stadium, the winter skies were gathering and darkening and roiling, preparing to unleash a savage storm on the landscape and the people below. Inside the stadium, as if huddled together for warmth and protection around their fierce joy, the Cincinnati fans paid ceaseless, frenetic homage to their heroes. The setting, the mood, the time of year, and the nature of the ritual combat down on the stadium floor all conspired to convince me that at last I could hit upon the key to football's hold on the American imagination.

The Civil War, as historians never tire of reminding us, was a watershed event in the history of warfare. It marked the most dramatic and irreversible change from premodern to modern war. Before the Civil War, battles were ritualized forms of combat, pitting against one another members of a carefully defined warrior class. War was a formal exchange staged under rules of combat rigorously adhered to by both sides. But with Civil War advances in weaponry came corresponding declines in morality. And as the spectators at Bull Run saw, war had become a disordered, uncontrollable mess.

It seemed to me no accident that football, with its military language and its soldier's instincts, was fostered and developed and refined by Civil War veterans. While they recognized the presence of nobility and magnificence in warfare, they also, having seen firsthand how hideous it had become, were groping for an alternative. In developing the war game called football, they were trying to give civilization a metaphor.

In the 123 years since the end of the Civil War, we have seen warfare grow into an all-devouring beast. In place of romance and valor, we now have computerized megadeath, in which the so-called warrior is nothing more than a bureaucrat punching computer keys as he takes aim at entire civilizations. There are no more combatants and noncombatants—there are only victims. And war, once rich in meaning, is now the ultimate expression of meaninglessness, purposelessness, disorder, chaos...

If Americans embraced football most fervently during the Vietnam era, and continue to embrace it in the era of mutually assured destruction, perhaps it is because we dimly recognize the ideals still inherent in this game defined by disillusioned warriors. We watch it, as they played it, out of nostalgia for a simpler, more ordered time—a time when war was civil.

Back to rejoin the battle on the banks of the Ohio came our present-day heroes and villains. In the Seattle locker room, Knox and his coaches had calmly gone about their business, shoring up weaknesses, making adjustments in the Seattle attack, and taking time to attempt inspiration. Before leading his troops back to the battlefield, Knox wrote on the locker room blackboard, "1. Nothing cheap. 2. Hit and hustle. 3. Talk. WIN."

After downing Cincinnati's kickoff in the end zone, Seattle started out with a crisp Krieg out-pass to Brian Blades, who slipped a tackle and slithered ahead for a 16-yard gain. Then, in a beautiful tactical moment, the Seahawks ran the John L. Williams screen in the identical manner that had brought them a 75-yard touchdown in Los Angeles. Cincinnati, completely fooled, left the left side of the field completely open to Williams and three blockers. But when Krieg turned to throw to Williams, he saw that his receiver had slipped on the turf and fallen. Krieg dumped the ball off to Warner, for a 1-yard loss. That missed-by-inches play was followed by another, when Krieg lobbed deep to Blades, who had a quarter-step lead on cornerback Lewis Billups. The ball, coming down directly over Blades's head, was underthrown just enough to allow Billups back into the play. Billups, while missing when he swatted at the ball, was nonetheless able to disturb Blades just enough to keep him from grasping the ball as it slipped through his hands. Two straight times Seattle had just missed breaking big plays.

Seattle punted, and Cincinnati—after having rushed for 165 yards in the first half, while passing for only 64—took to the air. This after a first half in which Bengal blockers had blasted Seahawk defenders off the line of scrimmage so thoroughly that running backs Ickey Woods and James Brooks had averaged over 6 yards per carry. After watching Esiason sandwich two woeful incompletions around a Joe Nash knee injury, I could see why Wyche liked to run the ball.

Suddenly Seattle kind of caught fire. Krieg hit Blades for another out-pass, then Cincy, blitzing, was caught off guard when Krieg completed a swing pass to Williams, and Williams promptly parlayed it into a 24-yard gain. Then, after missing connections with Blades—"I made a mistake in the huddle," Krieg said afterward—and getting sacked, Krieg threaded a needle so precisely that his pass hit a well-covered Blades in the facemask 24 yards downfield. Blades did not see the ball coming because he was trying to recover from a punch in the ribs delivered by Billups, for which Billups was flagged and which gave the Seahawks the ball at the Bengal 21. An ensuing run by Williams, followed by a pass to Williams, gave Seattle a first down at the Cincinnati 11.

At that point, Blades ran into the right corner of the end zone, then burst forward as Krieg rolled right and rifled a low pass at him. Billups, diving over Blades's back, couldn't quite reach the ball, and Blades caught it inches above the ground, for a touchdown. He rolled over, holding the ball proudly aloft, to see standing over him . . . an official signaling that he believed the pass to be incomplete.

Krieg, Blades, and half the Seattle team descended in a fury on the official. There was no doubt in any of their minds that Blades had caught the ball. The officials, for their part, conferred in apparent confusion. "The guy asked the other official," Krieg said later, "he said, 'Ron! Ron!' 'Cause he didn't know what it was. And the other guy, Ron, that he's talking to, said, 'I can't make a decision either.' So I'm going, 'Oh, man!' Then I knew we were in trouble. They didn't know what to call it."

So they called it incomplete, and the Seahawks finished the series with a fourth-and-two pass from the 3-yard line. Blades, distracted by the intervention of safety Rickey Dixon, juggled . . . juggled . . . and dropped the ball. For the second time in the game, Seattle was turned away scoreless from inside the Bengal 10.

Wyche then sent his troops on a punishing march for 15 plays, taking 7 minutes, 45 seconds. Brutalizing their opponents on the line of scrimmage, the Bengals ran the ball 11 times for 59 yards, passing for another 35, coming to rest with a fourth-and-two at the Seattle 3. Wyche, perhaps out of a love of symmetry, opted to try for a first down rather than kick a game-clinching field goal. Ickey Woods came up a yard short, Seattle took over on downs, and Krieg ended the quarter with a 4-yard completion to Williams.

Now Krieg was in a groove. Having thrown wildly off-target in the first half, he was now throwing as accurately as I had ever seen him throw—particularly considering the close coverage Bengal defensive backs were giving his receivers. After hitting Blades for a 24-yard completion, Krieg hit a double-covered Louis Clark, but Clark couldn't find the ball, and Eric Thomas, batting the ball in the air twice, managed to get it to fellow defensive back Solomon Wilcots. Two plays later, Esiason, back to pass at the Cincy 39, was hit by Jacob Green, fumbled, and the ball was miraculously recovered by the miraculously recovered Joe Nash. Immediately, Krieg beat the blitzing Fulcher just in time to hit Blades, crossing, for 17 yards, then he hit a crossing John Spagnola for another 7. Three plays later, the last being a perfect throw to Blades broken up by a perfect defensive play, Krieg, facing fourth-and-three at the Bengal 7, found Williams at the 5, and dumped him the ball. Williams then made one of the most remarkable plays I've ever seen: Running full tilt for the end zone, he vaulted one defender, and, airborne, met a waiting Fulcher at the goal line. Somehow Williams managed to accelerate while in midair, blasting Fulcher right in the head, knocking him to his knees, then flattening him in the end zone, for Seattle's first touchdown. Fulcher left the game, never to return.

The stadium, incredibly, was silent, Cincinnati fans realizing that their team had not scored since midway through the second quarter, and that the momentum had shifted Seattle's way. The Bengals had the ball for only three plays before punting it away again, and Krieg started out again from the Seattle 31. Completing three of four pass attempts, for 11, 32, and 10 yards, Krieg capped off the 3½-minute drive with a dive into the end zone, pulling his team to within 8 points with a full 5:54 remaining.

Largent, bent over awkwardly, hobbled out with Johnson to take his place as the holder. Fans, noticeably anxious, waited, too distracted even to blow their horns. Above the right upright, a confused array of sprites, fairies, gremlins, will-o-the-wisps, and assorted little creatures I didn't recognize were locked in chaotic combat, like insects maneuvering for position around a streetlight on a summer night. Back came the snap, down went the hold—all in perfect order—and off went the kick—*zip!*—shooting just wide to the right.

I looked it up: Until that moment, Johnson had successfully kicked 130 consecutive extra-point attempts, going back to 1985.

Johnson's miss by inches turned a suspenseful game into a cruel war of attrition. His miss grew more poetic by the play—particularly when Cincinnati, after Seattle's kickoff, once again ran three plays and punted. At the 4:47 mark, Seattle had the ball again, this time at the Seahawk 33. Had Johnson's kick been good, you would have heard the silence in Riverfront Stadium all the way to Seattle.

For the first time in the half, Seattle was stopped in three plays. The first was a near-completion to Williams, who turned inward, saw that Krieg had thrown to his outside shoulder, spun, and nearly made a one-handed catch. The second was an overthrown pass to Blades, running deep. The third was a 17-yard pass to Butler, running an out-pattern toward the left sideline. With a full step on his defender, Butler caught the ball and ran out of bounds as the referee closest to him came running up, signaling the completion. As the rest of the offense came charging up to regroup, though, another referee ran in, signaling that Butler had stepped out of bounds. The pass was ruled incomplete—and the replay showed that Butler, catching the ball with plenty of room to spare, had been just careless enough to come down with half of his second foot over the sideline. Seattle punted, and the crowd came to full-throated, renewed life.

After the punt, Cincinnati managed a 20-yard Ickey Woods run, then faltered again, punting to the Seattle 2. I was down on the field then, amazed at the player's-eye-view of the stands and its demented occupants. Down there, the noise was deafening, and the fans looked murderous. Shrieking, blowing horns, shouting, bellowing. . . the cacophony was the acoustic equivalent of a Hieronymus Bosch painting. Directly above me stood a young fan, leaning over the railing, screaming non-stop, in a hoarse falsetto, "AAAAAAAAAUUUUUUGH!" From his hand hung a little Seahawk doll, its neck in a noose, its body jerking spasmodically in time to the movements of the fan's hand.

At the far end of the field, Seattle—particularly Krieg and Williams—refused to give up. Inching out to the 18-yard line with completions on third and fourth down, Krieg hit Williams for 16 yards at the 2-minute mark. After missing connections with Blades, Krieg made his last completion of the day. Hitting Williams on a short sideline pattern, he watched the fullback spin out of a tackle and run 37 yards downfield. And there, to the rising tide of sound from the stands, the game ended, on four straight incompletions.

I was so caught up in the action and the noise that when the game ended I was caught by surprise, even though every play near the end had been run with the clock foremost in mind. As soon as the final gun sounded, the Seattle players ran as quickly as they could off the field, and I followed in their wake, along an endless curved tunnel that took me a good quarter of the way around the stadium. There, with the press, I waited.

After an interminable interval, we were ushered in to interview Knox, who had already showered and changed clothes. Looking drained and somber and slack, he uttered a few spiritless lines by way of analysis, then was asked almost immediately about Nash's knee. He answered in a curious way, insisting that Nash really had been hurt, then adding, "and we were able to get our substitutions in."

Now, this was his way of letting his audience know what he'd been up to. It was a rare acknowledgment, on his part, that journalists are intelligent enough to apprehend subtlety. But the Cincinnati contingent among his listeners was either too hostile or too thickheaded to take yes for an answer. The Cincy reporters pressed on, asking again and again whether Nash had been genuinely hurt. Hardening, Knox insisted each time that, yes, he had been.

"Really? All six times?" asked a particularly dullwitted writer. Knox, his eyes flashing, muttered, "I got nothin' more to say, pal!" And walked off.

A season-ending exclamation point.

The players, in various phases of anguish, sat immobile in the locker room. Most anguished of all was Williams, whose valiant efforts had accounted for 6 of Seattle's 13 points and 143 of his team's 294 yards. He had also, of course, accounted for the game's most poignant play—his first-half fumble at the Bengal 6. Normally a stoic's stoic, he now sat sobbing hysterically, so helpless and broken in his grief that Warner was moved to guide him gently out of the media's range.

Across the room, Krieg was spouting insights and anecdotes with his customary postloss enthusiasm. "It's hard," he was saying. "The finality of it is tough. It just ends so sudden, you know. The clock runs out... that's the hard part about it—you're done now for a long time."

To his mind, the game had been a reliving of his entire pro career as a starter. "It's frustrating, being in this position for so many years. It's been like this four or five times now. We were only 9-and-7 coming into this game, but I felt that we had as good a chance of getting to the Super Bowl as anybody. And to have this happen to you in this way, and then to be able to come back and kind of have time run out on you—it just is too sudden."

For that matter, the game had been a replay of Knox's career as a coach, if not of his whole life. He came into battle a determined, angry underdog, pulled himself and his team to the brink of victory, only to be undone by the tiny, inexplicable failing—the chance misbounce of the ball, or of the mind, or the body, or the will, or the official's eye. Every surge of his team in that game had been punctuated by the kind of mistake that has haunted Knox all his life.

A tired Paul Moyer was holding forth over by the exit from the locker room. "You know, really, their hurry-up offense didn't create any problems," he said. "You know, every time we needed to substitute on third down, Joe's knee was bothering him, so . . . you know, we got our substitutions in when we had to."

"Hopefully, Joe'll be ready for next season," someone said.

"Yeah," Moyer answered, grinning. "Well, you know, that happens in a game." "Was it his knee or his calf?" "I think it was both. It was hard to tell—he was grabbing his knee."

Asked what sort of season it had been, Moyer hesitated. "Hoo, I don't know," he said. "It's just been a strange year more than anything. It's just been a long season. God, there's just been so much going on this whole year. It was good that we won the division and it's disappointing and bad that we didn't get to keep playing. I think everybody wanted to keep playing football, you know. I really wasn't planning on not playing football next week. There's always an adjustment once the season's over. It's almost a deep depression. You don't go anywhere. You're used to going somewhere and hitting somebody and . . . And today, we played this team head to head, we spotted 'em 21 points. If we just could've made a play here or there! They won the first half, we won the second half. They just won the first half worse."

A season-ending confusion mark.

Just then Largent shuffled into view. "How you doin', Stevie?" Moyer asked.

"I don't know," Largent replied. He was bent almost double, twisted to one side. He was trying, without much success, to lean comfortably on a cane. Wedging himself against a trunk, he patiently answered questions. "When you lose in the playoffs," he said, "it's such a sudden ending. You come into this game, and you're not looking past it, but you're not thinking that this could be the end of the season, either. You're optimistic and confident and that's the way we were. And you know . . . BOOM! You lose the game and it's over, and it's like hitting a brick wall. It's kind of hard to accept. And there's just been a lot of things that I've had to deal with this year that I'm not accustomed to having to do, and that made it frustrating."

He turned and made his way haltingly out the door.

I made my way out of the stadium and walked back up to my hotel. It was nearly 11pm. The streets were awash in bacchanalia, and the hotel lobby nearly impenetrable, so thick and so besotted were the celebrants. Safely back in my room, listening to the sounds of riot in the streets below and in the hall outside, I turned on the television. There were the Bengal players, whining about Knox's one-downed-lineman defense. I couldn't believe that tactic had generated so much controversy. "Nash is a good football player," one lineman was saying heatedly, "but he is a bad actor."

Wyche, for his part, had calmed down considerably, even tossing Knox a compliment. "Actually," he said, "it was a good coaching tactic."

By midnight, the fireworks display down on the river was dampened somewhat by a tremendous deluge—the same storm that had visited me in Atlanta. It poured most of the night, and by morning the streets were bare and empty, the skies winter-bright and clear.

Picking up an *Enquirer* next morning, I read local accounts of the game. The Seahawks, Cincinnati reporters wrote, had mounted a "quasi-comeback." The near-upset that I thought I had seen was, in their eyes, nothing more than a long, anticlimactic running-out of the game clock.

Then I came across a remark that hit me with the force of religious revelation. Discussing Norm Johnson's missed extra point, a Cincinnati player, alluding to a Washington Redskin field goal attempt, a few weeks before, that had sailed wide of the same upright on the same goalpost, thus giving the Bengals a victory, said, "There must be some magical fairy-dust on that upright."

For the first time, it occurred to me that Johnson's miss could be subject to interpretations other than Seattle's. Every football game is really two games—or two versions of the same game. Each game is a chapter in two separate unfolding stories, with different high and low points, different symbol systems, different heroes and villains, different gods and ghosts, different morals and themes and subplots and authors. Just as I saw Johnson's kick being guided by Seattle demons, Bengal fans and chroniclers saw it being guided by Cincinnati's good fairy. And so it was with every play, every mistake, every injury, and every distracting scandal. Every Seahawk game that I had seen, and chronicled, was being recounted some- where else as part of some other city's civic myth.

And in Seattle's saga, I now understood, the story had been one of un- reasoning pride and determination, as an obsessive football coach set out to do the impossible: impose an order on human experience that would con- form to his own pathologically ordered visions. It was the story of a man both flawed and uplifted by his fierce pride, dragging through life the chains forged in his childhood. Each Sunday, he took to the playing field convinced that he could take on chaos and win. Dreaming constantly of what had been denied him in boyhood, he sought a world of perfect order and justice and harmony and predictability—one that he controlled, godlike, through his virtue, his ethics, his vision, and the strength of his will. Ultimately, of course, he would fail, as must anyone foolhardy enough to take up fighting chance for a living. In trying to make a science out of the art of survival, he might as well have been trying to control the bounce of a football.

Author Redux

24

A blunder—apparently the merest chance—reveals an unsuspected world, and the individual is drawn into a relationship with forces that are not rightly understood.
      —Joseph Campbell, *The Hero with a Thousand Faces*

Four days after Seattle's loss to Cincinnati, Knox looked at once contented, fulfilled, and stunned. Rested for the first time in six months, he was restored to something like health. His skin was clear, his jaw relaxed, and faint traces of color had returned to his cheeks. Although you still could see signs of exhaustion in his moist, red-rimmed eyes, his gaze had softened. His quest over, he was free of the turmoil that had consumed him while he was lost, body and soul, in the 1988 replay of his destiny.

Still, he had not yet recovered his equilibrium. Psychologically, he was flying through space like a man flung from an emotional merry-go-round that has come to a sudden stop. With the last loss of the season, everything that gave definition to his life had ceased. "I'd like to still be coaching," he said. "It's kind of like you've got to go cold turkey. Well, you've been going seven days a week since the 20th of July without one day off ever . . . then all of a sudden, bang! That's how final the daggone thing is."

Already he was beginning to work on the next season. "My coaches are off this week, and I'm cleaning up some loose ends here. I'll be in here." After the January 22 Super Bowl, he would proceed immediately to the Senior Bowl—a college all-star game that showcases players who will be entering the April player draft—and from there would go at the beginning of February to combine meetings, where coaches take close looks at the nation's top college-senior talent. "Then," Knox continued, "we'll sit down and map out a spring planning schedule for the coaches. And of course we'll evaluate everything we've done, take a look at areas where we need to improve, take a look at research and development, different concepts and things we want to explore, and always we're preparing for the draft—because you've got to have players. We want to know about this guy we might be taking:

Can he beat out who we have? Can we line up with him and can he win at that position week in and week out?" There was no question what his team needed most: "I think we still have the same number-one need that we had last year. We need an impact defensive lineman that can go rush the passer and still play the run."

Whether or not he found that player, there would be little rest for Knox between now and the beginning of next season. After the draft—held in the latter half of April—he would begin preparing for Seahawk minicamp, scheduled for May 10–12, and then begin preparations for the 1989 training camp in July.

His team, meanwhile, would be recuperating from the physical toll of the season. Brian Bosworth, still recovering from shoulder surgery, would undergo knee surgery in a few days, to remove a cyst. Eight of his teammates would also be having operations: Jeff Bryant had a knee cyst; Norm Johnson was to have a bone spur removed from his lower back; Steve Largent had nerve damage in his foot and ligament damage in his hand; Joe Nash would have cartilage removed from his knee; Bruce Scholtz would have bone spurs removed from his foot, which had been in a walking cast for most of the season; and Ron Mattes, Curt Warner, and Tony Woods had fingers and thumbs waiting for surgery. "I don't think any are really serious," said Knox. "Most of them are for minor things. But obviously we want to get them done as soon as possible, so that you have a longer period of rehabilitation and can get everybody ready for the minicamp."

Hard at work as he was on his next fight for football's Holy Grail, Knox had taken time to take stock of the '88 season, and came away more fulfilled, I think, than he realized.

He had seen his troops, first of all, come face-to-face with adversity— without which no football season, for Knox, would be complete. "We had some injuries that hurt us," he began. "David Krieg went out, Millard was out for two weeks, Patrick Hunter being out as a result of an automobile accident . . . " He had seen them fight through their shortcomings in a way that inspired him. "I thought that really our football team did a good job of holding the pieces and bits together, enabled us to be in position where we could win the division if we won the last two games. And it's a credit to the players and assistant coaches that got those people to do the things that they have to do." In the end, he found himself in a playoff game that had all the elements of the just-concluded season: key injuries, officials' mistakes, bad bounces, inexplicable blunders—all adding up to the early seizing of disadvantage—followed by the determined, heroic fight back. "We go to Cincinnati, we have a chance to win that football game. We didn't play well in the first half, we had a chance to make plays. And we didn't make 'em.

Turn the ball over inside the 5-yard line, the guy hasn't fumbled all year. We have a touchdown that clearly on film, looking at it, was a touchdown that we didn't get. You have to make those kinds of plays, or be good enough that if you don't make them, that you're strong enough in all areas that you can overcome it."

It was, in short, a quintessential Knox campaign—the best of seasons, the worst of seasons. In not winning the Super Bowl, his team had failed; but in doing better than expected, his team had succeeded. "So," concluded Knox on an appropriately ambiguous note, "if you ask me what kind of a year it was, that's the kind of year it was."

He took some consolation in the record he had compiled over six Seattle seasons. "You know, you sit there and you look at our six years, we got the sixth-best record in the NFL in that period of time. We're ahead of the Raiders, for example, and people like that. When we came here, they were out there ahead of us. And we're one of five teams not to have a losing season during that six-year period."

Knox also was gratified by the knowledge that he and his players had done their absolute best. They had overcome obstacles that would have daunted lesser men and had put themselves in a position to contend for the Super Bowl. "Our number-one goal in training camp was to win the AFC West. OK, we got that done. That was the number-one goal. Because if we get that, we were gonna be in the playoffs. So we accomplished that. The second goal was to get in the playoffs and go on and play in the AFC championship. We didn't get that done, OK? So there's satisfaction in achieving the one goal, and we fell short of achieving the other. And we can look at all the ratings and a lot of things happened to us, and I feel good about the way the team responded to the things that happened to us this year, the way they fought back and the way they came back when we were down 21–0 and came out that second half and just didn't flop around out there. So I feel good about that. You see, you're always unfulfilled at this time of year. And when it's all said and done, 27 head coaches in this league will be unfulfilled."

In repose, he could now allow himself the luxury of reflection. As if his having been "unfulfilled" had brought him heightened wisdom, Knox acknowledged that there was only so much of his destiny he could control. For all of his efforts, his fortune ultimately rode on the twists and turns of chance. Out of that humility rose a sense that his falling short of his ultimate goal was not a matter of personal failing, but of having been failed by fortune. And out of that conviction rose the determination to try again, for if he could keep fighting his way into the upper echelon of the NFL, eventually the breaks would fall his way, and he would win the Super Bowl.

"You're just two games away, then one game away," he said. "See, our first year, we were one game away. We beat the Raiders twice during the regular season, we go down there for the AFC championship game, and they beat us, and they go on and win the Super Bowl championship. So I just believe this: If you keep working to upgrade your football team personnel-wise, and if your football team's a competitive football team, and if they come to play hard every week, and they have a good attitude about things, and you do the job coaching, and you coach better next year than you did this year, and you work and sit down and analyze everything that you're doing, you're gonna put yourselves in a position where you're gonna be in contention, and you'll have a chance to win. And sooner or later, you're gonna win it. But you gotta put a lot of different things together. And it has to happen for you."

In that last line lay the transformation from the preseason to the post-season Knox. He had gone from the prideful conviction that he could make things happen—that he could take control of the workings of chance, and make them the residue of his designs—to the humble understanding that his efforts, however ingenious and energetic, were the efforts not of a god but of a man. After a season of lecturing and hectoring us from above, Knox now presented himself as one of us.

Lest we get too cozy with him, however, Knox served up one last morsel of offputting banality to the men who would be his fellows. When he was asked how Kelly Stouffer's development had come along, his eyes gleamed mischievously. "Well, I don't think you can put a limit on that. I don't think you can say, as I've said many times, it's not like cookin' that Christmas turkey. You put it in at 450 degrees, or whatever, and that sucker's ready for you in an hour and a half, and a little ol' thermometer pops up . . . "

Sitting in his office at the far end of the hall, contemplating the 1989 draft order taped to his desk, Mike McCormack, like Knox, was pondering the past and trying to prepare for the future. "This might have been the weirdest season we've ever had," he said. Then he paused thoughtfully, as if to compare the events of this season with those of seasons past—or perhaps even with those in the coming days—and seemed to reconsider. "But I think there are things that happen during the course of a season, sometimes they go for you and sometimes they go against you. You stay in this game long enough . . . I think it's been fairly normal."

Compared to what was looming on the horizon, he was right. When the season was winding down, rumor's vultures had been wheeling over his head in ever-tightening circles, as Ken Behring's men (most notably Mike Blatt, the agent McCormack publicly labeled a liar and an ignoramus during the previous offseason) persistently and anonymously insisted to Northwest reporters that McCormack would be fired when his contract expired on February 1. Now, with the season behind him, McCormack looked ahead with the same prescience he had exhibited at that CityClub luncheon some 10 months ago. He resigned himself in advance to his fate and took refuge, as Knox had done, in the long-term record of his franchise. "If they're gonna make a change here, I have no control over that," he said, his jaw hardening. "About the only thing I can do is do the best job I can. What comes after that, you know—that's in somebody else's hands. There's nothing I can do about it. But I'll tell you—I think that it will be made more palatable by the fact that we won our first division here. Something you can't take away, no matter what, is that in the seven years I've been here as head coach and general manager, six with Chuck, we haven't had a losing season. We had one 8–8 season, and every other season's been a winner. And there aren't many teams who can say that. Then you think of the organization—even though drafting from 18th to 23rd, we have been able to win, and win consistently. Hey—if they decide to make a change, that's their decision. But I think I'll leave the franchise in pretty good shape. So that doesn't bother me."

Over the next few weeks, as if it had been held in place only by the sheer force of Knox's fierce focus, the franchise began to dissolve. On January 12, Steve Moore abruptly resigned, leaving professional football altogether for a job at the Pacific Institute, a motivational feel tank. A few days later, defensive backfield coach Ralph Hawkins resigned to become defensive coordinator for the New York Jets. The two men had worked for Knox for 11 years and 8 years, respectively. For the rest of the month, while Blatt, et al, continued to insist that McCormack's days were numbered, Behring constantly and heatedly denied the rumors, saying at one point that he "didn't understand" why the local press kept asking him about McCormack's future. On January 30, after McCormack had spent several weeks—if not most of the season—slowly twisting in the wind, Behring called a press conference to announce that McCormack had been fired, that a search was on for his replacement, and that a "small raise" in ticket prices was coming.

The season over, Behring was taking full control, and showing his true colors in the process. As it turned out, a price hike announcement was already in the mail to season ticket holders. The "small raise" nearly doubled the cost of the cheapest seats, from $10 to $19. The price of the stadium's best seats took a 17 percent leap from $30 to $35, and the three remaining categories—formerly $15, $21, and $25—were folded into two considerably pricier categories, at $25 and $29.

Although Behring said at his press conference that he was interviewing "half a dozen" candidates for general manager, other Blackhawk sources said that Blatt had already been chosen. On February 3 Blatt set up shop at Seahawk headquarters, saying that "Ken and I are committed to building a dynasty here." It was to be a short-lived commitment. Blatt alienated public, press, and Seahawk employees so fast and so thoroughly that Behring found himself with a full-fledged public-image crisis on his hands. Four days after Blatt moved in, former Raider head coach Tom Flores announced that he and Behring were negotiating for Flores's assumption of McCormack's old position. Then, after Blatt spent two more weeks announcing to anyone who would listen that he was running the franchise, Behring announced the hiring of Flores, and Blatt disappeared.

Flores's first act as general manager was to leave for Maui on a two-week vacation.

While Flores fiddled, the Seahawk roster began to burn. In accordance with the NFL's new limited-free-agency plan, teams were allowed to list only 37 "protected" players currently on their rosters, meaning that the remaining players—in Seattle's case, 20—were free to sign a contract with another team. Unprotected players had from February 2 to April 1 to sign with new teams. During that time, they were not allowed to negotiate with their old team, and after April 1, if they had not signed elsewhere, their rights reverted to their original team and they were allowed to negotiate with no one else. The NFL had come up with the plan in an effort to weaken the players union antitrust suit against the league.

Left unprotected by Seattle were David Hollis, who had spent the last three games of the season on Seattle's inactive list; wide receivers Ray Butler and Paul Skansi; tight ends Mike Tice and John Spagnola; center Blair Bush and center/tackle Stan Eisenhooth; offensive guards Chris Godfrey and Alvin Powell; fourth-string quarterback Bruce Mathison; running back Tommy Agee; kick returner Bobby Joe Edmonds; nose tackles Ken Clarke and Roland Barbay; linebackers Darrin Miller, Sam Merriman, and Greg Gaines; and defensive backs Vernon Dean, Nesby Glasgow, and Kerry Justin.

By the time the free-agency signing period ended, the Seahawks had lost Gaines, Tice, Butler, Agee, Bush, Eisenhooth, Spagnola, and Edmonds to other teams. All but Gaines and Eisenhooth had played important roles the previous season, and three—Bush, Spagnola, and Edmonds—had been starters. By way of replacement, Seattle gained nine new players, none of whom had been starters in 1988, few of whom had even been on NFL active rosters, and one of whom—running back Tony Burse—had been cut by Seattle before the '88 season to make room for Tommy Agee.

On March 20, the NFL began its annual owners meeting, at which several new rules of particular interest to the Seahawks were passed. First came a rule penalizing home teams for excessive stadium noise by taking time-outs away from them if fans didn't quiet down when warned. The rule was aimed primarily at domed stadiums, and passed by one vote after having been voted down the year before. The league also voted to continue video review of controversial calls, but voted down the installation of electronic devices that would show on the replay official's screen exactly when during a given play a referee's whistle had blown. Finally, the league made faking injuries illegal, and tightened restrictions on the no-huddle offense.

On April 14, Kenny Easley sued the Seahawks, team doctors Pierce Scranton and James Trombold, private physician Dr. Gerald Pendras, trainer Jim Whitesel, and Whitehall Laboratories—distributors of the pain reliever Advil—for causing him, through improper treatment of injury, to contract the kidney disease nephrotic syndrome, then concealing his condition from him when it was discovered in 1986. The lawsuit promised to call into question every aspect of the treatment of athletes—particularly the goal of their medical treatment, which is heavily weighted toward getting them back on the playing field as soon as possible.

On April 23, the Seahawks, picking 15th in the NFL draft, selected Notre Dame offensive tackle Andy Heck, there being no quality defensive linemen available. The team would be going into the 1989 season with the same defensive front that had helped them finish 24th in the league in total defense.

On May 10, Terry Taylor was excused from the 1989 Seahawk minicamp to take care of what Knox called "personal problems."

On June 6, Brian Blades did his bit to help keep Seattle's name linked with scandal when he was named in a Florida paternity suit.

Matters were made even worse for Seattle when the '89 schedule was announced. The Seahawks would be playing three division champions (the 10–6 Philadelphia Eagles, 12–4 Buffalo Bills, and 12–4 Cincinnati Bengals), and would play their last seven games against perennially elite teams. As is dictated by the NFL's parity policy, they were being penalized in 1989 for winning their division in 1988.

With that kind of offseason, Knox was effectively heading into his next season behind by three touchdowns. The lone bright spot was Largent's decision, on the eve of Seattle's May minicamp, to return for one more year.

During the 1988 season, when not absorbed in Knox's dramatic quest, I watched in dismay as Behring gradually took form, changing from avuncular, folksy Ken "Bubba" Behring, football guy, into just another vulpine capitalist—the kind of man who is slowly taking over the entire National

Football League. Just as happened in major league baseball in the 1960s and 1970s, the old ownership—composed of men who understood and loved their game enough either to make it the focus of their professional lives or, Nordstrom-fashion, to entrust their franchises to those who knew the game best—is gradually being replaced by self-made multimillionaires who have made their fortunes in other fields, are accustomed to "winning" at everything they do, and expect success and profit to fall their way in gross quantities simply by virtue of their wanting it. A Super Bowl championship, to this breed of American, looks no more difficult to attain than a 25 percent return on their money or a prime cut of real estate that has long been held sacrosanct by generations of less profit-minded citizens.

But the more I looked at Behring, the more metaphorical he became, and the more importance he lent to the role Seattle professional football plays in the ongoing political, cultural, and demographic drama that is being played out in the Pacific Northwest. Behring's arrival, which was greeted with considerable fear and trembling by Seattle fans, and his subsequent machinations, which provoked even more fear and trembling, have caused me to regard Seattle football in a far different—and far grander—light than ever before.

I began the season intent simply on understanding the workings of the game I regard as America's least accessible professional sport. The complexity, scale, and speed of football, and the secretiveness of its players and coaches, make it far more difficult for fans to follow than baseball, with its stately pace, or basketball, with its small floor and small cast of characters. In the course of studying the game, however, I kept encountering far more engrossing football mysteries on and off the field, and as the season wore on, the scope of my exploration widened. Seahawk football turned from the odyssey of a team through a season's schedule into the odyssey of a single man—Knox—through a course marked with magic and symbolism of a kind that I thought existed only in fairy tales, myths, epics, religious texts, and psychiatric case histories.

Often during the season any understanding of the appeal of football seemed elusive. At various times, I thought Americans loved the game because of its violence, excitement, excess, militarism, or vulgarity, or because they saw allegorical representations of their own lives being played out on the gridiron. But as Knox gradually emerged as the central character in the Seahawk drama, and as everyone—Bosworth, Krieg, McCormack, Behring, the assistant coaches, the Seahawk players, Seattle sportswriters, and Seattle fans—took form around him as lesser characters in the story of his struggle, I began to understand that football in America is far more than a national pastime.

It is by now a truism that football is at least a parody of American religion, if not a new national religion in its own right. In allowing the game to take over the American Sunday, we have turned that day into a singularly secular sabbath. The faithful arrive at their places of worship on Sunday morning, gathering outside the stadium's gates to drink sacramental beverages and study texts on the ceremony they are about to attend. Once inside the sacred circle—the traditional form of all primitive places of worship—they watch an elaborate ritual battle, staged by exaggerated male archetypes, unfold on a field of symbols, while on its borders dance ecstatic, anatomically correct nuns—modern-day maenads.

In the days between Sunday ceremonies, the faithful pore over teachings, called sports pages, which interpret the ritual action and draw from it lessons that can be applied to their daily lives. And with each succeeding Sunday service, these pages of code words and coded numbers add up to an inspiring story of a quest by crusaders for a redemption in which, ultimately, all of their followers may share.

When we follow our football teams, we are indulging in the same rituals practiced by followers of mythical and religious heroes in ancient cultures. Just as the ancient Greeks followed the exploits of their Athenians — faithfully chronicled and characterized by that first great sportswriter, Homer—and just as the Arabs had their Saracen warriors and the medieval Christians their crusading knights, so do modern Americans have their Seahawks and Raiders and Broncos and Patriots. The NFL team is the modern American version of the premodern army in that most myth-soaked of texts, the epic. The grand, warlike scope of football, the season's march from one battle to the next, the quest for a transcendent reward—all are the stuff of epic and myth.

Dave Krieg, the field general who leads Seattle's army into its ritual battles, fits mythic tradition almost down to the last detail. The hero of any quest in any myth from any culture proceeds through clearly defined stages. First of all, the hero is a figure who is little different from the rest of his society, until he is called to adventure by a repulsive creature. The hero-to-be must overcome his instinctive distaste for the messenger, then embark on a journey through a region full of treasures, actions, creatures, and trials that are unimaginable in the mundane world. In order to survive his trials, the hero must have conferred upon himself supernatural powers, which he can acquire only from spirits he meets either in dreams or through death and resurrection.

In Krieg, Seattle fans have an unremarkable fellow mortal, outwardly indistinguishable from the rest of Seattle's male population, who was called to adventure by the loathsome Jack Patera. Believing that Patera represented the call of destiny, Krieg entered the quarterback's mythic battlefield—the football stadium, peopled by Dolphins, Lions, Falcons, Rams, Bears, Giants, and other supernatural beast-adversaries. At the two most pivotal moments in his career, Krieg found himself powerless before these monsters until he suffered symbolic death and resurrection. In 1986, when subjected to death-by-benching, he returned to close out the season as the NFL's best passer. And in 1988, suffering another "death" in the form of his shoulder separation, he again returned, imbued with remarkable and mysterious powers, to finish as one of the league's top two quarterbacks.

There remains in every hero myth one final passage in the change from mortal to immortal. The hero, turning his focus inward, withdraws from the world around him in order to integrate forces that give him supernatural power. He makes himself oblivious to everything but the task at hand. Obsessively introverted, he becomes Dave Krieg facing the press after a win.

My season with Seattle has convinced me that every NFL franchise is a symbol of its region, just as Homer's characters were symbols of their region. The franchise is an expression of its people's cultural values and preoccupations.

In this respect, nothing could be more perfectly timed than to have the Seattle Seahawks franchise taken over in 1988 by a land developer from California. The Nordstroms' sale to Behring comes at a time when the Northwest, beset by massive in-migration—80 percent of it from California—is being dramatically changed from rural paradise to ungainly sprawl of cities, suburbs, and exurbs. In watching Behring develop his new Northwest acquisition, we will be watching, with requisite agony, a microcosmic rendition of the ongoing destruction of the Northwest by profiteers and would-be exiles.

A team's saga, as narrated by its storytellers, embodies the aspirations of the people in whose name the heroes struggle. The image of a franchise, the style of football a team plays, the way it wins or loses, and—most importantly—the interpretation put upon its play by reporters and columnists, form a modern-day *Odyssey*, or Old Testament, that chronicles not only adventure but the character of the adventurer's culture. Thus the Raiders and the Rams present the two faces of Southern California; the 49ers are as trendy as their town; the Atlanta Falcons are as woebegone and broken in spirit as the post–Civil War South; and the Seattle Seahawks, Northwesterners to the core, are perennial underachievers.

In reading Knox's autobiography, I was mystified by one line in particular. "It sounded," he writes of Seattle, "like the perfect place to get my kind of job done." It was a line that made no sense at all until I understood exactly what "kind of job" it is that Knox does. He loses for a living—in a magical, moving way that closely mirrors the human condition. When Knox loses as only he can lose—winningly—he is carrying on, in a lesser, modern manner, the tradition of the most memorable stories from antiquity.

The tales we remember most, and from which we draw the most inspiration, are not the stories of all-powerful, dominant heroes, but of heroes who in one way or another are foiled by their own overreaching designs. Achilles, brought down by his heel, is far more heroic—more sympathetic, more human, more memorable—than Hector, the man who slays him. It is futility and determination and human failing that give the great myths their power and poignancy. The Holy Grail is never found; Paradise is lost; Prometheus is bound and tortured for bringing godly power to man; Moses never enters the Promised Land; Sisyphus, tireless and determined, always falls just short of his summit, and starts again, determined as ever, from the bottom of his hill; Oedipus is psychologically and physically mutilated; Lear is ruined; Seattle never reaches the Super Bowl. . .

This is why, in my memory at least, the season's three greatest games were losses—the 1-point defeat by the New Orleans Saints, the fateful loss to the Kansas City Chiefs in Arrowhead Stadium, and the season-ending loss to the Cincinnati Bengals. Seattle's victories, and its ascension to a division championship, were mere supporting events scripted to lend poignancy to these losses by raising in status the team that suffered them. In all three games, Knox's coaching, brilliant and determined as it was, could not overcome the invisible enemies he has fought all his life. Those losses, in lending definition and pathos to Knox's struggle, transformed the 16th volume of *The Knoxiad* from a mere sports story into a legitimate, sustaining work of art.

For this reason, I think Seattle football fans are mistaken in thinking that, in football, winning is everything. The team's paid promoters and the producers of its highlight films are wrong to concentrate on the "winning" features of the Seahawks. In the 1988 highlight film, for example, Seattle is described as having an aggressive, ball-hawking defense, and proof is shown in the form of linebacker Tony Woods intercepting a Kansas City Chiefs pass and returning it for a touchdown. But the film neglects to show the most characteristic part of that play. Instead of ending the sequence with Woods entering the end zone, it should have gone on to show what happened next—the play being called back because the Seattle defense was offsides. A true Seahawk highlight film, a great one, would concentrate on the near-misses, the crucial errors, the maddening mistakes and misbounces that lent the campaign its piquance—the agonizing satisfaction that comes from seeing ingenious, often superhuman effort undone by the even more ingenious, all-too-human penchant for screwing up.

For Seattleites, the Knoxian spectacle is made all the richer by the NFL's playoff and parity systems, which—in tying Knox's talent-acquisition hands, and in spreading the wealth of talent throughout enough of the league to enable Knox consistently to almost make it to the Super Bowl— heighten the suspense and increase the power of chance in each one of his yearly struggles. Just as there are no seasons when he stands no chance at all of contending, there also are no seasons when he can ascend effortlessly to the championship. The league thus constitutes a little model universe, built for the heightening of dreams and the deepening of disappointments. It is a perfect arena for the playing out, year after year, of Knox's psychological drama. It is a microcosm for the re-creation of his destiny—the destiny of a proven winner who always manages to lose magnificently.

Fred Moody grew up in Bellingham, Washington, where he graduated from Fairhaven College with a degree in English. He earned a master's degree in library science from the University of Michigan, and since then has worked as a janitor, Forest Service sawyer, warehouseman, bank messenger, typesetter, editor, entrepreneur, and sportswriter—but never as a librarian.

Moody, an award-winning writer, has covered the Seahawks for the *Seattle Weekly* since 1983. He lives with his wife, Anne, and three daughters on Bainbridge Island, Washington.